Building a House Divided

Building a House Divided

SLAVERY, WESTWARD EXPANSION, AND
THE ROOTS OF THE CIVIL WAR

Stephen G. Hyslop

UNIVERSITY OF OKLAHOMA PRESS : NORMAN

This book is published with the generous assistance of the Kerr Foundation, Inc.

Library of Congress Cataloging-in-Publication Data

Names: Hyslop, Stephen G. (Stephen Garrison), 1950– author.
Title: Building a house divided : slavery, westward expansion, and the roots of the Civil War / Stephen G. Hyslop.
Description: Norman : University of Oklahoma Press [2023] | Includes bibliographical references and index. | Summary: "Explores how an incipient rift between the states over slavery at the United States' founding lengthened and deepened, risking civil war, as the nation advanced westward"—Provided by publisher.
Identifiers: LCCN 2023002890 | ISBN 978-0-8061-9273-4 (hardcover)
Subjects: LCSH: Slavery—Political aspects—United States—History—19th century. | United States—Territorial expansion. | United States—Politics and government—1783–1865. | United States—History—Civil War, 1861–1865—Causes. | BISAC: HISTORY / United States / Civil War Period (1850–1877) | SOCIAL SCIENCE / Slavery
Classification: LCC E449 .H994 2023 | DDC 973.7/112—dc23/eng/20230418
LC record available at https://lccn.loc.gov/2023002890

Contents

Preface

This book examines how prominent American expansionists extended slavery and intensified disputes over it that divided the nation they hoped to consolidate. When Thomas Jefferson concluded the Louisiana Purchase in 1803 and advanced what he called an "empire of liberty," he believed that expansion would not endanger the Union, as some Americans feared, but would instead ease its strains. As he said during his second inaugural address in 1805: "The larger our association the less will it be shaken by local passions; and in any view is it not better that the opposite bank of the Mississippi should be settled by our own brethren and children than by strangers of another family?"[1] Yet the Louisiana Purchase aroused local passions among Federalists in New England opposed to Jefferson's increasingly dominant Republican Party. They suspected that those who settled in the western territory he acquired would not be their own northern brethren but southerners drawn to New Orleans and its vicinity, where slavery prevailed. Any state formed there would likely expand the southern base of Jefferson's party and add to its hefty share of congressional seats and electoral votes, enhanced by a clause in the Constitution counting each slave as three-fifths of a person for apportionment. When a bill authorizing statehood for Louisiana, the most populous part of the sprawling Louisiana Purchase, came before the House of Representatives in 1811, Federalist Josiah Quincy of Massachusetts assailed it. If the bill became law, he warned, northern states like his own, where slavery had been prohibited, would be at an intolerable disadvantage and justified in seceding, "amicably if they can, violently if they must."[2] That remark caused an uproar. Only after a bare majority in the House backed his right to continue speaking did Quincy complete his defiant address, which did not prevent the bill from passing and Louisiana from entering the Union as a slave state.

That was one of many times secession would be threatened when Congress debated admitting states or organizing territories where slavery was at issue.

Slavery embroiled American expansion in controversy and shadowed the lives and legacies of four major expansionists considered here, who extended slavery within the nation's boundaries or extended the nation to include slaveholding territory like French Louisiana. Three of those men were presidents from the South: Jefferson, Andrew Jackson, and James K. Polk. The fourth was a northern senator with presidential ambitions, Stephen A. Douglas, who lost his bid in 1860 amid convulsions that split his Democratic Party, which opposed the new Republican Party led by Abraham Lincoln. Collectively, those four figures spanned an epoch of phenomenal growth between 1776 and 1861 that made the nation great but ultimately brought it to grief. All of them held Black people as property and profited at their expense. But none of them was vociferously proslavery like the fire-eaters who prodded southern states to secede. They sought instead to maintain equilibrium between free states and slave states, an effort that faltered as the national expansion they pursued set northerners and southerners increasingly at odds over slavery in American territories. Unable to resolve the contradiction inherent in constructing a slaveholding empire of liberty, they built a house divided, as Lincoln described the imperiled Union not long before it broke apart.

Interacting with those four expansionists were influential southerners who relied on slavery but opposed risking disunion by seeking more ground for it, as well as determined northerners who grew more intent on resisting and restricting slavery as its proponents defended and extended it. All the historical actors considered here figured in the dramatic internal conflicts of a dynamic young republic that underwent violent upheaval on its arduous path to what Lincoln at Gettysburg called "a new birth of freedom."[3]

This book encompassing the nation's journey from independence to insurrection and emancipation is aimed not just at scholars well versed in the subject but more broadly at those studying American history or exploring it independently and interested in how slavery divided a country still reckoning with its bitter legacy today.

Introduction

Lincoln's Architecture and the Fault
in the Nation's Foundation

O n June 16, 1858, Abraham Lincoln accepted the Republican nomination for the U.S. Senate at the Illinois statehouse in Springfield. His legislative experience, which included several terms as a representative there and a single term as a congressman in Washington during the Mexican-American War, was slight compared with that of his Democratic foe, incumbent Stephen A. Douglas, who had helped establish several would-be western states as chairman of the Senate Committee on Territories. During their first debate two months later, Douglas would claim that Lincoln's stand in Congress against the war, which he argued was waged on false pretenses, proved so unpopular back home that he was "obliged to retire into private life, forgotten by his former friends."[1] In truth, Lincoln remained politically active after returning to Illinois and enhanced his reputation as a lawyer whose keen wit and vivid imagery cut to the heart of complex cases. His rhetorical gifts were on full display during his acceptance speech at Springfield when he memorably evoked the crisis facing the Union, beginning with a quote from Scripture and concluding with a jeremiad warning that a nation dedicated to liberty risked being fully exposed to slavery:

"A house divided against itself cannot stand." I believe this government cannot endure permanently half slave and half free. I do not expect the Union to be dissolved—I do not expect the house to fall—but I do expect it will cease to be divided. It will become all one thing, or all the other. Either the opponents of slavery will arrest the further spread of it, and place it where the public mind shall rest in the belief that it is in the course of ultimate extinction; or its advocates will push it forward, till it shall become alike lawful in all the States, old as well as new—North as well as South.[2]

Lincoln crafted this striking portrait of a dangerously divided Union by speaking figuratively. Strictly speaking, the nation was more than half-free. Congressional efforts to equalize free states and slave states had ended in 1850 when California joined the Union with a constitution prohibiting slavery. Minnesota became the country's seventeenth free state in May 1858, and Oregon's admission the following year would make that eighteen. Meanwhile, the number of slave states remained at fifteen and included border states such as Delaware and Maryland, both of which had substantial free Black populations. Representatives from free states held nearly two-thirds of the seats in the House based on the North's much larger population, which was swelled by immigrants. All things considered, the prospect of slavery overspreading the nation as a whole appeared remote.

Lincoln and his fellow Republicans were less heartened by the North's increasing strength, however, than they were alarmed by the resilience of what they termed the "Slave Power," wielded by southerners, who were concentrated in the Democratic Party. Those southern Democrats often relied on pliable northern "doughfaces" like President James Buchanan of Pennsylvania and his predecessor, President Franklin Pierce of New Hampshire, who won election with some support from free states but dealt generously with slave states when forming cabinets, signing or vetoing bills, and appointing judges, justices, and territorial officials. Lincoln cited two recent instances when the South's political or judicial power was exerted in a way that threatened to extend slavery. First and foremost was a notorious bill advanced by Douglas, backed by Pierce, and influenced by southern Democrats in the Senate: the Kansas-Nebraska Act of 1854, which repealed the Missouri Compromise of 1820 and allowed slaveholders access to territories where slavery had long been prohibited under that agreement. Seething northern opposition to Douglas's bill, which triggered armed conflict between proslavery and antislavery forces in "Bleeding Kansas," gave rise to a new Republican Party that, unlike its Jeffersonian predecessor, did not bridge the political gap between the South and the North, where the new Republicans flourished. They were further alarmed by the second provocation Lincoln cited: the U.S. Supreme Court's decision in *Dred Scott v. Sandford*, issued in 1857 by Chief Justice Roger B. Taney, a Maryland Democrat appointed by Andrew Jackson. Endorsed by Douglas and encouraged by Buchanan, who urged a northern justice to concur with the Supreme Court's southern majority, Taney's ruling held that slave owners were constitutionally entitled to take Black people they held as property to American territories without freeing them, even if Congress had prohibited slavery there.

Lincoln was among those who warned that the Supreme Court might extend slave owners' presumed property rights to northern states, making the South's "peculiar institution"—meaning peculiar to that section of the country—lawful throughout the United States. He portrayed Taney as plotting with Buchanan, Pierce, and Douglas to alter the "house divided" so that it accommodated slavery in every quarter, a nefarious project betrayed by "evidences of design, and concert of action, among its chief architects, from the beginning." That was conjecture on Lincoln's part, and he qualified his indictment by referring later in his speech to those "chief architects" or "bosses" as mere workmen, whom he addressed by their first names. One could not "absolutely know" if their project was "the result of preconcert," Lincoln conceded:

> But when we see a lot of framed timbers, different portions of which we know have been gotten out at different times and places and by different workmen—Stephen, Franklin, Roger and James, for instance—and when we see these timbers joined together, and see they exactly make the frame of a house or a mill, . . . in such a case, we find it impossible not to believe that Stephen and Franklin and Roger and James all understood one another from the beginning, and all worked upon a common plan or draft drawn up before the first blow was struck.[3]

Lincoln had reason to portray those "workmen" as following a Democratic plan to extend slavery, one that preceded the Kansas-Nebraska Act. Democrats had been instrumental in annexing Texas as a slave state in 1845 and embracing its far-fetched claim to historically Mexican territory, which led to war with Mexico and a bitter dispute between northerners and southerners over slavery in territory ceded by Mexico. Douglas had then helped enact the Compromise of 1850, which organized New Mexico and Utah Territories without restriction on slavery, leaving to their inhabitants the ultimate decision to allow or prohibit it. He later applied that same principle, known as popular sovereignty, to Kansas and Nebraska Territories, which helped him win support for the act from southern Democrats seeking compensation for California's admission as a free state. Douglas's efforts to appease those southerners—and perhaps smooth his path to the party's presidential nomination in the process—failed to pacify them, leaving them more insistent on guarantees for slavery when territories he organized proved unreceptive to it. But he was not plotting to make slavery lawful in free states, which would have been politically disastrous for him and other northern Democrats. As he stated while debating Lincoln, a Supreme Court decision overturning state prohibitions of slavery would be "an act of moral treason that no man on the bench could ever descend to."[4]

Lincoln was intent on discouraging former Democrats within Republican ranks from reverting to their old party and embracing Douglas, who had recently defied Buchanan by rejecting as unrepresentative the minority proslavery faction in Kansas and opposing its constitution and bid for statehood. That shift further weakened Lincoln's case against Douglas for conspiring to make the house framed by the nation's founders fully accessible to slaveholders. But Douglas, Buchanan, and others in the Democracy (as their party was known informally) could be arraigned for causing so much turmoil by backing Taney's disruptive decision and exposing Kansas to intrusions by proslavery Missourians that they were further dividing the house and placing it at risk of collapse. Lincoln and fellow Republicans hoped to repair that structure and make it "all one thing" by gaining control of the federal government and placing slavery "in the course of ultimate extinction." To extend his architectural analogy, that would mean excluding slave owners from the Union's expansive west wing, where numerous free states would emerge in due time and overwhelm the slave states and the Slave Power they exerted in Washington. Taney's ruling seemingly disallowed that, but it could be tested by a Republican Congress and overruled by a Supreme Court reshaped by Republican presidents. If slavery was strictly confined to the South, Lincoln reckoned it would gradually wither and die. If southerners resisted such confinement and seceded, they would be guilty in his view of bringing down the house.

Douglas and others who operated on the assumption that the nation should remain part slave and part free believed they were acting to preserve the house, but they did so in a way that disjointed it and made its eventual rupture all the more convulsive. By altering the plan for American expansion so as to admit slavery to what was long considered free territory, Douglas led northerners like Lincoln to constitute a party determined to throttle the Slave Power. And their victory in 1860 would in turn prompt southerners to secede. Although Douglas abhorred secession, his alterations to the nation's framework contributed to that outcome. He and those prominent expansionists who preceded him and extended American slavery—notably Presidents Jefferson, Jackson, and Polk—were not mere workmen on the house divided. Nor were they deliberate architects of disunion who intended to undermine the republic they cherished. They did not cause the rift between North and South over slavery, which was evident if not yet glaring when the Constitution was debated and drawn up. Yet they served in effect as master builders of the house divided by expanding a deeply imperfect Union stressed from its inception by slavery, the fault in the nation's foundation that made the structure increasingly unstable as they enlarged it. They feared disunion yet fostered it by maintaining part slave and part free a house subject to the same rule that applied to those who framed it in 1776: "United we stand, divided we fall."

□ □ □

Disunion long preceded secession and led gradually to that dire conclusion as the nation evolved. "It is a great mistake to assume that disunion can be effected by a single blow," stated John C. Calhoun of South Carolina in his final address, delivered in 1850 when he was so close to death that a fellow senator read the speech for him. "The cords which bind these States together in one common Union are far too numerous and powerful for that. Disunion must be the work of time. It is only through a long process, and successively, that the cords can be snapped, until the whole fabric falls asunder." Although Calhoun promoted disunion by urging southerners to unite politically in defense of slavery, he viewed secession as a last resort that states should undertake only after exhausting other means of asserting rights he believed were guaranteed them by the nation's founders, who themselves had progressed from gestures of disunion such as boycotting British goods to seceding from the British empire. He regarded George Washington as a model of resistance to overbearing authority and saw nothing in that founder's history to discourage disaffected southerners from leaving the Union "should it fail to fulfill the objects for which it was instituted. . . . On the contrary, we find much in his example to encourage us, should we be forced to the extremity of deciding between submission and disunion."[5]

Calhoun also drew lessons in resistance to misrule from another slaveholding founder from Virginia, Thomas Jefferson, who believed states had the right to nullify federal laws that exceeded the government's constitutional powers. But Jefferson did not envision or invite secession as perpetrated by Confederates long after he died. Americans should not think of separating from the Union, he wrote, "but for repeated and enormous violations" of their rights, to which secessionists had not been subjected when they formed the Confederacy.[6] Jefferson fostered disunion less as a political theorist than as an avid expansionist who furthered Black bondage within his so-called empire of liberty when he purchased French

Louisiana, which extended from the Mississippi River to the Rocky Mountains but would remain largely Indian country while Americans settled among French colonists in the would-be slave states of Louisiana and Missouri. Through that momentous acquisition, he renounced his earlier proposal to prohibit slavery in the West and laid the foundation for the first major political crisis over slavery when Missouri sought admission to the Union.

Lincoln revered the Declaration of Independence, drafted by Jefferson, and believed the rights it asserted applied to all Americans, including descendants of Africans brought to America in chains. Such was Jefferson's aspiration when he composed that document and deplored the international slave trade, but he did not oppose the domestic slave trade and often sold African Americans he owned to ease his debts. He was only half-free of the notion that liberty was meant for white men and remained half-slave to the view that Black people were "a subordinate and inferior class of beings," as Taney wrote in the *Dred Scott* decision.[7]

Several of those who administered western territories under the "Virginia dynasty" of Jefferson and his successors James Madison and James Monroe were themselves slaveholders from that state, including William Clark, who served as governor of Missouri Territory after completing his epic journey with the Corps of Discovery. Clark's reluctance to emancipate his enslaved manservant York, a veteran of that corps described by Clark as having such "a notion about freedom" that he was no longer of much service, exemplified the dependence on slavery that influenced Jefferson and the original Republican Party he established with Madison.[8] Fear of being overwhelmed politically as Republicans extended their southern, slaveholding base westward and gained support in the North prompted an abortive separatist movement during Jefferson's presidency by opposing Federalists in New England, which later became a bastion of resistance to the War of 1812. Yet that conflict advanced the territorial ambitions of northerners as well as southerners. General William Henry Harrison of Virginia, who as governor of Indiana Territory sought to circumvent the prohibition of slavery in the Northwest Territory, nonetheless secured that region for the development of free states by defeating the Shawnee chief Tecumseh, an adamant opponent of ceding tribal lands, and his British allies. That campaign would later help advance Harrison to the presidency, but his efforts were surpassed by those of Andrew Jackson in the Old Southwest beyond the Appalachians. By crushing the militant Red Stick faction of the Creek tribe—from which he demanded a huge land cession in what became the emerging Cotton Kingdom's fertile "Black Belt"—and annihilating British redcoats at New Orleans, Jackson won renown and emerged as a distinctly American Caesar, embodying the nation's republican ideals while furthering its imperial ambitions.

Faulted for exceeding orders when he invaded Spanish Florida in 1818, Jackson was defended by Monroe's secretary of state, John Quincy Adams of Massachusetts, who used the pressure Jackson applied to induce Spain to cede Florida and recognize American claims to the trans-Mississippi West above what would soon be Mexican Texas, New Mexico, and California. Jackson later vied politically with Adams and Henry Clay of Kentucky—who helped enact the Missouri Compromise as Speaker of the House—and avenged the supposedly "corrupt bargain" that made Adams president and Clay secretary of state in 1825 by defeating Adams when he sought reelection. Jackson then capped his relentless efforts to secure the South for white settlers and slaveholders by pressing for removal beyond the Mississippi of Cherokees and other tribal groups that were adopting Anglo-American practices. Although some of those he displaced held slaves, the Indian Removal Act of 1830 drew petitions and protests from men and women who would figure prominently in the antislavery movement, including Harriet Beecher, future author of *Uncle Tom's Cabin*, and abolitionist William Lloyd Garrison, whose opposition to removing Cherokees from the land of their birth set him firmly against colonizing emancipated slaves in Africa.

For Jackson, upholding the Union meant opposing northerners who urged abolition and southerners who threatened secession, as South Carolinians did when nullifying the federal tariff they blamed for imperiling their plantation economy. He sought to reconcile northern and southern interests in the nation at large and in the Democratic Party he established with his vice president and successor, Martin Van Buren of New York. For all his devout Unionism, however, Jackson did more than any expansionist since Jefferson to accommodate slavery and build the house divided that broke apart in 1861. Unlike Jefferson, he had no qualms about perpetuating Black bondage in a land of liberty. He thought slaves owed good service to their masters and deserved good treatment if they provided it and prodding or punishment if they did not. If they "behave well," he said of those enslaved at the Hermitage, his home and plantation near Nashville, their overseer should "treat them well."[9] Through conquest and Indian removal, he spurred the development of Mississippi, Alabama, and Florida as slave states, whose admission to the Union offset the admission of free states and reinforced the idea that extending slavery would allow the South to keep pace politically with the North and maintain sectional equilibrium. That policy proved deeply divisive, however, when applied at Jackson's urging to Texas, colonized by American planters led by Stephen F. Austin, who had reservations about introducing slavery there but considered it essential to his undertaking,

As president, Jackson tried in vain to purchase Texas from Mexico. After rebellious Texans led by Sam Houston defeated Mexican forces and declared independence in 1836, he recognized the Lone Star Republic but refrained from annexing it to avoid provoking Mexico and alienating northerners opposed to adding a vast slave state to the Union. Competing for their votes were leaders of the emerging Whig Party such as Clay and Daniel Webster of Massachusetts who favored developing the nation internally over engaging in hasty, disruptive expansion. As the prominent Whig editor Horace Greeley argued, "A nation cannot simultaneously devote its energies to the absorption of others' territories and the improvement of its own."[10]

Jackson thought otherwise and proved less cautious about Texas in retirement when President Harrison, the first Whig to occupy the White House, was succeeded at his death in 1841 by John Tyler of Virginia, a former Democrat committed to embracing Texas. Jackson used his considerable influence to warn of interference there by British abolitionists and urge its acquisition by the United States—a theme expanded on by Secretary of State Calhoun, who portrayed slavery as a virtuous institution that would be shielded by the annexation treaty Tyler concluded with Texas in 1844. That treaty was rejected in the Senate by Whigs and skeptical Democrats like Thomas Hart Benton of Missouri, who opposed taking Texas without Mexico's consent and favored pursuing continental expansion through trade and emigration along western paths that his son-in-law John C. Frémont surveyed and publicized with his eloquent wife, Jessie Benton Frémont. The fruitful Benton-Frémont partnership encouraged American settlement in far western territories largely inhospitable to slavery as practiced in the South, which did not bode well for efforts to avert sectional strife by preserving the expanding Union half-slave and half-free. Yet Jackson clung to that principle by backing for president a Democrat intent on admitting Texas as a slave state and acquiring Oregon as a likely free territory: his protégé and fellow Tennessean James Polk, who defeated Clay in 1844.

Although Polk managed to obtain Oregon up to the forty-ninth parallel through tense negotiations with Great Britain, his insistence that Mexico relinquish all the territory claimed by Texas, including Santa Fe and other New Mexican settlements east of the upper Rio Grande, precluded a peaceful settlement on that front. By sending U.S. troops to enforce that claim after slaveholding Texas joined the Union in 1845, Polk triggered a controversial war of conquest that led northerners in the House of Representatives to pass the Wilmot Proviso, which prohibited slavery in territory acquired from Mexico during the conflict, extending to California. The Senate prevented that proviso from becoming law, but the struggle over slavery in lands ceded by Mexico at the close of "Mr. Polk's War" raised tensions between North and South to a fever pitch. Southerners had been conditioned by Jefferson, Jackson, and other leaders amenable to slavery to believe they were entitled to a government that would further their peculiar institution and maintain sectional balance politically and territorially. But northerners were growing more populous, assertive, and intent on restricting slavery, as evidenced by the emergence in 1848 of the short-lived Free Soil Party.

The sectional crisis prompted by the Mexican-American War was eased briefly by the Compromise of 1850 but shook the nation's political foundations, dividing Democrats and contributing to the collapse of the Whig Party. Many southern Whigs ended up in the Democratic Party and gave it a more pronounced proslavery bias that persistent northern Democrats like Stephen Douglas had to reckon with when the Kansas-Nebraska Act failed to appease the party's southern wing. Other Democrats with free-soil convictions joined northern Whigs like Lincoln and Greeley in the new Republican Party, whose first presidential candidate, John Frémont, lost to Buchanan in 1856 but won most of the free states. Polk's aggressive expansionism in 1846 thus initiated a fateful realignment that set predominantly southern, proslavery Democrats against northern, antislavery Republicans, placing him in the company of Jefferson and Jackson as a builder of the house divided—one who no more intended to destabilize the nation than they did but increased the strain on its imperfect foundation.

Unlike those three presidents, Douglas never occupied the White House, an objective that eluded him in 1860 when southern Democrats rejected his candidacy and broke away. His refusal to yield to their demand for federal protection of slavery in American territories if settlers there refused to endorse or enforce it stemmed from his commitment to popular sovereignty rather than any sympathy he felt for African Americans, whether enslaved or free. What linked Douglas in outlook to Polk, Jackson, and Jefferson was not his belief in the superiority of his race, an assumption shared then by nearly all white Americans, but the fact that he held slaves as those southerners did. Technically, he was manager rather than owner of a plantation in Mississippi bequeathed by his father-in-law to his first wife, Martha Martin Douglas of North Carolina, and their two sons. But he profited from slave labor, receiving a share of the plantation's proceeds, and his position was little different from that of Polk and earlier southern presidents who, as absentee planters, relied on overseers to exploit those they held in bondage.

To what extent slaveholding governed the actions of politicians can be hard to gauge. Some prominent figures who owned slaves, such as Henry Clay and President Zachary Taylor of Louisiana, opposed efforts to extend slavery westward that risked disunion and civil strife. Others, including Jefferson, Jackson, Polk, and Douglas, were so intent on American expansion that they might have enabled the extension of slavery even if they had no stake in it. Profiting from slavery did not necessarily determine their policies, but accommodating it personally inclined them to advance it politically. They all lent impetus to the Slave Power, which was mythologized in antislavery rhetoric but was nonetheless real. That power was exercised not only by proslavery politicians and justices who wielded inordinate clout as the northern population far surpassed that of the South but also by slave owners who served as influential forerunners of southwestern expansion, advancing beyond the Appalachians before American territories were organized there, beyond the Mississippi before Louisiana was purchased, and beyond the Mexican border before Texas was annexed.

Such venturesome enslavers placed pressure on those in power to uphold their advances and serve their interests—as Jefferson did when he and his supporters in Congress overrode restrictions on slavery in the Louisiana Purchase to soothe Louisianans who deemed that institution essential "to the very existence of our country"; as Jackson did when he waged war in Florida against Seminoles and allied fugitive slaves on behalf of their owners; as Polk did when he enforced the claim that slaveholding Texas extended to the Rio Grande; and as Douglas did when he crafted the Kansas-Nebraska Act in consultation with Senator David Rice Atchison of Missouri, who then urged proslavery intruders to skew elections in Kansas and thwart abolitionists there, "forcibly if we must."[11] Halting the extension of slavery would have been difficult even for leaders fully committed to that objective. The fact that four of the nation's most accomplished expansionists were slaveholders, unwilling to prevent the brutal institution on which they relied from entering new American territories or proliferating there, left that task to be achieved by Lincoln and Republicans in Congress after the nation broke apart.

Those master builders of the house divided were not proslavery ideologues like Calhoun, and all might have deplored secession as Douglas did had they lived to witness it. Like commercial builders, they suited their plans to the lay of the land and the demands of their clients or constituents, which for those national political figures meant trying to reconcile the interests of southerners with those of northerners. They sought to avert a reckoning between North and South by balancing the extension of slavery with the extension of free territory. But that balancing act grew increasingly precarious as expansion advanced, and it intensified sectional disputes by encouraging southerners to expect and demand federal support for slavery as northern resistance to it mounted and prospects for new slave states dwindled.

Once southern planters had exploited the fertile ground and favorable climate for cultivating cotton in eastern Texas, there was not much American territory left for them to occupy securely and profitably. Not even repeal of the Missouri Compromise induced many slave owners to settle in Kansas. The bulk of the trans-Mississippi West lured farmers or prospectors who wanted territories they inhabited to be free soil, some of whom were nonslaveholding southerners, belying Calhoun's claims that prohibiting slavery in American possessions was an intolerable affront to the South as a whole. Southern expansionists continued to press their case in the 1850s, however, by urging the annexation of slaveholding Cuba, infiltrating New Mexico Territory, and seeking to divide the free state of California and permit slavery to the south. Emboldened by the belief that they were acting in the nation's venerable tradition of revolutionary defiance, proslavery insurgents fractured the Democracy by contesting Douglas's candidacy in 1860 and went on to fracture the democratic Union when Lincoln won election. He rejected any last-ditch congressional compromise that might appease such secessionists, further their designs on American territory, and set the republic on the path to becoming a "slave empire."[12]

□　□　□

The following chapters examine how the disruptive and divisive nature of Anglo-American expansionism, which involved enslaving, removing, or marginalizing those of other races or nations rather than incorporating them fully in society, disrupted and divided the Union internally prior to the Civil War. Indian removal, whether imposed by armed force or by treaty, enabled the extension of the free-labor North as well as the slaveholding South. As that process advanced, however, an expansionist impulse that once united Americans in opposition to tribes that resisted encroachment with support from European powers—notably the French in colonial times and the British during the American Revolution and the War of 1812—produced fierce sectional disputes over allowing Black bondage in lands wrested from Indians and Mexicans.

Northern opposition to slavery in American territories propelled Lincoln to the presidency and triggered the Confederate rebellion. But other factors contributed substantially to what Senator William H. Seward of New York in 1858 called an "irrepressible conflict between opposing and enduring forces," including economic and cultural differences between the free states and slave states and the emergence of a determined abolitionist movement in the North and an assertive proslavery movement in the South, whose adherents were as concerned with defending southern honor and repulsing any potential threat to their peculiar institution where it existed as they were with extending it.[13] The origins of that irrepressible conflict, however, lay not at the margins of the political spectrum but at its core, among prominent expansionists like Jefferson and Jackson who maintained the Union part slave and part free. They were central to the nation's development, and the center would not hold. Disunion stemmed from a critical fault in the nation's foundation, and those who built on that foundation increased the stressful disparity between America's fervent devotion to freedom and its shameful dependence on slavery until the house could no longer stand.

CHAPTER 1

Jefferson's Abandoned Stand against Slavery

Abraham Lincoln was not the first to ask whether a nation dedicated to the proposition that all men are created equal could long endure while divided by slavery. The founder whose words he invoked in his Gettysburg Address, Thomas Jefferson, had expressed a similar concern several decades earlier. Writing in April 1820 to John Holmes of Maine, who as a congressman had supported Missouri's admission to the Union as a slave state while many northerners opposed it, Jefferson likened that dispute famously to "a fire bell in the night," which "awakened and filled me with terror. I considered it at once as the knell of the Union." The alarm he felt was eased "for the moment" by the Missouri Compromise, which allowed slavery in that state but prohibited it elsewhere within territory acquired through the Louisiana Purchase above the line formed by Missouri's southern border. Yet that compromise was "a reprieve only," warned Jefferson: "A geographical line, coinciding with a marked principle, moral and political, once conceived and held up to the angry passions of men, will never be obliterated; and every new irritation will mark it deeper and deeper." A line meant to preserve the Union might, he feared, divide it irreparably.

Although the seventy-seven-year-old Jefferson professed to deplore slavery no less in 1820 than he did when he was a young apostle of liberty, he faulted Congress for restricting it geographically and clung to the wishful notion that diffusing it widely might reduce it to insignificance. "Of one thing I am certain," he wrote Holmes, "that as the passage of slaves from one state to another would not make a slave of a single human being who would not be so without it, so their diffusion over a greater surface would make them individually happier

and proportionally facilitate the accomplishment of their emancipation."[1] Yet
Jefferson had once considered slavery so at odds with liberty and the pursuit
of happiness that he proposed a barrier beyond which it would be forbidden.

In 1784, while representing Virginia in the Confederation Congress that presided before the Constitution was drawn up and ratified, Jefferson had helped draft
an ambitious plan for governing territory between the Appalachian Mountains
and the Mississippi River ceded by Great Britain at the end of the Revolutionary
War. Much of that expanse in fact remained tribal territory, inhabited by Indians
not yet dislodged by American forces or treaty makers. But the British cession left
various American states with claims to the trans-Appalachian West that would
be assumed by the federal government. Virginia ceded its claim to part of the
Northwest Territory, above the Ohio River, shortly before Jefferson and others
on a congressional committee he chaired drew up their plan. They anticipated
that all the land extending southward from the Ohio to the border of Spanish
West Florida would also become part of the national domain and envisioned
numerous western territories, each governed temporarily by legislators chosen by
"all free males of full age" until it reached a population of twenty thousand free
inhabitants and adopted a state constitution. States could seek admission to the
Union on an equal basis with the original thirteen states when their population
matched that of the least populous of those states and they met several other
conditions. One was that they shall forever remain part of the United States, a
rule Jefferson considered binding as long as the government did not flagrantly
abuse its powers and forfeit the consent of the governed. The last requirement,
which he proposed, was that after the year 1800 "there shall be neither slavery
nor involuntary servitude" in any of the trans-Appalachian states, "otherwise
than in punishment of crimes."[2]

When voting on that plan, known as the Ordinance of 1784, the Confederation
Congress narrowly rejected the slavery prohibition, which required approval by
seven of the thirteen existing states. As Jefferson explained in a letter to fellow
Virginian James Madison, only ten states had enough delegates present to cast
a vote. (Such absenteeism was chronic and had nearly prevented Congress from
ratifying the peace treaty with Britain before it expired.) The four New England
states in the Confederation then (Connecticut, Rhode Island, Massachusetts,
and New Hampshire) approved the prohibition along with New York and
Pennsylvania. Virginia joined South Carolina and Maryland in voting against
it because Jefferson was unable to dissuade the two other Virginia delegates
on hand from opposing the measure. North Carolina's delegates were evenly

divided and abstained. New Jersey "would have been for it," Jefferson reported, "but there were but two members, one of whom was sick in his chambers."[3] Had that ailing delegate joined the other and formed a quorum, it would have passed. "The voice of a single individual . . . would have prevented this abominable crime from spreading itself over the new country," Jefferson later lamented. "Thus we see the fate of millions unborn hanging on the tongue of one man, and heaven was silent in that awful moment!"[4]

Even if the weak Confederation Congress had approved the slavery prohibition, however, the ban would not have applied in 1800 unless upheld by the U.S. Congress (established in 1789), whose members showed no inclination to outlaw slavery in American territory below the Ohio. Not long after the first U.S. Congress convened, the Senate and House accepted North Carolina's cession of its trans-Appalachian territory (the future state of Tennessee), made on condition that Congress pass no law freeing slaves, whose substantial presence in that territory made white settlers wary of wholesale emancipation. Timothy Pickering of Massachusetts—who in 1783 had proposed the "total exclusion of slavery" from the Northwest Territory—complained that Jefferson's provision not only would have allowed slavery until 1800 in such areas below the Ohio where it was fast taking hold but also would have permitted it before then in areas above the river where slavery was scarce or nonexistent. To allow slaves "into countries where none now exist—countries which have been talked of, which we have boasted of, as asylums to the oppressed of the earth—can never be forgiven," Pickering declared.[5]

Jefferson's rejected prohibition did help prevent slavery from proliferating above the Ohio, however, by serving as the basis for Article VI of the Northwest Ordinance, adopted by the Confederation Congress in 1787 and affirmed by the U.S. Congress in 1789. Most southern representatives went along with that article barring slavery in the Northwest Territory. They had reason to believe that there would be no such congressional prohibition on slavery below the Ohio and were reassured by a provision in Article VI enabling slaveholders to reclaim fugitives who fled to the Northwest Territory. As stated in the ordinance: "There shall be neither slavery nor involuntary servitude in the said territory, otherwise than in the punishment of crimes, whereof the party shall have been duly convicted: Provided always, that any person escaping into the same, from whom labour or service is lawfully claimed in any one of the original States, such fugitive may be lawfully reclaimed, and conveyed to the person claiming his or her labour or service as aforesaid."[6] Enacted two months before the Constitutional Convention in Philadelphia completed its work in September 1787, the Northwest Ordinance with its slavery prohibition may have helped reconcile some northern delegates at the convention to a Constitution that included a fugitive-slave clause (Article IV, Section 2) similar to that in the ordinance as well as the clause counting each slave as three-fifths of a person when apportioning to states seats in the House of Representatives (Article I, Section 2), which in turn determined how many electoral votes each state would cast for president (Article II, Section 1).

James Madison, who figured prominently at the Constitutional Convention and documented the debates, stated that the "real difference of interests" was not between small and large states but between northern and southern states over the "institution of slavery & its consequences."[7] He favored applying proportional representation based on population (Virginia was then the most populous state) to the Senate as well as the House, which he argued would better reflect the will of the people and do more to promote political equilibrium between northern and southern states than giving them all equal representation in the Senate. Contrary to his expectations, allowing each state two senators—as delegates from small states insisted at the convention—would in decades to come give the less populous South parity in the Senate as long as the states remained sectionally balanced or nearly half-slave and half-free.

Arguments over slavery threatened efforts in Philadelphia to form what the preamble to the Constitution termed a "more perfect Union." Some northern delegates objected to allowing a state any additional political representation based on its enslaved population. Gouverneur Morris of Pennsylvania said that he "could never agree to give such encouragement" to the slave trade.[8] On the other hand, some southern delegates wanted each slave counted as a full person for apportionment and warned that they might shun the Union if slavery was not protected under the Constitution. To avoid a deadlock and disunion, the convention approved—and Morris was among those who signed—a Constitution containing not only the three-fifths and fugitive-slave clauses but also a clause barring Congress from prohibiting the importation of slaves before 1808 (Article I, Section 9), which some opponents tolerated because it allowed prohibition of the vicious African slave trade thereafter. By framing those clauses without specific reference to "slaves" or "slavery," delegates avoided an explicit endorsement of the idea that people could be held as property and allowed some abolitionists to argue later that their cause was consistent with the Constitution. But by defining those counted as three-fifths of a person as not free and not "bound to service for a term of years" like indentured servants, the Constitution acknowledged slavery and reinforced the notion among slave owners and their representatives that holding Black people in lifelong bondage was not just an American practice but an American right.

Jefferson was serving in France as U.S. minister (the equivalent then of ambassador) when the Constitution was framed and was not party to its compromises. When he returned to the United States and was appointed secretary of state by President George Washington, he welcomed the passage by Congress of the first ten amendments to the Constitution, which made up the Bill of Rights, ratified in 1791. Jefferson had argued for such a bill in correspondence with Madison, who represented his Virginia district in the House and was instrumental in framing those amendments, which established as law such fundamental rights as freedom of speech and religion and trial by jury. Because the amendments made no reference to race or slavery, however, they were subject to varying interpretations. Did the Fifth Amendment, requiring that no person "be deprived of life, liberty, or property, without due process of law," protect fugitives who sought liberty in free states from being reenslaved without due process such as trial by jury, or did it protect slaveholders from being deprived of those they claimed as property? Slaveholders in states that allowed them to own people believed that their property rights were inviolable because the Constitution did not forbid slavery and the Tenth Amendment provided that "powers not delegated to the United States by the Constitution, nor prohibited by it to the States, are reserved to the States respectively or to the people."

In the 1790s Jefferson and Madison emerged as champions of the powers reserved to states and the people by leading fellow Republicans in opposition to Federalists like Washington's successor, President John Adams, and Treasury Secretary Alexander Hamilton who were accused of assuming powers not constitutionally delegated to the government of the United States. Slavery was not a significant issue in that political contest. That Jefferson interpreted the Constitution as forbidding federal interference with slavery in the states was not unusual for one who extolled liberty as he did. As late as 1861, Lincoln stated at his inauguration that he had no intention or lawful right to prohibit slavery in the South. But Jefferson as president would depart from his earlier effort to confine American slavery when he purchased from France its claim to that vast expanse known as Louisiana. Though he favored prohibiting the international slave trade there, he did not back efforts to restrict slavery or promote emancipation in Louisiana under the constitutional provision empowering Congress to make "all needful rules and regulations respecting the territory or other property belonging to the United States" (Article IV, Section 3).

In one sense, Jefferson was following the familiar path of ambitious leaders who dispensed with youthful ideals they found inconvenient or impractical. Yet his disdain for slavery had long been qualified and muted by his utter dependence on it, which helps explain why the line drawn in 1820 between liberty and bondage across territory he acquired through the Louisiana Purchase touched a raw nerve in the elder Jefferson. The Missouri crisis revived an internal conflict he had first experienced as a prominent young slave owner and revolutionary idealist and never resolved—a conflict that would one day be enacted violently by the nation he dedicated to the pursuit of liberty, which led some Americans to regard slaveholding as intolerable and others to consider it their inalienable right, which if denied by the government justified altering or abandoning it.

A Fateful Inheritance

Born in Virginia in April 1743, Thomas Jefferson was the eldest son of Peter Jefferson, an enterprising planter, surveyor, and official who acquired some 7,500 acres and at least sixty slaves by the time he died in 1757. He bequeathed much of that land and nearly half those enslaved people to Thomas—who would come into that inheritance when he turned twenty-one—and also left the fourteen-year-old boy an enslaved body servant, described in Peter Jefferson's will as "my mulattoe Fellow Sawney."[9] By the time Thomas Jefferson entered the College of William and Mary in 1760, he was attended by another slave named Jupiter or Jupiter Evans, who was the same age as Jefferson and accompanied him to Williamsburg. Jupiter may have been Jefferson's companion since childhood, for enslaved children often served as playmates for white youths who were their masters. Such play could be amicable, but in his *Notes on the State of Virginia*, Jefferson described how the despotism of masters passed from one generation to the next: "The parent storms, the child looks on, catches the lineaments of wrath, puts on the same airs in the circle of smaller slaves, gives a loose to his worst of passions, and thus nursed, educated, and daily exercised in tyranny, cannot but be stamped by it with odious peculiarities. The man must be a prodigy who can retain his manners and morals undepraved by such circumstances."[10]

Jefferson generally exercised restraint toward those he held in bondage, but he was no moral prodigy and raged at Jupiter on one occasion for being insubordinate. Slaveholding was Jefferson's inheritance, and it brought him power, privileges, and happiness as well as the moral burden of depriving people under his authority of liberty, a bitter legacy that he might occasionally regret but would not disown any more than he would renounce his father. That burden fell not only on southerners like Jefferson but also on many northerners who practiced slavery during the revolutionary era or profited from it. As another slave owner and future president, James Polk, later remarked in Congress, slavery "had been entailed upon us by our ancestors" and was viewed when the United States won independence as "a common evil . . . affecting the whole Nation."[11]

Likening slavery to entailment was apt, for that legal means of bequeathing property to one's designated heirs was binding not just on the next generation but on subsequent generations. Practiced by some of the leading families in Virginia and other colonies before the Revolutionary War, entails kept wealth in the form of land and slaves firmly lodged within such families by providing that a designated heir might rent but could not sell to others what he or she inherited and thus deny that property to the next designated heir. Jefferson's inheritance was not entailed on him by his father, nor did he did inherit all his father's property as some eldest sons did under primogeniture. Peter Jefferson bequeathed the remainder of his land and slaves to his other children and to his wife, Jane Randolph Jefferson, for as long as she lived. Jefferson deplored entailment and primogeniture because he viewed those practices as bestowing wealth on people who did not necessarily merit it and promoting an entrenched aristocracy. The French term for entail, *mortmain* ("dead hand"), evoked a society bound by the past and its rigid conventions, which the forward-looking Jefferson disdained.[12] When revising the laws of colonial Virginia for the newly formed state of Virginia in 1776, he won passage of a bill abolishing entails, and legislators subsequently abolished primogeniture.

Prohibiting entailment, however, did not stop slavery from being entailed metaphorically on future generations of Americans, as Polk stated. Unentailed planters were free to sell people they enslaved, as Jefferson often did to relieve his debts, and such trade helped American slavery persist and expand. In that sense, the dead hand of the past continued to guide him and other slaveholders. The fatalistic notion that slavery was imposed or metaphorically entailed on them by their ancestors allowed some to absolve themselves of responsibility for perpetuating what they knew was contrary to the nation's revolutionary ideals.

One principle Jefferson adhered to throughout his career was opposition to the international slave trade. That cause gained support in Virginia and other American colonies during the eighteenth century for reasons that were not strictly humanitarian, including concerns that too many enslaved Africans were being imported, increasing the risk of rebellions. British companies figured prominently in the African trade, and in April 1772 the House of Burgesses in

Williamsburg petitioned King George III in vain to let Virginia curb that trade. "The importation of slaves into the colonies from the coast of Africa," the petition stated, "hath long been considered as a trade of great inhumanity, and under its present encouragement [by the Crown], we have too much reason to fear *will endanger the very existence* of your Majesty's American dominions."[13] Despite such fears, Virginians and other American colonists took part in that trade, among them Jefferson's father-in-law, John Wayles, a lawyer in Williamsburg. In October 1772, not long after his daughter Martha wed Jefferson, Wayles and his business partner, Richard Randolph, placed a notice in the *Virginia Gazette* offering for sale "about four hundred five healthy slaves" arriving from Africa on the ship *Prince of Wales*.[14] The actual number of Africans put up for sale was 280 because many who were crammed aboard the ship died during the voyage under dreadful conditions. The deal went awry for Wayles and Randolph when planters who purchased those slaves on credit amid a sagging market for tobacco, the colony's main cash crop, withheld payment.

John Wayles died in 1773 and bequeathed to Jefferson through Martha 135 enslaved people and extensive landholdings as well as debts resulting from his failed investment in captive Africans imported on the *Prince of Wales*, among other liabilities. Jefferson had good reason to deplore American participation in the Atlantic slave trade no less than the Crown's support for British companies involved in that commerce, which stifled Virginia's effort to stem the influx of enslaved Africans. When drafting the Declaration of Independence in 1776, however, he cast all the blame on King George III in a blistering indictment that his fellow delegates to the Continental Congress in Philadelphia excised. As Jefferson wrote of the king:

> He has waged cruel war against human nature itself, violating it's most sacred rights of life & liberty in the persons of a distant people who never offended him, captivating & carrying them into slavery in another hemisphere, or to incur miserable death in their transportation thither. . . . Determined to keep open a market where MEN should be bought & sold, he has prostituted his negative for suppressing every legislative attempt to prohibit or to restrain this execrable commerce.

Jefferson went on to denounce King George for offering freedom to slaves if they fled their masters and helped British forces put down the American rebellion, as stated in a recent proclamation by Virginia's royal governor, Lord Dunmore, that prompted some of Jefferson's slaves to seek freedom behind British lines.

Whereas the Declaration of Independence charged the king succinctly with exciting "domestic insurrections amongst us," Jefferson's excised passage accused him at length of causing slaves "to purchase that liberty of which *he* has deprived them, by murdering the people upon whom *he* also obtruded them; thus paying off former crimes committed against the *liberties* of one people, with crimes which he urges them to commit against the *lives* of another."[15]

One unfortunate consequence of omitting this indictment from the Declaration of Independence was that it made clear what some later apologists for slavery denied: Jefferson's celebrated assertion that "all men are created equal" and "endowed by their Creator" with the inalienable right of liberty included enslaved African Americans, as he emphasized by referring to them as "MEN," deprived by the king of their "*liberties*." By eliminating the passage, however, the Congress avoided casting all blame on the Crown for an African slave trade in which Anglo-Americans were complicit. Jefferson later acknowledged as much when he noted that his clause blaming King George for the trade was struck out in deference to those in South Carolina and Georgia who "still wished to continue it. Our Northern brethren also I believe felt a little tender under those censures; for tho' their people have very few slaves themselves yet they had been pretty considerable carriers of them to others."[16] He did not mention that Virginians had been eager buyers of captive Africans and thus responsible for swelling their enslaved population—which amounted to more than 40 percent of the state's inhabitants by 1790—or that his father-in-law had been involved in that deplorable commerce.

Jefferson's unwavering opposition to the international slave trade helped induce Virginia's assembly to forbid it in 1778 and later encouraged the U.S. Congress to pass an act he signed into law as president that prohibited importing slaves to the United States or its territories as of January 1, 1808, when the constitutional provision against doing so expired. But he did not oppose the cruel domestic slave trade that expanded as the international trade dwindled and that forcibly removed nearly one million African Americans from the Union's original slave states to new slave states by the time the Civil War erupted. Although Jefferson drafted a proposal, described in his *Notes on the State of Virginia*, to emancipate that commonwealth's slaves—a hypothetical measure that was not enacted—he called for those freed to be colonized elsewhere and thought them incapable of living peacefully and productively among his own race. He suspected that they were "inferior to the whites in the endowments both of body and mind" and added that the "unfortunate difference of colour, and perhaps of faculty, is a powerful obstacle to the emancipation of these people." Even if they were prepared for emancipation through education and training, he feared that allowing them free entrance to white society would result either in a race war or racial amalgamation, which he warned against. Roman slaves of the same race as their masters could be freed and intermarry with Romans without "staining" their blood, Jefferson noted, but Black slaves if emancipated should be "removed beyond the reach of mixture."[17]

How can Jefferson's opposition to racial mixture be reconciled with the fact that several of his most trusted household slaves were the mixed-race offspring of John Wayles and his enslaved mulatto mistress Elizabeth (Betty) Hemings? And how could Jefferson, following the death of his wife in 1782 and the subsequent publication of a book in which he deplored racial mixture, father several children by Betty's enslaved daughter Sarah (Sally) Hemings? He and many other white slaveholders evidently made a distinction between miscegenation that implied racial equality or amalgamation and their own practice of impregnating enslaved Black women and fostering a distinct class of mixed-race slaves or "servants," who remained subordinate but were endowed with some white traits, which Jefferson thought improved them "in body and mind" over those of wholly African ancestry. As diarist Mary Boykin Chesnut of South Carolina later remarked of slave owners in her social circle, they engaged in such miscegenation unabashedly, with results that were readily apparent in their households: "Like the patriarchs of old our men live all in one house with their wives and their concubines, and the mulattoes one sees in every family exactly resemble the white children."[18]

Jefferson's relationship with Sally Hemings became a political liability when it was alleged in print during his presidency, but he continued to have children by her—who reportedly bore some resemblance to him—and favored them. The four children who lived to adulthood were among the small number of slaves he freed during his lifetime or in his will, all of whom were mixed-race members of the extended Hemings family. (Sally Hemings became free after Jefferson died in 1826 without being formally emancipated, but others related to her were among 126 enslaved people sold at auction to cover his posthumous debts.) He may have seen no contradiction between fathering children by her and abhorring miscegenation that supposedly lowered whites to the level of Blacks, particularly when Black men fathered children by white women. When revising Virginia's laws, he eliminated or reduced some severe punishments imposed in colonial times but proposed a harsh penalty for white women who bore a child "by a negro or mulatto."[19] Those women were to be banished from the state or outlawed if they remained in Virginia, in which case they could be attacked with impunity. That drastic measure was not enacted.

Absent from Jefferson's ambitious proposal in 1784 to prohibit slavery in the trans-Appalachian West was any mention of how those who were not free inhabitants would be emancipated and what would then become of them. He envisioned the West ideally as populated by self-sufficient yeoman farmers. But in 1784 there were already several thousand slaves in that westernmost portion of Virginia known as Kentucky, and they would make up one-sixth of its nearly seventy-four thousand non-Indian inhabitants in the first national census, conducted in 1790, two years before Kentucky achieved statehood.[20] As Jefferson advanced toward the presidency in years to come, he would accept slavery below the Ohio River as essential to the development of the trans-Appalachian West, much as he came to accept slave labor as essential to his own prosperity and happiness. His overriding concern was to bind settlers between the Appalachians and the Mississippi to the Union and prevent them from falling into the grasp of the British to their north, who maintained forts around the Great Lakes, or Spanish authorities to their south and west, who had received Louisiana from France in 1762 and controlled the lower Mississippi. To enlarge the nation and hold it together, Jefferson would tolerate and facilitate the westward expansion of American slavery. Not until late in his life would he confront the prospect that binding East to West in that manner was deepening the divide between North and South.

Disunion on the Frontier

By the time Jefferson began serving as George Washington's secretary of state in 1790, emigrants had poured through Cumberland Gap and other passes in the Appalachians to populate the would-be states of Kentucky and Tennessee. That southwestern migration had begun not long before the Revolutionary War, during which settlers in the region battled defiant warriors aligned with the British, including Cherokees and Shawnees, some of whom would continue to oppose American encroachment after the United States achieved independence. Many early white settlers in what became Kentucky and Tennessee were largely self-reliant farmers and hunters, but planters claimed some of the best land there and raised cash crops like tobacco or hemp, used to make rope, by employing slave labor. Securing free navigation of the Mississippi was of particular concern to slave owners on the nation's southwestern frontier. They had much to lose if denied access by Spanish authorities to New Orleans, from which their trade goods could be shipped to either side of the Atlantic. In the mid-1780s, some men of property were rumored to be plotting to secede from the United States and join Spain—which upheld slavery in Louisiana as established there under French rule—if they were assured right of transit to New Orleans. In the case of James Wilkinson, an ambitious planter, merchant, and slave owner in Kentucky, those rumors were well-founded. His checkered career epitomized disunionist intrigue on the far side of the Appalachians.

After serving as an aide to Generals Benedict Arnold and Horatio Gates during the Revolutionary War, the Maryland-born Wilkinson resigned from the Continental Army and moved to Louisville, where he urged Kentuckians to separate not just from Virginia but from the American Confederation. Many enterprising settlers beyond the Appalachians felt betrayed when diplomat John Jay of New York proposed a treaty in 1786 that would give eastern merchants access to Spanish ports but would allow Spain to continue denying western traders access to the lower Mississippi River and New Orleans. James Madison was among those opposed to the agreement, which gave westerners cause to consider themselves "*sold by* their *Atlantic brethren*," he wrote Jefferson, and risked driving them into the hands of a foreign power.[21] The treaty was blocked in the Confederation Congress by Madison and other southern delegates, but it spurred efforts by Wilkinson and others in far western Virginia to form an independent state, which might then secure navigation rights from Spain. They spoke openly, for those advocating independence from the weak American Confederation were not considered traitorous unless they conspired with a foreign power against the United States. In 1787, however, Wilkinson did just that by venturing down the Mississippi to New Orleans, where he met with the governor of Louisiana, Esteban Miró, pledged allegiance to Spain, and began serving as a secret Spanish agent.

In a self-serving memorial that remained concealed in Spanish archives until long after his death, Wilkinson justified violating the oath he swore to his country as an American officer. "Born and educated in America," he wrote, "I embraced its cause in the recent revolution, and steadfastly I adhered to her interests until she triumphed over her enemy." Having fought for America's welfare, he now felt "at liberty" to seek his own welfare. Patriotism or love of country was rooted not in selflessness but in self-interest, Wilkinson declared, and he and like-minded Kentuckians were inclined to pursue their interests outside the American Union. He went so far as to suggest that Kentuckians as a whole would join him in becoming Spanish subjects if offered "certain privileges in political and religious matters." In the meantime, he advised that Spain deny Americans "intercourse by the Mississippi" with New Orleans while granting him a lucrative exception.

In return for serving as a Spanish agent, he asked permission to convey for sale in New Orleans up to $60,000 worth of merchandise, including "Negroes, live Stock, tobacco, Flour, Bacon," and other items.[22]

Although Wilkinson may never have sold slaves in New Orleans, he profited from slavery by selling tobacco and other goods consigned to him by those who held Black people in bondage as he did. For instance, Alexander Scott Bullitt, who raised tobacco on his sprawling Oxmoor estate in what became Bullitt County, Kentucky, held twenty-three slaves in 1789 and seventy by 1795. One of several "Kentucky notables" whom Wilkinson sought to draw into his plot, Bullitt balked and went on to endorse statehood for Kentucky within the Union, hoping that the United States would soon be strong enough to obtain concessions from Spain and guarantee American access to New Orleans. (That access was later achieved by Pinckney's Treaty in 1795 but was threatened anew when Spain retroceded Louisiana to France five years later.) Others linked to Wilkinson also withdrew from this so-called Spanish Conspiracy, and Kentucky went directly from being part of Virginia to the nation's fifteenth state without an intermediate phase as a territory. Bullitt helped uphold slavery in Kentucky's 1792 constitution, which stated that "the legislature shall have no power to pass laws for the emancipation of slaves without the consent of their owners."[23]

Before far western North Carolina became the Southwest Territory, established in 1790 by Congress without any restriction on slavery, it had its own version of the Spanish Conspiracy and a separatist movement by settlers who seceded from North Carolina and formed the short-lived state of Franklin. Such intrigue did not end when the Southwest Territory became the state of Tennessee in 1796. Territorial governor William Blount then became one its first two U.S. senators. A land speculator who faced ruin if France reacquired Louisiana and closed the lower Mississippi to Americans, Blount plotted to help Britain seize control of the region from Spain and keep the river open. Exposed before the scheme materialized by a letter he wrote indicating that he would be "at the head of the business on the part of the British," he was impeached by the House and expelled from the Senate.[24] Unlike Blount, Wilkinson managed to conceal the fact that he was aiding a foreign nation and remained a Spanish agent long after he returned to military service and took command of the U.S. Army as its senior officer in 1796, in which capacity he would later deceive President Jefferson.

Some Americans migrated to Spanish-held Louisiana and settled legally in what would later become the states of Louisiana, Arkansas, and Missouri by swearing allegiance to Spain and obtaining land grants there. Among those who

moved to the future Missouri while it was still Spanish territory were Daniel
Boone and Moses Austin, who left Virginia in 1798 with his wife and children—
including four-year-old Stephen Austin, the future "father" of American Texas—
and established a lead mine south of St. Louis worked by enslaved Black people.
Other emigrants from southeastern states settled with slaves they held around
Natchez, situated on the east bank of the Mississippi in what would become
Mississippi Territory, and began cultivating cotton there in the 1790s. Ceded by
Georgia, that territory was established by Congress in 1798 without restriction
on slavery after a motion by Congressman George Thatcher (or Thacher) of
Massachusetts to prohibit enslavement there was overwhelmingly rejected. Even
northerners with antislavery sentiments such as Timothy Pickering, serving then
as secretary of state under John Adams, favored allowing slavery in Mississippi
Territory because it was customary there among planters, some of whom had
remained loyal to Britain during the Revolution and settled in the area under
British protection. Pickering and Andrew Ellicott, an antislavery Quaker sent
to survey the boundary between the Mississippi Territory and Spanish West
Florida at the thirty-first parallel, feared that those former Loyalists and others
in the vicinity might seek British or Spanish aid and secede if slavery was not
upheld in the territory. To ensure their loyalty, Ellicott wrote, slavery should
be allowed there on "the same footing it is at present in the Southern States."[25]

As indicated by broad congressional support for establishing Mississippi
Territory without the restriction applied to the Northwest Territory, slavery was
not yet a divisive issue politically. The Union was severely strained, however,
by laws curbing dissent that were passed by Federalists in Congress in 1798
and signed by President Adams but strenuously opposed by Vice President
Jefferson and fellow Republicans. (Before adoption of the Twelfth Amendment
in 1804, the vice president was not the president's designated running mate
but the candidate who received the second-most electoral votes, as Adams's
opponent Jefferson did.) The Alien and Sedition Acts to which Republicans
objected aimed at suppressing opposition to Adams and his undeclared naval
war against revolutionary France, which prohibited trade with its enemy Great
Britain and seized American ships engaged in such commerce. Among the
targets of the legislation were French residents in the United States as well as
Republican journalists and editors, some of whom were charged with sedition
for vehemently denouncing the president and his party. Outraged at Federalists
for infringing on the rights of free speech and a free press, Jefferson drafted
resolutions declaring that the Constitution was a compact by which the states

Thomas Jefferson (1743–1826)
as vice president, circa 1797.
Courtesy Library of Congress
Prints and Photographs
Division (LC-pga-12975).

delegated to the federal government "certain definite powers" and that when the government assumed powers that have "not been delegated a nullification of the act is the rightful remedy." The Kentucky legislature adopted those resolutions in modified form, avoiding reference to nullification but declaring that when the federal government assumed undelegated powers, its acts were "unauthoritative, void, and of no force." The Virginia legislature adopted less defiant resolutions drafted by Madison, declaring the Alien and Sedition Acts unconstitutional and asserting the state's right to "interpose" when the government abused its powers.[26]

Jefferson anticipated the stance of some later proponents of states' rights not only by advocating nullification of those acts but also by contemplating secession should the federal government continue to infringe on the rights of the people or the powers reserved to the states when they formed the constitutional compact. As he wrote Madison in 1799, if the "true principles of our federal compact" were violated, we should "sever ourselves from that union we so much value, rather than give up the rights of self government which we have reserved, & in which alone we see liberty, safety & happiness." Influenced by the more cautious Madison, however, Jefferson conceded that "we should never think of separation but for repeated and enormous violations" by the federal government.[27] He chose not to forsake the Union but to reform it through the electoral process. By defeating Adams in the next election, he ushered in a new Republican era of federal restraint, which did not prevent him from concluding the Louisiana Purchase in 1803 in a manner he doubted was constitutional and added significantly to American territory in which slavery prevailed.

Jefferson's departure from his earlier effort to prevent slavery from expanding westward suited his political interests and his conviction that the authority to allow or prohibit it lay with the states and the people rather than with the federal government. It also corresponded with his efforts as a planter to rationalize slavery and make it not only more profitable but also less cruel and objectionable, in keeping with his belief that "our interests soundly calculated will ever be found inseparable from our moral duties."[28] Before becoming vice president, he had spent three years at his Monticello estate in Virginia, renovating the handsome home he had designed there and seeking to manage his enslaved laborers more prudently while continuing to exploit them for his own gain. To increase their efficiency, he relied more on "gratuities" or other incentives than on punishment. He did not want pregnant women burdened with hard tasks and reckoned that a child born every two years was "of more profit than the crop of the best laboring man. In this, as in all other cases, providence has made our interests & our duties coincide perfectly." Although he sold numerous slaves to relieve debts aggravated by the expense of enhancing Monticello, he sometimes did so to unite slaves he owned with their family members elsewhere and frowned on separating husbands from wives and parents from young children. Children aged ten or older, however, might be sold apart from other family members or set to work in shops like the one at Monticello where boys hammered out nails, the same task performed by some prison inmates. Jefferson kept track of what enslaved children accomplished on a daily basis at Monticello. He rewarded those who were diligent and urged those who were less productive to bear down. On one occasion later during his retirement, he told a girl who did poorly in the textile mill he established that "if there be no improvement, she must cease to spoil more cloth and go out to work with the overseer" in the fields.[29]

That Jefferson's material interests as a slaveholder trumped his moral scruples was demonstrated by his tolerance for overseer Gabriel Lilly, who was harsher than Jefferson might wish but made boys in the nailery work profitably. Around the time he became president, Jefferson removed Lilly—who whipped boys for truancy—but later returned him to the nailery when production lagged under his more lenient successor, William Stewart. The boys in the shop had become "a dead expense instead of a profit to me," Jefferson complained. "In truth they require a rigour of discipline to make them do reasonable work, to which he cannot bring himself." Lilly later tried to force one nailer who was ill, James (Jamey) Hemings, back to work by whipping him so severely that he fled Monticello. Jefferson did not send a slave catcher in pursuit of Hemings, who was not his own offspring but belonged to that mixed-race family to which he was linked. But neither did he discharge Lilly for his brutality. Not until the overseer demanded a hefty pay increase did his employer look elsewhere. "Certainly I can never get a man who fulfills my purposes better than he does," wrote Jefferson, who would have given Lilly "a moderate advance" but was unwilling to pay more if he could find another disciplinarian to suit his purposes.[30]

For all his dependence on slave labor, Jefferson never ceased to regard slavery as contrary to the principles of the American Republic that he helped articulate. As he wrote John Holmes in 1820, "There is not a man on earth who would sacrifice more than I would, to relieve us from this heavy reproach, in any *practicable* way." Yet his aversion to a racially mixed society meant that he could not abide wholesale emancipation unless it involved *"expatriation,"* or removing those freed from the United States by colonizing them abroad, which was not embraced by many slaveholders and not desired by most African Americans. "We have the wolf by the ear," he remarked bleakly of slavery, "and we can neither hold him, nor safely let him go." He was left with the hope that diffusing slavery westward might dissipate it and gradually remove that stain on the nation's moral fabric and his own conscience. Yet far from making enslaved people "individually happier" and facilitating their emancipation, as he assured Holmes, diffusion from the East to emerging plantations on either side of the Mississippi compounded their miseries and spread the stain wider.[31] Among the beneficiaries were southeastern planters who profited from the growing demand for their surplus slaves beyond the Appalachians and hoped to reduce the risk of slave uprisings in the process.

Fears that slaves might revolt were heightened, however, by a tumultuous rebellion launched in the 1790s by free and enslaved Black people in the French Caribbean colony of Saint-Domingue who forged what would become the independent nation of Haiti. As Governor Charles Pinckney of South Carolina warned, white southerners might one day "be exposed to the same insurrection."[32] That Haitian uprising set the stage for the Louisiana Purchase when an army sent by Napoleon Bonaparte to suppress the revolution in 1802 was devastated by disease and armed resistance, prompting him to abandon plans for the military occupation of Louisiana, reclaimed by France two years earlier but still administered by Spain. Renouncing his North American ambitions in exchange for funds to further his European campaigns, Napoleon countered President Jefferson's bid to buy New Orleans from France and secure American control of the lower Mississippi by offering to sell Louisiana as a whole to the United States. The epic purchase that Jefferson then concluded would entail both blessings and burdens on the nation by extending it far across the continent but miring what he called America's empire of liberty more deeply in slavery.

CHAPTER 2

A Contested Purchase

July 4, 1803, was a "proud day" for the president. So stated the *National Intelligencer and Washington Advertiser*, which favored Thomas Jefferson and announced his Louisiana Purchase on the twenty-seventh anniversary of his Declaration of Independence. "The Executive," as the official notice in that newspaper referred to him, had received confirmation of a treaty signed in Paris on April 30 by which the United States obtained from France "the full right to and sovereignty over New Orleans, and the whole of Louisiana, as Spain possessed the same."[1] The French claim to Louisiana, which King Carlos IV of Spain had secretly agreed to return to France in 1800 under pressure from Napoleon, extended westward from French settlements along the Mississippi to the headwaters of its major tributaries in the Rockies. The $15 million purchase gave the United States control of the Mississippi, a vital commercial artery for the burgeoning American states and territories of the trans-Appalachian West, and claim to a vast expanse beyond that great river. That larger claim was tenuous and subject to dispute, however. It would be contested not only by Spain—which had retroceded Louisiana to France on condition that it not be transferred to a third party and denied that it extended beyond the Mississippi Valley—but also by Indian tribes that occupied much of Louisiana and had not ceded their territory to France.

Unlike those who hailed the Louisiana Purchase for doubling the nation's territory at the stroke of a pen, a misconception that endures to this day, Jefferson recognized that the United States would not have firm possession of tribal lands in Louisiana until their inhabitants relinquished them. He acknowledged as much in a proposed constitutional amendment that he drafted in July 1803 because the Constitution did not give the federal government authority to annex foreign territory. "The rights of occupancy in the soil, & of self-government, are confirmed to the Indian Inhabitants, as they now exist," his amendment stipulated.[2] Jefferson initially envisioned all but the French-settled portions of Louisiana, including New Orleans and vicinity, as a vast Indian territory that would accommodate existing tribes as well as tribes induced to remove there from east of the Mississippi.

That proposed amendment was not submitted to Congress. Granting Native Americans constitutional rights of occupancy might have hampered efforts to pressure them to cede territory by treaty, which Jefferson pursued to the benefit of his land-hungry supporters in the West. In any case, his constitutional objections to the treaty shifted when he received the text that summer. Of particular concern to him was Article III, which stated that inhabitants of Louisiana would be granted "all the rights, advantages and immunities of citizens of the United States . . . and protected in the free enjoyment of their liberty, property, and the religion which they profess."[3] This article was broad enough to encompass both the territory's white residents, among whom were numerous slaveholders, and those designated in French as "*gens de couleur libres*" (free people of color), many of whom were of mixed African and French ancestry. Alarmed by a provision that might be viewed as promising people of color citizenship rights denied to free African Americans in the South and in some northern states as well, Jefferson began drafting another constitutional amendment, which specified that Louisiana's "white inhabitants shall be citizens."[4]

Had such language been adopted, it would have been the only article in the Constitution explicitly restricting citizenship on the basis of race. But Jefferson soon decided against introducing a constitutional amendment that would not soon be ratified to validate the Louisiana Purchase, which had to be ratified promptly. After learning that Napoleon was having second thoughts about the treaty, which would be void if the U.S. Senate failed to approve it within six months of the signing on April 30, Jefferson submitted it to Congress as written. He deemed Louisiana too precious an opportunity to pass up and decided, in effect, not to look that gift horse in the mouth. His Federalist opponents in Congress, on the other hand, viewed Louisiana as a Trojan horse, which, if brought within the nation, might devastate their party and degrade the Union. They were losing support even in their northern base, where states had abolished slavery or were gradually emancipating those enslaved there, and their chances

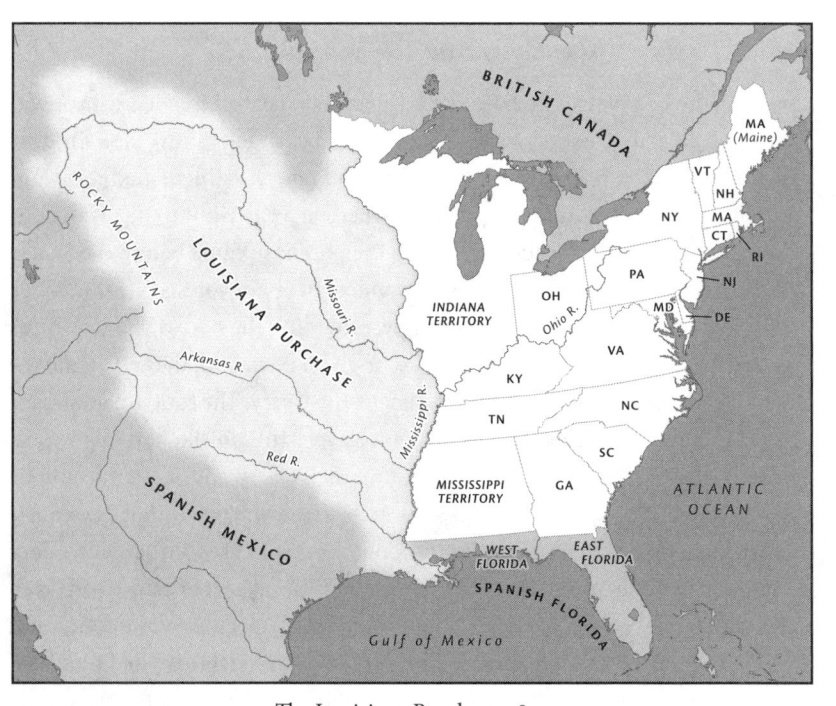

The Louisiana Purchase, 1803

of regaining the presidency or control of Congress might evaporate if Louisiana was admitted as American territory and gave rise to one or more slave states beholden to Republicans.

Some northern Federalists would sooner leave the Union than extend it to the benefit of Jefferson and his fellow Virginian and likely successor, Secretary of State Madison. That threat to secede would not be fulfilled, but sharp debate in Congress over the Louisiana Purchase foreshadowed further disputes in years to come when American expansion raised the specter of disunion. Relentless enlargement of the national domain—whether acquired from France, Britain, Spain, Mexico, or Indian tribes whose occupancy rights were honored in theory and flouted in practice—cast doubt on whether the American republic could preserve unity and integrity as it expanded and become a true empire of liberty, as Jefferson envisioned, or would instead suffer the fate of the late Roman Republic, whose conquests brought Rome more slaves than citizens and fostered fierce competition for control of the emerging Roman Empire, culminating in civil war.

At Odds with the "Negro President"

Opposing the Louisiana Purchase was an awkward stance for Federalists. Advocates of an assertive federal government, some had urged taking New Orleans by force in 1802 when Spanish officials, who had not yet relinquished control of Louisiana to French authorities, denied Americans the right to deposit goods at that port. When the treaty confirming the purchase came before the Senate in October 1803, however, Federalists provided all seven votes against it, while Republicans supported it overwhelmingly, providing the necessary two-thirds approval for ratification. Although badly outnumbered in both the Senate and the House, Federalists would continue to dispute the treaty. The fundamental issue that set them against the purchase was not slavery in Louisiana, though some deplored that practice, but the prospect that their party and section would be overwhelmed politically by slave states, which already enjoyed what Federalists deemed an unfair advantage under the Constitution's three-fifths clause. Foes of Jefferson derided him as the "Negro President" because that clause had given states with large numbers of slaves enough additional electoral votes to account for his slim margin of victory over John Adams.[5] Some who applied that label may also have had in mind Jefferson's reported intimacy with his slave Sally Hemings, alleged in print in 1802 by James Thomson Callender, who had been jailed under the Sedition Act for publishing diatribes against John Adams with Jefferson's help before being denied a patronage job and turning against him. "It is well known that the man, *whom it delighteth the people to honor*," Callender wrote, "keeps, and for many years past has kept, as his concubine, one of his own slaves. Her name is SALLY."[6] Republicans dismissed Callender's accusations as the ravings of a notorious scandalmonger and disappointed office seeker. For such skeptics, his death by drowning while intoxicated in July 1803 seemingly laid the matter to rest.

Federalists in Congress kept up their campaign against Jefferson's purchase by opposing enabling acts that would grant him funds and authority to implement the treaty and administer Louisiana. Leading that opposition in the House was Federalist firebrand Roger Griswold of Connecticut. In February 1798, Griswold had traded blows on the floor of the House with Republican Matthew Lyon of Vermont (who later that year became the first person tried for violating the Sedition Act, resulting in his conviction). Incensed after Lyon spat on him during a quarrel in the chamber and declared that "I did not come here to have my——kicked by everybody," Griswold caned Lyon, who grabbed fire tongs to defend himself.[7] Lyon, who had since been reelected to Congress while imprisoned in Vermont and now represented Kentucky, sparred verbally with Griswold when he questioned the validity of the Louisiana Purchase by introducing a resolution requesting from the president the text of the treaty that required Spain to return Louisiana to France, as well as any correspondence indicating whether Napoleon had honored that treaty and had clear title to Louisiana when he sold it to the United States. Lyon said that "he might have agreed to the resolution offered by the gentleman from Connecticut, had he brought it forward in a respectful manner. But the terms of the motion imply that the Executive has made a bargain for that, to which we have no right." Lyon objected to "the indecency of the motion" by the gentleman with whom he had once traded blows, but he later supported an amended version of Griswold's resolution, which was narrowly defeated.[8]

Thwarted in his efforts to prove that the Louisiana Purchase was invalid, as Spain protested, Griswold went on to denounce it on constitutional grounds. The government, he argued, had been formed by a "union of States," which probably would "never have consented to such a connexion, if a new world was to be thrown into the scale, to weigh down the influence which they might otherwise possess in the national councils." By opposing the purchase as contrary to the interests of northern states that consented to "become parties to the Union," Griswold was invoking the compact theory that Jefferson had asserted to uphold the right of states to nullify the Alien and Sedition Acts. "From this view of the subject," Griswold concluded, "I have been persuaded that the framers of the Constitution never intended that a power should reside in the President and Senate to form a treaty by which a foreign nation and people shall be incorporated into the Union, and that this treaty, so far as it stipulates for such an incorporation, is void."[9]

Several Republicans in the House rebutted Griswold's argument, including Virginian John Randolph of Roanoke, a cousin of Jefferson's, and Caesar Augustus Rodney of Delaware, who would later serve as attorney general under Jefferson. Rodney cited Article I, Section 8, of the Constitution, authorizing Congress to "provide for the common defence and general welfare of the United States" as ample grounds for enabling the treaty.[10] That same general welfare clause had been dismissed in 1791 by Secretary of State Jefferson as far too general to justify specific Federalist initiatives unspecified in the Constitution, such as chartering the Bank of the United States, the brainchild of Treasury Secretary Hamilton. Jefferson had denounced the bank's charter as "an act of *treason*" against the individual states because the Tenth Amendment reserved to them all powers not delegated to the United States in the Constitution, which he insisted gave the government no implied powers.[11] Federalists like Griswold who had supported the bank as a proper exercise of federal authority for the general welfare were now invoking states' rights in Jeffersonian fashion to oppose his treaty with France. Men on both sides in the Louisiana Purchase debate departed from core principles of their party to advance its interests.

To counter Federalist claims that incorporating foreign territory and its inhabitants in the Union was unprecedented and unconstitutional, Republican Samuel L. Mitchill of New York, a state where Jefferson's party was ascendant, cited the many treaties concluded with Indian tribes in the trans-Appalachian region that Great Britain had obtained from France in 1763 and ceded to the United States twenty years later:

> What, after all, was the amount of that cession by England? Certainly not a conveyance of a country which never was theirs, but rightfully belonged to the Indian natives; for it was, in its true construction, merely a *quit claim* of the pretensions or title to the land which the English had obtained by conquest and treaty from the French. By that negotiation, the United States obtained a bare relinquishment of the claims and possessions of those two powerful nations. But the paramount title of the original inhabitants was not affected by this. . . . The Indian tribes are as much aliens as any other foreign nations. Their lands are as much foreign dominion as the soil of France or Spain. Yet we have gone on to annex the territories which they sold us, to our present territory, from the time we acquired independence, and no mortal, until this debate arose, Mr. Chairman, has so much as thought that thereby a breach of the Constitution was made.[12]

In advancing this cogent argument for the purchase, Mitchill exposed just how slender America's claim was to that large portion of Louisiana situated west of the French settlements in the Mississippi Valley, which Spanish authorities would soon relinquish despite their objections to Napoleon's cession. To paraphrase Mitchill, what Jefferson purchased beyond those settlements and control of the Mississippi—vital assets worth a fortune to the nation—was a "bare relinquishment" of French pretensions to a vast Indian country whose tribes held "paramount title" to the land. French pretenses that Louisiana extended across the Great Plains to the Rockies originated with a grandiose assertion by explorer René-Robert Cavelier, sieur de La Salle, who in 1682 ventured down the Mississippi to its mouth and claimed for King Louis XIV of France the entire country drained by that river and "all rivers which discharge themselves thereinto."[13] Nothing accomplished by later French traders or officers who ventured up the Mississippi's western tributaries, including the Missouri, Arkansas, and Red Rivers, and dealt with tribes they encountered there gave France title to that Indian country or warranted the persistent American pretense that the Louisiana Purchase was a fabulous real estate deal, achieved at the trifling cost of a few cents an acre.

That was not the case because most of Louisiana remained unceded tribal territory. Jefferson acknowledged as much when he stated in his proposed constitutional amendment that Indians had "rights of occupancy in the soil," but he infringed on those rights when he urged removing beyond the Mississippi tribes that were not peaceful or prepared to adopt a settled way of life and relinquish much of their territory to white settlers. In 1803 he wrote Governor William Henry Harrison of Indiana Territory that "should any tribe be fool-hardy enough to take up the hatchet at any time," it should be stripped of its territory and driven across the Mississippi as an "example to others, and a furtherance of our final consolidation."[14] A year later, after Sac Indians killed some white intruders, Harrison imposed a treaty on chiefs of the allied Sac and Fox tribes that deprived them of their ancestral land east of the Mississippi and left them diminished territory within the Louisiana Purchase, where they had to contend with powerful tribal rivals such as Osages and Dakota Sioux. Decades of strife ensued, including a war waged in 1832 by American forces who repulsed Chief Black Hawk and his followers after they returned to Illinois. As such conflict demonstrated, the price paid to Napoleon for Louisiana was merely a down payment for a sweeping western claim that American officials, soldiers, and settlers would fulfill for the United States over the course of the nineteenth century at great effort and expense, including lives lost in Indian wars and in battles waged between Union and Confederate forces in Louisiana, Arkansas, Missouri, and other states or territories within Jefferson's contested purchase.

Exhilaration at gaining control of the Mississippi overwhelmed any such remote concerns in 1803, and Republicans easily prevailed in the House. Debate over enabling the Louisiana Purchase then shifted to the Senate, where opponents of the treaty warned of dire consequences for the Union. Federalist Samuel White of Delaware stated that possession of New Orleans and the Mississippi River was essential to the nation but that incorporating the "new, immense, unbounded world" beyond the Mississippi would be "the greatest curse that could at present befall us; it may be productive of innumerable evils, and especially of one that I fear even to look upon." White was alluding to the threat of disunion, which other foes of the purchase mentioned along with the danger of war with Spain.

Federalist Timothy Pickering observed that Spain contested the purchase "and, by her remonstrances, warns the United States not to touch Louisiana." He feared that "war was in the prospect, as the final result of our pacific measures—measures deemed so wise as to have been ascribed to divine inspiration!"[15] Although the threat of war would soon recede when Spanish authorities relinquished New Orleans, St. Louis, and other settlements along the Mississippi, it would resurface a few years later when Spain and the United States quarreled over the border between Louisiana and Texas, one of numerous disputes during the nineteenth century along the contested Spanish-Mexican-American frontier.

Pickering and his Federalist colleague, Senator Uriah Tracy of Connecticut, believed that not even a constitutional amendment could legitimize admitting to the Union a foreign country like Louisiana and its alien inhabitants, most of them French-speaking Catholics, whom Protestant New Englanders disdained as papists and had formerly been at odds with along the Canadian border. Those "people are probably as hostile to our Government, in its true construction, as they can be," Tracy claimed, "and the relative strength which this admission gives to a Southern and Western interest, is contradictory to the principles of our original Union." Annexation could be rightfully accomplished only "by universal consent of all the States or partners to our political association," he concluded. "And this universal consent I am positive can never be obtained to such a pernicious measure as the admission of Louisiana, of a world, and such a world, into our Union."[16]

Some critics of the Louisiana Purchase warned that a West embracing Louisiana would be too distant and distinct from the East to remain long attached to the Union. John Breckinridge of Kentucky, a close ally of Jefferson in the Senate, countered such objections by denying the theory that a republic "confined within narrow limits" was safer and more durable than an expansive republic. "Is the Goddess of Liberty restrained by water courses?" he asked. "Is her dominion on this continent confined to the east side of the Mississippi?" Furthermore, he insisted that "the people of the Western States are as sincerely attached to the Confederacy," by which he meant the Union, "and to the true principles of the Constitution, as any other quarter of the Union. A great portion of them have emigrated from the Atlantic States, and are attached to them by all those ties which so strongly bind societies together." Yet he admitted that such bonds could fray and warned that Kentuckians and other westerners might not remain forever devoted to the Union if denied such rights as the freedom to migrate to Louisiana secure in the knowledge that it was American territory. The present generation might endure that and cling to the Union, he stated:

But can you hope that those attachments, or dispositions to acquiesce in wrongs, will descend to our sons? Let no such calculations, I pray you, be made. . . . There is a point of endurance beyond which even the advocates for passive obedience and non-resistance cannot expect men to pass. That point is at once reached the moment you solemnly declare, by your vote, that a part of your citizens shall not enjoy those natural rights and advantages of which they are unjustly deprived, and which you have not the complete power to restore to them. Then it is that gentlemen may talk of danger to the Union; then it is I shall begin to tremble for my country; and then it is, and not till then, I shall agree with gentlemen that the Confederacy is in danger.[17]

More than a half century would elapse before the words "Union" and "Confederacy" took on starkly different meanings for a divided America. The tensions evident in Congress in 1803 did not reflect a fundamental conflict over slavery between rival parties or sections. There were antislavery Republicans and proslavery Federalists, including Charles Cotesworth Pinckney of South Carolina, a cousin of South Carolina's governor and senator Charles Pinckney and a former U.S. minister to France who would be the Federalist candidate for president in 1804 and 1808. Only Tracy, Pickering, White, and two other senators voted against funding the Louisiana Purchase, which was popular not only in the South and West but also among many northerners who cared more about enlarging the republic than about confining slavery. Nearly twelve thousand African Americans were still enslaved in New Jersey and more than twenty thousand in New York, where full emancipation would not be achieved for decades. Alexander Hamilton, who favored emancipation there, supported the Louisiana Purchase as a measure so clearly in the national interest that it outweighed any moral or political harm done by annexing territory where slavery prevailed. Broad acceptance of the treaty, however, did not preclude sharp debate over whether the inhabitants of Louisiana would be governed with or without their consent—and whether the presumed right of Americans to hold people as property and sell them to the highest bidder should be restricted or left unrestrained there.

Liberty for Louisiana?

On December 20, 1803, in New Orleans, General James Wilkinson and Governor William C. C. Claiborne of Mississippi Territory formally took possession of Louisiana from French officials, who had received it from Spanish authorities three weeks earlier. Claiborne would soon be appointed governor of Orleans Territory (the future state of Louisiana), divided in March 1804 from the District of Louisiana (including the future Missouri Territory), which would be administered by Wilkinson. While in New Orleans, Wilkinson renewed his contract as a secret Spanish agent by meeting furtively with the Marqués de Casa Calvo, former military commander of Spanish Louisiana, who paid him twelve thousand dollars for his services as a spy. In return, Wilkinson advised his paymasters on how to block American expansion beyond the Mississippi Valley. Spain should drive back "every illegal usurpation toward the region of Texas," Wilkinson urged, and intercept any American parties advancing up the Red River or Arkansas River toward Santa Fe, capital of Spanish New Mexico, from which the mineral-rich Mexican heartland might be invaded. Wilkinson went so far as to inform on the Lewis and Clark expedition, which was initiated by Jefferson and would head up the Missouri River from St. Louis in May 1804 on its way to the Pacific. Spanish troops should "intercept Captain Lewis and his party," he advised, "and force them to retire or take them prisoners."[18] Spanish forces sent in pursuit of Lewis and Clark failed to catch the Corps of Discovery, but other Spanish troops would later deter a Red River expedition dispatched by Jefferson in 1806. That party, led by Thomas Freeman and Peter Custis and accompanied by soldiers under Captain Richard Sparks, would turn back to avoid arrest after reaching what was later the Texas-Oklahoma border.

While Wilkinson was earning his keep as a Spanish agent in New Orleans, Congress was considering Jefferson's plan to divide Louisiana in two and form a government for Orleans Territory. (Those who debated that plan for Orleans Territory assumed its provisions would apply to Louisiana at large.) Jefferson chose not to claim authorship of the legislation, for reasons he explained when he sent his draft to Senator Breckinridge: "I must do it in confidence that you will never let any person know that I have put pen to paper on the subject . . . I am thus particular, because you know with what bloody teeth & fangs the federalists will attack any sentiment or principle known to come from me, & what blackguardisms & personalities they make it the occasion of vomiting forth."[19]

Those obstreperous Federalists were not the only critics of the bill introduced by Breckinridge, which was based largely on Jefferson's draft and called for Orleans Territory to be administered by a governor appointed by the president and a legislative council appointed by the governor. The bill denied Orleans an elective legislature, which less populous American territories obtained when their free adult male population reached five thousand. Senators William Cocke and Joseph Anderson of Tennessee, a state that backed Jefferson, denounced the governance bill vociferously. Let the people of that country "have liberty & a free government," said Cocke, according to the record of the debate kept by Senator Plumer (who often used dashes, suggesting that he was quoting speakers selectively and not transcribing their every word). "This bill I hope will not pass," Cocke added, "it is tyrannical." Anderson charged that the legislation reneged on the Louisiana Purchase Treaty, which promised the inhabitants "free enjoyment of their liberty." The bill, he added, "has not a single feature of our government in it—it is a system of tyranny, destructive of elective rights." Despite such objections, a majority in the Senate upheld the provision for an appointed legislature and defeated an amendment favored by Anderson and Cocke that would have allowed the legislature to elect a nonvoting delegate to Congress. Timothy Pickering, who had opposed the treaty, sided with the majority because he believed there was no basis for incorporating in the Union foreign territory or its inhabitants, particularly those lacking exposure to representative government. The people of Louisiana "are incapable of performing the duties or enjoying the blessings of a free government," he said. "They are too ignorant to elect suitable men."[20] Pickering's view that Louisianans should be ruled as colonists was not well calculated to appeal to citizens of a republic conceived in rebellion against colonial rule. Even in New England, Federalists were increasingly viewed as antidemocratic elitists who favored restricting suffrage and leadership to men suitably well-bred.

One point on which most Federalists and Republicans in the Senate agreed was that once Louisiana became American territory, Congress could regulate slavery there under its constitutional authority to "make all needful rules and regulations" regarding territory of the United States. (Because the Constitution gave Congress no such authority over states once they were admitted, political disputes over slavery often involved American territories.) In the past, Congress had prohibited slavery in the Northwest Territory and prohibited the international slave trade in Mississippi Territory, a restriction that could not be imposed on states constitutionally before 1808. Jefferson supported a similar prohibition on the foreign slave trade in Louisiana, but he proposed no restriction on importing to Louisiana slaves from American states that prohibited that foreign trade. Leading the effort in the Senate to impose broader restrictions was Federalist James Hillhouse of Connecticut, who remarked that slavery was too prevalent around New Orleans to be abolished outright. (The federal census conducted in Orleans Territory in 1810 would count 34,660 slaves among a non-Native population of 76,556.) "I believe that slavery is a real evil," Hillhouse stated, "but I am sensible we must extinguish it by degrees . . . These slaves are men—they have the passions and feelings of men—And I believe if we were slaves, we should not be more docile, more submissive, or virtuous than the negroes are."[21]

Hillhouse launched his effort to regulate slavery in Louisiana with a proposal that most who shared Jefferson's opposition to the international slave trade would approve—an amendment prohibiting the importation of slaves from "without the limits of the United States" and providing that every such slave introduced illegally to Louisiana "shall thereupon become entitled to, and receive his or her freedom." A few senators objected, including James Jackson of Georgia, who claimed that slaves were well treated in America and lived better in bondage "than if they were free," since they were in his opinion "incapable of liberty." Federalist Jonathan Dayton of New Jersey reckoned that imported Africans would make better laborers than surplus slaves offered for sale by American planters and should be admitted to the territory because "slaves must cultivate Louisiana—white people cannot subsist there without them."[22] Hillhouse's amendment was approved by a wide margin, however, as was a related measure designed to prevent slaves from being imported to Louisiana from South Carolina or Georgia, the only states that still allowed the international slave trade before it was abolished nationwide in 1808. Among the minority opposed to those amendments was the eldest son of former president Adams, Federalist John Quincy Adams of Massachusetts, who disdained slavery but considered incorporating foreign territory and imposing laws on its inhabitants unconstitutional. He had reluctantly approved the purchase treaty as in the nation's interest, but he argued that neither the Constitution nor the people of Louisiana gave Congress authority "to legislate for them."[23]

Hillhouse was unable to win approval for a more ambitious amendment requiring that slaves brought to Louisiana from American states or territories not be held in bondage for more than a year after men turned twenty-one or women turned eighteen. To mollify senators from the South, he included a fugitive-slave clause and argued that restricting slavery in Louisiana would reduce the need to defend against slave uprisings. "Every slave increases the necessity of a standing army," he remarked. "Every slave weakens the power of the militia."[24] His emancipation proposal ran counter to Jefferson's thinking, however, and was opposed not only by Breckinridge and most other southern senators but also by northerners with constitutional objections like Adams, resulting in its defeat by six votes. Hillhouse then proposed an amendment aimed at excluding slave traders, which in its final form stated that no slaves could be introduced except by an American citizen who was their "*bona fide* owner" and entered the territory for "actual settlement."[25] Any slaves imported otherwise would be freed.

Maryland had enacted a similar law in 1796 that called for emancipating any slaves introduced there who were not held by people taking up "*bona fide* residence" in the state.[26] But several senators argued against applying that restriction to Louisiana. James Jackson, who had earlier argued that Black people enslaved in America had little cause for complaint, now warned that those freed would incite rebellion among those who remained enslaved and "render a standing army necessary" to protect the white inhabitants. "A very few *free negroes* in Louisiana would revolutionize that country," he claimed.[27] In fact, there were many such people living peacefully in and around New Orleans. (The 1810 census would record more than 7,500 free Black inhabitants of Orleans Territory.) Spanish officials had lowered barriers that prevented slaves in Louisiana from earning their liberty. Far from revolutionizing the country, free men of color served in a separate Black militia, established under French rule to help defend the colony, and petitioned Governor Claiborne to preserve their unit under American authority. He offered them assurances but worried that they might become an "armed enemy in the very heart of the Country." Jefferson wrote that they were to be "treated favorably" until a "better settled state of things shall permit us to let them neglect themselves."[28]

To Jackson's argument that freeing slaves would trigger a race war, Senator Breckinridge added the objection that the restrictions Hillhouse proposed on introducing slaves to Louisiana would thwart the diffusion or spread of slavery to the West from the South, where it was dangerously concentrated. "I think it good policy to permit slaves to be sent there from the United States," Breckinridge said of Louisiana. "This will disperse and weaken that race—& free the southern states from a part of its black population, & of its danger."[29] Jefferson might not have argued in such stark terms for diffusing slavery westward, but he shared Breckinridge's assumption that doing so would ease the burden of slavery in existing southern states and make it less prevalent and troubling there. That argument failed to account for the natural increase of the enslaved African American population, which enabled the formation of seven new slave states by 1845 without reducing the enslaved population in the older South as a whole or easing fears of slave uprisings among its white inhabitants. Such fears were not unfounded, but those few attempted slave rebellions of any magnitude that were not exposed and crushed in advance proved less deadly for white southerners than for Black rebels, suspects, or scapegoats. Nat Turner's rebellion in 1831, which he called a "struggle for freedom," was by far the costliest such uprising in the South for its intended victims, claiming the lives of at least fifty-five white Virginians, but far more Black people were executed or lynched in response, most of them uninvolved in the rebellion.[30]

The main benefit of diffusion for eastern planters like Jefferson was not that it reduced the risk of slave rebellions but that it provided a market for their surplus slaves in southwestern territories and states. He remained troubled by slavery and clung to the hope that diffusion would ameliorate it, but slaves forcibly removed from Virginia and other states east of the Appalachians to plantations on either side of the Mississippi were often separated from family members in the process and subjected to harder labor and harsher treatment. As one Virginian in Richmond noted in 1807, "There is a very great aversion amongst our Negroes to be carried to distant parts, & particularly to our new countries." Those purchased by traders in eastern states were driven in shackles overland to slave auctions in the Southwest or shipped there in wretched conditions reminiscent of the notorious transatlantic trade. In 1810 a trader newly arrived in Mississippi Territory advertised for sale "twenty likely Virginia born slaves" stored like cargo in his flat-bottomed boat at Natchez.[31] That unconscionable domestic slave trade cast a dismal shadow over Jefferson's so-called empire of liberty.

Such were the conundrums of his political philosophy, which inspired abolitionists as well as slaveholders, that some Jeffersonians shifted positions during debate on the Hillhouse amendments. Breckinridge favored replacing the requirement that slaves imported illegally to the territory be freed with a provision that traders who violated the act pay a fine and forfeit their slaves, who could then be "recovered by any person who shall sue for the same."[32] But when that motion failed, he voted for the amendment as proposed by Hillhouse, which passed by a substantial margin and embodied the contradictions of the Jeffersonian era by recognizing both the rights of bona fide slave owners and the wrongs of the slave trade. Another Republican senator who wavered during the debate was Stephen R. Bradley of Vermont, who had stated early on that he opposed restricting slaveholding in Louisiana because it was a right people there claimed, and "by the treaty we are bound to grant it to them." When Hillhouse continued to press the matter, however, he forced Bradley to choose between the supposed property rights of slaveholders and the inalienable right to liberty of those they enslaved. Bradley ended up supporting both the ambitious emancipation amendment that failed and the successful amendment that prohibited importing slaves from existing states or territories for sale in Louisiana, using

"Gang of Slaves Journeying to Be Sold in a Southern Market." Engraving
in J. S. Buckingham, *The Slave States of America* (1842). Courtesy Library
of Congress Prints and Photographs Division (LC-cph-3c08055).

strong words that included a biblical injunction against seizing and selling people:
"I abhor slavery—I am opposed to it in every shape—*He that steals a man & sells
him ought to die*—I will on every question vote against slavery—I am very sorry
the question is *now* called up,—I have done everything I could to prevent it—but
since gentlemen, (& many of them from Slave States) will stir the question, I am
prepared & will on all occasions vote against slavery."[33]

Both Stephen Bradley and John Breckinridge were Jeffersonians and Republicans (also known as Democratic Republicans, a label distinguishing them from
Federalists wary of democracy). But the party that embraced their divergent
views of liberty for all and slaveholders' property rights would not long endure,
and their descendants would join rival parties. Bradley's son William would
oppose extending slavery to America's western territories and embrace the new
Republican Party, which he helped establish in Vermont in the 1850s. Breckinridge's renowned grandson, Vice President John C. Breckinridge, would run for
president in 1860 as the nominee of southern Democrats and would subsequently
join the Confederacy and wage war against the Union.

The prohibition against traders introducing slaves from American states to Orleans Territory that Hillhouse attached to the governance act of 1804 was an important precedent for later congressional efforts to restrict slavery. But it was quickly superseded when the Republican-controlled Congress passed and Jefferson signed a new governance act in 1805 designed to meet objections from Louisianans. They did not like having a legislative council imposed on them, a complaint remedied by the act of 1805, which provided for an elective legislature in Orleans Territory. But the main grievance of white Louisianans, including Anglo-Americans who settled among the French colonists, was the 1804 prohibition against traders importing slaves from the United States or abroad, which made establishing and maintaining labor-intensive sugar or cotton plantations more difficult and expensive. "On this point," Claiborne wrote, "the people here have united as one man!"[34] A petition to Congress protesting abolition of the slave trade and demanding statehood for Louisiana was approved in July 1804 at a meeting in New Orleans from which free people of color were excluded. Later that year, the Senate received a memorial or "remonstrance" from "planters, merchants, and other inhabitants of Louisiana," who argued that only "African laborers" could raise crops there and build levees on the banks of the Mississippi in "heat intolerable to whites." Without the "African trade," they warned, "cultivation must cease, the improvements of a century be destroyed, and the great river resume its empire over our ruined fields and demolished habitations." An anonymous satirist mocked those memorialists in a poem sent to Jefferson that ended: "Receive us to your arms as Brothers / And grant us to *make slaves of others*."[35]

The governance act of 1805 eliminated all slavery restrictions on Orleans Territory except the one that Jefferson favored: prohibition of the international slave trade. And that was eased by eliminating the clause in the 1804 act barring transshipment of slaves from American states that still allowed the foreign trade. Following passage of the 1805 act, notices appeared in the *Louisiana Gazette* offering Africans for sale—among them "12 Young Brute Negroes of the Mandingo and Congo nations, fit for a sugar estate"—and announcing the arrival of slave ships from Africa. One such vessel, the *Ethiopian*, delivered "140 Prime Congo Negroes" to New Orleans in 1807 by way of Charleston, South Carolina, where the ship docked long enough to give the sale of its captives in Orleans Territory the veneer of legality.[36] After such commerce was prohibited nationwide in 1808, an illicit foreign slave trade would be carried on by pirates and smugglers like Jean Lafitte, operating out of Barataria Bay at the mouth of the Mississippi. Slave traders had less incentive to infiltrate the remote District of Louisiana administered at St. Louis. There were fewer slaveholders there than around New Orleans, but they pressured American authorities to grant them a separate governance act in 1805 that made no mention of slavery and thus enabled that practice to flourish unimpeded in what was redesignated Missouri Territory when Orleans Territory became the state of Louisiana in 1812. Seven years later, Missouri would follow Louisiana's lead and apply for admission as a slave state, triggering a bitter sectional dispute that confounded some of the same legislators who debated restricting slavery in 1804.

Jefferson could not foresee that crisis when he followed the path of least resistance as president and endorsed acts that accommodated slaveholders within the Louisiana Purchase. He was in no position to condemn them, having made his own accommodation with slavery, and he wanted to bind proslavery Louisianans to the Union and prevent separatist schemes of the sort that sprouted in the trans-Appalachian West as Kentucky and Tennessee advanced to statehood. That extending slaveholding territory in the Southwest and free territory in the Northwest in an effort to balance the republic and mediate its sectional differences might instead accentuate those differences would not be evident until the Missouri controversy erupted.

Disunion appeared a remote threat when Jefferson was resoundingly reelected in 1804 with broad support from northerners and southerners alike. But there were signs that this fast-growing young republic might not be immune to dissension and division, including a separatist scheme hatched by New Englanders shortly before that election and a plot enacted subsequently by outgoing vice president Aaron Burr in conjunction with General Wilkinson. That conspiracy would revive Jefferson's fears that the West he viewed as the nation's ultimate land of promise might yet slip from its grasp—and would serve as a test case for determining what constituted treason and whether Americans were legally entitled to promote secession.

Yankee Separatists and the Burr Conspiracy

Prominent New Englanders who sought their own confederacy following the Louisiana Purchase felt they were losing their rightful place in the nation. What troubled defiant Federalists like Timothy Pickering, leader of that separatist scheme, was not just the political advantage Republicans would gain as slave states emerged beyond the Mississippi but the decline of his own party in the Northeast, where men of modest means increasingly favored Republicans. If Federalism was "crumbling away in New England," Pickering wrote, "there is no time to be lost, lest it should be overwhelmed." He hoped for a northern league that would include populous New York, which "must be made the center of the confederacy."[37]

That was a tall order for a separatist movement limited to a handful of influential figures from a few New England states, including Pickering of Massachusetts, Plumer of New Hampshire, and Hillhouse, Tracy, and Griswold of Connecticut. In January 1804 they met with Vice President Aaron Burr, hoping to recruit him to their cause. Burr knew that he would soon be discarded by Jefferson, who had distrusted him ever since the two received the same number of electoral votes in the presidential election of 1800 and Burr, his presumed running mate, remained in contention until the House of Representatives decided in Jefferson's favor. Burr was now preparing to return to New York, which he had helped carry for Republicans in 1800, and seek the governorship. He had support among Federalists there because he was not beholden to the southern base of his party and was as well-bred as any Federalist dignitary, having graduated at sixteen from Princeton (then the College of New Jersey), where both his father and his maternal grandfather, theologian Jonathan Edwards, had served as president. Pickering and company queried Burr to see if he might back their plan for a northern confederacy including New York. When Hillhouse predicted that two separate governments would soon form within the country, Burr gave Plumer the impression that "he not only thought *such an event would take place—but that it was necessary it should.*" Reflecting on the meeting afterward, however, Plumer concluded that Burr had not committed himself and that "perhaps no man's language was ever so apparently explicit, & at the same time so covert & indefinite."[38]

Alexander Hamilton was alarmed when he learned that those Yankee separatists had met with Burr, whom he considered fully capable of severing the Union. In February 1804, Hamilton warned Federalists convening in Albany—who had no hope of electing one of their own governor and had to choose between Republican candidates—not to back Burr, who would draw New Yorkers and New Englanders into a northern confederacy by exploiting resentment of Jefferson "and jealousy of the ambition of Virginia." It would suit Burr, Hamilton added, to serve as chief of those seeking "dismemberment of the Union . . . And placed at the head of the state of New York no man would be more likely to succeed."[39] Hamilton's portrait of Burr as a secessionist mastermind added fuel to their combustible rivalry. But it was not as damaging to Burr's cause as the relentless attacks on him in print by scandalmonger James Cheetham, who backed the successful candidate Morgan Lewis, favored by the powerful Clinton family. Shortly before the election, Cheetham claimed that Burr invited "gentlemen of color" to a ball at his home, described as a bordello with mirrors on the bedroom walls, where they were offered indecent "amusements." That was meant to turn white voters against Burr, who owned slaves but had supported gradual emancipation in New York, as Hamilton did. But any values held in common by those archrivals, who had both served with distinction as officers in the Revolutionary War, were set aside when Burr suffered a stinging defeat in late April following scurrilous charges by Cheetham, who claimed that Hamilton had accused Burr of "atrocious" acts. Either Burr was guilty as charged, Cheetham added, or he dared not challenge Hamilton and was the most "despicable bastard in the universe."[40]

Cheetham could not have chosen a more inflammatory word to precede "bastard" than "despicable"—considered an affront to a gentleman's honor, which depended on whether he was respected or despised by his peers. During the campaign, Burr refused to respond to such taunts and promised his married daughter, Theodosia, to whom he remained devoted following the death in 1794 of his wife, Theodosia, that he would send her "some new and amusing libels against the vice president."[41] But he was not amused when he learned in June of a letter published shortly before the election describing a dinner party where Hamilton called Burr a "dangerous man and one who ought not to be trusted with the reins of Government" and went on to express a "still more despicable opinion" of him, which remained unspecified.[42] That implied something worse than Hamilton's attacks on Burr's political character, something so sordid it could not be mentioned in print. Burr demanded a prompt "acknowledgment or denial" that his rival had ever uttered such an opinion. Hamilton responded that he would not be "interrogated as to the justness of the *inferences* which may be drawn by *others* from whatever I may have said of a political opponent in the course of a fifteen years competition."[43] Their tragic affair of honor ended on July 11, 1804, when they dueled on the west bank of the Hudson River in New Jersey and Burr mortally wounded Hamilton, who died the next day.

Following the duel, the notorious Burr seemingly confirmed some of the worst things Hamilton had said about him. His detractors found him doubly despicable for taking a life of far greater value to the republic than his own and then allegedly seeking to separate the West from the Union. But others were reluctant to condemn him. Although indicted in New York for dueling and in New Jersey for murder, both charges were eventually dropped. Many Americans still considered it proper for a man to defend his honor at gunpoint. Even Federalists like Plumer were impressed when Burr concluded his vice presidency by presiding impartially over the Senate impeachment trial of Supreme Court Justice Samuel Chase, a stern Federalist enforcer of the Alien and Sedition Acts and outspoken critic of Jeffersonian democracy, whose acquittal irked the president. "He can never I think rise again," Plumer wrote of Burr before he left office in March 1805. "But surely he is a very extraordinary man, & is an exception to all rules."[44] Jefferson would conclude that he defied all rules and was just what Hamilton took him to be: a dangerous man capable of dismembering the Union.

In the spring of 1805, Burr journeyed down the Ohio and Mississippi Rivers to New Orleans. Among those he visited along the way was Andrew Jackson, who commanded the Tennessee state militia. Jackson had little regard for Spanish sovereignty in North America and contracted with Burr to purchase boats and provisions for an assault on Spanish territory, to which Jackson would commit militia in the event of war. Among the borderlands that beckoned to American expansionists as Spain grew weaker were Texas and East and West Florida (two Spanish territories divided at the Apalachicola River, from which West Florida extended along the Gulf of Mexico to the Mississippi River). Jefferson himself staked a speculative claim to Texas and West Florida by asserting wishfully that they were included in the Louisiana Purchase. Burr's ultimate goal was evidently to wrest control of the Mexican heartland from Spain, but lightly defended Texas or the Floridas could be targeted with fewer forces. When later told that Burr planned to seize American territory as well, Jackson found that hard to believe but wrote that if he really meant "to become a traitor," being torn to pieces and "scattered with the four winds of heaven would be too good for him."[45]

In 1806, Joseph H. Daveiss, U.S. district attorney in Kentucky, wrote Jefferson that Burr was plotting with General Wilkinson and others to "cause a revolt of the Spanish provinces, and a severance of all these western states and territories from the union."[46] A Federalist who reviled Burr for killing Hamilton, Daveiss lacked proof that he was a separatist but had reason to suspect Burr of conspiring with General Wilkinson to seize Spanish territory. They had been considering such a foray since May 1804, when Wilkinson arranged a clandestine meeting with Burr at his home in New York City. "I propose to take a Bed with you this night," Wilkinson wrote, "if it may be done without observation or intrusion." Wilkinson brought with him maps of Mexico and had ties to other notable figures with designs on that country, including John Adair, who represented Kentucky in the U.S. House and Senate. In a letter to Wilkinson, Adair described Kentuckians as "full of enterprise" and "as greedy after plunder as ever the old Romans were. Mexico glitters in our Eyes—the word is all we wait for."[47] As commander of the

Aaron Burr (1756–1836). Courtesy Library of Congress Prints and Photographs Division (LC-USZ62-52550).

U.S. Army, Wilkinson was in position to anticipate, and perhaps precipitate, a border war that might legitimize a filibuster or unauthorized invasion. If war was not in the offing, Wilkinson could ensure that no U.S. troops intervened to halt a foray that many westerners would welcome. He seemingly had no more qualms about betraying his Spanish paymasters than he did about betraying American secrets to them.

Did Burr seek command of a western empire embracing American as well as Spanish possessions, as charged when he was later tried for treason? Apparent confirmation would surface many years later in a report to London by Anthony Merry, British minister to the United States. Merry stated that Burr offered in 1804 to "lend his assistance to His Majesty's Government in any Manner in which they may think fit to employ him, particularly endeavoring to effect a Separation of the Western Part of the United States." Burr may have fed Merry that story, however, hoping in vain for British aid he might then use to invade Spanish territory. By 1806 the main grievance of westerners—foreign control of New Orleans and the lower Mississippi—had been eliminated by Jefferson's purchase. As John Adams later remarked, the vast plot attributed to Burr, including inciting rebellion in Republican strongholds like Kentucky and Tennessee, made him sound like "an idiot or a lunatic."[48] He certainly did not fit that description, but he may have flirted with separatism, and he stood to gain favor and followers in the West if his would-be Mexican filibuster went as planned.

One American possession of keen interest to Burr was New Orleans. He knew from his visit there in 1805 that it contained likely recruits for a filibuster, including members of a conspiratorial association for whom "liberating" Mexico glittered as brightly as plundering it did for Adair's Kentuckians. Using New Orleans as a base from which to invade Mexico, whose core could be reached much quicker by sea from that city than overland, would not violate the Neutrality Act of 1794 if the United States went to war with Spain. By mid-1806, conflict appeared imminent on the disputed boundary between Orleans Territory and Spanish Texas. Wilkinson was ordered to depart St. Louis, where he was governing the District of Louisiana, and defend that frontier. Before leaving, Wilkinson dispatched a small party of soldiers led by Lieutenant Zebulon M. Pike on an arduous expedition that carried them up the Arkansas River to its frigid headwaters in the Rockies and then southward to New Mexico, where they were arrested by Spanish troops in February 1807 and conducted first to Santa Fe and thence to Chihuahua for interrogation and confinement. Pike and men of his party were eventually released, but he would be shadowed by his association with the nefarious Wilkinson and suspicions that he was somehow involved in the Burr Conspiracy. Wilkinson had informed Secretary of War Henry Dearborn in advance of Pike's expedition, however, stating that a military reconnaissance of the route to New Mexico might be useful if U.S. forces were called on to "take possession" there. Dearborn approved and wrote that such an invasion might perhaps "become necessary."[49] Seizing Mexico would long intrigue dutiful officials like Dearborn and ambitious officers like Pike as well as conspirators like Burr and Wilkinson. Four decades after Pike's expedition, American troops would set out on the Santa Fe Trail he helped pioneer to occupy New Mexico and invade Chihuahua.

When Wilkinson approached the Texas boundary in September 1806, rumors were surfacing in print that he was plotting with Burr, who planned to convey several hundred recruits down the Ohio and Mississippi Rivers to New Orleans. Wilkinson concluded that he was in too precarious a position to further the conspiracy and instead exposed and exaggerated it. In late October he wrote Jefferson that a "powerfull association, extending from New York through the Western States, to the Territories bordering on the Mississippi, has been formed with the design to levy and rendezvous eight or Ten thousand men in New Orleans at a very near period; and from thence, with the co-operation of a Naval Armament, to carry an Expedition against Vera Cruz," the strategic port on Mexico's east coast from which invaders could advance on Mexico City. Wilkinson claimed that "the revolt of this [Orleans] Territory, will be made an auxiliary Step to the main design of attacking Mexico." He did not initially identify the "prime mover" of that plot, but Wilkinson later wrote Jefferson that he intended to arrest Burr.[50] Having turned informer, he had no ulterior motive to wage war and came to terms with the opposing Spanish commander on the contested border by establishing the Neutral Ground between Orleans Territory and Texas, an outcome that Jefferson welcomed. Wilkinson then set out with troops to defend New Orleans against Burr's supposedly massive forces. "Let us save it if we can," he wrote his second-in-command, Colonel Thomas H. Cushing, "and if necessary let us be buried together in the place we shall defend."[51] Wilkinson imposed martial law in New Orleans and jailed numerous suspects, including men aware of his involvement in the conspiracy.

Burr's expedition collapsed before he or his recruits could reach that city. He was arraigned that November in Kentucky—where lawyer and future political luminary Henry Clay helped him avoid indictment by a grand jury convened by Joseph Daveiss—and was cleared again in early 1807 by grand jurors in Mississippi Territory. He was then taken into custody by federal officers and conducted in March to Richmond, Virginia, to be tried there for treason. Jefferson informed Congress before the proceedings began that Burr was guilty "beyond question."[52] He professed not to be alarmed should westerners ever choose freely to separate from the Union, but the prospect of losing the West he cherished to the perfidious Burr appalled him. He credited self-serving accusations by Wilkinson as well as claims by Daveiss and others at odds with Burr that his designs on American territory went far beyond New Orleans. He did not just plan to invade Mexico and "place himself on the throne of Montezuma," Jefferson wrote; he meant to "extend his empire to the Allegany [Appalachians]," seizing on New Orleans "as the instrument of compulsion for our Western states."[53]

Even if all that were true, however, Burr's conduct was not necessarily treasonous. As ruled by Chief Justice John Marshall, who presided over the trial in Richmond, "conspiring to subvert by force the government of our country" was not treason, which involved only overt acts against the government as specified in the Constitution.[54] The prosecution had to prove that Burr had levied war against the United States or assembled troops for that purpose, a hard case to make and one complicated by the fact that the star witness, Wilkinson, was rendered suspect by his intimate knowledge of the plot. A grand jury indicted Burr, but some on the panel wanted to indict the general as well. Their foreman, John Randolph of Roanoke, now a political adversary of his cousin Jefferson, called Wilkinson "a mammoth of iniquity," and Andrew Jackson added his voice to those in Richmond who charged Wilkinson with hiding his own guilt by denouncing Burr. Yet Jefferson assured the general that "no one is more sensible than myself of the injustice which has been aimed at you."[55]

Burr, who took part in his own defense, objected in court that Jefferson drew partly on press accounts to portray him and his confederates as rebels engaged in "a civil war." For months, authorities had been seeking evidence of that war in vain, Burr claimed: "There was, to be sure, a most terrible war in the newspapers, but nowhere else."[56] Witnesses other than Wilkinson testified that Burr spoke to them of disunion, but Marshall's ruling made clear that talk did not constitute treason. On September 1, 1807, Burr was acquitted of that crime by jurors who remained suspicious of him and qualified their verdict by stating that he was "not proved to be guilty." Later that month in Richmond, he was also acquitted of violating the Neutrality Act. His defense as asserted by his chief counsel, John Wickham—that his expedition was planned "in concurrence with General Wilkinson, against the dominions of the king of Spain, in case of a war"—had prevailed in court.[57]

Although pleased that westerners had not been seduced by Burr, Jefferson was exasperated by his acquittal, which came as the president was struggling to assert the nation's maritime rights as a neutral in the ongoing war between France and Britain, whose Royal Navy intercepted American ships and seized sailors suspected of deserting British vessels, contributing ultimately to the War of 1812. Jefferson accused Federalists he regarded as monarchists and British sympathizers of making "Burr's cause their own, mortified only that he did not separate the union or overturn the government." And he blamed the verdict in Richmond on his distant relative John Marshall, a Federalist appointed by John Adams. "We had supposed we possessed fixed laws to guard us equally against treason & oppression," Jefferson wrote. "But it now appears we have no law but the will of the judge."[58] What Marshall required to prove treason, however, was based on strict construction of the Constitution and the rights it afforded Americans. Those rights were dear to the president, who abhorred the Sedition Act of 1798, which made it a crime to "counsel, advise, or attempt to procure" insurrection and might have been used against Burr had not Jefferson allowed the act to expire to protect freedom of speech.[59] Yet he feared for his empire of liberty if men like Burr could defy the government with impunity. The problem Jefferson faced was that empire and liberty were often at odds. Constitutional liberty allowed Americans to urge secession without being arraigned as traitors. Furthermore, those who defied federal law by filibustering against friendly or neutral countries were seldom convicted, and they frequently infringed on

Spanish or Mexican territory that if acquired by the United States would heighten sectional tensions and foster disunion.

Empire and liberty seemingly went hand in hand when troops or treaty makers enabled Anglo-Americans to advance freely across the continent, but that often involved taking liberties with those of other nations or races. Under Jefferson and his successor Madison, huge land cessions were extracted from tribal leaders deceptively in peacetime or punitively in wartime by men at the forefront of American expansion such as William Clark, William Henry Harrison, and Andrew Jackson. They were furthering an imperial scheme like that attributed to Burr but driven by the continental ambitions of Jefferson and subsequent presidents, fulfilled at mid-century when U.S. troops forced Mexico to cede a vast area from Texas to California by seizing its capital, once the seat of the Aztec ruler Montezuma, on whose fabled throne Burr supposedly planned to perch. His plot may not have been as treacherous as Jefferson imagined, but it foreshadowed that later American assault on Mexico, which would intensify disputes over slavery in an empire dedicated to liberty and strain the Union to the breaking point.

CHAPTER 3

Lewis and Clark, William Henry Harrison, and the Northwestern Frontier

On September 23, 1806, Meriwether Lewis and William Clark returned with the Corps of Discovery to St. Louis, completing their epic journey to the Pacific and back. "We were met by all the village and received a harty welcom from it's inhabitants," noted Clark, whose irregular spelling was not uncommon among literate Americans then.[1] St. Louis was still largely a French town dominated by venturesome fur traders like Pierre and Auguste Chouteau, but Anglo-American residents joined such notables at a banquet honoring the explorers. Lewis and Clark launched the festivities by proposing a toast to President Jefferson, "the polar star of *discovery*." Many toasts followed, among them a cautionary tribute to the American states, concluding that *"united they stand—but divided they fall."*[2] That refrain, popularized during the American Revolution, may have referred on this occasion to the political rift between Jefferson's Republicans and opposing Federalists or to rumors that Aaron Burr was plotting to break the Union apart. Few at the ball could have imagined that Americans would one day be at odds over the fate of their sparsely settled Louisiana Territory—redesignated Missouri Territory in 1812 and fiercely debated when Congress took up Missouri's application for admission as a slave state in 1819.

The overriding concern in St. Louis in the last years of the Jefferson administration was not slavery but how to reconcile tribes in the area to the influx of American settlers from east of the Mississippi. Of the territory's twenty thousand or so non-Native inhabitants enumerated in the census of 1810, about three thousand were slaves. Gradual emancipation could have been undertaken there without drastic upheaval, as happened in some northern states. But there were few abolitionists among the territory's French inhabitants, who were accustomed to slavery even if they did not practice it, or among American newcomers, who came largely from the Upper South and often brought slaves with them. Some slaveholders from Virginia or Kentucky who might otherwise have settled in the Northwest Territory, where slavery was prohibited, went to Missouri instead. Lewis and Clark were Virginia-born slave owners, and each would serve as territorial governor of Missouri. Neither they nor the Virginians who appointed them, Jefferson and Madison, considered it their mission to uphold slavery. They were more concerned with tribal matters, which was Clark's sole responsibility as U.S. Indian agent in St. Louis before he became governor in 1813. But their authoritative presence in Missouri signaled that slaveholding would not be challenged there as the territory advanced toward statehood. Clark's handling of his slaves—notably York, his manservant—was representative of slavery as practiced and perpetuated in Missouri, where it was not relentlessly brutal but conditioned masters who might be conscientious in other respects to treat African Americans as movable property or chattel (a word derived from the same root as "cattle"), to be trounced if recalcitrant, hired out to the highest bidder, or sold down the river.

"My Man York"

Born in 1770, William Clark was placed as a boy under the care of York, who was perhaps a few years older than him. In addition to serving as Clark's helpmate, York was probably his playmate. The two may have hunted together, for trusted slaves like York were allowed to handle guns, and he later shot elk, bison, and other game while with the Corps of Discovery. In 1785 the Clark household settled near Louisville, where they established a new home called Mulberry Hill. When his father died in 1799, Clark inherited that estate and eight slaves, including York and a couple listed in the will as old York and his wife, Rose. (Old York was York's father, and Rose may have been his mother or more likely his stepmother.) Before setting out across the continent in 1804, Clark met his future wife, Julia Hancock of Virginia—a girl who was then about twelve years old—and York married an enslaved woman in Louisville.

York was one of two people attached to the Corps of Discovery who belonged to someone else, the other being Sacagawea, a young Shoshone woman who had been captured by Hidatsa warriors and was later purchased, or won in a gamble, by her husband Toussaint Charbonneau, a French-Canadian trader. Lewis and Clark hired Charbonneau as an interpreter, but Sacagawea also proved

William Clark (1770–1838).
Courtesy Library of Congress
Prints and Photographs
Division (LC-USZ62-10609)

quite useful to them in that capacity. Her contribution to the success of the
corps would be duly acknowledged, but York's role was more significant than
indicated by his reputation as the expedition's odd man out, whose race made
him remarkable to Indians who had never encountered a Black person. He was
indeed viewed by people of various tribes, including Arikaras the corps met
with along the Missouri River in October 1804, as "big Medison [medicine]," or
imbued with spirit power which they attributed to impressive strangers. But his
power depended on fulfilling their expectations and sustaining that impression
rather than appearing fearful or weak. "Those Indians wer much astonished at
my Servent," Clark wrote of the Arikaras, "they never Saw a black man before,
all flocked around him & examind him from top to toe, he Carried on the joke
and made himself more turribal than we wished him to doe."[3]

Clark may have worried that York would alarm and antagonize Arikaras
with his performance, but it enhanced his "medicine." Clark later told Nicholas
Biddle, who composed the first full narrative of the expedition, that an Arikara
man invited York to his lodge and stood guard at the entrance while York had sex
with his wife. Various members of the corps probably had sexual relations with

Native American women at one time or another during the expedition. Clark himself was said to have fathered a child in that way, a rumor that later caused him trouble when he unsuccessfully sought election as the first governor of the state of Missouri. York proved his mettle as a member of the corps not just by demonstrating to Indians his spirit power, sexually or otherwise, but by hunting skillfully, tending men who fell sick—including the expedition's lone casualty, Sergeant Charles Floyd, who died of a ruptured appendix in August 1804—and searching for Clark, Charbonneau, and Sacagawea when they were stranded by a flood near the Great Falls of the Missouri in mid-1805. When he found them, Clark noted, York was "greatly agitated, for our wellfar." In his journals, Clark referred to York not just as his servant but as "my black man York" or simply "my man York."[4] His standing was not much different from that of other men in the corps, who were free but subject to the authority of Lewis and Clark, as he was. When the expedition ended, York had reason to feel that he had earned his freedom, but he remained enslaved and his relationship with Clark deteriorated.

In October 1806, York accompanied Clark back to Mulberry Hill. According to family lore recorded by Clark's nephew William Clark Kennerly, York displayed Indian mementos to "the prideful joy" of his father and others in the household: "Little work was done that first day, and candles burned late in the cabins as York recited his adventures with dramatic pose."[5] Reunited with his wife in Louisville after more than two years away, he did not want to be separated from her again. But after Clark wed Julia Hancock in January 1808, he took York and other slaves to St. Louis, where he began serving as Indian agent and rented a house that required less care than Mulberry Hill. "I have hired out most of my negrows," he wrote his older brother Jonathan in Kentucky, "and Shall if possible live in a littl Snug way."[6]

As Clark's manservant who helped keep him snug, York was probably not hired out, but he soon made it clear that he wished to return to Kentucky. In November, Clark allowed him to spend a few weeks there with his wife but told Jonathan to keep an eye on him. If he tried to run off or refused to perform "his duty as a Slave," Clark instructed, "I wish him Sent to New Orleans and Sold, or hired out to Some Severe master untill he thinks better of Such Conduct." Clark did not consider himself severe, but he berated York by referring to him uncustomarily as a slave and threatening to sell him downriver to New Orleans, notorious for the brutal conditions on nearby sugar plantations. Clark evidently regretted that outburst, for he softened his tone in his next letter to Jonathan: "I wrote you the other day about york, I do not wish him Sold if he behaves himself well . . . he does not like to Stay here on account of his wife being there . . . perhaps he will See his Situation there more unfavourable than he expected & will after a while prefur returning to this place." The crux of their dispute, Clark wrote later, was that York "has got Such a notion about freedom and his emence Services, that I do not expect he will be of much Service to me again." Although York had been at his side for three decades, seeing to his needs and welfare, Clark did not think his services so great as to warrant emancipation. York returned to St. Louis after several months but remained at odds with Clark, who found him "insolent and Sulky" and took him to task. "I gave him a Severe trouncing the other Day and he has much mended Sence," wrote Clark, who still considered himself a kind master and believed that if York were placed under "a Severe master he would See the difference and do better."[7] He eventually hired York out to a man named Young in Louisville, which allowed him to see his wife but exposed him to a neglectful master, according to a letter Clark received in 1811 from his nephew John O'Fallon, who wrote: "I apprehend that he has been indifferently clothed if at all by Young as appearance satisfactorily prove—he appears wretched under the fear that he has incurred your displeasure and which he despairs he will ever remove."[8]

The last chapter in York's life was related in 1832 by Clark to Washington Irving, who visited the old explorer and took notes of their conversation. Clark told Irving that he had freed three of his slaves, including York, to whom he gave "a large waggon and team of six horses to ply between Nashville and Richmond." According to Clark, York did not fare well as a free man and self-employed wagon master: "He could not get up early enough in the morn'g—his horses were ill kept—two died—the others grew poor. He sold them and was cheated—entered into service—fared ill. 'Damn this freedom,' said York, 'I have never had a happy day since I got it.' He determined to go back to his old master—set off for St. Louis, but was taken with the cholera in Tennessee and died." That sounds like a second- or thirdhand tale that may have been shaped by Clark or his informants to suit their assumption that slaves were better off under the care of white masters than when emancipated. York may indeed have fallen on hard times, particularly if he was caught in the Panic of 1819, when many white Americans went broke and prospects were even worse for free African Americans. His fate may then have been sealed when he contracted cholera or yellow fever, which plagued Tennessee in the early 1820s. Whatever York's plight, he had such a "notion about freedom," in Clark's words, that he would more likely have cherished his liberty than cursed it, even in adversity. Clark told Irving that all the slaves he freed "repented and wanted to come back."[9] But he himself had cause for repentance as a slave owner, and his belief that they would rather return to him than remain free may have helped ease his conscience.

From Indian Country to Slave State

That William Clark was a man of some conscience was shown by his dealings with Indians. As leaders of the Corps of Discovery, he and Lewis fulfilled their instructions from Jefferson, who stated: "In all your intercourse with the natives treat them in the most friendly & conciliatory manner which their own conduct will admit."[10] Later, as Indian agent and ultimately superintendent of Indian Affairs at St. Louis, Clark applied his diplomatic skills to treaty negotiations with various tribes, honoring chiefs with gifts, which they prized but some white settlers considered excessive. Yet Clark knew that the compensation he offered tribal leaders to induce them to cede territory was far less than the land was worth. In September 1808 he concluded a treaty with Osage chiefs by which they ceded "near 50,000 square miles of excellent country," by his estimate, for goods and other considerations worth about $5,000—or ten cents a square mile at a time when a single acre of public land (amounting to 1/640 of a square mile) sold for as much as two dollars. Clark assured Secretary of War Dearborn that "no unfair means had been taken on my part" to induce chiefs to yield so much for so little.[11] Yet Osages appealed to Governor Lewis, who had overall responsibility for tribal affairs in Missouri, and told him that the chiefs only meant to concede hunting rights on that land and had not obtained the consent of their tribal council. Lewis then had the treaty renegotiated. The paltry compensation was increased to include an annuity or yearly distribution of goods worth $1,000, but the amount of territory ceded by the Osages also increased. Clark later wrote of his part in the deal that if he were "damned hereafter, it would be for making that treaty."[12]

To their credit, both Lewis and Clark tried to prevent white settlers from intruding on land reserved for tribes. In April 1809, Lewis ordered intruders and squatters prohibited within five miles of towns established by Shawnees and Delawares, who were adopting the settled ways that Jefferson and other American authorities wanted Indians to embrace if they wished to retain land and be left in peace. That order did little to ease the pressure from settlers that eventually forced Shawnees and Delawares to abandon those towns. For his efforts to shield those Indians, Lewis faced mounting criticism from incoming Americans, who also faulted him for not imposing their laws and their land claims on earlier settlers of the French or Spanish era. Harried and depressed, Lewis died on his way back to Washington in October 1809, an apparent suicide.

When Clark was appointed governor four years later, he too tried to protect tribal lands from squatters, who were asserting their claims not just against Native Americans but against white speculators. Those who considered Lewis and Clark too kind to Indians ignored the fact that treaties they negotiated cleared the way for poor settlers as well as for wealthier newcomers who brought slaves with them. One difference between those two groups was that many poor, land-hungry people were prepared to risk intruding on tribal territory, whereas slaveholders were often wary of entering contested borderlands where Indians might abduct their slaves or offer them refuge, as happened in lower Georgia and Alabama where some slaves fled to Spanish Florida and were harbored by Seminoles. Slave owners were thus among the prime beneficiaries of Indian removal in those American territories or states where their peculiar institution was upheld. By inducing the Osages and other tribes to withdraw westward, Lewis and Clark helped make Missouri safe for slavery. Even their efforts to protect settled or peaceful tribes from intrusions, to the extent that those efforts preserved order in the territory, made it more attractive to their fellow slaveholders—and to self-reliant white settlers of less means. As Lewis remarked of Missouri, this territory seemed to offer more advantages than any other part of the nation "to the farmer, the mechanic, [the] inland merchant or the honest adventurer who can command money or negroes."[13] Lewis and Clark served the interests of their fellow southerners who settled in sufficient numbers with the African Americans they commanded to make Missouri a would-be slave state, triggering the sectional crisis that later alarmed Jefferson "like a fire bell in the night."

Harrison's Northwest Passage

Ten years old when Virginia ceded its claims above the Ohio River to the United States in 1783, William Henry Harrison would later apply the values he imbibed as a Virginian to the Northwest Territory by seeking land and opportunity for white settlers while circumventing the congressional prohibition against slavery there. The youngest child of Benjamin Harrison, an elite planter who signed the Declaration of Independence and was later governor of Virginia, he inherited his father's political acumen but had to seek his own fortune and fame. After serving as an aide to General "Mad" Anthony Wayne, whose resounding victory over confederated tribes in the Battle of Fallen Timbers in 1794 cleared the way for white settlement of Ohio, Harrison became secretary of the Northwest

Territory under Governor Arthur St. Clair. He went on to represent that territory in Congress, where he had no vote but helped secure passage in 1800 of an act making public land more accessible by reducing the minimum purchase from 640 to 320 acres and allowing payment in installments.

Shortly before Jefferson became president in 1801, Harrison was appointed governor of Indiana Territory, which originally embraced much of the old Northwest Territory except for Ohio (admitted to the Union in 1803). There were about two hundred enslaved people there when he took office, most of them held by French inhabitants in what later became Illinois. Article VI of the Northwest Ordinance, stating that there "shall be neither Slavery nor involuntary Servitude" in the Northwest Territory, had been interpreted by Governor St. Clair as applying strictly to the importation of slaves, meaning that those held in bondage before the United States took possession did not have to be freed. Harrison, for his part, defied Article VI outright by bringing one or two slaves with him to Vincennes, his capital on the Wabash River, and encouraging settlers with slaves to enter the territory. In late 1802 he held a convention at Vincennes where delegates petitioned Congress for approval to suspend Article VI for ten years. When Congress declined to do so, Harrison and his supporters in the territorial legislature enacted a law in 1805 permitting slaves to be brought into the territory and held under contract as indentured servants. The law allowed them to be indentured for life, under terms of service lasting up to ninety-nine years, and allowed their children to be held as servants into adulthood. Opponents of the act complained to Congress that it was "absurd to speak of the agreement between the master and a slave as a 'contract,' since slavery by its very nature made a person incapable of contracting."[14]

Harrison's proslavery efforts faltered in 1810 after Illinois Territory (including what later became Wisconsin) was separated from Indiana Territory and the indenture act was repealed by a new legislature representing Indiana's nonslaveholding majority—among them white settlers of little means from Kentucky and western Virginia who remained southerners at heart but wanted nothing to do with slaves or their owners. Thereafter, the ambitious and adaptable Harrison helped Indiana develop as a free territory by intensifying his efforts to obtain land cessions from tribal leaders. Unlike William Clark, he had no qualms about pressuring chiefs to sell land for a pittance or sign away tracts over which they had little or no authority. Following a treaty he concluded with Miami chiefs in 1805, he apologized to Jefferson for offering them "about one cent per acre. This is much higher than I could have wished it to have been but it was impossible to make it less."[15] Although he had guaranteed Miamis possession of their remaining land, he hoped to pare that down in future negotiations.

When Harrison demanded additional concessions from Miami chiefs at Fort Wayne in 1809, they refused unless he offered them what their land was worth to his government: two dollars an acre. That was only for the best land, Harrison replied, and if they sold that they would have only bad land left to inhabit. He insisted that they instead accept payment in the form of additional annuities and pressured them to do so by withholding annuities for land they had ceded previously. Other tribal leaders invited to the council—where Harrison dispensed liquor freely despite his professed disdain for that practice—had little claim to the territory he was seeking and urged Miamis to yield so that their own annuities would increase. In council with the chiefs, Harrison portrayed the deal he offered as one that would preserve peace and amity between Miamis and other tribes represented at Fort Wayne, including Potawatomis and Delawares. "I love to see you all united," he declared. "I wish to hear you speak with one voice the dictates of one heart . . . The consent of the whole is necessary."[16] In truth, Harrison liked to see tribal leaders divided rather than united in opposition to his demands. He obtained their consent at Fort Wayne by using Delawares and Potawatomis to wear down the resistance of Miamis, who eventually gave in. In exchange for modest increases in annuities—which made tribes more dependent on American authorities and more susceptible to their demands for further concessions—he secured nearly three million acres of Indian country for future white settlers. That brought his total acquisitions through such treaties to some thirty million acres, or seven million acres more than encompassed by the future state of Indiana.

The Treaty of Fort Wayne set Harrison at odds with the Shawnee chief Tecumseh, who was seeking what Harrison professed to love but actually feared: unity among tribes, whose leaders might speak with one voice and refuse to yield any more ground to the Americans. Born in 1768, Tecumseh had distinguished himself as a war leader of the confederated tribes defeated at Fallen Timbers. That setback left him convinced that American expansion could be halted only by a broader and stronger confederacy, one he hoped would reach beyond the Northwest and include many tribes between the Appalachians and the Mississippi. Shawnees were not directly affected by the Fort Wayne Treaty, but Tecumseh was appalled by the concessions extracted from Miamis and confronted Harrison during a council at Grouseland, his Vincennes estate, in August 1810. Tecumseh's speech on that occasion, approximated in English by Harrison's interpreter, described the land Indians occupied as their shared inheritance, which Americans were appropriating by inducing chiefs to sell what did not belong to them:

> You endeavour to make destructions, you wish to prevent the Indians to do as we wish them to unite and let them consider their land as the common property of the whole . . . Brother, when you speak to me of annuities I look at the land, and pity the women and children. . . . Brother, they want to save that piece of land, we do not wish you to take it. It is small enough for our purposes.[17]

Harrison was impressed by Tecumseh and described him in a letter to Secretary of War William Eustis as "one of those uncommon geniuses, which spring up occasionally to produce revolutions and overturn the established order of things."[18] In fact, Harrison and his fellow Americans were the revolutionaries, imposing a convulsive new order on Indian country, whereas Tecumseh and his brother Tenskwatawa—a visionary known as the Shawnee Prophet—were calling on Native people to return to an idealized past, when they held the land in common as their sacred trust. Harrison did not think Tecumseh so formidable as to lead a successful pan-Indian uprising against American expansion without military aid from the British. Indeed, Harrison had long blamed the British for inciting tribal opposition that his own voracious treaty making did much to arouse. That view contributed to his decision to mount the initial campaign of what might be called America's second British and Indian War, which began in 1811 and continued as the War of 1812. The first such conflict had occurred during the American Revolution, and though this one resulted in defeat for neither the Americans nor the British, it was catastrophic for defiant tribes of the trans-Appalachian West.

Tecumseh was reluctant to trust in the British, whose past support for tribes of the Northwest had been withdrawn when American forces gained the upper hand there in the 1790s. But he had little doubt that the tribal confederacy he was forming would be forcefully opposed by Americans and sought British aid. By 1811 he had recruited such traditional allies as Miamis, Potawatomis, and Delawares as well as tribes around the Great Lakes with ties to the British, including Ottawas and Winnebagos. It was not a comprehensive confederacy, because elements of various tribes, including some Shawnee bands, were unwilling to oppose the Americans. But Tecumseh felt sufficiently emboldened to head south with a retinue of warriors in August 1811 and seek support among Creeks—to whom he had family ties—and other tribes of the southern woodlands. Harrison learned of his departure and decided to attack Prophetstown, established near the Tippecanoe River by Tenskwatawa, a former alcoholic who had renounced liquor and all other curses or customs associated with Americans, whom he called children of the Evil Spirit. Prophetstown was also home to Tecumseh and hundreds of his warriors. His absence, Harrison wrote Eustis, "affords a most favorable opportunity for breaking up his Confederacy."[19]

In late September, Harrison advanced north from Vincennes toward Prophetstown with nearly 500 Indiana militiamen and mounted riflemen, 300 U.S. Army troops, and 120 mounted volunteers from Kentucky led by Joseph Daveiss, the U.S. district attorney at Louisville who had reported the Burr Conspiracy to Jefferson. On November 6 they camped near Tenskwatawa's village, where Harrison planned to meet with the Prophet the next day. Neither side expected those talks to avert hostilities, and Tenskwatawa decided to strike first. Before dawn on November 7, several hundred warriors attacked Harrison's camp, which he had not fortified, and wreaked havoc before they were driven away. Daveiss was among sixty-eight Americans who perished, which exceeded the death toll among their tribal foes. Tenskwatawa and his followers then abandoned Prophetstown, which Harrison torched. The Battle of Tippecanoe failed to break up Tecumseh's confederacy and brought retaliation against American settlers. But President Madison praised the "dauntless spirit and fortitude victoriously displayed" by Harrison and his men, and his supposed triumph at Tippecanoe was later touted when he ran successfully for president as an Ohioan in 1840 with John Tyler of Virginia as his running mate.[20]

Unlike Madison, Andrew Jackson viewed the Battle of Tippecanoe as a setback for Harrison and wrote him expressing condolence for "the loss you sustained." Jackson offered to "march with five hundred or one thousand brave Tennesseans" and scourge those hostile Indians, supposedly incited by the "secret agents of great Britain."[21] Fears of a British-Indian alliance in the West added to the war fever of Republicans in Congress, incensed at the British for violating American maritime rights and impressing sailors. (Word that the British government had suspended the Orders in Council, which had caused American merchant ships to be seized, reached Washington too late to avert conflict.) The war declared against Great Britain in June 1812 drew considerable opposition in New England, voiced largely by die-hard Federalists whose British sympathies and commercial ties to Canada exposed them to accusations of disloyalty. In the South and West, most Americans supported the conflict and viewed it as an opportunity for national expansion, whether in the direction of Canada or

East and West Florida, loosely controlled by Britain's ally Spain. A rebellion by Anglo-American settlers in 1810 had prompted Madison to claim for the United States much of West Florida between the Mississippi River and the Perdido River (the future boundary between Alabama and Florida). U.S. troops would complete the American takeover in that sector by occupying the strategic port of Mobile in 1813 to prevent the British from seizing it, thus confining West Florida to a narrow zone between the Perdido and Apalachicola Rivers.

In September 1812, Governor Harrison became General Harrison, in command of the Army of the Northwest, made up largely of militiamen. In the spring of 1813 his troops were besieged in Ohio at Fort Meigs by a combined force of British soldiers under General Henry Procter and warriors led by Tecumseh. Kentuckians sent by Harrison to spike British siege guns were lured into an ambush by Tecumseh's forces and overwhelmed. Several hundred militiamen were killed or captured, and some of the captives were massacred before Tecumseh intervened to spare others. Despite those losses, Harrison withstood the siege. In September 1813, Captain Oliver Hazard Perry defeated a British naval squadron in the pivotal Battle of Lake Erie and wrote Harrison triumphantly: "We have met the enemy and they are ours."[22] That victory caused Procter and Tecumseh to withdraw into Canada. Harrison pursued them with a reinforced army that outnumbered his opponents nearly three to one. Attacked along the Thames River on October 5, Procter's beleaguered troops broke and ran. Tecumseh's men kept fighting at his urging until he was killed. Harrison's troops then mutilated his body and those of other warriors.

The Battle of the Thames left Tecumseh's confederacy in tatters. Some bands found refuge in Canada, which remained under British control at war's end, but most yielded to Harrison, who wisely refrained from demanding any further territorial concessions from them in the battle's immediate aftermath. Any hope they had of resisting American encroachment was shattered, however. As their tribal domain dwindled, white settlers poured into Indiana—which achieved statehood in 1816—and Illinois, which entered the Union in 1818. Both were admitted as nominally free states, but the Illinois constitution specified that slavery and involuntary servitude could not be introduced thereafter, meaning that Black people held in 1818 as slaves (of which there were nine hundred or so then in Illinois) or as indentured servants on lifetime contracts did not have to be emancipated. No longer bound by the Northwest Ordinance, proslavery Illinoisans proposed amending the state constitution to their liking in 1824. Voters rejected altering the constitution, but slavery would not be prohibited in Illinois until 1848, thus freeing a few hundred Black people who remained in bondage there. Prior to abolition, lower Illinois, known as Egypt or Little Egypt, was home to some slaveholders and many nonslaveholding settlers of southern origin. There and in lower Indiana and Ohio, southern customs, accents, and attitudes would long persist, providing fertile ground for an emerging Democratic Party, which operated on the principle that the Union should remain part slave and part free, as the Constitution allowed. "Let the north vote as she may," wrote a southern Illinois Democrat after the new Republican Party emerged in the 1850s, "one thing is certain, Egypt will stand as firm as the hills, giving a heavier democratic vote than she has ever done, in behalf of the constitution and the Union."[23]

The party that Egypt favored was forged by Andrew Jackson, whose exploits against British and Indian forces during the War of 1812 surpassed those of Harrison and earned him greater acclaim. A man of common origins and exceptional determination lifted to high office by the rising tide of American democracy, Jackson would help make the interests and ambitions of the slaveholding South palatable to a substantial portion of the northern electorate until the last years of his life, when the annexation of Texas that he promoted became an abundant source of sectional strife.

CHAPTER 4

Jackson's Southern Strategy

Unlike William Henry Harrison, whose career as an armed American expansionist ended with the War of 1812, Andrew Jackson capitalized on his exploits during that conflict to further Indian removal afterward and expand U.S. territory at Spain's expense. Americans who dreamed of conquering Canada had to accept coexistence with British subjects to their north at war's end, but Jackson would not rest until the United States nullified the claims of all competing nations, whether Native or European, between the Ohio River and the Gulf of Mexico. His aggressive southern strategy endeared him to settlers and slaveholders in that section but also won him admirers in the North, where many people were pleased to see Americans triumph over British, Spanish, or Indian adversaries and were not necessarily opposed to the extension of slavery below the Ohio.

Jackson launched his campaign to secure that region for white southerners in 1813 by scourging Creek insurgents known as Red Sticks for the painted war clubs they wielded. Their uprising was a violent reaction by tribal traditionalists to concessions sought by Anglo-American traders and Indian agents, who pressured southern tribes to cede land by placing them in debt for goods they received and urging them to forsake hunting and adopt the settled ways of white farmers, thus taking up less territory. Some adaptable Creeks—and their counterparts among Choctaws, Chickasaws, and Cherokees—emulated white planters and cooperated with American authorities. Others resisted yielding territory to Americans, including a chief named William Weatherford, a mixed-race Creek who prospered as a slaveholding planter but sided with the Red Sticks. They drew inspiration when visited in 1811 by Tecumseh, who urged them to defend their ancestral land and way of life.

The Creek War waged by Jackson and other American commanders began as a struggle within the tribe between Red Sticks and those who supported the Creek National Council, which made concessions to the United States and yielded to demands by Indian agent Benjamin Hawkins that Creeks who killed white settlers along the tribe's contested borders be seized and executed. In July 1813, Red Sticks incensed by those executions were returning with ammunition obtained at Pensacola in West Florida—where Spanish officials allowed allied British officers and traders to arm Indians at odds with Americans—when they were attacked by Mississippi Territory militiamen at Burnt Corn Creek. After repelling that assault, Red Sticks led by Weatherford vented their fury in late August by storming Fort Mims. They slaughtered some 250 people, including opposing Creeks and white settlers who sought shelter with militiamen there, and killed or seized their Black slaves. The massacre shocked Tennesseans and gave Andrew Jackson, in command of Tennessee militiamen and volunteers, a war to fight. The murderous attack on Fort Mims cried out "for retaliatory vengeance," he told his men, who set out under the tough commander they dubbed "Old Hickory" to annihilate Red Sticks wherever they found them.[1] Crushing that uprising was the first step in Jackson's campaign to bring the South fully under American control by subduing and displacing Indians, repulsing British forces, and nullifying Spanish claims.

Born in 1767 in the Waxhaws region along the border of North and South Carolina, the combative Jackson was a product of the southern frontier and the American Revolution, during which his two elder brothers died while serving the patriot cause and he was slashed by a British officer for refusing to clean the man's boots. That conflict, which also claimed his mother's life when she fell ill while nursing stricken American troops, gave him cause to hate the British and dread disunion, which plagued the Carolinas as American Tories loyal to the Crown fought American revolutionaries. One of many southerners who migrated beyond the Appalachians after the Revolution hoping to improve their fortunes, Jackson settled in the budding town of Nashville in 1788 and prospered as a lawyer, trader, planter, and land speculator before becoming Tennessee's first U.S. congressman in 1796. Although he went on to serve briefly in the U.S. Senate before being appointed a superior court judge in Tennessee, the position he most coveted was major general of the state militia, which he achieved in 1802 when Governor Archibald Roane decided the election for that post in his favor over a formidable competitor, former governor John Sevier.

Jackson, whose father died around the time he was born, proved as adept at befriending elders like Roane who helped him advance as he was at defying those like Sevier, Tennessee's most accomplished officer, who stood in his way. Jackson's military experience was negligible by comparison, but various enemies felt his wrath as he rose to prominence, including men who dared insult him or his beloved wife, Rachel, with whom he eloped to Natchez and cohabited before her estranged first husband divorced her. When Sevier, whom Jackson accused of furthering a fraudulent land scheme, disparaged him by saying he knew of "no great service you rendered the country, except taking a trip to Natchez with another man's wife," Jackson challenged him to a duel.[2] He was taking aim at Sevier when their seconds intervened and arranged a truce. Charles Dickinson, a young lawyer who allegedly spoke ill of Rachel and denounced Jackson in print as a scoundrel, was less fortunate. When he and Jackson faced off in 1806, Jackson shot Dickinson to death after taking a bullet that remained lodged near his heart for the rest of his life. That did not stop him from fighting those who later impugned his honor and reputation. As he rode off to challenge the Red Sticks in October 1813, he was suffering from bullet wounds in the shoulder and arm sustained in a clash with Jesse Benton and his brother Thomas Hart Benton, who had served as an officer under Jackson and would later reconcile with him in Washington when they met again there as senators.

Jackson's forces and other American troops scourged Red Sticks in several battles that fall but grew restive over the winter as rations dwindled and their terms of enlistment expired. Several American commanders involved in the Creek War withdrew, but Jackson persuaded some of his troops to remain in camp and barred others from departing at gunpoint before substantial reinforcements arrived in late winter, swelling his forces to several thousand American troops and allied Creeks and Cherokees at odds with the Red Sticks. On March 27, 1814, they attacked about one thousand of those defiant Creek warriors barricaded along the Tallapoosa River at Horseshoe Bend (Tohopeka) and all but annihilated them. It was a crushing blow not just for the Red Sticks, whose surviving forces fled south into Spanish territory, but for the Creek nation as a whole. Jackson spared Red Stick leader Weatherford, who surrendered to him after Horseshoe Bend, but stunned Creek chiefs who had opposed the uprising by summoning them to a council in August at Fort Jackson (in what became Alabama) and demanding

they cede nearly twenty-three million acres to the United States. When asked
why they were being punished despite standing by him, he blamed them for not
seizing Tecumseh and his followers when they incited the Red Sticks. As related
by his aide John Reid, Jackson told the Creeks:

> You know that the part [of Creek territory] you desire to retain is that
> through which the intruders and mischief-makers from the lakes reached
> you. . . . Through it leads the path Tecumseh trod, when he came to visit
> you: that path must be stopped. Until this be done, your nation cannot
> expect happiness, nor mine security. . . . This evening must determine
> whether or not you are disposed to become friendly. Your rejecting the
> treaty will show you to be the enemies of the United States—enemies even
> to yourselves.[3]

The treaty that Creek chiefs signed reluctantly on August 9 made Jackson
the nation's foremost agent of Indian removal, a part he would continue to play
forcefully until most Creeks, Choctaws, Chickasaws, and Cherokees had been
driven west of the Mississippi. Intent on clearing ground for American settlers,
Jackson cared little whether or not they owned slaves as he did. But his efforts
facilitated the westward expansion of slavery across the Lower South as planters
cultivated short-staple cotton, which thrived in the interior (unlike the long-staple
cotton grown in coastal areas) and could be cleaned of its seeds using cotton
gins like that patented by Eli Whitney in 1794. The huge cession extracted from
the Creeks at Fort Jackson in 1814, combined with an influx of cotton planters
and their slaves, helped swell the non-Native population of the emerging state of
Alabama (admitted to the Union in 1819) from about 9,000 in 1810, when it was
still part of Mississippi Territory, to 128,000 a decade later, one-third of whom
were enslaved. Most who took part in that land rush came from older slave states
like North Carolina, where one planter who remained behind complained that
"Alabama Feaver rages here with great violence and has carried off vast numbers
of our Citizens."[4] Speculators caught that fever as well and obtained large lots
by bidding well above the minimum price of two dollars an acre when public
land was auctioned, reckoning that its value would soar. Easy credit terms fueled
such speculation as well as bids by settlers of modest means, who entered the
market as the 320-acre minimum for purchases was reduced to 160 and then
80 acres. By the time Alabama achieved statehood, however, cotton prices had
plummeted and banks were calling in loans, triggering the Panic of 1819, which
depressed the American economy for several years.

That setback did not halt the phenomenal increase in American cotton production, which nearly doubled each decade between 1810 and 1850, by which time cotton grown in the South made up three-fourths of the world's output and nearly two-thirds of the nation's exports in value. That raw cotton went largely to mills in Britain, which initiated production on mechanized looms in the late 1700s, but it also supplied factories in the North that were producing rough cotton fabric by 1820, some of which was used to clothe enslaved laborers on southern plantations. Cotton transformed the South as planters seeking fertile land advanced westward from the Carolinas to the lower Mississippi Valley and beyond, extending slavery and compounding its miseries for those uprooted in the process. Cotton also enriched the North as merchants and bankers in New York financed those planters, mill workers in New England manufactured their produce, and farmers in the Northwest helped feed them and their slaves. Such economic ties nurtured political ties between North and South. But the wealth and power southerners gleaned from cotton would eventually encourage them to risk seceding when northerners opposed extending slavery. As Senator James Henry Hammond of South Carolina declared overconfidently to his northern colleagues a few years before the Union broke apart: "No, sir, you dare not make war on cotton. No power on earth dares make war upon it. Cotton is king."[5]

The huge land cession Andrew Jackson secured from the Creeks contributed to formation of the Black Belt, which stretched across central Alabama to Mississippi (admitted 1817). So called for the dark soil in which cotton was planted there, that Black Belt acquired an additional meaning as enslaved African Americans outnumbered white settlers in some areas, causing them to fear rebellion and oppose emancipation. Montgomery, incorporated in 1819 within the Black Belt, would become the Alabama state capital in 1846 and the first capital of the Confederacy in February 1861. Some planters who migrated to the Black Belt and other fertile areas beyond the Appalachians had inherited slaves, but other settlers acquired them as they gained wealth and social standing. Jackson, for example, did not become a slaveholder until he began practicing law in Tennessee and purchased an enslaved woman named Nancy. He and his wife, Rachel, later inherited two slaves bequeathed by her father, John Donelson, and Jackson occasionally traded in slaves before distancing himself from that unsavory practice as he became more prominent. When Tennesseans published a letter of condolence to Charles Dickinson's widow, Jackson responded by publicly accusing the man he had killed of "purchasing Negroes in Maryland and carrying them to Natchez & Louis[ian]a and thus making a fortune of speculating in human flesh."[6] Jackson could ill afford to be recognized as a slave trader after denouncing that business as inhumane, but he continued to purchase Black people to labor at the Hermitage, his plantation near Nashville, where he held nearly one hundred slaves by the time he became president in 1829. More than a dozen would accompany him to the White House, some of whom were separated from family members in the process.

Unlike Jefferson or James Polk, Jackson regarded slavery not as something imposed or entailed on him by his Scotch-Irish ancestors but rather as an asset that he earned and was entitled to so long as he did not mistreat those he enslaved. Often absent from the Hermitage, he asked Rachel to ensure that they were well fed and clothed and not abused by their overseer. "I do not want them in any way oppressed," he wrote, "and if they behave well I am sure [the overseer] knowing my wishes will treat them well."[7] Rachel died shortly before Jackson was inaugurated, a loss that devastated him, and he left the Hermitage in charge of their adopted son, Andrew Jackson Jr., and overseer Graves W. Steele. As president, Jackson worried that Steele was acting rashly and might have caused the death of an enslaved man named James. He did not dismiss Steele but warned him in writing against mishandling the valuable people and livestock Jackson entrusted to him. An overseer "is accountable to his employer *for all losses sustained through his neglect*," insisted Jackson, who complained that he had suffered "great losses in stock and negroes" since placing his plantation under Steele's management. Jackson gave him one last chance to manage his task properly. "But when I say I have concluded to retain you another year," he wrote Steele, "it is on the express conditions that you treat my negroes with humanity, & attention when sick; & not work them too hard, when well—that you feed & cloath them *well*, and that you *carefully attend to my stock* of all kinds, & particularly to my mares & colts, & see that they are well taken care of. . . . This I have a right to expect from you for the wages I give you."[8]

Jackson did not want those he held in bondage treated leniently in all circumstances. He expected defiant slaves to be reined in and lashed as his horses were when unruly. As he instructed the overseer on another plantation he established, in Alabama: "Subordination must be obtained first, and then good treatment." Enslaved people who remained insubordinate might be "ruled with the cowhide," as Jackson said of a woman named Betty he ordered whipped if she defied Rachel, or "secured with irons" and sold "down the river," as he threatened when a fugitive named Gilbert was recaptured. Following a subsequent escape attempt, Gilbert resisted being whipped and was killed by his overseer. Jackson himself exposed an escaped slave to potentially deadly punishment by placing a notice in the *Tennessee Gazette* in 1804 that offered anyone recapturing a "Mulatto Man Slave, about thirty years old" who could "pass for a free man," a reward of fifty dollars, "and ten dollars extra, for every hundred lashes any person will give him, to the amount of three hundred."[9]

A National Hero

After crushing Creek insurgents at Horseshoe Bend and attaining the rank of major general in the U.S. Army, Jackson struck another blow on behalf of the expanding American empire with his staggering defeat of British troops at New Orleans on January 8, 1815, two weeks after a treaty ending the war was signed in Europe but before word of that settlement reached the United States. Jackson's forces—who killed, wounded, or captured some two thousand Redcoats while suffering fewer than one hundred casualties—included free men of color from New Orleans and were shielded by fortifications built by slaves as the Americans targeted their woefully exposed British opponents, among whom were Black soldiers from the West Indies.

Jackson's triumph at New Orleans made him a national hero and cheered Americans, who had been humiliated when British troops sacked Washington in 1814 but now felt vindicated. Opposition to the war had been rampant in New England, where governors refused to commit state militias to battle and some Federalists urged a separate peace with Britain or secession from the Union. Such critics spoke disparagingly of "Mr. Madison's War," but Madison portrayed the conflict as a struggle to secure lasting independence from Britain and blamed northern opponents for encouraging the enemy to withhold concessions. Federalists who convened at Hartford in December 1814 denounced the "ruinous war" and proposed constitutional amendments that would curb the Virginia-led Republican Party, including revoking the three-fifths clause in the Constitution, limiting the president to one term, and barring consecutive terms by presidents from the same state.[10] They stopped short of endorsing secession or a separate peace, but their ill-timed objections to the war, delivered shortly before Jackson's victory at New Orleans and announcement of the peace treaty, made Federalists appear disloyal and doomed their party. That ensured the resounding election of another slaveholding Republican president from Virginia, James Monroe, inaugurated in March 1817.

With the opposition in disarray, Monroe forswore partisanship and chose a former Federalist, John Quincy Adams, as his secretary of state, a post that

Andrew Jackson on horseback at the Battle of New Orleans. Courtesy Library
of Congress Prints and Photographs Division (LC-USZ62-19603.)

Jefferson, Madison, and Monroe had occupied on their way to the presidency.
Adams had entered foreign service as a boy when he accompanied his father to
the French court in Paris during the American Revolution and went on to become
secretary to the U.S. minister to Russia at the age of fourteen. He emerged as
an eager young statesman, convinced that Americans would have to present a
united front against European powers if the United States were to fulfill its great
potential. He parted ways with fellow Federalists in New England when they
resisted an embargo on foreign trade that Jefferson imposed to avoid entangle-
ment in the war between France and Britain. States had no right to defy federal
authority, insisted Adams, who later supported the War of 1812 and helped
resolve the conflict as head of the American delegation that held out against
British demands for galling American concessions and obtained a settlement
that left neither side at a loss. He considered the day on which he signed the peace
treaty the "happiest of my life" and worked diplomatically thereafter to secure
the nation and extend its boundaries.[11]

The treaty that Adams and his fellow delegates concluded helped set the
stage for an agreement with Britain in 1818 that established the forty-ninth

parallel as the U.S.-Canadian border between the Great Lakes and the Rocky Mountains. That pact also established joint British-American occupation of the Oregon country beyond the Rockies, where few American settlers would arrive before the early 1840s. While that agreement was being negotiated in London, Secretary of State Adams was meeting in Washington with Luis de Onís, Spanish minister to the United States. Adams hoped to induce Spain to accept in full America's claims under the Louisiana Purchase and cede East Florida and what little remained of West Florida. His talks with Onís went haltingly until spurred along by Old Hickory. Jackson had declined to implement a provision in the peace treaty with Britain requiring the United States to restore to tribes the "possessions, rights, and privileges" they had before the war began, which would have meant returning to Creeks the territory ceded at Fort Jackson.[12] Doing so would have infuriated American settlers, and neither Madison nor Monroe compelled Jackson to honor that provision or refrain from extracting further concessions from southern tribes over the next several years that substantially reduced the territory of Cherokees, Chickasaws, and Choctaws.

With his authority as military commander in the South enhanced, Jackson expanded his theater of operations to include the Floridas, where Seminoles—a tribal group largely of Creek origin—offered refuge to Red Sticks as well as fugitive slaves seeking freedom. Some of those Black freedom seekers and their tribal allies had been armed during the War of 1812 by the British, who built the so-called Negro Fort in Spanish territory on the Apalachicola River and left it at war's end to forces that included about fifty Indians and "upwards of two hundred & fifty negroes," Jackson reckoned, "many of whom have been enticed away from the service of their Masters, Citizens of the United States." The fort's Black defenders were "well armed clothed and disciplined," added Jackson, who described them as the "property" of American citizens, to whom they must be "forthwith restored." Their armed resistance "would not be tolerated by our government," he warned the Spanish commandant at Pensacola in late April 1816, "and if not put down by Spanish Authority will compel us in self Defence to destroy them." In fact, Jackson had already authorized General Edmund P. Gaines to attack the fort at his discretion. If it induced "the Slaves of our Citizens to desert from their owner's service," he wrote Gaines in early April, "this fort must be destroyed."[13] On July 27, 1816, troops dispatched by Gaines blew up the fort, killing most if its defenders. Black survivors of the assault were reenslaved in the United States, signaling that Jackson was prepared to wage war not just to extend the national domain but to enforce the presumed property rights of slaveholders.

Jackson soon had the pretext he needed to invade the Floridas without a declaration of war on Spain. In November 1817, troops sent by General Gaines torched
Fowltown, situated in Georgia just above the Spanish border and inhabited by
Miccosukees, Seminoles of Creek heritage led by Neamathla, who had joined the
Red Stick uprising and refused to abandon Fowltown after Creeks ceded the area
at Fort Jackson in 1814. Seminoles retaliated for the destruction of that village
by attacking forty American soldiers and a dozen or so women and children as
they headed up the Apalachicola River to Fort Scott in Georgia, killing most of
them. Like the Fort Mims massacre, the attack brought swift retaliation from
Jackson. The resulting conflict became known as the First Seminole War, but it
also involved allied Red Sticks and other Creeks who had fled to Florida as well
as Black fugitives who joined Seminoles in their epic struggle against American
forces, which would continue long after Jackson's campaign ended. His ulterior
motive was to subvert Spanish officials, whose weak grip on the Floridas he hoped
to replace with American rule.

In early January 1818, Jackson wrote the president, stating that Monroe need
only signal to him indirectly that "possession of the Floridas would be desirable
to the United States, & in sixty days it will be accomplished."[14] Monroe later said
that he was ill when that letter arrived and did not read it until after Jackson's
Florida campaign began. Monroe did, however, send Jackson instructions in late
December 1817 placing him in command of troops "acting against the Seminoles,
a tribe which has long violated our rights, & insulted our national character."
He added that Jackson might have "other services to perform" and that "until
our course is carried through triumphantly . . . you ought not to withdraw your
active support from it."[15] Monroe may not have ordered hostile action against a
nation with which the United States was officially at peace, but Jackson concluded
that staking an American claim to territory which Spain might then concede by
treaty would be of service to his country and its president.

Launching his invasion in March 1818, Jackson waged war not just against
Seminoles and their Black allies but also against Spanish officials and British
agents who aided or harbored those opponents. In April he ordered the execution of two Seminole chiefs in his custody as well as two British subjects he
captured at the Spanish fort of San Marcos de Apalache (St. Marks) and had court-
martialed: Robert C. Ambrister, an ex–Royal Marine who served as a military
adviser to Seminoles; and Alexander Arbuthnot, a Scottish merchant who had
traded guns, powder, and other goods to Indians but denied any role in their
attacks on Americans. In May, Jackson proceeded to Pensacola and forced its

surrender. He mischaracterized the capitulation of Colonel José Masot, the commandant and governor of West Florida, as a "complete cession" of that territory and established a provisional American government there before concluding his campaign and declaring victory. On June 2 he wrote Rachel that he had visited the "Just Vengeance of heaven" on those who incited "the Indian war, and horrid massacre of our innocent weomen and children . . . I have destroyed the babylon of the South, the hot bed of the Indian war & depredations on our frontier, by taking St Marks and pensacola—which is now garrisoned by our Troops, and the american flag waving on their ramparts, we have Sufferred privation but we have met them like Soldiers."[16] His troops had torched tribal villages and destroyed food stores, but the Seminoles and their allies had largely eluded pursuit and would stoutly resist American authority for decades to come. More significant was the blow Jackson dealt to Spanish authority, which may not have been his assigned task but was one he carried out with gusto, confident that he was advancing American interests.

Rebuked and Redeemed

Much to Jackson's dismay, his actions proved controversial in Washington. Although he had campaigned on behalf of settlers and slaveholders on the nation's southern frontier, some prominent southerners in Congress and the cabinet were alarmed by his conduct. They feared he might use military force to defy the Constitution and act tyrannically—or might emerge as a formidable political rival, elevated to high office by popular acclaim for his generalship like George Washington. Secretary of War John C. Calhoun of South Carolina wanted Jackson called to account for defying orders by targeting Spanish forts. And Speaker of the House Henry Clay of Kentucky rebuked Jackson not only for provocative and unwarranted actions during the Seminole War but also for sowing the seeds of that conflict with his punitive treaty at Fort Jackson, which demonstrated that "hard and unconscionable terms, extorted by the power of the sword and the right of conquest, served but to whet and stimulate revenge." To thank Jackson rather than censure him, Clay concluded, would be "a triumph of the principle of insubordination—a triumph of the military over the civil authority—a triumph over the powers of this House—a triumph over the Constitution of the land."[17]

Jackson's chief defender within the administration, on the other hand, was a northerner, Secretary of State Adams. Jackson's campaign had been purely defensive, he claimed, and did not require a declaration of war. Denouncing Jackson would weaken America's bargaining position in negotiations with Spain,

Adams argued, and might lead the British to conclude that America was renouncing its bid for the Floridas. Adams composed a defense of the campaign that could not have been more emphatic if written by Jackson himself and circulated that letter to ministers representing the United States in European capitals to ensure that Spanish and British authorities alarmed by the invasion got the message. The president, he wrote, would "neither inflict punishment, nor pass a censure upon General Jackson," who demonstrated "the purest patriotism" by defending Americans against hostile forces in the Floridas, which impotent Spanish authorities left open to "every enemy, civilized or savage, of the United States." Adams justified the executions of Ambrister and Arbuthnot, which Clay had denounced, by claiming that the British were not just guilty of arming and inciting Seminoles and their allies along the Spanish-American border but were the root cause of tribal hostility throughout frontier America. From "the period of our established independence to this day," Adams claimed, "*all* the Indian wars with which we have been afflicted have been distinctly traceable to the instigation of English traders or agents. Always disavowed, yet always felt; more than once detected, but never before punished."[18] Similar charges were leveled by Americans who blamed their former colonial masters for slavery. Adams's accusation served to absolve not just Jackson but the nation as a whole of responsibility for Indian wars that the British often abetted but were largely incited by American expansion. His argument for Jackson's innocence was also a plea for America's innocence, which Adams asserted publicly while privately opposed to extending slavery, a cause furthered by Jackson's campaign.

Congress did not condemn Jackson. Monroe returned Pensacola to Spain but refrained from denouncing the general for actions he took on his "own responsibility."[19] Negotiations between Adams and Onís soon resumed in earnest against the backdrop of Jackson's intimidating foray. In early 1819 they reached an agreement by which Spain would yield East and West Florida to the United States for five million dollars and would recognize American territory in the trans-Mississippi West above Spanish Texas, New Mexico, and California, with the forty-second parallel forming the Spanish-American border between the Rocky Mountains and the Pacific Ocean (although Oregon, above that border, was claimed jointly by Britain and the United States). Adams was aware that Jackson and other American expansionists hoped for possession of Texas, which they envisioned far more broadly than Spain did by projecting the winding Rio Grande del Norte as its southern and western border. In recent years Americans had participated in filibusters aimed at Spanish Texas, including an expedition launched jointly in 1812 by West Point graduate Augustus W. Magee and Mexican revolutionary José Bernardo Gutiérrez de Lara, whose combined forces seized control of San Antonio before Spanish troops struck back with a vengeance and ended the incursion.

Neither Spanish nor Mexican control of Texas would satisfy ardent expansionists like Jackson, but Adams hoped that he would approve the proposed treaty boundary when he viewed a map showing the impressive extent of U.S. territory as recognized by Spain, extending across the continent. Adams described their meeting on February 3, 1819, in a diary entry later published in his memoirs:

> General Jackson came to my house this morning, and I showed him the boundary line which has been offered to the Spanish Minister . . . He said there were many individuals who would take exception to our receding so far from the boundary of the Rio del Norte . . . but the possession of the Floridas was of so great importance to the southern frontier of the United States, and so essential even to their safety, that the vast majority of the nation would be satisfied with the western boundary as we propose, if we obtain the Floridas.[20]

Adams took this as Jackson's assent to the treaty, which represented a compromise not just between the United States and Spain but between Americans who favored expansion at Spain's expense and those who worried that incorporating Spanish territory might benefit the South at the expense of the North. If Adams had induced Spain to cede both Florida and Texas, whose fertile country bordering Louisiana and the Gulf of Mexico was an alluring objective for slaveholding planters, the treaty he signed with Onís in February 1819 might have aggravated beyond compromise a dispute that erupted simultaneously: the intense debate in Congress over admitting Missouri as a slave state, which some northern representatives opposed morally and many opposed tactically because it would increase the political clout of the slaveholding South.

Adams remarked in 1820 to Senator Ninian Edwards of Illinois that, "as an Eastern man, I should be disinclined to have either Texas or Florida without a restriction excluding slavery from them."[21] He would later emerge as an antislavery stalwart, but as a loyal member of the Monroe administration, which was seeking both national expansion and national unity, Adams defended Jackson's invasion of Florida and pursued annexation of that future slave state without reference to slavery. He trusted that Jackson would respond in kind by not opposing the treaty because it left Spain in possession of Texas. Jackson voiced no objections when the treaty was signed and wrote Calhoun in late 1820 that "our Treaty with Spain as it respected our limits and the possession of the Floridas, was a good one—Texas for the present we could well do without."[22] In later years, however, after Jackson became a political opponent of Adams, succeeded him as president, and urged American annexation of slaveholding Texas as an elder statesman, he would fault Adams for renouncing that prize to Spain. Both men were proud expansionists. But as demonstrated by the unfolding Missouri crisis, the mutual pride Americans felt when their national boundaries advanced gave way to rancor and recriminations when hard lines were drawn on their map between freedom and slavery.

CHAPTER 5

Missouri Compromised

Thomas Hart Benton, who had clashed with Andrew Jackson in 1813 in a vicious brawl that had none of the decorum of a duel, was doubly fortunate to emerge from that fight with no serious injury—and with so many detractors in Nashville that he later set out for St. Louis, which boomed in the aftermath of the War of 1812 and boosted him to prominence. Born in North Carolina in 1782 to a lawyer and overambitious land speculator who was deeply in debt when he died in 1790, Benton was expelled from the University of North Carolina for stealing cash from his roommates. Unrepentant after wounding Jackson, Benton maintained his combative posture as a lawyer in Missouri Territory. His quarrel with an opposing attorney, Charles Lucas, reportedly turned venomous when Lucas challenged Benton's right to vote, "alleging in the presence of the judges that he had not the necessary property qualification." Benton defended his right to vote by stating that he owned slaves, "paid a tax upon them, and was qualified; and concluded by calling Lucas an insolent puppy." In September 1817 they faced off at ten paces on a dueling ground amid the Mississippi called Bloody Island, and Benton shot young Lucas dead. Denounced as "Bully Benton," he later wrote that he would have "given the world" to see his victim "restored to life."[1]

Thereafter, Benton dueled only in the political arena. In 1818 he became the first editor of the *St. Louis Enquirer* and used that platform to promote western expansion and statehood for Missouri, whose non-Native population was now about sixty thousand, the number stipulated for new states in the Northwest Territory that served as an unofficial standard elsewhere. Nearly ten thousand of those inhabitants were enslaved. A few prominent figures in St. Louis—including

Joseph Charless, editor of the rival *Missouri Gazette*, and Judge John B. C. Lucas, father of Benton's victim—favored modest restrictions on slavery, such as barring settlers from bringing people they held as property to Missouri at some future date. But Benton opposed infringing in any way on the privileges of fellow slaveholders there. Like most Missourians, he thought the state should be admitted without restriction on slavery, as Louisiana and Mississippi had been within the past decade. On February 13, 1819, however, Republican congressman James Tallmadge of New York proposed an amendment to the Missouri statehood bill in the House of Representatives that prohibited "the further introduction of slavery or involuntary servitude" there and provided that "all children of slaves, born within the said State, after the admission thereof into the Union, shall be free at the age of twenty-five years."[2]

Tallmadge exemplified those northerners who opposed extending slavery not just because it might give southerners a political advantage in Washington but because it demeaned America and its dedication to liberty—a sentiment that increased as the nation's internal slave trade spread cancerously, shattering hopes that prohibiting the international slave trade might cure the disease. Although the term "African slavery" would long remain in use, it was now largely African American slavery, denying to those born in America the "blessings of liberty" promised to the people of the United States in the preamble to the Constitution. Tallmadge's amendment offered eventual freedom only to those born into slavery after Missouri achieved statehood and did not require that those held in bondage when it joined the Union ever be freed. Nonetheless, the legislation would if adopted set a congressional precedent for restricting and ultimately eliminating slavery in would-be states where that dismal and increasingly divisive institution existed.

Speaker Henry Clay, later hailed as the Great Compromiser, struck an uncompromising tone for the congressional debate on the amendment by opposing it and comparing the condition of Black slaves in the South favorably to that of "white slaves" who performed menial labor in the North.[3] He and others who supported Missouri's admission without restrictions believed that states had a constitutional right to allow or prohibit slavery that Congress must not tamper with. But when Ohio was authorized to seek admission as a state, Congress had required that its constitution not be "repugnant" to the Northwest Ordinance, prohibiting slavery above the Ohio River.[4] That precedent was cited by Representative John W. Taylor of New York, who spoke in favor of the amendment and noted that Indiana and Illinois had also been required to conform to the Northwest Ordinance. "These

States have all complied with it, and framed constitutions excluding slavery," said Taylor, who neglected to mention that the Illinois constitution allowed those who held slaves there before statehood to retain them. Taylor also argued selectively when he stated that "Missouri lies in the same latitude" as the states of the old Northwest, "and the same principles of government should be applied to it." Missouri also lay in the same latitude as slaveholding Virginia and Kentucky, and Congress had not restricted slavery in states such as Tennessee where it had been allowed when they were territories, as was the case in Missouri.

The congressional debate grew sharper when it shifted from legality to morality. Clay had entered that moral minefield when he spoke of white slavery, and Taylor responded in kind when he chided southerners for portraying slavery as a regrettable legacy from their colonial past:

> How often, and how eloquently, have they deplored its existence among them? What willingness, nay, what solicitude have they not manifested to be relieved from this burden? How have they wept over the unfortunate policy that first introduced slaves into this country! How have they disclaimed the guilt and shame of that original sin, and thrown it back upon their ancestors! I have with pleasure heard those avowals of regret and confided in their sincerity. . . . Gentlemen have now an opportunity of putting their principles into practice; if they have tried slavery and found it a curse; if they desire to dissipate the gloom with which it covers their land; I call upon them to exclude it from the Territory in question; plant not its seeds in this uncorrupt soil.

Couched as an appeal to slaveholders with tender consciences, this speech was in fact meant to chide them for their willingness to allow an institution they professed to deplore to spread across the continent. Taylor overstated his case by portraying Missouri, where the seeds of slavery had been sown before Americans settled there, as "uncorrupt soil" and urging legislators not to reject the amendment and suffer that "evil, now easily eradicated, to strike its roots so deep in the soil that it can never be removed."[5]

Eradicating slavery was never easy, and doing so in Missouri had become more difficult since senators in 1804 rejected the Hillhouse amendment that would have freed any slaves introduced there once they reached adulthood and Congress in 1805 placed no restrictions on slavery in that territory. Since 1810 the number of slaves in Missouri had tripled, and resistance to freeing them had increased as their presence did. Tallmadge sought to overcome that resistance by proposing gradual emancipation that would take several decades to achieve. But debate over his amendment often portrayed it as something drastic and immediate, ranging from Taylor's plea to eradicate the evils of slavery before it took root in supposedly free soil to warnings by southerners of the evils that would result should slavery be rashly uprooted in Missouri. Opponents of the Tallmadge amendment were less intent on arguing that slavery was virtuous than that forced emancipation was vicious and reckless. To declare that slaves had a right to liberty, charged Representative Edward Colston of Virginia, was to "excite a servile war." Tallmadge himself stated that he would not advocate prohibiting slavery in Alabama, which was about to achieve statehood, because emancipation there could agitate slaves in surrounding states, "and a *servile* war might be the result."[6]

That concession did little to reassure Tallmadge's foes in the House. Philip P. Barbour of Virginia denounced his amendment as "tantamount to the prohibition of the emigration of the Southern people to the State of Missouri," ignoring the fact that many nonslaveholding southerners had emigrated to Ohio, Indiana, and Illinois as well as Missouri Territory. John Scott, the nonvoting delegate from that territory, warned Tallmadge and his supporters that "they were sowing the seeds of discord in this Union, by attempting to admit States with unequal privileges and unequal rights; that they were signing, sealing, and delivering their own death warrant; that the weapon they were so unjustly wielding against the people of Missouri, was a two-edged sword." Tallmadge took such language as advocating disunion and rebellion and replied defiantly: "Sir, if a dissolution of the Union must take place, let it be so! If civil war, which gentlemen so much threaten, must come, I can only say, let it come!"[7]

A Divided House

Contrary to the fears of some Federalists at the time of Louisiana Purchase, the three-fifths clause in the Constitution did not give the South enough representation in the House to match the fast-growing population of the North, which had about two dozen more congressmen than the South did by 1819. On February 16, the House approved the first part of the Tallmadge amendment, forbidding the further introduction of slavery to Missouri, by a vote of 87 to 76. The second part, requiring slaves born after Missouri achieved statehood to be emancipated by the age of twenty-five, passed by a narrower margin, 82 to 78. Northerners largely favored the amendment and southerners mostly opposed it. The national unity that Monroe sought was challenged in this case not by rival parties but by opposing northern and southern blocs. The Senate was more closely matched sectionally—with eleven free states and ten slave states (Alabama would make that eleven when admitted in December 1819)—and most of its members were reluctant to pursue the path proposed by Tallmadge. On February 27, they rejected his gradual emancipation plan for Missouri by a wide margin and opposed the prohibition against introducing slaves there by a vote of 22 to 16. Voting to defeat the amendment were both senators from Illinois, Jesse Thomas and Ninian Edwards, who as governor of Illinois Territory in 1815 had offered for sale twenty-two slaves, among them "several of both sexes between the years of ten and seventeen."[8]

After the House and Senate failed to reach agreement on Missouri and the Fifteenth Congress adjourned in March, the Tallmadge amendment remained a matter of public debate, which went beyond whether slavery should be restricted in new territories or states to whether it was justifiable in the nation at large. Northerners objected that admitting Missouri without restriction on slavery would disgrace the Union and flout the constitutional requirement that the United States "guarantee to every State in this Union a republican form of government" (Article IV, Section 4). Slavery was "contrary to republican principles," insisted Joseph Blunt of New York, "and stains our national honor." Southerners argued that respect for property rights was essential to the American Republic and that the right to hold people in bondage was upheld by the fugitive-slave clause, among other provisions in the Constitution. Some cited justification for slavery in an even more revered text: the Bible. Opposition to the Tallmadge amendment among Missourians was based less on constitutional principles than on their revolutionary right, affirmed in the Declaration of Independence, to alter or abolish their government if it became destructive of their safety and happiness. Benton's *St. Louis Enquirer* vowed that Missourians would never submit to a law that would drive slaveholders from the state and allow scheming, self-righteous New Englanders to gain "supremacy in this country." The threat that Missouri might secede if Congress restricted slavery there or denied it statehood revived old fears of disunion in the West even as tensions between the North and South rose menacingly, causing Henry Clay to worry that if the crisis were not resolved, the nation might be divided "into three distinct confederacies."[9]

Fear of disunion transformed Clay from a partisan firmly opposed to the Tallmadge amendment to one of several prominent figures in Washington who helped implement the Missouri Compromise. Prior to that accommodation, he was known in Congress as a keen political combatant. First elected Speaker of the House in 1811 by his fellow Republicans at the age of thirty-four, Clay had no

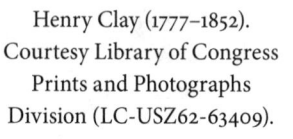

Henry Clay (1777–1852).
Courtesy Library of Congress
Prints and Photographs
Division (LC-USZ62-63409).

intention of compromising with the British and figured prominently among those "War Hawks" in Congress who invited a conflict in 1812 for which the nation was ill prepared. He likened the burgeoning American Republic to a young officer who had to fight a duel with an overbearing rival to prevent "being bullied."[10] He later served as a founding member of the American Colonization Society, which sought a middle ground between abolitionists and ardent defenders of slavery by promoting gradual, voluntary emancipation and the settlement of freed slaves abroad. Although the society's prescription failed to remedy slavery and Clay himself did not free most of the fifty or so Black people he owned, the Missouri crisis impressed on him the danger that extending slavery posed to the Union.

When the Sixteenth Congress convened in December 1819, Clay was among those who recognized a basis for compromise in efforts by residents of Maine, which was then part of Massachusetts, to form their own state. He suggested linking a vote to admit Maine as a free state with a vote to admit Missouri without restriction on slavery. President Monroe, for his part, backed a similar proposal by Senator James Barbour of Virginia, who was more inclined than his brother Philip in the House to subordinate states' rights and slaveholders' property rights to the cause of national unity. Joining that effort in the Senate was Thomas of Illinois, a former slaveholder from Kentucky who still held several permanently indentured Black servants in his adopted state. To make admitting slaveholding Missouri along with Maine more palatable to northerners like those settling in Illinois, he linked Barbour's initiative to a proposal introduced by Congressman Taylor the previous February. After the House narrowly defeated his effort to restrict slavery in the newly organized Arkansas Territory—which initially included much of what later became the state of Oklahoma—Taylor had then proposed that "neither slavery nor involuntary servitude shall hereafter be introduced into any part of the Territories of the United States, lying north of 36 degrees and 30 minutes north latitude," the boundary line between Arkansas Territory and Missouri Territory.[11] That too was rejected in the House. But when Thomas attached the prohibition of slavery in territory above 36°30' to Barbour's proposal for admitting Missouri and Maine as states jointly, southerners in the Senate largely supported the compromise, as did enough northerners to pass it by a margin of four votes.

Clay ushered the compromise through the House by separating its two parts, which if voted on jointly risked being rejected by northerners opposed to admitting Missouri without restriction on slavery and southerners opposed to prohibiting slavery in territories above 36°30'. Enough northerners wary of disunion and soothed by the admission of Maine as a free state joined the entire southern delegation to approve admitting Missouri as a slave state by a margin of three votes. With that concession in hand, roughly half the southerners in the House, many of them from states bordering the North, joined northerners in prohibiting slavery above the compromise line by a wide margin. "We have gained all that was possible, if not all that was desired," concluded John Taylor.[12] He had helped preserve the bulk of the Louisiana Purchase as free territory. Yet rejection of the Tallmadge amendment was a fateful defeat for efforts to confine slavery by prohibiting or gradually eliminating it in newly admitted states. Some southerners had threatened secession if that amendment passed. But the Missouri Compromise fostered disunion in the long run by signaling that slavery was not a relic of the nation's past but part of its expansive future, allowed below a line that many southerners would favor extending to the Pacific when the nation spanned the continent—an extension many northerners would oppose. The compromise would also strain the Union in decades to come by reinforcing the notion that balancing the admission of free states with slave states was incumbent on Congress, which encouraged southern expectations and demands at odds with the increasing political clout of the numerically superior North and the poor prospects for exporting the South's peculiar institution to far western territories.

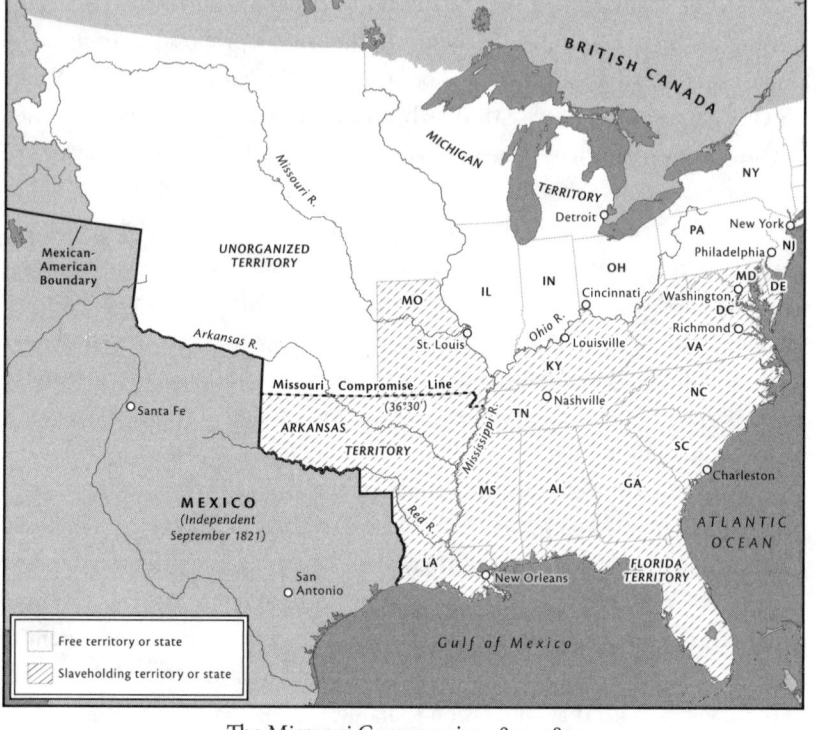

The Missouri Compromise, 1820–1821

A Repugnant Constitution

In the summer of 1820, Missourians reignited the crisis that Congress had seemingly resolved by adopting a state constitution declaring that its general assembly could not emancipate slaves without the permission of their owners and must pass laws to "prevent free negroes and mulattoes from coming to, and settling in this state, under any pretext whatsoever."[13] Those provisions were proof that diffusing slavery from southern states to western territories failed to loosen its grip either on those held in bondage or on the minds of white settlers, who seldom welcomed free African Americans in free states but abhorred them where their presence might conceivably make slaves more inclined to seek liberty. Prohibiting free Black people from entering Missouri conflicted with the congressional requirement that the state's constitution not be repugnant to the U.S. Constitution, which stated that the "citizens of each State shall be entitled to all privileges and immunities of citizens in the several States" (Article IV, Section 2).

When the issue came before the House of Representatives in early 1821, Charles Pinckney, a delegate at the Constitutional Convention in 1787 before he served as governor of South Carolina, said he knew then that there was no such thing in the Union "as a black or colored citizen" and still did not believe that there were any legitimate Black citizens, considering the "comparatively few rights" they had in northern states.[14] Although free Blacks were prohibited from voting and denied other civil rights in several northern states, opponents of the Missouri constitution argued that they were nonetheless citizens, entitled to such basic constitutional protections as not being deprived of life, liberty, or property without due process of law, and thus could not be barred from entering Missouri. The House narrowly voted to refuse admission to Missouri because of its repugnant constitution. The Senate voted otherwise, resulting in a deadlock. When results of the 1820 presidential election, won by the uncontested incumbent Monroe, were certified by Congress in February 1821, two tallies resulted—one approved by the Senate awarding Missouri's three electoral votes to Monroe, and the other withholding those three votes, as insisted by the House.

Later that month, Henry Clay contrived a second compromise by winning approval for a resolution he drafted, which let the controversial Missouri constitution stand but stated that "no law shall be passed in conformity thereto, by which any citizen, of either of the states in this Union, shall be excluded from the enjoyment of any of the privileges and immunities to which such citizen is entitled under the constitution of the United States."[15] That brought the House into alignment with the Senate on admitting Missouri but did not prevent the new state's general assembly from enacting statutes that effectively prevented free Black people from settling there, including an 1825 law requiring them to present certificates of citizenship that were difficult if not impossible to obtain. Laws aimed at curbing such immigration were also enacted in some northern states.

Settlement of the Missouri crisis came soon after final ratification of the Adams-Onís Treaty, delayed by political upheaval in Spain and its rebellious American colonies. Two boundaries of great significance for American expansion now divided the trans-Mississippi West—one separating American from Spanish territory, which was about to become Mexican territory, and the other separating free soil from land open to slavery within the Louisiana Purchase. The Adams-Onís line was already under attack from American expansionists like Benton, who protested that Adams had surrendered to Spain "an immense country between the Red River and the Rio Grande del Norte."[16] Benton's support for extending the nation's boundaries and his opposition to congressional restrictions on slavery in Missouri helped elevate him in late 1821 to the U.S. Senate, where he would represent that state for the next three decades. Around the time he entered that chamber, American traders and settlers began crossing the Adams-Onís line in ways that gradually eroded it, among them venturesome Missourians like William Becknell, who inaugurated commerce with New Mexico along the Santa Fe Trail, and Stephen Austin, who established an American colony in Mexican Texas. Southern critics of the Missouri Compromise like Thomas Ritchie, editor of the *Richmond Enquirer*, recognized that although the agreement left slaveholders firmly entrenched on the far side of the Mississippi from Missouri to Louisiana when there were no emerging free states beyond that river, it left only one avenue for extending slavery farther west: into Mexican territory. "If we are cooped up on the north," Ritchie wrote, "we must have elbow room to the west."[17] Austin's initiative enabled American slaveholders to elbow their way into Texas and eventually seize that territory, leading to a war that would greatly enlarge U.S. territory and foster fierce new disputes over slavery.

That the Missouri Compromise might ultimately fail to avert disunion was foreseen by two of the nation's most accomplished expansionists. Thomas Jefferson called it "a reprieve only" in his letter to John Holmes of Maine, whose state gained admission through the compromise he backed. Andrew Jackson described the crisis as "the entering wedge to separate the union." He feared it might cause slaves to rebel and blamed the "Eastern interest," represented by Tallmadge, for raising the slavery issue. "They will find the southern & western states equally resolved to support their constitutional rights," warned Jackson, who hoped he would not live to see the evils "that must grow out of this wicked design of Demagogues."[18] Yet Jackson went on to embrace the assumption on which the Missouri Compromise was based: that this democratic republic could and should remain part slave and part free. Southerners who shared that belief expected their government to uphold slavery and advance it in a way that maintained equilibrium between free states and slave states. As the nineteenth century progressed, however, northerners would grow more populous and politically assertive as their determination to restrict slavery increased. The line drawn across the West in 1820 that Jefferson deplored was indeed ominous. It postponed a reckoning between North and South over western expansion, but it set them apart like those lines drawn in war zones to separate opposing forces who nursed their grievances during a truce that might be prolonged but would eventually break down.

CHAPTER 6

Stephen Austin's Invasive Colony

American expansion entered a new phase in the early 1820s as traders and colonists from the United States infiltrated the emerging nation of Mexico. Previously, Americans had often expanded their domain through conquest or coercive treaties that removed Indians from territory claimed by the United States from Britain, France, or Spain. Eventually, conquest and coercion would be applied in similar fashion to Mexico and tribes occupying the far Southwest. But that takeover was preceded by disarming overtures made by Anglo-Americans in Texas, New Mexico, and California who dealt peacefully with Mexicans and began settling among them. Such cultural infiltration could be compared to biological colonization, by which an invasive species adapts to a new environment and intermingles with its hosts before supplanting them. No agent of American expansion entering the Mexican borderlands was more adaptable or adept at colonization than Stephen Austin, who embraced Mexican citizenship and cultivated close ties with Mexican authorities even as he drew American slaveholders to Texas, which would serve as the wedge by which the United States severed northern Mexico from that nation's heartland.

Born in Virginia in 1793, Stephen Austin went west as a child when his venturesome father, Moses Austin, resettled his family on a land grant he obtained south of St. Louis in Spanish Louisiana. Although Moses pledged allegiance to Spain to secure that grant, he raised Stephen as an American in what became U.S. territory in 1803 and sent him at the age of eleven to an academy in Colchester, Connecticut. Austin's sojourn in the state where his father was born—and where Black children who were free or would be emancipated by law as adults attended a school adjacent to his academy—may have made him less accepting of slavery than many southerners who later colonized Texas. But as a young man he owned a slave named Richmond and employed slave labor while managing a lead mine his father established in what was then Missouri Territory. That business faltered during the Panic of 1819, and both father and son were deeply in debt when Moses Austin traveled with Richmond to Texas in late 1820 and obtained permission to settle three hundred American families there. Ailing when he returned to Missouri, he died the following June after assuring Stephen Austin in writing that "a new chance presents itself" in Texas and urging him to seize that opportunity.[1]

Leaving behind his law studies in New Orleans, Austin set out for Texas, where he learned in August 1821 that Mexico had won independence from Spain. That was "glorious news," he wrote, but he would have to obtain Mexican approval for the land grant on which Spanish officials had authorized his late father to found a colony.[2] By the time he reached Mexico City in the spring of 1822, he had recruited colonists and was fluent enough in Spanish to lobby for his cause. Prepared to swear loyalty to Mexico as his father had sworn to Spain, he distinguished himself from militant American expansionists such as James Long, a Virginian who defied Spanish sovereignty in Texas by mounting two filibusters there between 1819 and 1821, both of which failed.

Austin's approach was far more accommodating. In a petition to Agustín de Iturbide, the short-lived emperor of Mexico who would abdicate in 1823 and be executed a year later, he sought permission to colonize Texas by pledging loyalty to "his Imperial Majesty" and allegiance to his empire, using language as effusive as a Spanish courtier might have employed:

> This solemn act cuts me off from all protection or dependence on my former government—my property, my prospects, my future hopes of happiness, for myself and family, and for the families I have brought with me, are centered here. This is our adopted Nation: . . . I therefore supplicate that his Imperial Majesty will have the goodness to take the Settlement I have formed under his protection, and that we may be received as Children of the great Mexican family.[3]

This was not mere flattery of Iturbide by Austin, who believed that Mexico, having long been subject to the king of Spain, would fare better under a constitutional monarch than under a representative government. "These people will not do for a Republic," he wrote; "nothing but a Monarchy can save them from Anarchy."[4]

Iturbide dissolved the Mexican Congress in late 1822 and replaced it with the junta, a legislative council beholden to him. Anticipating that slaveholders would be the mainstay of his colony, Austin urged the junta—which was considering a colonization bill that would free within ten years all slaves introduced to Mexico—to amend that act "so as to make them slaves for life and their children free at 21 years." By his own account, he "talked to every member" of the council and shaped the bill they approved, which required only that slaves introduced by colonists not be sold and that their children be "free at the age of fourteen."[5] The law was annulled after Iturbide fell from power in 1823, but the emperor had by then approved Austin's grant for a colony in eastern Texas between the San Jacinto and Lavaca Rivers, entering respectively into Galveston Bay and Matagorda Bay.

When Mexico emerged as a republic in 1824, Austin set aside his concern that anarchy would result and made the most of its constitution, which gave Mexican states such as Coahuila and Texas—combined as one because Texas had too few Mexican inhabitants for statehood—broad authority to implement federal statutes, including a new colonization law intended to help populate the country's sparsely settled northern frontier with immigrants loyal to the nation. Aided by the Baron de Bastrop—a Dutch immigrant with an assumed title who had helped Moses Austin obtain his grant and now represented Texas in the state legislature at Saltillo—Austin overcame doubts among delegates there that Americans could be trusted as colonists. The law as implemented at Saltillo allowed them to settle in Texas under Austin and other authorized empresarios, none of whom proved as successful as he did. All colonists had to swear allegiance to Mexico and profess Catholicism, the country's established religion. In practice, however, they did not have to worship as Catholics. For Austin's settlers, becoming Mexican did not mean renouncing their American identity—or their commitment to the revolutionary principle of 1776 that government derived its just powers from the consent of the governed and could rightfully be altered or abolished if it forfeited their consent.

During the 1820s, Mexican authorities gave colonists from the United States little cause for complaint, exempting them from most tariffs and taxes while affording them representation in the national congress and in the state legislature, where Austin was among those who served as a delegate. He affirmed his loyalty to Mexico by helping to put down a reckless uprising by American-born empresario Haden Edwards, who declared independence in December 1826 before fleeing with rebels to Louisiana a month later when their so-called Fredonia Republic collapsed. Austin did what he could to suppress such rebelliousness within his own colony. As he put it, he had "an unruly set of North American frontier republicans to controul who felt that they were sovereigns." Some of them resented the authority he exercised over them as much as they did Mexican authority. He tried to persuade them that they were fortunate to live under so little restraint. "The policy of this Gov' to emigrants is liberal beyond parallel," he wrote.[6]

When Mexican authorities proposed liberating slaves, however, they alarmed Americans who had settled in Texas, most of them southerners accustomed to slavery. A census of Austin's colony in 1825 revealed that about one-fourth of its 1,800 inhabitants were enslaved. Having fulfilled his original contract to settle three hundred families in Texas, Austin sought approval to admit five hundred more families. Texas was emerging as an extension of the Cotton Kingdom, and its colonists were increasingly reliant on slave labor. The government should authorize them "to bring in their Slaves and Servants," Austin urged Governor Rafael Gonzáles, and grant colonists "right of property" in them and their descendants. Otherwise, he argued, "these fertile lands, instead of being occupied by wealthy planters, will remain for many years, in the hands of mere shepherds, or poor people, who will scarcely raise a sufficiency for the sustenance of their families."[7]

Although slavery was not yet authorized in Coahuila and Texas, as Austin urged, neither was it forbidden. He lured planters from southern states by placing advertisements in newspapers promising them fertile land in Texas and by basing how much land they received on how many enslaved people they introduced. No one benefited more from Austin's inducements than planter Jared Groce, who arrived from Alabama with nearly one hundred slaves and received a hefty land grant of some forty-four thousand acres. Austin's policy was to exclude from the colony "men of infamous character and bad conduct," but he tolerated Groce, who had fled Georgia to escape a $10,000 debt to business partners and may not have been the rightful owner of all those he enslaved.[8] Many other southerners suffering from the lingering effects of the Panic of 1819 found refuge from their debts in Texas. Austin himself owed thousands of dollars to creditors in Missouri and hoped that the extensive acreage he claimed for serving as empresario would enable him to meet those obligations and prosper when land values increased along with crop yields.

The cotton trade on which Austin's colony depended was speculative, exhaustive, and expansive. Although modest amounts of that cash crop were produced by southern farmers without resorting to slave labor, much of it was laboriously planted, tended, and harvested by enslaved people on plantations whose owners flourished when cotton prices rose and faltered if prices tumbled and they could no longer cover loans they took to purchase land, slaves, or goods. Expanding to Texas offered indebted planters or those who had exhausted their soil a chance to profit anew—and would-be planters of limited means an opportunity to improve their fortunes—so long as they retained firm control of their indispensable laborers. The legal code Austin instituted for his colony, based partly on slave codes in the American South, imposed steep fines on anyone who helped slaves escape or evade recapture and called for slaves to be whipped severely if they were accused of theft or left their owners without a pass.

Jared Groce leased enslaved people as needed to colonists who had none or held only a few, as Austin did. (He had sold Richmond before leaving New Orleans, but he later owned a manservant named Simon and a woman he purchased as his housekeeper.) Groce also sent armed slaves to bolster militiamen campaigning against defiant Indians, who had long raided San Antonio, Goliad, and other Hispanic settlements. The politically savvy Austin, who had served in the Missouri territorial legislature and with Missouri militia forces campaigning against hostile tribes, hoped that helping defend Texas would earn his slaveholding colonists concessions from Mexican officials. In 1826, concerned by reports that slavery might be abolished in Mexico, he warned José Antonio Saucedo, who served under the governor as political chief in Texas, that emancipation would end the protection the colony's militiamen provided against tribal threats. "We are not well prepared here to resist an attack," he wrote. "More than one half of these people are awaiting the decision of Congress in regard to their slaves, as they intend to leave the Country if their emancipation is decreed. . . . The remainder of the settlers are so disheartened that they have no energy to make an effort. Therefore, if the slaves are emancipated the government must not depend upon the assistance of this militia."[9] Austin may have been overstating his case, but slave owners were indeed reluctant to inhabit territory where their legal right to hold people in bondage might be denied.

Austin's lobbying did not dissuade legislators at Saltillo from approving a state constitution in 1827 that recognized slavery but prohibited the importation of slaves and freed children born to slaves henceforth. Austin responded by promoting a scheme like that introduced earlier by Governor Harrison in Indiana Territory to skirt prohibition of slavery in the Northwest Ordinance. Planters destined for Texas would place their slaves under indenture contracts that bound them to serve their masters for up to ninety-nine years. Representatives from Texas won approval for such contracts at Saltillo by claiming they were intended to allow Americans to immigrate with free laborers who agreed to become indentured servants. Austin's scheme for contractual slavery was publicized in New Orleans, where one newspaper reported: "The law of Mexico, prohibiting slavery, is evaded by having negroes bound to serve an apprenticeship of 99 years. There are several planters who number 50 or 60 such apprentices."[10]

Pressure from Above

Not long after Austin met one challenge to his plan for a prosperous slaveholding colony, he faced another, which emanated from Mexico City and proved more formidable. In 1828, General Manuel de Mier y Terán toured Texas to assess whether it was secure against threats such as that posed recently by Haden Edwards and the Fredonia rebels. He dealt cordially with Austin, whose respect for Mexican authority earned him the trust of liberals as well as conservatives like Terán and Lucas Alamán, minister of relations in Mexico City, who would act on Terán's recommendations. Austin's settlers occupied "the best land that exists in all the extent of Texas; his dedication and economy have made it very productive," Terán reported. The main threat to security came not from Austin's colonists, Terán concluded, but from the many Americans who were settling illegally in Texas, particularly around Nacogdoches, near the Louisiana border. "The North Americans have conquered whatever territory adjoins them," he warned, and might soon take Texas unless American immigration was curbed and colonists from Mexico or nations that posed no threat were sent there along with Mexican troops.[11] Alamán drew on Terán's recommendations to formulate a comprehensive law passed by the Mexican Congress on April 6, 1830, which barred further American immigration to Texas, imposed tariffs on imported goods there, prohibited the importation of slaves, and authorized sending troops to enforce compliance. Austin circumvented the ban on immigration by pledging to admit only those he had previously "contracted" to accept as colonists—a commitment he then flouted by issuing blank certificates with his signature that were distributed to immigrants at the border with no assurance they were destined for his colony.[12]

Although strictly enforcing the new rules in Texas would have taken far more Mexican troops than were sent there, the Law of April 6, 1830, signaled to Austin that his plan for Texas was increasingly at odds with Mexico's intentions, particularly in regard to slavery, which President Vicente Ramón Guerrero had abolished by decree in 1829. Texas was exempted from that decree, but it was yet another indication that the racially diverse Mexican Republic, in which

Stephen F. Austin (1793–1836).
Courtesy Library of Congress
Prints and Photographs
Division (LC-USZ62-4220).

those of pure Spanish ancestry were a small minority, might not long tolerate incursions by American slaveholders, even if they swore allegiance to their adopted homeland. Racial prejudice toward mestizos, who were partly of Native American ancestry and made up much of the Mexican population, was common among Anglo-Texans. Austin was no exception, having written in 1823 after traveling to Mexico City and back that "the majority of the people of the whole nation as far as I have seen them want nothing but tails to be more brutes than the Apes."[13] He proved capable of dealing cordially with prominent mestizos. But continued immigration by his colonists and other Americans who enslaved Black people and often disdained Mexicans as racially inferior reinforced doubts among authorities that such immigrants belonged in this country and would in fact remain loyal to it.

Faced with mounting Mexican opposition to slavery, Austin considered embracing a proposal by Terán and Alamán that European immigrants be recruited as colonists. Soon after the Law of April 6, 1830, was enacted, Austin suggested in writing that self-reliant German or Swiss immigrants might make better colonists than American planters and would help shield Texas from the nightmare scenario of slave rebellions:

> They will introduce the culture of the vine, olive etc., they are industrious and moral . . . *and above all they will oppose slavery*. The idea of seeing such a country as this overrun by a slave population almost makes me weep. It is in vain to tell a North American that the white population will be destroyed some fifty or eighty years hence by the negros, and that his daughters will be violated and Butch[er]ed by them . . . Slavery is now most positively prohibited by our Constitution and by a number of laws, and I do hope it may always be so.[14]

Like other ambivalent exponents of slavery, Austin feared that it might become so pervasive that white settlers in Texas would be outnumbered and overwhelmed by rebellious slaves. In another letter written a few days later, Austin worried that annexation by the United States would commit Texas irrevocably to slavery:

> It has been, and is, my ambition to redeem Texas from the wilderness, and to lay a solid foundation for its future prosperity. I do not believe that, that object can be effected by any kind of union with the U. S. for such an union would of course intail slavery on this fair region, which may be made the Eden of America—satan entered the sacred garden in the shape of a serpent—if he is allowed to enter Texas in the shape of negros it will share the fate of Eden.[15]

Austin appeared oblivious to the fact that he and his colonists had already entailed slavery on Texas. Far from suggesting that they had blighted this would-be "Eden of America" by doing so, he portrayed their slaves as serpents in the garden and shifted blame for proliferating slavery and its hazards to the United States as if he and his settlers were not products of American society, steeped in its vices as well as its virtues. Earlier American leaders like Jefferson had reacted similarly by blaming the British from whose society they emerged for the African slave trade and the threat of slave rebellions and citing those as grounds for declaring independence.

In a letter written in December 1831 to his cousin Mary Austin Holley shortly after she visited him in Texas, Austin doubted that Texas was ready for independence but acknowledged that possibility:

To remain as we are, is impossible. We have not the right kind of material for an Independent Government, and an union with the United States would bring Negro Slavery—that curse of curses, and worst of reproaches, on civilized man; that unanswered, and unanswerable, inconsistency of *free* and liberal republicans. I think the Government will yield, and give us what we ought to have. If not, we shall go for *Independence* and put our trust in our selves, our riffles, and—our God.[16]

In fact, one essential thing many Anglo-Texans thought they ought to have from the Mexican government was an end to restrictions on that "curse of curses" slavery, which was so vital to Texas and its plantation economy that Austin soon reaffirmed his commitment to it. As he wrote emphatically in May 1833, "Texas *must be* a slave country. . . . It is the wish of the people there, and it is my duty to do all I can, prudently, in favor of it."[17]

Austin's change of heart came after Texans began offering armed resistance to Mexican authorities responsible for collecting tariffs and enforcing other provisions enacted by Congress in 1830. Among those officials was Colonel Juan Davis Bradburn, born John Bradburn in Virginia in 1787. Raised in Kentucky and involved in filibusters against Spanish authority during the Mexican War of Independence, he became a Mexican citizen with a Mexican wife, loyal to his adopted nation and intent on upholding its laws. Sent by General Terán to Texas with 170 troops, he did what he could to enforce customs regulations and prohibitions against settlement by incoming Americans. Bradburn also alarmed settlers from southern states by refusing to return to their owners fugitive slaves from Louisiana who sought refuge at his fort in Anahuac, situated at the north end of Galveston Bay, outside Austin's colony.

Any Mexican officer who took those actions would have faced opposition, but the rigor with which the American-born Bradburn upheld Mexican statutes made him all the more repugnant to recent immigrants like William B. Travis. A young lawyer from Alabama, Travis was emerging as a leader of those Anglo-Texans who remained proud Americans at heart and felt entitled to resist Mexican infringements on their liberty or their interests as slave owners. When Bradburn arrested Travis and another defiant lawyer, Patrick C. Jack, in May 1832, armed supporters clashed with Bradburn's troops at Anahuac. Further conflict there was averted by Colonel José de las Piedras, who outranked Bradburn and relieved him before releasing the two prisoners. But Piedras and his troops were then challenged in early August by rebellious settlers at Nacogdoches, who killed or wounded more than eighty Mexicans and captured Piedras after his hard-pressed soldiers turned against him. Rebellious Texans might have faced severe reprisals had they not linked their cause with a broader revolt by Mexican federalists, who favored the Constitution of 1824 that left Mexican states largely in control of their own affairs. Led by General Antonio López de Santa Anna, who had repulsed a Spanish effort to reclaim Mexico in 1829, federalists defeated centralists loyal to President Anastacio Bustamante, who sought to concentrate power in Mexico City and was ousted by the insurgents. Among those who perished in that internal conflict was General Terán, who committed suicide in July 1832 after concluding that his centralist forces could not halt the federalist uprising and that Mexico was too divided to prevent Texas from slipping away. "How could we expect to hold Texas when we do not even agree among ourselves?" he wrote.[18]

Victory for federalists prompted Texans to seek greater autonomy by demanding statehood apart from Coahuila, which would enable them to limit if not avoid tariffs and restrictions on American immigration and slavery under the Law of April 6, 1830, which remained in effect. Austin embraced that statehood movement not only as a way of averting secession from Mexico—which he considered a last resort, to be pursued only if other remedies failed—but also as a means of maintaining his influence in Texas, where many unauthorized American immigrants arrived hungering for land or hoping to profit from it by engaging in what Austin called a "horrible *Mania* for speculation," as he himself had done as a young man.[19] He still commanded the respect of Anglo-Texans as a whole, and he tried to reconcile their demands with the concerns of Tejanos, who were now outnumbered nearly ten to one by the thirty thousand or so American immigrants in Texas. Some Tejanos opposed separate statehood for Texas because it would be dominated politically by Anglos, and others favored it only if accomplished lawfully, as Austin intended when he returned to Mexico City in 1833 to lobby for that outcome. But a reckless letter he wrote that October, urging ayuntamientos (town councils) in Texas to unite and "organize a local government independent of Coahuila, even though the general government withholds its consent," caused him to be arrested and jailed in the capital.[20]

Road to Rebellion

Austin's confinement, which lasted from early 1834 until Christmas Day that December, further alienated his supporters in Texas from the new regime in Mexico City, which was reverting to centralism under the nation's mercurial president and commander in chief, Santa Anna. After assuming the presidency, he had remained in seclusion until the federalist policies backed by Vice President Valentín Gómez Farías—who made some concessions to Texans, including allowing them the right to trial by jury—lost favor in the capital. By 1835, Santa Anna was centralizing power in Mexico aggressively. The ultraconservative Congress he instituted nullified the Constitution of 1824 and dissolved state legislatures, provoking rebellion in several states, including Coahuila and Texas. In late June 1835, Texans led by William Travis seized the fort at Anahuac and ejected Mexican troops. General Martín Perfecto de Cos, related to Santa Anna and loyal to his centralist regime, then ordered Travis and other troublemakers arrested and warned Texans that the cost of defying the government would "bear heavily upon them and their property." Some viewed that as a threat to free slaves in Texas and turn them against insurgents. Texans also feared that slaves would try to free themselves if war erupted, and one such revolt would in fact occur along the Brazos River in Austin's colony, where an uprising by some one hundred enslaved people would be crushed that October. Like some Americans who rebelled against Britain, militant Texans warned fellow colonists that they would be reduced to political slavery if they did not defend their freedom. In the town of Liberty, established north of Anahuac in 1831 within ten leagues of the coast, where American immigrants were not authorized to settle, residents formed a committee of public safety and declared that "the contest is for liberty or slavery, for life or death."[21]

Some Texans disdained impulsive rebels like Travis and formed an unofficial "peace party" in opposition to the "war party." But hopes for reconciliation with the Mexican government waned when Texans learned that Santa Anna's forces had brutally suppressed rebellion in the state of Zacatecas that May. When Austin returned by ship to Texas by way of New Orleans in August 1835, he concluded that the time had come for Texans to resist Mexico and recast themselves as American revolutionaries. In a memorable letter he wrote that month to his beloved cousin Mary, with whom the unmarried Austin shared thoughts he seldom revealed to others, he stated that Americanizing Texas had long been his objective, with the ultimate goal of attaching it to the United States:

> It is very evident that the best interests of the United States require that Texas should be effectually, and fully, *Americanized*—that is—settled by a population that will harmonize with their neighbors on the *East*, in language, political principles, common origin, sympathy, and even interest. *Texas must be a slave country. It is no longer a matter of doubt.* . . . A gentle

breeze shakes off a ripe peach. Can it be supposed that the violent political convulsions of Mexico will not shake off Texas so soon as it is ripe enough to fall[?] All that is now wanting is a great immigration of good and efficient families, this fall and winter . . . The fact is, we must, and ought to become a part of the United States. . . . For fourteen years I have had a hard time of it, but nothing shall daunt my courage or abate my exertions to complete the main object of my labors—*to Americanize Texas.*[22]

How can Austin's admission here that he colonized Texas to promote American expansion be reconciled with his frequent and seemingly sincere professions of loyalty to Mexico? Was it all a bluff, which fooled even those wary of American designs on Texas like Terán? Raised in Missouri on the shifting Spanish-American frontier, Austin was well prepared to function credibly as a loyal Mexican while retaining his American identity. His capacity to cross borders and assume the character and concerns of those whose country he infiltrated—including their misgivings about slavery—was essential to his success at introducing slaveholding American settlers who would help shake Texas free from Mexico and eventually attach it to the United States. That may not have been his intention when he entered the country, but it became his "main object." His adaptability enabled him to occupy middle ground between such transparent and truculent Americans as William Travis, who could never have won permission to colonize Texas, and a fully assimilated Anglo-Mexican like Juan Bradburn.

"WAR is our only resource," Austin wrote in September 1835 after Mexican troops led by General Cos occupied San Antonio. "There is no other remedy than to defend our rights, our country and ourselves by force of arms."[23] Austin briefly led Texas troops that fall before serving as a commissioner of the provisional revolutionary government to the United States. In a widely published letter he wrote in that capacity in May 1836, after Texas troops were annihilated at the Alamo and massacred at Goliad, he described them as victims of a "war of extermination . . . waged by the mongrel Spanish-Indian and Negro race, against civilization and the Anglo-American race."[24] In fact, rebellious slaves did not join forces with Mexican troops, and Texans led by Sam Houston had avenged Goliad and the Alamo in April by crushing forces led by Santa Anna in the decisive Battle of San Jacinto, news of which had not reached Austin when he composed that letter. His harsh language was indicative of a revolution whose success would enhance the liberty of Anglo-Texans but embed slavery in the constitution of their new republic and further marginalize Tejanos by attracting to their homeland tens of thousands more American settlers, who too often viewed them as Austin described them.

After Texas broke free, Austin lost the presidential election there to Houston and served briefly as secretary of state before he died of pneumonia in December 1836. He had not loomed large in the war for independence, but his skill at conciliating Mexican officials and discouraging a premature revolt by American colonists contributed as much to the outcome as the efforts of those who led the fight. As he stated suggestively in his letter seeking support for the revolution, he had worked "like a slave to *Americanize* Texas." Like Jefferson and Jackson, Austin extended American slavery and helped build the house divided that shattered in 1861 without seeking that convulsive outcome. He foresaw that Texas might eventually enter the Union as a slave state under the political bargain between North and South that kept their share of stars on the American flag equitable. What he did not foresee was that the bargain would break down, in large part because of sectional disputes resulting from the American annexation of Texas and the ensuing war with Mexico. The ultimate price that Anglo-Texans and other southerners would pay for perpetuating their peculiar institution was not a bloody revolt by African Americans they held in bondage, as Austin feared, but carnage resulting from their own ill-fated rebellion against the Union, which the rebellion of Texans against Mexico anticipated and helped precipitate.

CHAPTER 7

Houston, Jackson, and
the Southwestern Frontier

O n November 20, 1836, Sam Houston, president of the Texas Republic, wrote two letters, one official and one confidential, to the president of the United States, Andrew Jackson. "*Dear Sir,*" the official note began: "Allow me the pleasure of introducing to the notice, and kind attention of your Excellency, General Antonio Lopez de Sant[a] Anna, the President of the Republic of Mexico."[1] Having captured Santa Anna after crushing his Mexican forces at San Jacinto in April, Houston was now sending him under escort to Washington. That would spare him from possible execution as a war criminal for ordering captured Texas troops put to death and would preserve him as an asset in the new republic's bid for international recognition. Although Mexico rejected the treaty Santa Anna signed under duress in captivity, Houston hoped that his pledge to acknowledge the independence of Texas would encourage Jackson to recognize, if not annex, the Lone Star Republic.

In his confidential letter to Jackson, Houston confessed that while he and other authorities in Texas gave the impression that they could stand up to any threat, "I am free to say *to you* that we cannot do it." Well aware that Santa Anna's surrender was no guarantee against a renewed invasion by Mexico or incursions by European powers, Houston appealed to Jackson to wrap Texas in America's protective embrace: "My great desire is that our country Texas shall be annexed to the United States and on a footing of Justice and reciprocity to the parties. . . . I look to you as the friend and patron of my youth and the benefactor of mankind to interpose in our behalf and save us."[2]

Jackson had indeed been his patron and paragon since 1814 when twenty-one-year-old Lieutenant Sam Houston was gravely injured battling Creek warriors at Horseshoe Bend. The wounds he suffered in that battle, Jackson's first major victory, long plagued him and prevented him from taking part in Old Hickory's triumph at New Orleans the following January. But he followed closely in his patron's path in years to come. General Jackson was gratified when Houston regained strength and began serving in 1817 as subagent to Cherokees he had lived among in Tennessee after leaving home in his teens. They were to be removed by treaty beyond the Mississippi River. Although Jackson was ruthless in pursuing the removal of Indians, he justified doing so by arguing that they would be better off when distanced from white settlers. Houston performed that task conscientiously by preventing the sale of liquor to Cherokees. As he wrote his patron: "You know General Jackson? how difficult it is to keep Indians sober? and also how impossible it is to transact business with them when intoxicated?"[3] Houston himself sometimes found it difficult to keep sober, and he would not use liquor to dull the senses of Cherokees he had to induce to leave their homeland. Among them was a chief named Oolooteka, who had adopted young Houston after his father died and would offer him refuge in years to come.

After overseeing removal of those Cherokees, Houston was elected to Congress in 1823 with Jackson's blessing. Jackson returned to Washington as a senator from Tennessee around the same time and was among four candidates for president in 1824 as the Republican Party splintered. John Quincy Adams was well placed to succeed outgoing president James Monroe after serving as secretary of state but had little support beyond the Northeast. Many southerners and westerners favored Jackson, who despite the wealth and elite status he acquired in Tennessee was viewed as a champion of the common man, meaning white men without wealth who were gaining voting rights. Jackson finished first in the election that November with about 42 percent of the popular vote and fifteen more electoral votes than Adams. But Speaker Henry Clay and Treasury Secretary William H. Crawford of Georgia garnered enough support to deny Jackson an electoral majority and send the race into the House of Representatives, where each state delegation would cast one vote. Clay, who had carried his home state of Kentucky as well as Missouri and Ohio, helped deliver all three to Adams, who won the presidency with votes from thirteen states, a bare majority. When Adams then appointed Clay secretary of state, Jackson's supporters took that as proof of a "corrupt bargain" between the two. Apart from any reward Clay anticipated from Adams, however, he had no interest in aiding his rival Jackson, whom he had disparaged as a "military chieftain." Jackson hit back by calling Clay a designing politician who had never "risked himself for his country, sacrificed his repose, or made an effort to repel an invading foe."[4]

Jackson's vendetta against his victorious foes, which would lead him to challenge and defeat Adams in 1828, was not just personal but philosophical. It foretold a major political realignment as Democratic Republicans in the Jeffersonian mold who favored limited government in Washington and due regard for states' rights gravitated to the new Democratic Party led by Jackson. Others like Adams and Clay favored a somewhat larger role for the federal government—as endorsed by Madison after the War of 1812 and his successor Monroe—and became National Republicans and later Whigs. Adams had begun his political career as a Federalist and remained committed as president to the national bank conceived by Hamilton (now the Second Bank of the United States) and to raising enough revenue from tariffs and land sales to fund internal improvements such as roads and canals, fostering commerce and communication in a largely rural society where an overland journey of a few hundred miles could take a week or two. Clay held similar views and advocated what he called the American System, employing tariffs and internal improvements to promote domestic industries and provide accessible home markets for them. He favored developing the nation's existing states and territories over territorial expansion to avoid provoking conflict and aggravating sectional tensions, which he had helped suppress as Speaker by implementing the Missouri Compromise. Adams was a more eager expansionist than Clay, but he was also the nation's leading diplomat. He preferred acquiring territory through negotiations and treaties like the one he had concluded with Spain to obtain Florida, and using diplomatic pressure to discourage European imperial intervention in the Americas, in keeping with the Monroe Doctrine he had formulated as secretary of state.

Jackson, for his part, believed that Americans had an inherent right to expand across the continent that nullified the competing claims of other nations or tribes. That his fellow slaveholders would benefit from Indian removal, his first priority as president, did not trouble him, for he did not harbor misgivings about slavery, as Adams did, or put much stock in plans to emancipate slaves on a voluntary basis and colonize them in Africa, as Clay did. Jackson's main concern was that agitation in defiance or defense of slavery might threaten the Union. His respect for the rights of states did not extend to recognizing their right to nullify federal law or secede, which he would strenuously oppose when asserted by South Carolina.

And he would wield presidential authority brazenly by removing federal deposits from the national bank, which he viewed as a foul nest of privilege and greed polluting American democracy. Foes of "King Andrew" accused him of exceeding his powers and became known as Whigs for those in Britain and America who had opposed royalist Tories during the revolutionary era.[5]

Fervent supporters of Jackson like Sam Houston blamed the 1824 defeat of their hero—who retired temporarily to the Hermitage, his plantation in Tennessee—on the supposedly corrupt bargain between Adams and Clay. Houston insisted that Jackson was "manifestly the choice of the majority of the people" (which was not quite the case in terms of the popular vote) and disdained all those associated with the incoming administration.[6] He invited trouble when he stated in print that the new postmaster at Nashville appointed by Adams, John P. Erwin, was not of good character. Erwin then sent a challenge to Houston delivered by two men, one of whom, General William White, quarreled with Houston and challenged him to a duel in Erwin's place. After practicing for that confrontation at the Hermitage, where the veteran duelist Jackson advised him to bite on a bullet to steel his nerve and steady his aim, Houston faced off against White and shot him in the groin, a wound similar to one Houston had suffered at Horseshoe Bend that still troubled him. White survived, and Houston emerged intact and was elected governor of Tennessee with Jackson's support in 1827.

A year later, Jackson defeated President Adams handily, receiving nearly twice as many popular votes as were cast for all four candidates in 1824, reflecting an increasingly democratic process for white men as most states now allowed them to vote without meeting property qualifications and to participate in presidential elections rather than leaving that decision to state legislators. The expansion of white male suffrage—accompanied in some states by the restriction of voting rights for free Black men—brought to the polls voters of little means who found Jackson's ascent from humble origins to national prominence inspirational and helped him defeat the privileged and supposedly corrupt Adams. It was a victory not just for Jackson but for what became known as Jacksonian democracy, which relied on a broader electorate and what he called "the virtue of the people" to make the government more representative if not more virtuous. Whereas Adams had declared that the nation's leaders should "not be palsied by the will of their constituents," Jacksonians believed that the will of the people, as represented by the hero they elected president, was imperative.[7]

Jackson's eager thirty-five-year-old protégé Houston appeared destined for higher office before his calamitous courtship of Eliza Allen, whom he wed in

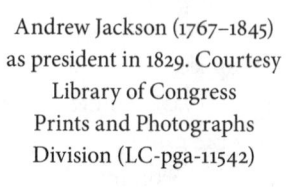

Andrew Jackson (1767–1845)
as president in 1829. Courtesy
Library of Congress
Prints and Photographs
Division (LC-pga-11542)

January 1829 when she was nineteen. Urged to marry him by her family, she seceded from that union in short order, returning home amid reports that he was insanely jealous of her attachment to a previous suitor—or that his lingering war wound rendered him repugnant to her. He wrote her father that she "was cold to me, & I thought did not love me. She owns that such was one cause of my unhappiness."[8] Bereft and humiliated, Houston resigned as governor in April. He spent much of the next three years among the western Cherokees he had earlier helped remove from Tennessee and who now inhabited what became known as Indian Territory, which would remain unorganized until its diminished tribal lands were subsumed within the new state of Oklahoma in 1907.

Houston was so often intoxicated that Cherokees sometimes referred to him not by his honorary name "Raven" but as "Big Drunk." Although he would not be legally divorced from Eliza Houston until 1837, he lived as husband and wife with Tiana Rogers Gentry, the part-Cherokee daughter of Scottish trader John Rogers and the widow of David Gentry, a white man killed by Osage warriors at odds with the Cherokees he lived among. They recognized Houston as a citizen of their nation, and he claimed the right to trade with fellow Cherokees (and import liquor strictly for his own use) without obtaining a license from a U.S. Indian agent, as required for Americans engaging in such commerce. But

Attorney General John M. Berrien ruled in December 1830 that Cherokees did not constitute a sovereign nation of which Houston was a citizen and that "by establishing himself within the limits of this tribe, and incorporating with it," he was not exempt from federal law and authority.[9] The U.S. Supreme Court ruled similarly in January 1831 that tribes such as the Cherokee were not sovereign foreign nations but "domestic dependent nations," in the words of Chief Justice John Marshall, who likened their relationship to the federal government to that of wards to their guardian.[10]

Those rulings came amid President Jackson's convulsive campaign to remove from the South all those Cherokees and members of other tribes who remained there. The Indian Removal Act he advanced provoked one of the most intense political debates in Congress and the country at large since Missouri sought admission as a slave state in 1820. Like that crisis, this dispute concerned whether white Americans and their elected representatives would continue to deny liberty and justice to those of other races or nations who came under their authority.

Contesting Removal

Although the Removal Act applied broadly to Indians in any state or organized territory who might be induced to exchange "lands where they now reside" for lands in unorganized territory west of the Mississippi, Jackson indicated in his first message to Congress in December 1829 that the legislation was aimed at southern tribes.[11] He mentioned by name Cherokees, Creeks, and Choctaws, who along with Chickasaws and Seminoles would become known as the Five Civilized Tribes for adopting customs and practices introduced by white traders and missionaries. Some in those tribes had already been removed like the Cherokees joined by Houston, but some sixty thousand Indians remained in southern states, occupying considerably more land than the scattered tribal groups inhabiting small reservations in northern states. Among their chiefs were men of mixed race, partly descended from white traders. But the exposure of those southern tribes to Anglo-American culture did not lessen their conviction that they constituted distinct Indian nations, linked to the United States by treaties but self-governing. Cherokees in northwestern Georgia formed a national council and passed a law that made ceding tribal land without the council's consent punishable by death. A gold rush on their territory increased pressure for their removal, and the Georgia legislature placed them under state authority but delayed pressing for their eviction until June 1830, hoping that Jackson would by then have congressional authority to remove them in keeping with an earlier commitment by the federal government to extinguish Indian title to land within the state's borders.

In his message to Congress, Jackson argued that attempts by Cherokees and other tribes in southern states to form independent governments violated the constitutional requirement that "no new State shall be formed or erected within the jurisdiction of any other State" without that state's consent. He advised those Indians to "emigrate beyond the Mississippi or submit to the laws of those States." (The Supreme Court would rule in 1832 that Cherokees and missionaries aiding them were not subject to Georgia's punitive laws because the Constitution made the federal government responsible for all intercourse with Indians, but Jackson would not enforce that ruling.) Hostility and "decay" awaited tribes if they remained under state authority, Jackson warned in his address to Congress, whereas removal to federal lands beyond the Mississippi would secure them "governments of their own choice." Their emigration, he concluded, "should be voluntary, for it would be as cruel as unjust to compel the aborigines to abandon the graves of their fathers and seek a home in a distant land."[12]

The Removal Act seemingly confirmed that the process was voluntary by authorizing Jackson to set aside federal lands beyond the Mississippi "for the reception of such tribes or nations of Indians as may choose to exchange the lands where they now reside, and remove there." Furthermore, the act pledged that "the United States will forever secure and guaranty to them, and their heirs or successors, the country so exchanged with them."[13] Jackson's promise not to compel removal, however, ran counter to his previous actions as a treaty maker, including issuing threats, as he did at Fort Jackson in 1814 when he stated that Creek chiefs who refused to surrender much of their territory to the United States would be regarded as enemies. The implied threat in his message to Congress was that he would do nothing to stop states like Georgia from dispossessing Indians who spurned federal removal treaties, which would not in fact last forever because the government reserved the right to renegotiate treaties with tribes and impose new terms on them.

Opposition to the Removal Act was fervent, particularly among Americans who supported mission efforts to convert and "civilize" those targeted by the legislation, who were doing what Indians had long been asked to do if they wished to retain their land and become productive members of American society. Senator Theodore Frelinghuysen of New Jersey, future president of the American Bible Society, preached devoutly against the act when it came before the Senate. "Do the obligations of justice change with the color of the skin?" he asked. "Is it one of the prerogatives of the white man, that he may disregard the dictates of moral principles, when an Indian shall be concerned?" Like Frelinghuysen, many who spoke against the Removal Act or denounced it in petitions to Congress also opposed slavery and believed that people of other races were endowed with the same inalienable rights as white Americans, whose customs and institutions members of the five tribes were emulating. As Frelinghuysen said of Cherokees: "Prompted and encouraged by our counsels, they have in good earnest resolved to become men, rational, educated, Christian men; and they have succeeded beyond our most sanguine hopes. They have established a regular constitution of civil government, republican in its principles." Americans had a civic and religious duty to honor that government and oppose removal, insisted Frelinghuysen, who warned that abandoning Cherokees to the menacing jurisdiction of Georgia would offend "God, and call down the thunders of his wrath."[14]

Such righteous rhetoric incensed Representative Wilson Lumpkin, who defended the Removal Act before the House and would be elected governor of Georgia in 1831. The "common comforts of civil and domestic life" were enjoyed by a minority of Cherokees who were partly white, he contended, whereas most other Cherokees remained "a poor degraded race of human beings," whose lot would only worsen if they remained in close proximity to white settlers, as pious opponents of removal urged. Lumpkin denounced those reformers as malignant meddlers: "If the wicked influence of designing men, veiled in the garb of philanthropy and christian benevolence, should excite the Cherokees to a course that will end in their speedy destruction, I now call upon this Congress, and the whole American people, not to charge the Georgians with this sin; but let it be remembered that it is the fruit of cant and fanaticism, emanating from the land of steady habits, from the boasted progeny of the pilgrims and puritans." Such verbal assaults on high-minded northerners who opposed removal now that few Indians remained in their region echoed similar denunciations of puritanical abolitionists who hailed from states where relatively small numbers of slaves had been emancipated and condemned southerners for not freeing multitudes. Lumpkin was aware that some of those crusading against the Removal Act viewed it as designed to expand the domain of white slave owners. He quoted from an article that assailed removal with abolitionist fervor and suggested that disunion would be preferable to preserving a nation tainted by the sins of the South:

> The Indians had better stand to their arms and be exterminated, than march farther onwards to the Pacific, in the faith that the coming tide of

civilized population will not sweep them forever until they mingle in its depths. Better thus than remain to be trampled as the serfs of Georgia, to have their faces ground by the pride and oppressions of their slave-holding neighbours. . . . God forbid that the prayers which have ascended for the Indians, and the exertions which may be made in their behalf, should fail; it would be better that half the States in the Union were annihilated, and the remnant left powerful in holiness, strong in the prevalence of virtue, than that the whole nation should be stained with guilt. . . . We would rather have a civil war, were there no other alternative, than avoid it by taking shelter in crime.[15]

Lumpkin attributed this article to William Penn, the pseudonym of Jeremiah Evarts, a prominent New England missionary and reformer whose essays opposing the Removal Act were widely published. But this was the work of George B. Cheever, a devout abolitionist who later wrote an influential book entitled *God Against Slavery*. Many who would loom large in the emerging antislavery movement opposed the Removal Act, including young Harriet Beecher, who joined a women's petition drive organized by her sister Catharine Beecher at Hartford Female Seminary. "Last night we teachers sat up till eleven o'clock finishing our Cherokee letters," wrote Harriet Beecher, who added that "the excitement, I hope, is but just begun. So 'great effects come from little causes.'"[16] Tens of thousands of men and women, most but not all of them northerners, urged Congress in writing to reject the Removal Act—an outpouring that anticipated the flood of antislavery petitions to Congress that in 1836 led opponents in the House to pass the gag rule, causing such petitions to be tabled without being considered or printed in congressional records.

Opposition to the Removal Act caused some antislavery orators and authors to reconsider their support for colonizing freed slaves in Africa. Lumpkin in his speech referred sarcastically to Clay, who opposed the Removal Act, as that "distinguished orator of the West," who introduced the subject of Indian removal into one of his speeches in favor of African colonization and expressed his "deep feelings of interest for the suffering sons of Africa and the forest."[17] If it was charitable to remove freed slaves from the South to Africa, skeptics like Lumpkin wondered, why should Indians not be removed beyond the Mississippi? That question troubled those who were not seeking compromises between North and South, as Clay was, and were vehemently opposed to slavery. William Lloyd Garrison, who had earlier supported African colonization, turned decisively against it around the time he began denouncing Indian removal. By the early 1830s he had joined Black abolitionists in decrying the notion that freed slaves should be exiled from the land of their birth. They were "as unanimously opposed to a removal to Africa," Garrison wrote, "as the Cherokees from the council-fires and graves of their ancestors."[18]

Both sides in the congressional debate over the Removal Act invoked Thomas Jefferson, for he initiated the process of exchanging tribal lands east of the Mississippi for federal lands west of the river but also hoped for peaceful coexistence between white settlers and those Indians who adopted Anglo-American customs and culture. "None can fail to perceive the spirit of justice and humanity which Mr. Jefferson cherished towards our Indian allies," stated Frelinghuysen, emphasizing Jefferson's lofty principles rather than his less charitable policies. "He was, through his whole life, the firm unshrinking advocate of their rights, a patron of all their plans for moral improvement and elevation."[19] Representative George Evans of Maine opposed the Removal Act by quoting Jefferson's cautionary words about slavery:

> Sir, it was said by one often quoted upon this floor, and in reference to a subject not dissimilar to the present, (Mr. Jefferson,) "I tremble for my country when I remember that God is just, and that his justice will not sleep forever." And although the particular mode of retribution which was in his mind on that occasion may not now be anticipated, yet let us recollect "that the Almighty has no attribute which can take side with us" in a conflict between power and right—between oppression and justice.[20]

Left unmentioned by Evans and most of those who spoke on either side of the debate in Congress was that some members of the southern tribes targeted for removal held Black slaves. Representative Edward Everett of Massachusetts—an orator who was not then opposed to slavery but would later precede Lincoln as a speaker at Gettysburg in 1863—offered one veiled reference to Cherokees as slave owners during a compelling speech in which he foresaw that the federal government would fail to secure tribal lands beyond the Mississippi against white encroachment. "What, are you indeed going to abandon this region to the Indians?" he asked supporters of removal. "Can we stop the wave of population that flows toward it? . . . Precisely the same process which has gone on in the East will go on in the West." Southern tribes removed to territory occupied by Plains tribes would never be as secure as they were at present, Everett insisted, because they were "essentially a civilized people," able to support themselves without infringing on white settlers and clashing with them. To bolster his case, he cited the results of a census of Cherokees and their property, including 18 schools attended by 314 students, 36 gristmills, 13 sawmills, 762 looms, 2,486 spinning wheels, 172 wagons, and 2,923 plows to sustain a population of 15,560, including 610 "male negroes" and 667 "female negroes."[21] Everett refrained from mentioning that they were enslaved.

Drawing attention to the slaves held by southern tribes did not suit the rhetorical purposes of northern opponents of removal—or southern supporters of removing Indians who had more in common with them than they cared to admit. Had slaveholding tribes been destined for an organized Indian Territory, eligible for statehood, the Removal Act might have faced even stiffer resistance from northerners and been defeated in the House, where it received just enough support from northern Jacksonians to pass by a margin of five votes, 102 to 97. Senators from Indiana and Illinois where Jackson was popular and some people still considered Indians a threat helped the Removal Act prevail in their chamber by a vote of 28 to 19, but fifteen of the nays came from the North and the other four came from states bordering that section.

Nullifying the Nullifiers

Passage of the Removal Act was a cautionary triumph for Jackson, one that played well in the South and West but alienated the Northeast—a cause for concern because Jackson feared sectionalism and abhorred separatism of the sort that flared up earlier in New England in response to the Louisiana Purchase and the War of 1812. Although his expansionist agenda enhanced the slaveholding South, he would not tolerate resistance to federal authority there. He demonstrated as much when South Carolinians proposed nullifying the so-called Tariff of Abominations enacted in 1828, which they blamed for depressing their plantation economy with duties placed on imported goods to protect northern industries. In fact, other factors did more to hurt South Carolina economically, including competition from planters who migrated westward to more fertile areas where they harvested cotton and other cash crops in abundance. But South Carolinians were wary of federal assaults on their livelihood and way of life, dependent as it was on slavery and congressional deference to states' rights.

Nullification distanced Jackson from his vice president, John Calhoun, who had backed the first protective tariff in 1816 but opposed the tariff of 1828 by arguing that the Constitution's general welfare clause did not allow the government to impose tariffs benefiting particular industries or regions rather than the country as a whole. The rift between Calhoun and Jackson was signaled when toasts were offered at a dinner in April 1830 celebrating the late Thomas Jefferson's birthday. "Our Union," Jackson declared: "*It must be preserved.*" To which Calhoun responded: "The Union. Next to our liberty, the most dear. May we all remember that it can only be preserved by respecting the rights of the states and by distributing equally the benefits and the burdens of the Union."[22] Jackson believed that states had ample means to redress wrongs and ease their burdens within the Union and no justification for defying or abandoning it. He was more tolerant of tariffs than some Jacksonians he inspired, who thought they benefited men of wealth and privilege at the expense of ordinary Americans, but he would have deplored nullification even if he felt the grievances of its perpetrators were warranted.

Although the tariff was revised in 1832 with lower duties on some goods, that failed to mollify South Carolinians, who adopted an ordinance nullifying it that November, soon after Jackson was reelected by a wide margin over his closest competitor, Clay, who was now in the Senate. Calhoun, who had been replaced as Jackson's running mate by former secretary of state Martin Van Buren of New York, resigned as vice president in December to represent South Carolina in the Senate. He was not yet an outspoken defender of slavery and did not link that issue publicly to his stand against the tariff. But Robert J. Turnbull, an ardent proponent of nullification who took the pen name Brutus, warned his fellow South Carolinians that if the federal government could impose burdensome tariffs on them under the Constitution's general welfare clause, it might use the same pretext to abolish slavery. "Congress, some fifteen or twenty years hence," he wrote, might decide "that the *gradual* emancipation of the slaves in the United States ought to take place, as essential to 'the general welfare.' . . . Is there any son of the South, who would be willing to submit to any judges, much less the judges of the United States, whether such a law was constitutional or not, and to stand *pledged* to abide by *their* judgment? It would be madness."[23]

Like Turnbull, Calhoun argued that states need not defer to the Supreme Court when determining that a federal law was unconstitutional and intolerable. Such laws should be binding, he proposed, only if representatives from three-fourths of the states convened and upheld them, providing ratification of the sort required for amendments to the Constitution. Like Jefferson, Calhoun based his support for nullification on the theory that the constitutional Union was a compact

between the states, which created the federal government and were not subject
to it if it exceeded its powers. But he did not regard tariffs, however abominable,
as sufficient cause for South Carolina to withdraw from that compact. He saw
only one prospect that might warrant secession. Nothing could break the Union,
he stated, "but the slavery question, if that can."[24]

Calhoun's reservations about secession were not shared by those who passed
South Carolina's nullification ordinance, which stated that if the federal government tried to "enforce the acts hereby declared to be null and void, otherwise than
through the civil tribunals of the country," South Carolinians would be "absolved
from all further obligation to maintain or preserve their political connection with
the people of the other States, and will forthwith proceed to organize a separate
government."[25] Jackson responded to South Carolina's defiant stance by issuing a
proclamation rejecting nullification. For a state to claim the right to annul a law
of the United States was, he underscored, "*incompatible with the existence of the
Union, contradicted expressly by the letter of the Constitution, unauthorized by its
spirit, inconsistent with every principle on which it was founded, and destructive
of the great object for which it was formed.*" Jackson went on to denounce the
compact theory of the Union and those who believed it allowed for secession,
advancing an argument that would later be echoed by Unionists at odds with
those secessionists who formed the Confederacy:

> This right to secede is deduced from the nature of the Constitution, which,
> they say, is a compact between Sovereign States, who have preserved their
> whole sovereignty, and therefore, are subject to no superior; that, because
> they made the compact, they can break it when, in their opinion, it has
> been departed from . . . But each State having expressly parted with so
> many powers as to constitute, jointly with the other States, a single nation,
> cannot, from that period, possess any right to secede, because such seces-
> sion does not break a league, but destroys the unity of a nation. . . . To say
> that any State may at pleasure secede from the Union, is to say that the
> United States are not a nation.

Jackson's conception of the Union was organic. It could grow by incorporating new states, but each incorporated state was a vital organ, which could not
be severed without imperiling the whole. His oath of office required him to
defend the nation and its Constitution, and he assured South Carolinians that
he would do so:

The laws of the United States must be executed. I have no discretion-
ary power on the subject—my duty is emphatically pronounced in the
Constitution. Those who told you that you might peaceably prevent their
execution, deceived you. . . . They know that a forcible opposition could
alone prevent the execution of the laws, and they know that such opposition
must be repelled. Their object is disunion, but be not deceived by names;
disunion, by armed force, is *treason*.

Jackson concluded his proclamation on a more conciliatory note. Much like
Lincoln at his inauguration in 1861, he vowed "to execute the laws—to preserve
the Union by all constitutional means—to arrest, if possible, by moderate but
firm measures, the necessity of a recourse to force."[26] But he anticipated armed
resistance in South Carolina, whose governor was calling for volunteers to uphold
the nullification ordinance, and Jackson obtained congressional approval to use
military force there, if necessary. As it turned out, he did not have to wield that
stick because it was accompanied by a carrot supplied by Clay, who enhanced
his reputation as a conciliator by conferring with Calhoun and securing passage
of a bill that would gradually lower the tariff and helped induce South Carolina
to comply with it.

Jackson's defiance of the nullifiers encouraged some northern Democrats
to challenge their party's pro-southern, proslavery bias, which he helped foster
by upholding states' rights and the interests of white settlers and slaveholders
through Indian removal—and by enabling his postmaster general, Amos Kendall,
to suppress delivery of abolitionist tracts to the South. In years to come those
antislavery Democrats would denounce southern planters as scheming oligarchs,
hostile to Jacksonian democracy and the Union he vowed to preserve. Jackson
himself viewed the revolt he deterred in South Carolina as a possible prelude to
a proslavery secessionist movement. "Nullification is dead," he wrote in April
1833, but he feared that nullifiers like Calhoun would eventually "blow up a storm
on the subject of the slavery question . . . for be assured these men would do any
act to destroy the union, & form a southern confederacy bounded, north, by the
Potomac river." The tariff they deplored "was only the pretext, and disunion &
a southern confederacy the real object," he stated a few weeks later. "The next
pretext will be the negro, or slavery question."[27]

That question had deep roots in the nation's history and was constantly
sprouting up. It had intensified debate over the Removal Act, and it caused

further controversy as that act was enforced under Jackson and his successor, President Van Buren. Some mixed-race, slaveholding tribal leaders such as Greenwood LeFlore, principal chief of the Choctaws, signed removal treaties opposed by tribal traditionalists. LeFlore remained in Mississippi and prospered on land granted him under the removal treaty he approved in late 1830 while thousands of Choctaws embarked on arduous treks to Indian Territory, during which many perished of disease, famine, or exposure. Other mixed-race chiefs who owned slaves resisted removal, notably John Ross, who held out in Georgia with the majority of Cherokees against a treaty signed in December 1835 by a small faction led by Major Ridge, who was assassinated as a consequence. The forcible removal between 1838 and 1839 of some fifteen thousand defiant Cherokees and enslaved Black people on the Trail of Tears, during which several thousand of them died, was not the last tragedy they or others exiled to Indian Territory would endure. Removal and slavery caused chronic factionalism and strife within the five tribes, including the Seminoles, most of whom would yield reluctantly in the 1840s to U.S. forces they had long opposed. Fugitive slaves who found refuge among Seminoles in Florida and joined their fight against removal were promised freedom in Indian Territory if they surrendered. But they risked being reenslaved there, and some would flee to Mexico, where Black Seminoles called "Mascogos" (for the Muscogees or Creeks who had authority over them in Indian Territory) helped defend the Mexican border against intrusions and clashed with Texans along the Rio Grande.[28]

Sidestepping Texas

Andrew Jackson's aversion to raising the slavery question made him cautious about acquiring Texas as his presidency progressed. He had entered office hoping to persuade Mexico to relinquish Texas by treaty, for which he would offer up to $5 million. He did not want Americans filibustering there in the meantime and disrupting negotiations. Around the time of his first inauguration, he heard that Sam Houston had sought refuge among western Cherokees not to drown his sorrows but to recruit warriors and seize Texas. Houston assured him by letter that he had no such intentions. "What am I?" he wrote plaintively, "an Exile from my home; and my country, a houseless unshelter'd wanderer, among the Indians! . . . Yet I am myself, and will remain, the proud and honest man! I will love my country; & my friends—You Genl. will ever possess my warmest love and most profound veneration!"[29] Jackson credited Houston's denial but disapproved of the turn his life had taken. "It cannot be possible you have

Sam Houston (1793–1863) in
Cherokee dress. Courtesy
Library of Congress Prints
and Photographs Division
(LC-USZ-92305).

taken the determination to settle with the Indians and become a savage," he
wrote Houston.

> I have heard, and it has been communicated to me, that you had the illegal
> enterprise in view of conquering the Texas; that you had declared that you
> would, in less than two years, be Emperor in that country by conquest. At
> the same time it was communicated that you were mad; and I really must
> have thought you deranged to have believed you had such a wild scheme
> in contemplation. . . . Your pledge of honor to the country is a sufficient
> guarantee that you will never engage in any enterprise injurious to your
> country, or that will tarnish your fame.[30]

Houston regained Jackson's full support on two visits he made to Washington
during his sojourn among western Cherokees, whose interests he represented
in the capital. He also pursued his own interests there by bidding for a contract
from Secretary of War John H. Eaton to supply rations to Indians subjected to
removal. Eaton did not award a contract to any of the bidders and resigned in 1831.
Representative William Stanberry of Ohio, a staunch anti-Jacksonian, later suggested in a speech to the House that Eaton was let go because his intention to grant
Houston the contract "fraudulently" risked being exposed and embarrassing

Jackson, who allegedly had "full knowledge" of that suspect deal.[31] Houston then defended his honor and Jackson's reputation by confronting Stanberry in the street and caning him, for which offense he was reprimanded by the House and fined five hundred dollars in federal court. Jackson subsequently remitted the fine.

In late 1832, Houston set out for Texas after parting with his Cherokee wife and leaving her their cabin and other assets, including two slaves held legally under tribal authority as well as federal law governing American territory below the Missouri Compromise line. Houston had been raised in a slaveholding family, which prepared him to settle among Anglo-Texans increasingly reliant on slavery. Jackson authorized him to meet in Texas with Comanches and discourage them from clashing with tribes removed to Indian Territory. But Houston's larger objective was to play a prominent role in Texas, which he recognized might soon break free from Mexico. In February 1833 he wrote Jackson a letter "calculated to forward your views if you should entertain any; touching the acquisition of Texas." If the United States "does not press for it," he added, England would "most assuredly obtain it" by some means. He and most other Anglo-Texans, however, would prefer American annexation. "I may make Texas my abiding place," wrote Houston, who became nominally Mexican and Catholic in order to obtain land in Austin's colony. But in "adopting this course," he assured Jackson, "I will *never forget* the Country of my birth."[32] Houston's letter did not prompt Jackson to press for Texas. His efforts to purchase it were faltering, and he knew that annexing a vast, would-be slave state would face opposition in Congress. In April 1834, Houston wrote James Prentiss, a financier and land speculator, that he "need not hope for the acquisition (if ever) by this Government of Texas during the Administration of Genl Jackson—If it were acquired by a Treaty, that Treaty, would not be ratified, by the present Senate—!!!"[33]

Houston's close ties to his patron suggested that he was serving as Jackson's agent in Texas, but Jackson influenced Houston's actions there less as president than as a general during the War of 1812, when Old Hickory molded raw volunteers into serviceable soldiers and led them to victory. Houston proceeded cautiously when Texans rebelled against Mexico and placed him in charge of their provisional "army," consisting of fewer than two thousand volunteers who initially answered to other officers. Some blamed him for retreating with the men remaining to him after disaster befell forces he did not command at San Antonio—where some 200 men led by William Travis and James Bowie were annihilated at the Alamo in March 1836 by 6,000 troops under Santa Anna—and at Goliad, where 350 volunteers led by Colonel James Fannin were captured and nearly all were executed by Santa Anna's order. But by waiting to attack until Santa Anna divided his forces and had fewer than 1,400 troops under his direct command—and until Houston had enough control over his 800 soldiers to harness their fury and spur them into concerted action under a battle flag emblazoned "Liberty or Death"—he triumphed at San Jacinto and delivered Texas from ignominy to independence.[34]

When Houston became president of the Texas Republic and urged annexation by the United States in the confidential letter he sent when he dispatched Santa Anna to Washington in November 1836, Jackson was in the final months of his presidency. Concerned with his legacy, the former "military chieftain" who had invaded Spanish Florida without compunction did not want the nation he now led to be charged with aggression against Mexico, which still claimed Texas and refused to recognize its independence. Yet Jackson had given critics some cause to accuse him of aggression. That July, two months after Houston's victory at San Jacinto, U.S. troops dispatched by General Edmund Gaines had crossed the Sabine River, separating Louisiana from Texas, and occupied Nacogdoches in response to rumors that Indians were being incited by Mexican authorities to attack Texans, who urged Gaines to intervene. He was acting on orders from Secretary of War Lewis Cass, who authorized him, if necessary for defense of the frontier, to advance to Nacogdoches, "which is within the limits of the United States, as claimed by this Government."[35] In fact, Nacogdoches was within Texas, contrary to Jackson's specious claim that the Neches River, west of Nacogdoches, was the main branch of the Sabine River and thus formed the boundary. What he and Cass defined as a defensive maneuver looked suspiciously like intervention on behalf of Texans, whose conflict with Mexico would continue sporadically for years to come.

Jackson's claim to Nacogdoches as asserted by Gaines—who called on volunteers from several states to help bolster his forces—drew criticism in Congress and the press. As the editor of the *National Intelligencer* stated, no one "even moderately acquainted with the geography" of the region would "regard the Neches as the main stream of the Sabine."[36] Amos Kendall, no longer postmaster general but still a trusted advisor to Jackson, warned him that the nation's honor and reputation were at stake. "Our *people* are already considered responsible for the warfare carried on against Mexico in Texas," he wrote, referring not just to American settlers there who had rebelled against Mexico but to volunteers from the United States who joined the war, many of them lured by promises of land grants in Texas. If U.S. troops backed Texas against Mexico, Kendall warned, anti-American sentiment would "gain strength, day by day, throughout the world." Jackson replied that he would maintain "strict neutrality" in the conflict between Texas and Mexico.[37] But though he urged Gaines in September to exercise caution, he authorized him to concentrate all his forces at Nacogdoches if there were actual hostilities on the frontier. Not until December 1836 did Gaines withdraw American troops from Texas.

Jackson still wanted Texas attached to the Union, but he would not seek its annexation during his last days as president, and concern for the nation's honor was not the only reason. Texans had reconfigured their boundaries in a way that made Jackson's effort to shift the American frontier from the Sabine to the Neches look piddling by comparison. By claiming the Rio Grande as their border with Mexico rather than the Nueces River—which formed the southern border of Texas under Spain and Mexico and gave it far less territory than would the Rio Grande—they all but assured that Mexico would remain hostile to Texas and view its annexation by the United States as cause for war. Relinquishing everything north and east of the Rio Grande would mean abandoning Mexico's indisputable claim to longstanding Hispanic settlements that were never part of Texas, including Santa Fe and other New Mexican towns. Jackson could not embrace a Texas bordered by the Rio Grande without inviting conflict with Mexico and leaving that burden to his vice president and successor, Martin Van Buren.

Known as the "Little Magician" for his short stature and political wizardry, Van Buren had envisioned the Democratic Party when he first backed Jackson for president as an alliance between "the planters of the South and the plain Republicans of the north," like that achieved earlier by the Republican Party of Jefferson and Madison.[38] Preserving that alliance meant avoiding actions that would incite sectional disputes over slavery. That gave Jackson all the more reason not to annex the Texas Republic, whose constitution barred its Congress from emancipating slaves and stated that "no free person of African descent, either in whole or in part, shall be permitted to reside permanently in the Republic, without the consent of Congress."[39] Former president John Quincy Adams, back in Washington as a congressman from Massachusetts, denounced the rebellion in Texas as a civil war "for the re-establishment of slavery where it was abolished . . . a war between slavery and emancipation." Should the United States side with Texans against Mexico, he warned, the result would be civil war within the Union, a conflict "between emancipation and slavery."[40]

Recognizing the independence of Texas would be less inflammatory than annexing it, and many expected Jackson to propose doing so in his final message to Congress in December 1836. Instead, he advised against too-early recognition of that fledgling republic to avoid heightening suspicions that the United States had designs on that country. Texans were crestfallen, but that was not Jackson's last word on the subject. When he met with Santa Anna in January 1837, he resuscitated the idea of purchasing Texas and proposed extending the deal westward to include California. Santa Anna stated that the authority to make such a bargain rested with the Mexican Congress. Indeed, Santa Anna had been deposed as president of Mexico after yielding to the victorious Texans, and he had no authority to negotiate with Jackson. Nonetheless, William H. Wharton, whom Houston sent to Washington as the republic's envoy, was alarmed when informed by Jackson of his meeting with Santa Anna. Before engaging in any talks with Mexico that might affect the Texas Republic, Wharton insisted, the United States must first recognize its independence. Jackson would ultimately do so with congressional approval on March 3, just before he left office. But he reminded Wharton that recognizing Texas was one thing and annexing it was another—a step sure to be opposed by antislavery northerners. Jackson suggested that Texas might counter such opposition by extending its territorial claims beyond New Mexico to California, an objective as alluring to enterprising northerners as it was to expansive Texans like Houston's successor as president of the Lone Star Republic, Mirabeau Buonaparte Lamar, who imagined his country "stretching from the Sabine to the Pacific."[41]

Jackson was envisioning even broader boundaries than that for the United States as his presidency drew to a close. A greater American West that embraced Texas as well as California, which appeared ill-suited for slavery as practiced in the South, was an enticing prospect for him and avid Jacksonians who believed that the American empire should span the continent while remaining roughly half-slave and half-free. Incorporating a wider West stretching to the Pacific would prove difficult and disruptive, however, for it would not be covered by the Missouri Compromise, which applied only to territory encompassed by the Louisiana Purchase. Congress would have to strike a new bargain between North and South as the national argument over slavery intensified. Casting aside the concerns that restrained him as president, when he prophetically envisioned that proslavery zealots inspired by nullifiers like Calhoun might sever the Union, Jackson in retirement would urge the annexation of Texas that Calhoun promoted—and would bequeath to his fellow Tennessean and political disciple James Polk the perilous task of greatly enlarging an increasingly divided nation.

CHAPTER 8

Benton, Frémont, and the Westward Course of American Empire

By the time Andrew Jackson left office in March 1837, he had no more reliable defender in the U.S. Senate than the man who twenty-four years earlier had battled him in Nashville, Thomas Hart Benton. After his brother Jesse shot Jackson there, Benton took the sword the general dropped and broke it over his knee, as if shattering any possibility that he and Jackson might reconcile. But when Jackson entered the Senate in 1823, he ended up sitting next to Benton. Their truce evolved into a fruitful alliance when Benton backed Jackson in the hotly contested presidential election of 1824 and then helped him carry Missouri four years later and win election.

Firmly attached to the Democracy, as the Democratic Party that Jackson forged during his presidency was known, Benton backed him when he pressed for Indian removal and destruction of the Second Bank of the United States. Benton's support for Jackson often set him at odds with Henry Clay, who emerged as the congressional leader of the opposing Whigs. But no senator was more detested by Benton than John Calhoun, an idiosyncratic Democrat who sometimes sided with the Whigs and joined Clay in censuring Jackson for abusing his powers during his so-called Bank War. Benton later erased that blot on Jackson's record by inducing the Senate to expunge the censure, but he would never forgive Calhoun for aggravating sectional tensions by supporting nullification of the federal tariff by South Carolina and rekindling debate in Congress over slavery and its extension. "Mr. Clay's efforts were limited to the overthrow of President Jackson," Benton wrote in his memoir *Thirty Years' View*, published in 1854.

"Mr. Calhoun's extended to the overthrow of the Union, and to the establishment of a southern confederacy of the slave States."[1]

Calhoun never went quite so far as to urge secession, but Benton had reason to fault him for encouraging defiance if not disunion by southerners in defense of slavery. Soon after President Martin Van Buren—raised in a slaveholding family in upstate New York in the late 1700s—promised in December 1837 to thwart any attempt by Congress to abolish slavery in the District of Columbia, Calhoun sought further protection for the South's peculiar institution by introducing a resolution against prohibiting it in any American territory. During the debate that followed, he claimed that slavery was "as much under the protection of the Constitution here [in the District], and in the Territories, as in the States themselves." Calhoun regretted his earlier support for the Missouri Compromise, which he now considered a "dangerous measure" that barred slavery in territories above 36°30' and fostered efforts to prohibit it elsewhere on American soil. If Congress did not uphold slavery, he warned, the "assaults daily made on the institutions of nearly one-half of the States of this Union" might compel their citizens "to take the remedy into their own hands. They will then stand justified in the sight of God and man; and what, in that event, will follow, no mortal can anticipate."[2] That warning did not sway the Senate, which replaced Calhoun's stringent resolution with a milder one, stating that prohibiting slavery in a territory where it existed with congressional consent such as Florida would be "a violation of good faith."[3]

Benton remained firmly committed to the Missouri Compromise, which brought his state into the Union, and regarded Calhoun's rejection of it as undermining efforts by Democrats to soothe sectional differences within their party and the nation at large. To that end, applications for admission from Arkansas as the nation's thirteenth slave state and Michigan as the thirteenth free state were linked in the Senate and "kept as nearly together as possible," noted Benton, who sponsored the application by Michigan (admitted in 1837) while his fellow Democrat, Senator James Buchanan of Pennsylvania, sponsored the application by Arkansas (admitted in 1836). Benton considered that arrangement "a most beautiful illustration of the total impotence of all attempts to agitate and ulcerate the public mind on the worn-out subject of slavery."[4]

In truth, that subject was far from worn-out when Arkansas and Michigan achieved statehood and would prove ever more divisive in the years to come, particularly for the Whig Party, whose northern members would become increasingly antislavery and alienate southern Whigs in the process. Benton's party was more cohesive, having proclaimed officially in 1835 that no one could "even wish to interfere" with slavery in the South and "call himself a Democrat."[5] Northern Democrats were far more likely to vote with southern members of their party on legislation involving slavery than were northern Whigs. As Calhoun's influence increased among the Democracy's southern stalwarts, however, some northern Democrats previously supportive of slavery like Van Buren would defy them. Fearful of such divisions within his party and the nation as a whole, Benton came to view stridently proslavery ideologues like Calhoun as even more disruptive than northern abolitionists. And he would oppose not only Calhounites but also many fellow Jacksonians who backed taking Texas with the Rio Grande border it claimed, which Benton had once supported but worried would provoke a convulsive war with Mexico.

Various factors led Benton to that unorthodox stance for a leading slave-state Democrat, including his long-held conviction that American expansion across the continent could be better achieved through commerce, settlement, and negotiation than through conquest. To be sure, Benton was not free of belligerence or racism. Although he had reportedly kept a free woman of color from New Orleans as his mistress in St. Louis for "some two or three years" before he joined the Senate, he defended Missouri's right to perpetuate slavery and prevent free Black people from entering the state.[6] And he faulted John Quincy Adams not only for yielding Texas to Spain in 1821 but also for compromising the American claim to Oregon by allowing Britain joint occupation there with the United States. Yet he believed that the westward advance of American empire should be led not by armies but by explorers, traders, trappers, and settlers like those who fanned out energetically from Missouri and sought paths across the continent.

Benton took particular interest in the Santa Fe Trail, down which traders led by William Becknell first ventured in wagons from Franklin, Missouri, in 1822 to sell their wares in New Mexico. Augustus Storrs, who joined a larger caravan in 1824 that carried some $30,000 worth of trade goods to Santa Fe and vicinity, informed Benton that the merchandise consisted largely of cotton fabrics as well as some woolens and other articles "necessary for the purposes of an assortment." The traders received in return "Spanish milled dollars, a small amount of gold and silver, in bullion, beaver fur, and some mules."[7] Mules would come to symbolize Missouri, but it was the silver dollars that most intrigued Benton, who blamed the state's travails during the lean years following the Panic of 1819

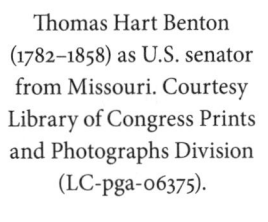

Thomas Hart Benton
(1782–1858) as U.S. senator
from Missouri. Courtesy
Library of Congress Prints
and Photographs Division
(LC-pga-06375).

on a shortage of coins and a surplus of suspect banknotes, which encouraged speculative frenzies that ended in crashes. Benton's belief that hard money was the only reliable currency—a conviction he shared with Jackson—earned him the title "Old Bullion" and led him to tout the Santa Fe trade as a tonic for all those among whom the cash earned by those traders circulated.

When Benton sought appropriations in 1825 to survey the Santa Fe Trail and treat with tribes that might obstruct the trade, he gave the prosaic report he received from Storrs a poetic gloss: "It sounded like romance to hear of caravans of men, horses, and wagons, traversing with their merchandise the vast plain which lies between the Mississippi and the Rio del Norte." Benton overstated the national significance of that trade by noting that its profits came largely in exchange for goods made of cotton, "which grows in the South, is manufactured in the North, and exported from the West." In fact, much of the cotton grown in the South was exported to Britain and manufactured there. Benton succeeded in obtaining federal funds to support what he immodestly called "my road to Mexico."[8] But neither the survey of the Santa Fe Trail conducted at his initiative nor military efforts to protect traders from Indian raids by escorting them as far as the Mexican border did much to promote that commerce. Merchants marked the trail with the wheels of their heavily loaded wagons and saw to their own defense by wielding weapons when necessary or negotiating with Native Americans and offering them gifts.

Those self-sufficient Santa Fe companies were not unlike the resourceful companies of mountain men who enlisted at St. Louis to gather beaver pelts and ventured up the Missouri River, from which they found better paths to the Rockies and the Pacific coast than the lengthy route followed by Lewis and Clark. By the time Benton touted the Santa Fe trade before the Senate, the expert mountain man turned explorer Jedediah Smith had located South Pass, an inviting corridor through the northern Rockies that would later enable emigrants in wagons to reach Oregon and California, or what Mexicans termed Alta California (as opposed to Baja California). Smith went on to lead trappers across the Great Basin and Mojave Desert in 1826 to Mission San Gabriel Arcángel, near the small Mexican town of Los Angeles. Some American merchants had already reached California by sea and gained footholds there by trading with Californios (Hispanic Californians) and intermarrying with them. One of those adaptable merchants vouched for Smith to California's governor, who allowed him to purchase fresh horses and supplies but insisted that he depart by an assigned route under military escort. Determined to "take my own course," Smith and his company instead slipped away to trap beaver in the Central Valley, serving as forerunners of those American emigrants who began arriving overland in California the early 1840s and settled without authorization in the interior, where they would defy Mexican sovereignty.[9]

Far from relying on the U.S. Army or officials in Washington for direction and support, venturesome companies of trappers and traders set the westward course of American empire on their own initiative and influenced statesmen like Benton. Their profitable expeditions into Mexican territory reinforced his preference for commercial expansion over conquest or colonization, which he admired as practiced by Stephen Austin in Texas but set the stage there for a conflict he worried might imperil America's lucrative give-and-take with Mexico, including maritime trade between Mexican ports and New Orleans that he reckoned brought in more than $8 million worth of "silver coin and bullion" in 1836 alone.[10] Furthermore, the Americanization of Texas alarmed those opposed to extending slavery in a way that American trade, settlement, and possible acquisition of new territories in the Far West did not. Involuntary servitude had long existed in New Mexico and California in the form of peonage by Hispanics or forced labor by Indians who were captured, purchased, or confined at Franciscan missions. But neither of those territories appeared well suited for slavery as practiced in the South.

Unlike Texas when Austin founded his colony there, New Mexico was relatively populous, inhabited in the 1820s by more than forty thousand Mexicans and

Pueblo Indians who cooperated in defending their settlements against raids by hostile tribes. The dry climate there limited opportunities for profitable agriculture largely to irrigated fields near the upper Rio Grande, where newcomers would have to compete with established residents for water and arable land. In 1824, 150 Missourians led by John G. Heath—who had joined Becknell's 1822 trading expedition to New Mexico along with other men in "Mr. Heath's company"—departed Franklin in flatboats, descended the Missouri and Mississippi Rivers to New Orleans, set sail for the Gulf Coast of Mexico, and trekked overland to El Paso, where the town council had earlier granted Heath land in the Mesilla Valley.[11] By the time his party arrived there, however, Heath's grant had been denied by higher authorities, who rebuked the council for allowing foreigners access to land and water to the disadvantage of New Mexicans. As that setback demonstrated, New Mexico with its limited agricultural resources was not receptive to American colonization like that instituted by planters in eastern Texas employing slave labor, although some slaves accompanied the Santa Fe traders.

In sparsely settled California, which had only about seven thousand non-Native inhabitants as late as 1846, the barriers to intrusions by American slave-holders included official Mexican opposition to slavery—which Austin's colonists and other settlers in Texas managed to circumvent—as well as the hazards and expense of reaching distant California by land or sea and the risk of raids by Indians who evaded the missions or fled them. (That risk was even higher in New Mexico, where settlers were subject to raids by the formidable Apaches and Navajos.) Some foreigners who entered Mexican California, however, considered it susceptible to slavery. Jedediah Smith noted that, under the Mexican Republic, mission Indians were "declared free and the fathers were ordered to inform them of the fact." But padres spoke of freedom "in such a way that it appeared to them a change not to be desired," he added, which had the effect of keeping them in "real slavery without the desire of freedom."[12] When the missions were secularized in the 1830s, many Indians left them and were employed by wealthy Californios, for whom they herded cattle, raised crops, and performed domestic chores, often receiving no compensation other than food, clothing, and shelter of the sort slaves in the South received. Sir George Simpson of the Hudson's Bay Company, who visited California in the early 1840s, remarked that Americans who infiltrated the Sacramento Valley were "ready for all sorts of mischief" and might rebel against Mexico and make California a slave territory unless the British, who had abolished slavery throughout their empire by act of Parliament in 1833, took control there first. "Either Britain will introduce her well-regulated freedom of all classes and colors," he wrote, "or the people of the United States will inundate the country with their own peculiar mixture of helpless bondage and lawless insubordination."[13]

Not many Americans, however, envisioned such an outcome if California, New Mexico, or Oregon became U.S. territories. The Far West had considerable allure for expansionists who disdained slavery or those like Benton who accepted it where it was but did not want the nation's growth clouded by that divisive issue. While in the Senate, Benton remained the owner of several slaves and cast no aspersions on slaveholders who seized Texas from Mexico and appealed for American recognition of their republic, which he favored. But he opposed arguments by Calhoun and other southerners that slavery was virtuous and should be exported to American territories. "If there was no slavery in Missouri today," he stated as the national argument over its extension intensified, "I should oppose its coming in."[14] Benton's outlook was partly the result of representing a state that bordered the North and was attracting settlers who wanted nothing to do with slaves or believed that enslaving people was wrong, a conviction shared by many of the German immigrants inhabiting Missouri by the 1840s.

Benton's views on slavery were also influenced by family members, including his wife, Elizabeth, whom he wed soon after entering the Senate. The daughter of Colonel James McDowell, a wealthy Virginia planter, she inherited many of his forty slaves, whom she then freed, employing those who chose to stay as servants in the Benton household. Even more influential were Benton's gifted daughter Jessie—who wrote that he gave her the attention and instruction a cherished "son would have had"—and the man with whom she eloped in 1841 at the age of seventeen, twenty-eight-year-old John C. Frémont.[15] His exploits in years to come as a celebrated surveyor and "pathfinder" of the American West would reinforce Benton's conviction that expansion to the Pacific was too vital to the nation to be hindered by incendiary disputes over extending slavery.

Patrons of the Pathfinder

Frémont was a southerner by origin, but the circumstances of his birth distanced him from the genteel slaveholding society in which his mother was raised. Wed at seventeen in Richmond, Virginia, to Major John Pryor, a man far older than her, Anne Whiting Pryor endured a loveless marriage until her husband discovered her affair with her French-born tutor, Charles Fremon, and the young couple fled. John Pryor filed for divorce in 1811 soon after they left, but his petition was denied. Anne and Charles Fremon thus were not legally married in 1813 when she bore their first child John Charles, who later altered his last name to Frémont as if to accentuate his French heritage. His father died when John was four and left him no bequest, but he went on to attract one generous patron after another—men of substance who helped educate him in Charleston, South Carolina, where his mother had settled, and later helped boost him to prominence. By his late teens, he was a protégé of Joel R. Poinsett, an eminent Charlestonian who had traveled widely in Europe and South America before serving as the first U.S. minister to Mexico in the 1820s. A Jacksonian, Poinsett differed with many of his fellow slaveholders in South Carolina by opposing nullification and helped instill in Frémont devotion to the Union rather than loyalty to South Carolina or the South at large.

When Poinsett became secretary of war under President Van Buren, he helped Frémont secure appointment as a lieutenant in the U.S. Army Corps of Topographical Engineers and join the accomplished French-born scientist and cartographer Joseph Nicollet in surveying the region between the Mississippi and Missouri Rivers. By the time they returned to Washington in late 1839 to map the area they had explored, Nicollet's health was deteriorating and Frémont was poised to succeed him as the foremost topographer of the West, aided by connections to powerful figures like Poinsett and Benton, whom he met in 1840 when the senator inquired about the recent expedition. "The results of our journeys between the two great rivers had suggested to him the same work for the broader field beyond the Missouri," Frémont recalled. "The thought of penetrating into the recesses of that wilderness region filled me with enthusiasm—I saw visions."[16] Although impressed with the precocious lieutenant, Benton did not favor his courtship of young Jessie. By wedding her without permission, Frémont demonstrated a penchant for defying authority that his superiors would resent. But Benton could not long remain at odds with Jessie. And when he reconciled with her, he also embraced her husband and became his ultimate patron, one who furthered Frémont's career substantially along with his own expansionist agenda.

Benton was disappointed but not unduly alarmed when President Van Buren was defeated in November 1840 by the Whig candidate, William Henry Harrison, whose handlers likened the prosperous Virginia-born former governor of Indiana Territory ludicrously to rugged pioneers of the old Northwest who lived in log cabins and drank hard cider. More problematic for Benton than Harrison, hailed by Whigs for his supposed victory in 1811 over defiant Indians at Tippecanoe, was his running mate John Tyler of Virginia, a former Democrat who had turned against Andrew Jackson and joined the Whigs. After succeeding

Harrison, who died soon after his inauguration in March 1841, Tyler vetoed a bill backed by Clay to recharter a national bank and opposed other measures favored by the Whig Party, from which he was then ousted. Although Tyler found allies among southern Democrats who shared his proslavery views and devotion to states' rights, he was disdained by Benton, who considered him too reckless in pursuing the annexation of Texas and too timid in asserting American claims to Oregon. In fact, Tyler favored expansion on both fronts, but he was wary of conflict with Britain over sprawling Oregon—which extended from the northern border of Mexican California at the forty-second parallel to the southern border of Russian Alaska at 54°40'—or over other contested areas along the U.S.-Canadian frontier, disputes that he hoped to resolve diplomatically.

Secretary of State Daniel Webster, who remained in the cabinet after other Whigs resigned, obliged Tyler by settling a boundary dispute with the British in northern Maine. Benton, meanwhile, used his clout as chairman of the Senate Military Affairs Committee to persuade Colonel John J. Abert, chief of the Corps of Topographical Engineers, to dispatch Frémont up the Platte River and tributaries as far as South Pass at the Continental Divide. Although scientific in nature, this expedition had the strategic objective of promoting a route that American emigrants had begun following to Oregon, where Benton hoped they would help make the forty-ninth parallel America's northern boundary rather than the lower Columbia River, as Britain proposed. Influenced by Benton's jaundiced view of Tyler, Frémont stated that they had to proceed cautiously to avoid alarming the president, who threw "the weight of his administration against any measure to encourage and aid the emigration to Oregon." For the first time, Frémont felt he was "being drawn into the current of important political events: the object of this expedition was not merely a survey; beyond that was its bearing on the holding of our territory on the Pacific."[17]

Embarking from western Missouri in June 1842, Frémont enhanced his expedition by enlisting the services of Christopher "Kit" Carson and other trail-wise mountain men, some of whom had earlier followed the Platte River route to trap beaver in the Rockies. Their ventures had emboldened small parties of American emigrants to set out along that trail not just to Oregon but to California, which they reached by way of a route that left the Oregon Trail on the far side of South Pass and crossed the Great Basin along the Humboldt River to steep passes through the Sierra Nevada. None of those pioneers had yet succeeded in reaching the Pacific coast in wagons, which were essential to support large-scale emigration by Americans hauling their supplies and belongings to new homes in the Far West. Although touted later as the "Pathfinder," Frémont's task on this expedition was to chart the established route to South Pass by way of the Platte, North Platte, and Sweetwater Rivers and document topographical features such as streams that had to be forded or changes in elevation that might be arduous for heavy wagons. He also surveyed natural resources such as plants and wildlife and collected specimens.

After his party reached South Pass in August, the urge to explore terrain that had not been surveyed led Frémont to turn northward along the towering Wind River Range and ascend what he mistook for the highest mountain in the Rockies, later dubbed Frémont Peak. It was a reckless detour for him and his companions, who were ill-equipped for mountain climbing and suffered from hunger, cold, and altitude sickness. But by including in his popular narrative of the expedition—which he drafted or dictated to Jessie and she refined—a stirring account of how he ascended that peak, gauged its elevation by barometric pressure at 13,570 feet, and planted at the summit an American flag emblazoned with an eagle, Frémont cast himself as a heroic figure in what Benton envisioned as the epic progress of Americans to the Pacific and the beckoning wealth of Asia. Later, when rails had been laid across the continent on a path that Frémont surveyed in part, Walt Whitman would celebrate that as America's "Passage to India," a route "Tying the Eastern to the Western sea, / The road between Europe and Asia."[18]

Such poetic flights were inspired in part by ventures promoted by Benton, conducted by Frémont, and transcribed and embellished by Jessie Benton Frémont, who helped romanticize America's imperial expansion. The western poet Joaquin Miller was entranced as a boy by the narrative of Frémont's 1842 expedition, published by Congress the following March and excerpted in many newspapers. He imagined men ascending "the savage battlements of the Rocky Mountains, flags in the air, Frémont at the head, waving his sword, his horse neighing wildly in the mountain wind, with unknown and unnamed empires on every hand." That vision filled young Miller with "a love for action, adventure, glory, and great deeds away yonder under the path of the setting sun."[19]

Oregon Fever

In practical terms, Frémont's well-publicized expedition encouraged emigration to Oregon, as Benton hoped it would. "The Oregon fever is raging in almost every part of the union," stated the *Niles' National Register* in May 1843, which predicted that there would be "at least five thousand Americans west of the Rocky Mountains by next autumn."[20] That same month, nearly one thousand men, women, and children set out from Independence, Missouri, on the so-called Great Migration to Oregon. Aided by Marcus Whitman, a physician and missionary who had reached the Columbia River on horseback in 1836, they became the first emigrants to arrive there in wagons on the Oregon Trail, which they improved for that purpose as they proceeded. Whitman stated that he considered the settlement of Oregon "by Americans rather than by an English colony" to be of utmost importance and was "happy to have been the means of landing so large an emigration on the shores of the Columbia."[21] But the mission work of Whitman and his wife, Narcissa, would end tragically in 1847 when Cayuse and Umatilla Indians who resented the influx of white settlers and blamed him for the deaths of people he treated during a measles epidemic killed the Whitmans and suffered reprisals for that attack.

In March 1843, with Benton's encouragement, Colonel Abert ordered Frémont to lead a second expedition, during which he would chart the remainder of the Oregon Trail from South Pass to the Columbia River. That would complement the recent naval reconnaissance of the northwest Pacific coast by Lieutenant Charles Wilkes and provide a comprehensive survey of what Abert emphatically termed "*our* continent" from the lower Missouri River to the mouth of the Columbia.[22] Benton stated that the Tyler administration deserved no credit for this expedition and was "innocent of its conception." But efforts by Benton and fellow Missouri senator Lewis F. Linn to promote emigration to Oregon could not have escaped Tyler's notice. There was little any president could do to hinder American settlement in Oregon, which would have proceeded even without help from Benton, Frémont, or the Corps of Topographical Engineers. In fact, emigration to Oregon served Tyler's purpose by increasing pressure on Britain to yield diplomatically. In late 1843 he would encourage "Oregon fever" by claiming that the United States had "rights" to that entire country up to 54°40', which may well have been a bargaining ploy in boundary negotiations with the British that he hoped would reach a "speedy and happy" conclusion.[23]

When Abert learned in May 1843 that Frémont was arming his company with a howitzer to defend against possible Indian attacks during the forthcoming expedition, he sent a stern letter to the explorer at the Benton home in St. Louis, stating that such a weapon had no place in what was meant to be "a peaceable expedition, similar to the one of last year, an expedition to gather scientific knowledge." If Frémont could not safely manage that assignment without heavy armament, Abert added, "you will immediately desist in its further prosecution and report to this office."[24] By the time the letter arrived, Frémont had left St. Louis and asked Jessie to forward any important correspondence to Westport Landing (within the future Kansas City), where his party would assemble and embark up the Missouri. Jessie read Abert's letter and withheld its contents from Frémont to spare him from having to disobey his superior. "Start at once," she wrote her husband, "ready or not ready."[25] Her father approved her course. Like Jessie, he thought Frémont could do no wrong and blamed efforts to restrain or rebuke him on jealous West Pointers in his corps, "to whose pursuit of easy service Frémont's adventurous expeditions was a reproach."[26]

In late 1843, after a journey that included a detour from the Oregon Trail to reconnoiter the Great Salt Lake, Frémont reached the lower Columbia River. As Benton later wrote, his assignment ended there:

> To complete his survey across the continent, on the line of travel between the State of Missouri and the tide-water region of the Columbia, was Frémont's object in this expedition; and it was all that he had obtained orders for doing; but only a small part, and to his mind, an insignificant part, of what he proposed doing. People had been to the mouth of the Columbia before, and his ambition was not limited to making tracks where others had made them before him. . . . He might then have returned upon his tracks, or been brought home by sea, . . . and if he had been a routine officer, satisfied with fulfilling an order, he would have done so. Not so the young explorer who held his diploma from Nature, and not from the United States' Military Academy.[27]

In Benton's view, it was only natural that this avid student of nature should embark on a return journey that crossed national frontiers in order to survey geographical features transcending those boundaries.

As 1843 drew to a close, Frémont set out to circumscribe what he labeled the Great Basin by heading south from the Columbia along the eastern flank of the Cascade Range and the Sierra Nevada. In the process, he would enter Mexican territory below 42 degrees latitude, which he was capable of determining with his instruments. Crossing that line where there were no Mexican settlements, as was the case when he descended earlier to the Great Salt Lake, involved little risk that he would be challenged by Mexican authorities or troops. The greater risk he faced was that a winter's journey on the rugged margins of the Great Basin would ruin his horses and leave his company stranded and famished. He hoped to avoid that fate by locating the fabled Buenaventura River, which supposedly descended from the Rockies on a westerly course to San Francisco Bay and was shown on some early maps of the West. His goal, he asserted, was to pass safely "to the banks of the Buenaventura, where, in the softer climate of a more southern latitude, our horses might find grass to sustain them, and ourselves be sheltered from the rigors of winter and from the inhospitable desert."[28]

Was Frémont unaware that others who traversed the region before he did, among them far-ranging mountain men like Jedediah Smith, had come to doubt or deny the existence of the Buenaventura? Such ignorance on his part seems unlikely, given his exposure to such men, although he did have some reason to think that river might possibly exist. According to Benton, John McLoughlin—who oversaw the Hudson's Bay Company in Oregon and met with Frémont there—believed in the Buenaventura "and made out a conjectural manuscript map to show its place and course." Yet it would have been uncommonly naïve of Frémont to base his plans that winter on the assurance of finding a river that had never been documented (and was in fact mythical). He may well have entered Mexican territory east of the Sierra Nevada with the idea of crossing into California, if necessary, to replenish his supplies and obtain fresh horses. And that would not be a regrettable diversion for him but a welcome opportunity to help direct the course of American empire toward California. Under Benton's tutelage, he had come to appreciate the strategic significance of exploration, and his actions during this journey and his third expedition, launched in 1845, were those of a proud expansionist, eager to encourage emigration to Mexican California and stake an American claim there. As stated later by Benton, who shared the widely held misconception that the British intended to seize California, Frémont's "second expedition led to a third, just in time to snatch the golden California from the hands of the British, ready to clutch it."[29] Benton neglected to mention that California was in fact snatched from Mexico, although he had more regard for Mexican sovereignty than most American expansionists.

In mid-January 1844, Frémont's party reached Pyramid Lake, fed by a river descending from the Sierra Nevada that was later dubbed the Truckee for a Paiute chief friendly to American settlers. The river was teeming with tasty cutthroat trout and had "tolerably good grass" along its banks, Frémont noted, but he chose not to linger there and instead risked crossing the snow-clogged Sierra in midwinter, a decision he attributed to the poor condition of his foot-sore horses and mules and the lack of iron to reshoe them. Trail-hardened mountain men with Frémont such as Thomas Fitzpatrick and Kit Carson, who had reached California with a trapping party in 1831, looked forward to entering the lush Sacramento Valley and stoically endured a frigid trek over the mountains while

John C. Frémont (1813–1890).
Courtesy Library of Congress
Prints and Photographs
Division (LC-ppmsca-03210).

subsisting on horses, mules, and dogs they slaughtered. "We were nearly out of provisions," Carson said of that ordeal, "but we had to cross the mountains, let the consequences be what they may."[30]

Anticipating trouble in California from Indians, and perhaps from Mexican soldiers, Frémont insisted on hauling the howitzer up the eastern slope of the Sierra before abandoning that heavy gun, which had never been fired at foes. "If we had only left that ridiculous thing at home," wrote artist and cartographer Charles Preuss, who lost his way after the company's dreary slog down the western slope in February before reuniting with Frémont and his advance party at their campsite near what a Spanish-speaking Indian they encountered called the "Río de los Americanos" (American River).[31] That Americans were associated with that pristine river testified to their growing presence in the area, dominated by the man whose fort near the Sacramento River Frémont was seeking, the German-born, Swiss-bred adventurer and entrepreneur John Sutter.

Sutter had arrived in California in 1839 by sea from Hawaii with a letter of introduction from King Kamehameha III, which he presented to California's governor, Juan Alvarado. Alvarado was increasingly concerned about foreigners of little means who were settling without authorization in California, many of them Americans who jumped ship or arrived overland as trappers or traders. Some of them had helped him take power in 1836 during a brief rebellion against Santa Anna's regime that ended when Alvarado reconciled with the government in Mexico City. But in 1840 he evicted scores of foreigners after accusing Kentuckian Isaac Graham, who operated a distillery and grogshop near California's capital, Monterey, of plotting to overthrow him. To help stabilize and develop sparsely settled California, Alvarado counted on reputable foreigners like Alfred Robinson, an American coastal merchant who purchased hide and tallow from California's prosperous rancheros, became a Mexican citizen, and was linked by marriage to one of its leading landholders. Sutter appeared to be similarly reliable, and Alvarado appointed him justice of the peace in the Sacramento Valley, with responsibilities that included guarding against American intruders. Instead, Sutter allowed incoming Americans to settle near the fort he built with Indian labor and treated them as colonists on his personal domain, where he hoped to be "absolute master."[32] Unlike Texas empresario Austin, however, he soon lost control of American settlers, who reckoned that they rather than Sutter would be masters of the valley. And contrary to Sir George Simpson's warning that Americans might introduce slavery in California as they had in Texas, those settlers were not generally inclined to rely on forced labor other than the sort Sutter imposed on Indian servants or subjects.

By the time Frémont reached Sutter's Fort in March 1844, its proprietor suspected that Americans might indeed seize California—a takeover foreshadowed in October 1842 when Commodore Thomas ap Catesby Jones, in charge of the U.S. Pacific Squadron, mistakenly thought the United States was at war with Mexico and occupied Monterey before withdrawing after learning of his error. Robinson predicted that there would soon be enough Americans in California to "play the Texas game" there.[33] Sutter hoped by cooperating with American officials and earning their gratitude to preserve his domain if they took charge. He greeted Frémont cordially, sold him twenty-five horses and sixty mules, and delayed notifying authorities in Monterey long enough so that when Mexican troops reached Sutter's Fort to investigate in April, Frémont and his men were safely on their way back east. Furthermore, Sutter agreed to inform Thomas Larkin, U.S. consul in Monterey, on matters "of consequence" concerning Americans, including the arrival of emigrant parties at the fort.[34] Sutter thus became an American agent while still serving as a Mexican official, a commitment he felt he could safely make after Frémont's armed company entered California undetected and slipped away unscathed.

The next time Frémont entered California, American settlers would be ready to play the Texas game and snatch that golden prize. But unlike Texas, California would frustrate southerners intent on extending African American slavery across the continent and would strain their ties to a nation whose westward course eluded their control. Benton and his son-in-law—and those merchants, mountain men, prospectors, and farmers who trod paths that Frémont surveyed—pursued a continental empire whose far western geography and demography (consisting of Hispanics and incoming Anglos who relied mostly on their own efforts or on Indian labor) helped determine that the peculiar institution would remain largely confined to the South. Tyler would contribute unwittingly to that outcome by seeking the annexation of Texas, leading to a war that culminated in the annexation of New Mexico, California, and other Mexican territory unreceptive to slaveholding planters, thus nullifying any advantage the South would gain politically when the Lone Star Republic became the Union's last slave state.

CHAPTER 9

Tyler, Calhoun, and the "Reannexation" of Texas

By the time John Frémont completed his epic circuit of the West and returned to Missouri in late July 1844, American interest in the Far West had become intertwined with President Tyler's campaign to draw Texas into the Union. Born in 1790 on a plantation in the Virginia Tidewater, Tyler had long maintained that those who owned slaves as he did were entitled to settle with them in any American territory. Indeed, he had held that view longer than its leading exponent, John Calhoun. Unlike Calhoun, Tyler had opposed the Missouri Compromise while serving as a young congressman, arguing that it infringed on the property rights of his fellow southerners and slaveholders. The Louisiana Purchase was "our property in common with the inhabitants of the North," he stated, "and no principle of justice can sanction an act which shall have the effect of excluding from it any member of our society. Our property in our slaves is as full and complete as in our plantation utensils and with equal semblance of propriety might it be contended that we should not carry with us into the western forests an axe or an hoe."[1]

Tyler acknowledged during debate over the Missouri Compromise that slavery was a "dark cloud" hanging over the South, but like Jefferson he argued that the cloud could be dispersed by wafting it westward. By "diffusing this population extensively," he said of enslaved African Americans, "you increase the prospects of emancipation." By the time Tyler became president, the notion that slavery could be eradicated or ameliorated through diffusion had been exposed as a poor excuse for allowing it to proliferate. Yet that theory would be resuscitated by Senator Robert J. Walker of Mississippi and other proponents of Tyler's controversial plan to annex slaveholding Texas, which meant extending the vicious domestic slave trade that Tyler professed to disdain. Like his father, Judge John Tyler Sr., he had deplored the Atlantic slave trade, and he found the local trade conducted in the nation's capital so distasteful that he proposed prohibiting slave auctions there while serving as a U.S. senator in 1835. But he denounced as inflammatory the abolitionist crusade to end slavery in Washington and had proposed selling a Black woman he held in bondage, a house servant named Ann Eliza, on the block at Brooke and Hubbard's auction house in Richmond after his brother-in-law, Dr. Henry Curtis, declined to purchase her. "I have to request," Tyler wrote Curtis in 1827 when in need of cash to launch his senatorial career, "that if you cannot meet with a *ready sale* in your neighborhood, which I would prefer, that you will hand her over to the Hubbard's for public auction."[2]

As president, Tyler hoped that annexing Texas might help him secure a second term and refute those who derided him as "His Accidency" for succeeding William Henry Harrison at his death in 1841. Embraced in Washington neither by Democrats, whose ranks he had abandoned, nor by Whigs—who had abandoned him soon after he took office and deviated from the party line—Tyler needed a signal achievement to have any hope of winning election. Taking Texas, he reckoned, would not just be the "salvation of the Union" but would salvage his presidency.[3] His plans allowed for balancing the annexation of that slaveholding republic with the admission of Oregon as a free territory, if a satisfactory British-American boundary could be negotiated there. Acquiring Oregon had long been a goal of Senator Benton, who hoped that California, to which his son-in-law Frémont would soon return, might fall into American hands as well. At some political risk, however, Benton opposed Tyler and those in Missouri and elsewhere who proposed embracing Texas regardless of Mexican opposition. He favored doing so only if it could be achieved without provoking war with Mexico. Tyler, in his annual message to Congress in December 1843, urged the "representatives of a brave and patriotic people" not to be deterred by Mexico's threat to declare war on the United States if it annexed Texas.[4] But Benton recognized, as Tyler and most other American expansionists did not, that taking Texas with the Rio Grande boundary it claimed would be "an act of unparalleled outrage on Mexico."[5]

Benton's hopes for achieving transcontinental expansion without causing conflict—and a convulsive debate over extending slavery that might threaten disunion—were doomed by a series of events that made Texas an international bone of contention. In 1841, after succeeding Sam Houston as president of the

Lone Star Republic, Mirabeau Lamar had dispatched to New Mexico more than three hundred so-called pioneers, including merchants and soldiers, on what was ostensibly a commercial venture intended to divert some of the profits of the Santa Fe trade to deeply indebted Texas. But Lamar also dispatched those Texans to assert their claim to New Mexico east of the Rio Grande. To that end, he issued a proclamation in English and Spanish expressing his hope that New Mexicans would "join, peacefully, the Texan standard" and stating that if they were not so disposed, the expedition would "retire immediately."[6] When pioneers worn down by their grueling trek across the barren Staked Plains of western Texas were seized in New Mexico carrying Lamar's proclamation, Governor Manuel Armijo concluded that their intentions were not peaceful but hostile. Several Texans were executed, and others died during a brutal march to prison in Mexico City. The disastrous expedition reignited hostilities between Texas and Mexico.

Houston, who returned as president by being elected in late 1841, concluded that Texas was too vulnerable and debt-ridden to stand alone in defiance of Mexico. He welcomed overtures from British officials and hinted that Texas would remain independent and well disposed to them if they induced Mexico to recognize his republic. But he also calculated that flirting with Britain might cause the United States to react by annexing Texas, the outcome he had long sought. To that end, his private secretary, Washington D. Miller, sent a message to President Tyler in early 1843 portraying Great Britain as a suitor fast gaining favor in Texas. "Every day that the action of the US is delayed," Miller claimed, "the prospects of GB are brightening."[7]

Tyler needed little prompting from Texas to foil Britain's supposedly nefarious designs there. He received warnings from editor Duff Green, his special agent in London, that the British might compensate bankrupt Texas if it would forgo American annexation, free its slaves, and ally with their recently emancipated empire. Green went to such lengths to portray the British as intent on abolitionizing Texas that John Quincy Adams described him as the administration's "ambassador of slavery."[8] Furthermore, Tyler suspected British abolitionists of aiding their American counterparts, including Joshua Leavitt, who asserted in his journal the *Emancipator* that Tyler had fathered two children by an enslaved woman he owned. In May 1843, Tyler prevailed on Secretary of State Daniel Webster, who opposed annexing Texas, to resign and replaced him with Abel P. Upshur of Virginia, a Calhounite Democrat intent on drawing Texas into the Union before it became what he and other proslavery ideologues dreaded: an emancipated British colony. Britain's foreign minister, Lord Aberdeen, assured

Upshur in writing in late 1843 that although Great Britain would use its influence to encourage abolition "throughout the world," it would not interfere with slavery in Texas, the United States, or any other foreign country.[9] By then, however, ominous reports to the contrary were circulating publicly, including an alarming series of articles entitled "The British Conspiracy," attributed to Upshur and published in the *Daily Madisonian*, the organ of the Tyler administration.

Texans in fact had no intention of emancipating their slaves, who sustained their economy and would make up more than one-fourth of their population by 1850. Yet Houston continued to give the impression that he might come to terms with Britain, which he later said was meant to "turn public opinion in the United States in favor of annexation."[10] Andrew Jackson, who had refrained from annexing Texas as president, now urged it on Houston in writing. Houston responded in February 1844 that although he favored that outcome, "Texas with peace could exist without the U. States, but the U. States cannot, without great hazard to the security of their institutions, exist without Texas." Among those institutions was slavery, which would be bolstered in the South with the addition of Texas, enhancing America's lucrative cotton trade. In return, Texas sought American support if annexation caused Mexico to wage war. Given such assurance, Houston wrote, Texas was ready to tie the knot with the United States, "as a bride adorned for her espousals." Were she to be spurned, however, "she would seek some other friend."[11]

Echoing Houston, the ailing, seventy-seven-year-old Jackson then warned in a letter intended for publication that failure to annex Texas "may throw her in the arms of Great Britain," his old enemy and America's great rival. "Should that take place, how easy can Britain by an overland movement, turn all our fortifications, raise a servile war, take New Orleans, arouse the Indians . . . throw our whole west into flames that would cost oceans of blood & hundred[s] of millions of money to quench." In another such letter, Jackson envisioned the British adding Texas and Oregon to their empire along with Canada and the West Indies and forming "an iron Hoop around the United States."[12] In a similar vein, Democrat Michael Hoke, while campaigning for governor of North Carolina, imagined Britain "winding herself about us like the terrible anaconda."[13]

Some northerners shared such claustrophobic Anglophobia and thought the British intended not just to thwart American expansion but to encircle the nation and throttle it. Like most northern Democrats in Congress, Representative Charles J. Ingersoll of Pennsylvania supported annexing Texas, which he portrayed as a defensive measure against perfidious Albion, "whose territorial possessions by land and water hem us in on every side."[14] Many southerners were even more fearful of being hemmed in by British imperialists hostile to slavery, who might then deny the South a profitable outlet for its surplus slaves and encourage them to flee or rebel, waging what Jackson called "servile war." Ashbel Smith, a Texas envoy in London, charged that Britain's ultimate objective was to "make Texas a refuge for runaway slaves from the United States, and eventually a negro nation," thus confining the South and depleting its captive labor force.[15] Such fears, amounting to paranoia in some cases, would be eased when Texas was admitted as a slave state, only to intensify in the 1850s when a new Republican Party emerged opposing any further extension of slavery.

Calhoun's Gambit

In April 1844, after being assured by Tyler of American military support if Mexico retaliated, Texas concluded an annexation treaty with the United States stating that Texans would be "protected in the full enjoyment of their liberty and property," which included slaves under their constitution.[16] John Calhoun had recently been appointed secretary of state following the death of Upshur, among those killed when a naval gun exploded during a demonstration aboard a warship in the Potomac. Calhoun viewed confirming that treaty in the Senate not as an end in itself but as part of his ongoing campaign to unite southerners politically and make defending and extending slavery incumbent on the federal government if it meant to retain their allegiance. Born in 1782 in western South Carolina, he was of Scotch-Irish descent like Andrew Jackson. But he was better off than young Jackson as the son of a prosperous planter, slaveholder, and state legislator and far better educated as a graduate of Yale and Tapping Reeve's law school in Litchfield, Connecticut, where various leaders of the early American republic learned their craft. After breaking with Jackson and resigning as vice president, he continued to harbor presidential ambitions. But he was too stridently southern and proslavery to appeal to many northern Democrats and dropped out of the race for the party's nomination in 1844, which Van Buren was seeking in a bid to reclaim the presidency. Calhoun realized he might never lead the nation but still hoped to rally southerners, whom he viewed as threatened by majority rule, which might soon favor northerners in the Senate as it did in the House and subject the southern minority and its peculiar institution to what he considered legislative tyranny. As his predecessor Upshur told him, southerners were "far too lethargic" in defending slavery: "They ought to be roused and made of one mind."[17]

To that end, Calhoun defined the annexation treaty in a way that ended up increasing the odds against it in the Senate—where achieving approval by two-thirds as required would be quite difficult—but made admitting Texas a pressing issue in the upcoming presidential race that neither Van Buren nor his likely Whig opponent, Henry Clay, could duck. Included in the papers Calhoun submitted to the Senate in April as it considered the treaty was a letter he wrote to Richard Pakenham, British minister to the United States, in which he denounced Britain for seeking to interfere with slavery on foreign ground and dismissed Lord Aberdeen's claim to the contrary. Black people were not fit for freedom, Calhoun claimed, and were better off enslaved by their supposedly charitable masters in America. In no other condition or country, he asserted, had "the negro race ever attained so high an elevation in morals, intelligence or civilization."[18]

If Calhoun hoped to unite southern senators behind annexation by accentuating the slavery issue, he was disappointed. When the treaty came up for a vote in June, Benton and nearly all the Senate's Whigs joined a number of northern Democrats in rejecting the deal by a hefty margin, 35 to 16. That did not settle the matter, however, because annexation had by then become a hot issue in the presidential race, as Calhoun wished. Not long before Democrats held their nominating convention in Baltimore in May, Van Buren opposed annexing Texas anytime soon, citing the risk of war with Mexico, which might "do us more real, lasting injury as a nation, than the acquisition of such a territory, valuable as it undoubtedly is, could possibly repair."[19] That stance caused Jackson to abandon him, thus straining the alliance those two master politicians had nurtured between southern and northern Democrats. Henry Clay came out against immediate annexation about the same time as Van Buren, raising suspicions that they conspired to eliminate Texas as a campaign issue. Tyler planned to give voters a say by forming his own party and seeking reelection on a pro-annexation platform. But any realistic hope of sustaining his candidacy faded when Democratic delegates—including many from the South who agreed with Calhoun that opposing the treaty meant opposing slavery—turned against Van Buren and sought a candidate ready to embrace Texas.

At the Democratic convention, some delegates pledged to Van Buren backed a motion by his opponents requiring a two-thirds majority for the nomination—a high standard he could not reach, leaving loyal Van Burenites embittered. (The two-thirds rule would remain in effect at Democratic conventions through 1860, giving southern delegates veto power over northern candidates whose commitment to slavery they doubted.) Deadlocked after eight ballots, the delegates

settled on James Polk, who despite having served as Speaker of the House and
governor of Tennessee was not a commanding figure in the party. Calhoun
was pleased to see Van Buren discarded in favor of a candidate committed to
annexing Texas. But no one was more gratified by the outcome than Andrew
Jackson, who favored his protégé Polk. As firm an expansionist as Old Hickory,
"Young Hickory" was not a proslavery zealot like Calhoun. But he would seek
political parity for the South by ushering Texas into the Union as a slave state
along with Florida to offset the anticipated admission of Iowa and Wisconsin
as free states and the hoped-for annexation of Oregon as a likely free territory.

Polk was nominated on a platform stating that America's claim to "the whole
of the Territory of Oregon is clear and unquestionable" and endorsing "the
reoccupation of Oregon and the reannexation of Texas, at the earliest practicable
period."[20] Some delegates who shared Van Buren's concern that hasty expansion
would set the nation at war with Mexico, Britain, or both were reassured by the
words "at the earliest practicable period." But the rest of that plank was fodder
for those hungering for territories to which their nation supposedly had prior
claims. Fort Astoria—an American trading post founded near the mouth of the
Columbia River by John Jacob Astor's Pacific Fur Company in 1811 and sold to
British traders two years later—did not constitute occupation of Oregon, which
was Indian country when the United States and Britain agreed to occupy it
jointly in 1818. By 1844 several thousand Americans had settled in the Willamette
Valley below the Columbia River. The Strait of Juan de Fuca below Vancouver
Island offered American as well as British ships access to sheltered waters and
fine harbors near the forty-ninth parallel, but Americans had no hold on interior
Oregon above that line, where forts of the Hudson's Bay Company formed the
nucleus of what would become British Columbia.

If American "reoccupation" of Oregon was pablum for naïve expansionists,
"reannexation" of Texas appeared somewhat more plausible and palatable as
dished out by Senator Walker, who was elected in Mississippi but had been born
in Pennsylvania and promoted expansion across sectional lines by appealing
to the ambitions and anxieties of white northerners and southerners alike. In
a lengthy letter published in early 1844 that attracted wide attention, Walker
based his case for reannexation on claims by Jefferson and other American
expansionists that Texas had been part of Louisiana when France sold that territory and thus belonged to the United States when John Quincy Adams allegedly
surrendered Texas to Spain by treaty in 1819. Those assertions were founded
on what Walker touted as the "discovery and occupation of Texas, as a part of

Louisiana, by Lasalle, for France, in 1685," which followed Spanish exploration of Texas but preceded Spanish colonization there in the early 1700s.[21] The struggling little settlement that La Salle planted along Matagorda Bay in 1685 lasted only a few years, however, before it was extinguished by disease, famine, and Indian attacks. It did not give France claim to Spanish Texas at the time of the Louisiana Purchase any more than the ill-fated French settlement at Fort Caroline in 1564—wiped out by Spaniards who arrived a year later and founded nearby St. Augustine—gave France claim to Spanish Florida. If the prior inhabitants of a territory had enduring claim to it, then Texas was rightfully Indian territory and the assertions of Walker and other reannexationists were moot.

More insidious than Walker's contention that the Louisiana Purchase entitled the nation to reclaim Texas was his assertion that diffusing American slavery to Texas would eliminate it from states bordering the North and ultimately disperse it from the nation as a whole. He aimed this argument at northerners concerned that slaves who escaped from states in the Upper South or were emancipated there would flood neighboring free states and compete with white workers or become public burdens. Citing the same flawed 1840 census report used by Calhoun to defend slavery—which erroneously claimed vastly higher rates of insanity and other debilities among free Blacks in the North than among slaves in the South—Walker painted a bleak picture of northern states afflicted by a ruinous influx of former slaves: "They would still be a degraded caste, free only in name, without the reality of freedom. A few might earn a wretched and precarious subsistence, by competing with the white laborers of the North, and reducing their wages to the lowest point in the sliding scale of starvation and misery; whilst the poor-house and the jail, the asylums of the deaf and dumb, the blind, the idiot and insane, would be filled to overflowing; if, indeed, any asylum could be afforded to the millions of the negro race whom wretchedness and crime would drive to despair and madness." All this could be avoided, Walker insisted, if northerners opposed to extending slavery instead embraced Texas and allowed it to serve as a "safety-valve," absorbing slaves from the Upper South, who might otherwise overrun the North. With Texas as an outlet for slaves in states bordering the North, he predicted, "slavery will disappear from Delaware in ten years, and from Maryland in twenty, and have greatly diminished in Virginia and Kentucky."[22]

Neither past nor future census figures bore out that claim by Walker. Between 1840 and 1860, the enslaved population of the five states bordering the North—Delaware, Maryland, Virginia, Kentucky, and Missouri—would increase altogether by more than 15 percent, which was considerably less than the entire population increased in those states but hardly indicated that slavery was evaporating there. In Kentucky, about one-fifth of the population was enslaved in 1860, nearly the same ratio as in 1810. In Virginia, about two-fifths of the population was enslaved in 1860, nearly the same ratio as in 1800. Neither in Delaware—where slavery was never prevalent and roughly 90 percent of the Black population was free by 1840—nor in Maryland, where almost 50 percent of the Black population was free by 1860, was there a massive exodus of free Blacks to the North such as Walker envisioned, in part because they were unwelcome there or discouraged from entering by law in some states. Nor did the presence of numerous free Black people in Maryland and Delaware result in calamitous slave uprisings or race wars as predicted by proslavery doomsayers who warned against emancipation. Not even in Delaware and Maryland did the number of enslaved people fall appreciably between 1840 and 1860. Meanwhile, the enslaved population increased by about 150,000 in Virginia, Kentucky, and Missouri combined, despite the admission to the Union of that supposed safety valve Texas, where the enslaved population increased threefold to more than 180,000 during the 1850s.

Not content to claim that slavery in the Upper South would be reduced to insignificance through diffusion to Texas, Walker promised that slavery would ultimately be dispersed entirely from the nation through diffusion from Texas to Latin America:

> Again, then, the question is asked, is slavery never to disappear from the Union? This is a startling and momentous question, but the answer is easy, and the proof is clear; *it will certainly disappear if Texas is reannexed to the Union*; not by abolition, but against and in spite of all its frenzy, slowly, and gradually, by diffusion, as it has already thus nearly receded from several of the more northern of the slaveholding States, and as it will continue thus more rapidly to recede by the reannexation of Texas, and finally, in the distant future, without a shock, without abolition, without a convulsion, disappear into and through Texas, into Mexico and Central and Southern America.[23]

This was sheer propaganda, concocted by an astute politician who knew that Mexico would no longer tolerate slavery as practiced by rebellious American settlers in Texas and that the Mississippians he represented in the Senate wanted Texas in the Union to keep slavery secure in their home state and serve as a profitable outlet for those who held more Black people in bondage than they required. Walker himself had profited from the diffusion of slavery after joining his brother in Mississippi in the 1820s by speculating in land and slaves as the Cotton Kingdom expanded—and he stood to gain from investments in Texas if it was annexed.

Although Walker's deceptive promotional efforts helped add Texas to the roster of slave states that would later secede and form the Confederacy, he was in fact a Jacksonian Unionist who had opposed nullification in South Carolina and would side with his native Pennsylvania rather than his adopted Mississippi during the Civil War. His divided sectional loyalties in the prewar years made him an enthusiastic advocate for the main issue on which Polk campaigned: balancing the interests of North and South by annexing Texas as a slave state and Oregon as free territory. Oregon would not be populous enough to seek statehood for some time, but it appealed to northern expansionists and enabled Walker to link their animosity toward Britain along the Canadian border with southern fears of British interference in Texas. "Look at her forts and her traders, occupying our own undoubted territory of Oregon," he wrote of Britain. "Though saturated with blood, and gorged with power, she yet marches on her course to universal dominion; and here, upon our own borders, Texas is to be her next prey." Echoing charges of disloyalty leveled at Federalists who had opposed the Louisiana Purchase and the War of 1812, Walker branded anyone who might be willing to surrender Oregon and Texas to Britain "a monarchist . . . an Englishman in feeling and principle," who would help the British "recolonize the American States."[24] He thus defined Britain not in Calhoun's terms as a threat to slavery in the South but as a menace to the nation as a whole, offering a broader argument for Polk's national campaign.

Some northern expansionists still hoped that much if not all of British Canada would become part of their nation. That ambition inspired the slogan "Fifty-four Forty or Fight," voiced by those who wanted Oregon in its entirety. The saying was not part of Polk's campaign but emerged afterward. Urged by his friend and advisor Cave Johnson to avoid "speaking or writing from now until the election," Polk made a few cautious pronouncements but did not address concerns that his expansionist agenda risked conflict with Britain over Oregon or with Mexico over Texas—a danger emphasized by opposing Whigs and their candidate, Henry Clay, who warned of sectional strife between North and South if Polk fought to acquire slaveholding Texas. A Whig newspaper in New York denounced Polk as one "who would instantly plunge us into a disgraceful war, which he has not the ability to conduct—who would set in motion causes which could not fail to result in disunion and civil war."[25] To avoid further controversy over his expansionist agenda, Polk concealed his interest in acquiring California, which would be among his chief goals as president. That would mean a wider war if Mexico refused to yield ground.

Clay's Southern Dilemma

If Polk risked appearing warlike, Clay risked looking like someone backing down from a challenge and unwilling to fight, which American voters generally and those in the South particularly considered dishonorable. To be sure, Clay was not averse to dueling. While serving as secretary of state in 1826, he had faced off against Senator John Randolph and exchanged shots with him, albeit harmlessly. But Jackson had questioned Clay's patriotic fortitude by stating that he had never risked himself for his nation. To reassure those who wondered if he would stand up to Britain or Mexico if pressed, Clay pledged that he would not allow any foreign country to subvert the sovereignty of the Texas Republic. His problems in the South were compounded, however, by his support for voluntary emancipation and African colonization and the impression that he was bowing to northern antislavery sentiment by declining to embrace Texas. In July 1844, Clay issued two "Alabama letters," published in Tuscaloosa, in which he stated that he did not oppose taking Texas because it upheld slavery—which he thought was "destined to become extinct" there and elsewhere "at some distant day"—and that he would gladly annex the republic if that could be achieved "without dishonor, without war, with the common consent of the Union, and upon just and fair terms."[26] Those letters alienated some northern Whigs, but Clay could ill afford to lose the support of southern Whigs, including planters or merchants financially dependent on slavery who differed with Democrats on other issues. Some blamed Jackson's annihilation of the national bank—and his requirement in 1836 that federal land purchases be backed by gold or silver—for the Panic of 1837 and its bitter aftermath, which helped swing previously Democratic Louisiana, Mississippi, and North Carolina to the Whigs in 1840.

Clay's call for a fiscally sound federal government that would fund internal improvements appealed to enterprising southern Whigs such as Albert Pike, a transplanted northerner who prospered in Arkansas as a journalist and politician. A former schoolmaster in Massachusetts, Pike had embarked in 1831 on a western odyssey that took him out along the Santa Fe Trail to New Mexico, from which he then journeyed to Arkansas Territory through the emerging

Indian Territory, where he would later seek treaties with slaveholding tribes as Confederate Indian commissioner. After evoking his early western travels in a fine book that flopped, Pike settled down as a Whig editor in Little Rock. Like Benton and other ambitious southerners of limited means, he improved his prospects through marriage, wedding the daughter of a wealthy planter whose dowry included slaves Pike then mortgaged to purchase the *Arkansas Advocate.* By 1835 he could describe himself as "a great man in Israel," although he remained somewhat disdainful of this would-be state on the nation's rugged southwestern frontier: "I imagine I am settled here for my life time. After all there is something to being looked up to—even in Arkansas." He saw much room for improvement there that Clay's American System might help provide. "All along our roads are abandoned huts, shattered fences, deserted fields overgrown with weeds," Pike wrote long after arriving in Arkansas. "Except a few cotton-planters, nobody seems to have any energy, confidence, or hopefulness."[27] Most southern Whigs in Congress backed Clay on Texas, but Pike and others in the party's southern wing were prepared to fight if annexation resulted in war with Mexico. During that conflict, Pike would lead Arkansas volunteers into battle there.

One southerner who turned firmly against slavery and challenged Clay on that issue was Kentucky-born James G. Birney, who had failed as a planter in Alabama in the 1820s while seeking to treat his slaves humanely but succeeded as a lawyer. Opposed to Andrew Jackson, he counseled Cherokees seeking to avoid removal from the Southeast and served as an agent for the American Colonization Society before concluding that sending emancipated slaves to Africa was akin to evicting Indians from their southern homelands. Unlike Clay, who continued to promote colonization but emancipated few of the people he owned, Birney moved north, freed his slaves, and published an abolitionist newspaper in Cincinnati whose press was targeted by mobs. Nominated for president in 1840 by the newly formed Liberty Party, he received only about 7,000 votes. He fared better four years later when Clay's equivocation over Texas and Birney's forthright declaration that "we cannot receive Texas as a slave territory" attracted like-minded northerners who might otherwise have backed Clay against Polk. The 15,800 votes cast for Birney in New York in November 1844 may well have determined the outcome in a state that Polk won by barely 5,000 votes, capturing 36 electoral votes that would have altered the outcome had they gone to Clay. His defeat could also be attributed to his poor showing in two regions where there was strong sentiment for taking Oregon, Texas, or both: the old Northwest or emerging Midwest, where he won only Ohio, and the Lower South, where he was shut out by Polk. Nonetheless, many northern Whigs blamed Birney for handing New York and the election to a Democrat committed to annexing Texas. Birney offered no apologies. He did not trust a slaveholding compromiser like Clay to advance abolition, a cause sacred to Birney, who later wrote a pamphlet titled *The Sinfulness of Slaveholding in All Circumstances*.[28]

Tyler, who had withdrawn as a candidate and supported Polk, interpreted the agonizingly close election—in which Polk received fewer popular votes than Clay and Birney combined—as a mandate for "immediate annexation" of Texas, which he sought to achieve in the last months remaining to him as president.[29] Rather than amending the rejected Texas annexation treaty and resubmitting it to the Senate, Tyler pressed for a joint congressional resolution to admit Texas as a state, which required a simple majority in both the Senate and the House. Despite objections that there was no constitutional basis or historical precedent for admitting to the Union a foreign country like the Lone Star Republic that was not first annexed by treaty, the resolution on which the House voted called for Texas to be granted statehood "subject to the adjustment by this Government of all questions of boundary that may arise with other Governments."[30] In addition, the resolution allowed for the eventual formation of up to four additional states within the boundaries of Texas, provided that slavery would not be allowed in any such state embracing territory claimed by Texas north of 36°30'. That provision was introduced by a young Democrat who would loom large in Congress in years to come, Stephen Douglas of Illinois. He may have intended it to counter the impression among opponents of annexation, which he firmly endorsed, that he was a "subservient tool of the slaveholders," as a Boston newspaper labeled him.[31] But the restriction he offered left a vast area open to slavery and offered no solace to those who rejected the Texas Republic's outlandish claim to a panhandle extending northward from the source of the Rio Grande in what would become Colorado to the forty-second parallel in what would later be Wyoming.

Among the staunchest congressional opponents of admitting Texas was John Quincy Adams, who had tried unsuccessfully to purchase Texas from Mexico during his presidency with the approval of Secretary of State Clay. But Adams said that there was a difference between "purchase and burglary," or taking territory that Mexico declined to cede to the United States. A fervent critic of Texas for perpetuating "the crime of slavery" there after Mexico abolished it, he said he would not embrace that republic even if it were "ten thousand times more valuable than it is."[32] Some of his fellow Whigs in the House shared his abhorrence for slavery, and even many who did not feared that waging war against Mexico over slaveholding Texas might shatter the fragile accommodation between northerners and southerners in their party and the nation as a whole. "As certain as truth and God exist," Representative Daniel D. Barnard of New York warned, "the admission of Texas into the Union will prove, sooner or later, an element of overwhelming ruin to the Republic."[33]

Of the eighty Whigs in the House who cast votes, only eight favored the resolution, all of them from the South. But it passed with solid support from the opposing party. Despite defections by free-state congressmen partial to the spurned Van Buren, two-thirds of northern Democrats backed the resolution, swayed by their desire for party unity and by arguments that admitting Texas was not just a southern concern or "a mere sectional measure," in the words of Representative Chesselden Ellis of New York, but a national imperative that would expand "our institutions over a magnificent domain." Like Senator Walker, Ellis linked Texas and Oregon to the nation's long-running contest with Britain, which began as a war for independence and was now a struggle for preeminence. "From the day when Texas and Oregon are brought under the sway of American enterprise," he declared, begins the decline and ultimate "downfall of the British empire."[34]

In the Senate, Benton—a longtime Jacksonian who parted with Old Hickory on annexation and shared Van Buren's concerns—proposed an alternative to the House resolution that made no reference to forming additional states within Texas and called for it to be admitted to the Union after a new agreement was reached to replace the treaty rejected in 1844. His resolution would appropriate funds for diplomatic "missions and negotiations," which he hoped would yield a settlement with Mexico on the Texas boundary.[35] When it became clear that the House resolution could not pass the Senate on its own, Walker proposed attaching it to Benton's resolution along with a clause allowing the president to choose between the two. Walker made that proposal at Polk's urging, and Benton trusted in assurances that Polk rather than Tyler would implement the terms and be guided by Benton's resolution. He and four like-minded senators voted in favor of the combined resolutions, which passed the Senate in late February 1845 by a margin of two votes. With Calhoun's encouragement, Tyler then took it upon himself to offer Texas admission under the House resolution on March 3, one day before he was succeeded by Polk, who exasperated Benton by letting Tyler's decision stand. Calhoun's gambit, by which he had linked annexation to slavery and lost the treaty in the Senate, thus succeeded in the long run. But this victory had far-reaching consequences he would come to regret.

Benton later cried foul, stating that Texas was hustled into the Union "by a deception, and by deluding five senators out of their votes. It was not a barren fraud, but one prolific of evil, and pregnant with bitter fruit."[36] Yet Benton had been outmaneuvered because he left Tyler an opening to do so—and left Polk free to follow the House resolution that Tyler set in motion. Although Benton urged negotiations with Mexico on the disputed Texas boundary in a speech supporting his resolution, he did not specify that in the text and accepted the clause allowing either president to opt for the House resolution with its vague language on adjusting boundary questions, which Tyler and Polk ignored. Benton's stand against annexing Texas with a boundary inimical to Mexico was unpopular in Missouri, and he had faced a stiff challenge there before state legislators reelected him to the Senate in 1844. If he pressed his case against annexation without Mexican consent to the hilt, he risked losing influence with Polk and his party. Benton was, after all, an ardent expansionist who maintained that the United States was entitled to Texas within its historical boundaries and shared Polk's keen interest in Mexican California. He thus bore some responsibility for the looming war he feared—and for the sectional dispute it exacerbated, which would eventually make his son-in-law Frémont the first standard-bearer of a new party that would denounce Benton's cherished Democratic Party for extending slavery.

CHAPTER 10

Mr. Polk's War and Manifest Destiny

When James K. Polk learned that he had been nominated for president by Democratic delegates in Baltimore in May 1844, he declared his intention to serve only a single term if elected. He thus risked being transformed in short order from a dark horse—chosen by weary delegates after more prominent candidates fell short—to a lame duck, without enough staying power to overawe opposing Whigs or command obedience within his own ranks. Yet Polk managed to avoid that fate. His self-imposed term limit helped appease powerful Democrats who did not want their own presidential aspirations deferred for eight years and lent him a sense of urgency as he pursued a drastic campaign of expansion that altered the nation's destiny.

At his inauguration on March 4, 1845, the forty-nine-year-old Polk became the nation's youngest president to date, but the constant pressures he faced wore on him, and he would die soon after completing his term. He would thus be spared from witnessing the Union he greatly enlarged break apart, an outcome to which men present at his inaugural ceremony contributed. Administering the oath of office to Polk was Chief Justice Roger Taney, who would issue the convulsive *Dred Scott* decision. Standing beside Polk as he swore to defend the Constitution was the outgoing president, John Tyler, who would endorse secession by Virginia in defense of slavery.

Polk, for his part, would frown on any suggestion that he was serving the interests of the South and its peculiar institution. Yet he was a substantial slaveholder who continued to buy enslaved African Americans as president while concealing those purchases from the public. Through his wedding to Sarah Childress on New Year's Day, 1824, he had acquired an adept partner who enhanced his political career and brought to their union nine slaves inherited from her father, a prominent planter like Polk's father, who would bequeath to him about a dozen slaves and land in western Tennessee. Polk established a plantation there that he placed under overseers while he served in Congress and became Speaker of the House, in which capacity he helped implement the controversial gag rule, stating that all petitions relating to slavery or its abolition shall "be laid upon the table, and that no further action whatever shall be had thereon."[1]

Among those enslaved people who served Polk personally was one who would proudly bear his surname when emancipated: his manservant Elias Polk, a wedding present from his father. According to a tall tale attributed to Elias by a reporter, he accompanied President Polk to Pennsylvania, where he was asked why he did not seek freedom there. He would never desert Polk, he replied: "No, sir . . . I'd sooner die than run off." Polk supposedly overheard the conversation and was so moved that he offered to free Elias, who would not hear of it. In fact, Elias made no such trip with the president, and Polk did not free him. With an eye toward posterity, Polk stated in his will that he intended to emancipate all his slaves at his death if he survived Sarah—and that if she survived him, he hoped she would free their slaves at her death. She long outlived Polk, however, and Elias was still enslaved at her home in Nashville when the Civil War erupted. Freed under the Thirteenth Amendment at war's end, he became a vocal supporter of the Democratic Party formerly led by President Polk. The Radical Republicans who implemented Reconstruction, Elias Polk declared on one occasion, were sowing "confusion and strife" by enfranchising ex-slaves and disenfranchising ex-Confederates in a cynical effort to "keep power."[2]

Elias Polk was not the only slave held by James Polk who fared well enough in his service to emulate or speak favorably of him. Among his most resourceful enslaved laborers was a skilled blacksmith named Long Harry, who at his own request was hired out by Polk to employers in Carroll County, Mississippi, which enabled him to rejoin his enslaved wife there and raise a family. That was not the only time James and Sarah Polk acted to unite spouses or family members enslaved on separate plantations. But such benevolence was mingled with self-interest in the case of Harry, a valuable asset. In one year, he earned Polk more than four hundred dollars in hiring fees, enough to cover the annual salary of an overseer Polk employed. Harry also earned cash on his own account by working as a blacksmith in his free time. Having learned to read and write, he sent Polk flattering letters designed to dissuade his owner from removing him from a position close to his family. In 1844 he placed bets that Polk would be elected president and campaigned for him locally: "I tell you Master Jimmy that I made some big speaches for you," he wrote, "and though an humble negro I made some votes for you."[3] As president, however, Polk was unable to collect debts owed by Harry's employers and had him return to the plantation, thus separating him from his family.

Among those who vouched for Polk's virtues as a slaveholder was his friend Gideon J. Pillow, who would later serve as a Confederate general. To counter accusations that Polk profited by buying and selling slaves, Pillow asserted in print that the slaves Polk purchased were "Family Negros," who wished to remain part of the extended Polk or Childress families. "I never heard of his buying but one slave," Pillow added, and that was a woman Polk purchased in order to unite her with her husband, "a man of his own." But slavery as practiced by Polk was by no means strictly a family affair. Until he became president, he derived only a modest income from the elective offices he held or his law practice, which he abandoned when he entered Congress. His wealth consisted largely of the land and enslaved people he owned, and the value of both fluctuated as the cotton trade flourished or faltered. In the mid-1830s, when his cotton plantation in western Tennessee failed to yield much income, he sold it and established a new one with his partner and relative, Dr. Silas M. Caldwell, on land in northern Mississippi vacated by Choctaws during the Indian removal led by Polk's political patron, Andrew Jackson. "I am resolved to send my hands to the South," Polk wrote before dispatching most of his slaves to Mississippi. "I am determined to make more money or loose [lose] more."[4]

Polk's calculated gamble meant hardship and disruption for those "hands" and other slaves he bought, many of them children or young adults who did not belong to the Polk or Childress families and were subject to wrenching separations from their own kin. Overseers he hired faced resistance from slaves who fled to avoid hard labor or punishment or rejoin family members in Tennessee. One overseer wrote Polk that they believed Tennessee was "a place of parridise" to which "all want to gow back." Established plantations in Tennessee were no paradise, but raw plantations in Mississippi like Polk's were hell by comparison for those exiled to them. More than half the children born on his wet, low-lying, malaria-ridden property there died by the age of fifteen. Some brave souls who were old and strong enough to do so defied brutal overseers. One man named Chunky Jack responded to a whipping by grabbing a stick and breaking it over the head of his overseer, who then wielded his knife, stabbed Jack twice, and placed him in chains. Jack remained intransigent and was probably sold to a trader and relegated to an even worse form of bondage in the "lower country," such as laboring on a sugar plantation in Louisiana. Another man enslaved by Polk, Henry Carter, who was in his twenties and one of the plantation's best workers, was forced to strip naked before being whipped by his overseer and responded by grappling with the man, who called on other slaves to come to his aid. They refused and fled, as did Carter, who obtained clothing and sought refuge in Tennessee with Silas Caldwell, who had ended his partnership with Polk. Caldwell did not send Carter back to the Mississippi plantation until Polk hired another overseer, who proved to be as cruel as his predecessor. He whipped a man named Addison so severely that when the victim fled to Dr. Caldwell and he examined the wounds, he wrote Polk that it "appears that the Overseer intended to kill Him."[5]

Faced with such grim reports, Polk sought to distance himself from the harsh realities of slavery as he advanced politically. As president, he bought slaves for his Mississippi plantation confidentially, sometimes using Sarah Polk and her brother John W. Childress as intermediaries who conveyed cash and the president's requests to the actual purchaser. Polk instructed one such agent, his cousin Robert Campbell Jr., that "as my *private business* does not concern the public, you will keep it to yourself. There is a great disposition with many persons, to parade every thing connected with the President whether *private or not* before the public." Concern for his reputation as a slave owner may have influenced Polk's decision to offer those who labored on his Mississippi plantation financial incentives. Beginning in 1844, slaves there could earn cash for cotton they cultivated in their spare time. "It is right and proper to pay the negroes for their cotton," Polk wrote Campbell, "and I desire that it shall be done." But this was not a charitable scheme. Enslaved men and women who took part received no more than their cotton was worth on the market. They earned on average less than seven dollars per person for their efforts in 1846, expended at no loss to Polk, who benefited because slaves awaiting payment were less inclined to flee the plantation, which earned him more than $3,700 that year. He told Campbell that he would apply the "proceeds" for the next few years "to the increase of my force" at the plantation, which would be his "only source of income" when he left office.[6]

Although Campbell mainly bought slaves as Polk's agent, he wrote the president in October 1846 that he had sold a boy named Jim, purchased previously for $392, "to the Widow Colbern for $450 & bought a girl (Jane) 20 lb heavier for $425." Campbell said she was "likely 12 or 13 years old" and considered it "one of the best trades I have made."[7] Seven of the nineteen slaves purchased for Polk while he occupied the White House were under fourteen, providing him with pliable youngsters who were less likely to flee than older slaves and who might in time produce numerous offspring who would became his property as well. One enslaved girl named Daphney, whom Polk bought before he became president when she was about ten, became pregnant not long after she reached puberty. The father was a young slave named Giles. He and Daphney were made to "claim one another," a woman enslaved with them recalled, and that was "all the wedding they had."[8] Although four of Daphney's children died, three survived to adulthood, thus profiting Polk and his wife, who inherited them, despite the plantation's high mortality rate.

Although he would insist that his public actions as president had nothing to do with slavery and his own involvement in it, Polk raised that issue in his inaugural address and warned of disunion if attempts were made to restrict the rights of states and subvert their "domestic institutions," notably that dismal institution peculiar to the South. He regretted that "in some sections of our country misguided persons have occasionally indulged in schemes and agitations whose object is the destruction of domestic institutions existing in other sections—institutions which existed at the adoption of the Constitution and were recognized and protected by it." If those agitators achieved their goal, he added, "the dissolution of the Union and the consequent destruction of our happy form of government must speedily follow." Antislavery agitation was of particular concern to Polk because he would soon fulfill Tyler's initiative by annexing Texas, a slaveholding republic larger than the slaves states of Louisiana, Arkansas, and Missouri combined. To preserve the Union, Polk insisted, "the compromises which alone enabled our fathers to form a common constitution for the government and protection of so many States and distinct communities, of such diversified habits, interests, and domestic institutions, must be sacredly and religiously observed." Those in free states who objected to slavery would not diminish it, he argued, if they refused to compromise and barred Texas from the Union. The same principle that would deny statehood to Texas "because of her local institutions," he concluded, would have prevented the founders "from forming our present Union."

Although Polk expected states of the Union to compromise by tolerating one another's interests and institutions, he appeared unwilling to compromise with the neighboring state of Mexico over Texas and its boundary claims, which included much Mexican territory. Polk hoped to purchase Mexico's compliance

James K. Polk (1795–1849) as president in 1845. Courtesy Library of Congress Prints and Photographs Division (LC-pga-10650).

and professed no hostile intentions. But his insistence that the United States was reclaiming its rightful territory by annexing Texas and would not tolerate resistance to that acquisition threatened war if Mexico remained defiant—a war waged by the nation as a whole to secure territory for a domestic institution only some states honored. He insisted that other countries had no right to interfere with the forthcoming "reunion" between the United States and Texas or take exception to it: "Foreign powers do not seem to appreciate the true character of our Government. Our Union is a confederation of independent States, whose policy is peace with each other and all the world. To enlarge its limits is to extend the dominions of peace over additional territories and increasing millions."

Such professions of innocence by a president who would wage what opponents called "Mr. Polk's War" to achieve his goals shifted the blame for hostilities from what he mischaracterized as a "confederation of independent States" (which were interdependent under the Constitution) to any nation that dared dispute America's right to expand. Polk likely had Mexico in mind as well as Great Britain and France—which also hoped to prevent American annexation of Texas—when he warned against foreign interference with that republic's supposed reunion with the United States. And he challenged Britain directly on another front when he added: "Our title to the country of the Oregon is 'clear and unquestionable,' and already are our people preparing to perfect that title by occupying it with their wives and children."[9] Yet Polk harbored a grudging respect for British power that would make him more inclined to yield part of Oregon than relinquish to Mexico any territory claimed by Texas.

Left unmentioned in Polk's inaugural address was California. George Bancroft, who served as secretary of the navy under Polk, recalled a conversation soon after the inauguration in which Polk described acquiring California as one of several "great measures" he hoped to achieve as president. Revealing that objective publicly might have helped him in one respect by confirming that his expansionist agenda went beyond territory where slavery as practiced in the South existed or might readily be introduced. Southern expansionists dreamed of a slaveholding empire extending westward from Texas to California. But since the early 1800s, California had been of particular interest to maritime merchants in the Northeast, whose ships rounded Cape Horn and visited ports such as San Diego and San Francisco (originally Yerba Buena) while engaged in whaling, the fur trade, or the hide-and-tallow trade, conducted with enterprising Californios who herded cattle by the thousands. As Polk told Bancroft, he hoped to obtain all of California or at least a "large district" on the Pacific coast.[10] That would further American interests in Hawaii, which traders and missionaries were colonizing, and China, which the Tyler administration had induced to open several of its ports to merchant ships carrying goods that included raw cotton and cotton fabric. In that regard, Polk's expansionism was not just continental but global.

Although acquiring California might broaden the appeal of his expansionist agenda, Polk had reason to keep quiet about that objective. For if Mexico refused to yield territory, a war of conquest that embraced California would be broader, deeper, and more disruptive than a campaign waged strictly to secure the Rio Grande boundary for Texas and the United States. Polk's muddled prewar efforts to purchase what lay between the upper Rio Grande and the California coast would stiffen resistance to his demands by Mexican authorities and lead to a conflict in which he targeted their capital. That in turn would provoke substantial opposition from Americans who considered such an invasion dishonorable if the purpose was to seize Mexican territory—and intolerable if the objective was to extend slavery.

Might and Right

Young Hickory was not an acclaimed commander like Old Hickory and could not count on wholesale support for Mr. Polk's War, a label evoking Mr. Madison's War against the British. But Polk would have the advantage of calling on volunteers to fight for their country at a time when Americans were increasingly sure of their

John Quincy Adams (1767–
1848) as U.S. representative
from Massachusetts, ca. 1843.
Courtesy Library of Congress
Prints and Photographs
Division (LC-pga-06984).

right to exert their might and extend their borders. Polk's expansive rhetoric was
restrained compared with that of some in Congress who considered every inch of
Oregon up to 54°40' to be God's gift to America, not to be surrendered to British
imperialists. John Quincy Adams, for one, was as intent on asserting the nation's
right to Oregon in its entirety as he was on denouncing the annexation of Texas.
Speaking in the House in early 1846 like a preacher addressing his flock, Adams
based that right on biblical precepts. In a dispute "between Christian nations," he
stated, "the foundation to title to land is laid in the first chapter of Genesis," from
which he asked the clerk of the House to read the passage commanding those
created in God's image to be "fruitful and multiply, and replenish the earth, and
subdue it." Adams also had the clerk read a verse from the Psalms that his Puritan
antecedents in Massachusetts had cited to justify subduing Native Americans
and taking their land: "Ask of me, and I shall give thee the heathen for thine
inheritance, and the uttermost parts of the earth for thy possession" (Psalm 2:8).

Throughout history, Adams argued, nations had cited various justifications
for seizing territory, such as discovery and exploration. But discoverers and
explorers did not have true title unless they possessed the land and replenished
it, he said: "There is nothing complete in the way of title, but *actual possession*;
and that is the only thing we now want, to have a perfect, clear, indisputable, and
undoubted right to the territory of Oregon." The United States rather than Great
Britain had that right, Adams concluded, because the British did not improve

or replenish the land by settling there and tilling the soil but kept it in "a savage and barbarous state" for traders of the Hudson's Bay Company and tribes they dealt with. And therein lay the difference between British and American claims, he declared: "We claim that country—for what? To make the wilderness blossom as the rose, to establish laws, to increase, multiply, and subdue the earth, which we are commanded to do by the behest of God Almighty."[11]

If that was the basis for laying claim to Oregon, however, a similar argument could be made for annexing Texas, which Stephen Austin had foretold would "present a second Eden to posterity" as Americans settled there and made the wilderness blossom using slave labor.[12] Unlike Adams, expansionists less troubled by slavery such as editor John L. O'Sullivan justified annexing not only Oregon or California but also Texas and other alluring places dependent on enslaved labor such as Cuba, a Spanish colony eyed acquisitively by Polk and later presidents. Born in 1813, O'Sullivan grew up in New York City and graduated from Columbia College before joining with his brother-in-law in 1837 to found the *United States Magazine, and Democratic Review*. As its editor, he extolled the "democratic genius" of the nation in general and the Democratic Party in particular. O'Sullivan proclaimed in 1839 that the United States was "destined to be *the great nation* of futurity." Unlike European nations that were rooted in the past and sacrificed the interests of the many "to the aristocracy of the few," the American nation looked forward and promised

> freedom of conscience, freedom of person, freedom of trade and business pursuits, universality of freedom and equality. . . . For this blessed mission to the nations of the world, which are shut out from the life-giving light of truth, has America been chosen; and her high example shall smite unto death the tyranny of kings, hierarchs, and oligarchs, and carry the glad tidings of peace and good will where myriads now endure an existence scarcely more enviable than that of beasts of the field.[13]

That eloquent assertion of American exceptionalism epitomized the Young America movement, consisting mostly of eager young Democrats like O'Sullivan whose ambitions for their dynamic young country were boundless. They were idealistic when supporting national liberation movements in Europe such as Young Italy and Young Ireland but imperialistic when asserting the right of their own nation and race to dominate North America and vicinity. O'Sullivan was careful, however, not to associate national supremacy with its unsavory partner white supremacy. He extolled his country's "blessed mission" to the world by avoiding mention of slavery, whose persistence in the United States demonstrated that it had not yet escaped the ancient history of oppression that subjected many to the demands of a few and condemned those who resisted enslavement to be whipped like beasts of the field.

Slavery was so bound up with Texas when Polk proceeded with annexation that O'Sullivan could no longer rely on lofty tributes to American liberty when upholding the policy of his party and president, as evidenced in his 1845 editorial that articulated Manifest Destiny. (He was responsible for that unsigned article, which spoke for him even if some other contributor to his magazine—such as journalist Jane McManus Storm Cazneau, an avid expansionist with close ties to Texas—had a hand in it.) Compared with "The Great Nation of Futurity," O'Sullivan's editorial on "Annexation" was defensive and dismissive. It disparaged those who greeted the admission of slaveholding Texas to the Union with "the most ungracious frowns of aversion and words of unwelcome." All true Americans should embrace Texas, he insisted: "Ill betide those foul birds that delight to [de]file their own nest, and disgust the ear with perpetual discord of ill-omened croak." The nation must unite behind Texas, he argued, if only to resist interference there by the British and French, who were conspiring against America "for the avowed object of thwarting our policy and hampering our power, limiting our greatness and checking the fulfillment of our manifest destiny to overspread the continent allotted by Providence for the free development of our yearly multiplying millions."[14]

In that memorable passage, O'Sullivan linked Manifest Destiny and Providence—terms evoking the nation's Puritan heritage and the Calvinist doctrine that God predestines the fate of individuals and nations—to the remarkable growth of the American population (which had increased fivefold since 1790) and the biblical injunction to be fruitful and multiply and subdue the earth. By avoiding direct references to God or Scripture of the sort Adams invoked in his speech, however, he made Manifest Destiny part of the nation's civic religion along with such patriotic pieties as "the land of the free and the home of the brave." Manifest Destiny assured Americans of any faith or no faith that they were meant to proliferate and predominate.

Continental expansion in the 1840s was driven not just by the population pressure O'Sullivan cited but by the political pressure he and other influential Democrats exerted. Even in the more populous North, there was ample room within the nation's existing boundaries to accommodate land-hungry farmers. Minnesota would have barely six thousand settlers when organized as a territory in 1849. Yet Democratic expansionists argued that the nation must seek additional ground to preserve freedom and opportunity for present and future generations. As claimed in an article O'Sullivan published in 1842 under the provocative headline "White Slavery," Americans could avoid the industrial woes of Britain, where white laborers were supposedly treated worse than Black slaves, by overspreading their bountiful continent and tending its soil:

> Nature has pointed out the course which we ought to pursue for perhaps half a century to come . . . till happy plantations shall have been formed on the deserted domains of the Indian huntsman from the Atlantic to the Ohio, and from the Mississippi to the Pacific. She has directed us to cling to the bosom of mother Earth, as to the most fertile source of wealth, and the most abundant reward of labor. She has told us to remain planters, farmers, and wood-cutters—to extend society and cultivation to new regions.[15]

Similar arguments that recalled Jefferson's idealized view of rural America were made by other Democratic editors and politicians to promote expansion to the southwest as well as the northwest. In truth, lands on which farmers first settled in Oregon were not deserted by Indians, and plantations in Texas were not happy for those enslaved there. But Americans were restless in pursuit of more fertile sources of wealth or sustenance, and the party that promised to extend cultivation to new regions benefited when western states it helped attach to the Union sent Democrats to Congress, as Texas soon would.

O'Sullivan dismissed fears that expansion would promote disunion by arguing that new modes of transportation and communication, including railroads, steamships, and telegraph lines, would unify a country stretching from the Atlantic to the Pacific. The day was not too distant, he assured readers in "Annexation," when railroads would convey elected representatives

> from Oregon and California to Washington within less time than a few years ago was devoted to a similar journey by those from Ohio; while the magnetic telegraph will enable the editors of the "San Francisco Union," the "Astoria Evening Post," or the "Nootka Morning News," to set up in type the first half of the President's Inaugural before the echoes of the latter half shall have died away beneath the lofty porch of the Capitol, as spoken from his lips.

Significantly, those were examples linking East to West. Given Polk's warning against disunion in his inaugural address, O'Sullivan could not promise readers that technological ties would bind North to South and prevent telegraphs, railroads, and steamships from becoming strategic assets in a calamitous civil war. Ominous sectional resentments were evident even among those who favored annexing Texas. O'Sullivan complained in print that Calhoun did "great wrong" to northerners who took that stance by defining annexation as a proslavery initiative essential to southerners, "a relative minority in the Union of about one-third to two-thirds."[16] In years to come, the mathematics of Manifest Destiny would offer little solace to southerners increasingly at odds with yearly multiplying northerners who so outnumbered them.

In late 1845, as the Anglo-American dispute over Oregon intensified, O'Sullivan again invoked Manifest Destiny in an editorial in the *New York Morning News*. Much like Adams, he argued that traditional grounds for claiming territory were insufficient and instead tried to place America's claim to Oregon on a higher moral ground. "Away, away with all these cobweb tissues of rights of discovery, exploration, settlement, continuity, etc.," he wrote. If Britain had a stronger case in all those respects, he added, the United States would still have the superior claim: "And that claim is by the right of our manifest destiny to overspread and to possess the whole of the continent which Providence has given us for the development of the great experiment of liberty and federative self-government entrusted to us."[17] O'Sullivan reformulated Manifest Destiny here by linking it not to the "free development" of the nation's millions—which was also an imperative for Britain and other populous countries—but to America's distinctive democratic system. Yet American liberty was fostered in part by the British parliamentary tradition, which limited the Crown's power and enabled American colonists to form assemblies that nurtured self-rule and the desire for independence. Ardent American expansionists believed that Canada would be free only if absorbed by the United States, but it would achieve self-government as a confederated British dominion. The liberty that O'Sullivan considered America's unique gift from Providence and the nation's unique gift to the world served as a rationale for claiming "the whole of the continent," in his words, to the detriment of neighboring countries that were evolving from colonial rule to self-rule.

O'Sullivan was no warmonger. He did not think that Mexicans would fight for territory over which their government supposedly had no real authority. And when, to his surprise, they proved as intent on preserving their country in its entirety as Polk and like-minded Americans were on extending their boundaries, he did not celebrate the resulting conflict, which contradicted his notion that America would spread peace and glad tidings abroad. Critics of Manifest

Destiny like Congressman Charles Goodyear of New York—who favored a negotiated settlement with Britain that would give the United States possession of Oregon up to the forty-ninth parallel—charged that, far from placing the nation's territorial ambitions on higher ground, that doctrine debased them by invoking a self-righteous "claim to universal dominion" of the sort used to justify "every act of wholesale violence and rapine that ever disgraced the history of the world." Americans, Goodyear added, should heed the lesson of Rome and other fallen empires, which signaled that a nation "destined to extend its territory by conquest, is equally fated to perish in the midst of its victories."[18]

In an address entitled "The Young American," Ralph Waldo Emerson—who influenced O'Sullivan and other Young Americans but offered a more complex and cautionary view of the nation's destiny—stated in 1844 that "America is the country of the Future . . . a country of beginnings, of projects, of vast designs, and expectations." But how America's future would be shaped by the "Genius, or Destiny" that guided humanity toward gradual improvement was unpredictable, he added: "This Genius, or Destiny, is of the sternest administration, though rumors exist of its secret tenderness. It may be styled a cruel kindness, serving the whole even to the ruin of the member." Emerson saw the cruel kindness of destiny at work in American industries that were scarring the natural landscape he loved to make the nation more productive and cohesive. "This rage for road building is beneficent for America," he noted, but with the building of railroads came disruption and destruction:

> The tunneling of mountains, the bridging of streams . . . the encounter at short distances along the track of gangs of laborers; the energy with which they strain at their tasks; the cries of the overseer or *boss*; the character of the work itself, which so violates and revolutionizes the primal and immemorial forms of nature; the village of shanties, at the edge of beautiful lakes . . . around which the wives and children of the Irish are seen . . . the blowing of rocks, the explosions all day, with the occasional alarm of frightful accident.[19]

The cruel lot of those Irish immigrants who dug tunnels, laid tracks, and perished in accidents proved beneficial for the nation and for their own descendants, who built a better world for Irish Americans on the foundation they laid. Some called them wage slaves and pitied them, but they would not have changed places for a moment with the Black slaves on which southern prosperity and the livelihood of many northerners depended. Emerson understood destiny or historical evolution as a process of creative destruction or rather destructive creation—one in which the Civil War that stemmed from the Mexican-American War he opposed amounted to a stern administration of justice to America before it sought redemption in a new birth of freedom.

Edging toward Conflict

Soon after Polk became president and pledged to bring Texas into the Union, Juan Nepomuceno Almonte, Mexico's minister to the United States, protested annexation as an "act of aggression" and left the country, thus severing diplomatic relations.[20] That complicated efforts by Polk and Secretary of State James Buchanan to resolve the Texas boundary dispute in America's favor and made their approach to Mexico less direct and more secretive than their approach to Great Britain, whose minister to the United States, Richard Pakenham, remained in place as tense negotiations over Oregon proceeded. Indirection and secrecy suited Polk, however, because he hoped to resolve the dispute with Britain through compromise while leaving Americans largely in the dark as to the greater risk of war he incurred by demanding galling concessions from Mexico.

The question of whether the United States would annex Texas with the Rio Grande boundary it claimed in defiance of Mexico was not resolved by the joint congressional resolution that outgoing president Tyler set in motion and Polk then implemented. That resolution called for boundary adjustments, and the envoy dispatched by Tyler to offer Texas annexation—Andrew Jackson Donelson, nephew of Andrew Jackson—assumed that meant negotiating a boundary acceptable to Mexico. He told Sam Houston that the United States would try to secure as much of the Rio Grande claim as it could "without manifest injustice to Mexico."[21] Avoiding such injustice was not Polk's policy, however. He was willing to compensate Mexico for ceding what Texas claimed but meant to obtain that territory in full. Soon after his inauguration, he sent additional envoys to instruct and bolster Donelson, who then joined them in assuring Texans that Polk would back their claim. "You may have no apprehensions with regard to your boundary," Polk wrote Houston on June 6, 1845. Texas was "once a part of the Union," he asserted, "and we will maintain all your rights, of territory, and will not suffer them to be sacraficed."[22]

Houston remained influential in Texas, but he had been succeeded as president there in December 1844 by Anson Jones, who was more cautious about merging with the United States if that meant war with Mexico. Jones withheld support for American annexation while Britain and France sought an agreement by which Mexico would recognize Texas in exchange for its pledge to remain independent. American envoys did all they could to subvert that initiative, including spreading rumors of a Mexican invasion and encouraging a plot by Texans to incite a border war that would draw in American troops. That scheme proved unnecessary because there was little support in Texas for reconciling with Mexico and remaining independent. When Jones presented the proposed treaty with Mexico in June 1845, the Texas Congress rejected it and voted to accept annexation pending approval by delegates who would convene in Austin on July 4. Before they met, Polk authorized General Zachary Taylor to embark with troops from Fort Jesup in Louisiana to a position "on or near the Rio Grande" and wrote Donelson that he would of course "maintain the Texas title to the extent which she claims it to be."[23] That meant enforcing Texas's claim to Santa Fe and other New Mexican settlements east of the upper Rio Grande as well as its claim to territory between the Nueces River (the historical boundary of Spanish and Mexican Texas) and the lower Rio Grande. Polk acted without adjusting boundary questions with Mexico as the joint congressional resolution on Texas implied he should. Instead, he assumed the Rio Grande boundary for the United States in defiance of Mexico and won approval for annexation from all but one of the fifty-six delegates voting in Austin.

Polk thought that forcefully backing Texas's claim might avert rather than incite war by intimidating Mexico into ceding territory. He and others doubted that Mexicans were willing or able to defend their northern frontier against determined opposition. Such was the opinion of the secret agent he sent to Mexico City in 1845 to see if diplomatic relations could be restored and negotiations held: William S. Parrott. A poor choice for that assignment, he had filed the largest of numerous American claims against Mexico for financial losses blamed on that country. In a dispatch to Washington, Parrott portrayed Mexicans as all bluster and bravado until they were thrashed. They can "never love or respect us, as we should be loved and respected by them," he wrote, until given "positive proof of our superiority." They would yield more readily in talks, Parrott suggested, if they were first "well flogged by Uncle Sam's boys."[24] He wanted Mexicans punished the way southern masters flogged recalcitrant slaves. Polk, for example, was offended when told that a political foe had said he should be treated like an "ugly Negro who was unruly . . . give him a d——n drubbing at the start, and he would learn to behave himself."[25]

Parrott changed his tune after the proposed treaty between Texas and Mexico fell through and Mexicans could no longer count on British or French support.

They were now suitably chastened, he thought, and would yield readily to American offers. "An Envoy possessing suitable qualifications," he wrote Buchanan in late August 1845, "might with comparative ease, settle, *over a breakfast*, the most important national questions."[26] Encouraged by Parrott's report, Polk met in September with his cabinet, which approved his proposal to send Congressman John Slidell of Louisiana to Mexico City to "adjust a permanent boundary," language suggesting that Polk meant to comply belatedly with the congressional resolution on Texas. But the boundary he envisioned with Mexico would extend far beyond Texas, reaching the Pacific below the harbor at San Diego. He supposed that could be purchased from Mexico for $15 million or $20 million, but he was "ready to pay forty millions for it, if it could not be had for less."[27]

The more detailed instructions that Buchanan issued to Slidell offered Mexico various options, which ranged from ceding the entire area from Texas to California for $25 million to ceding just Texas within the Rio Grande boundary, in which case the United States would assume the financial claims of U.S. citizens against Mexico, an offer that Mexican authorities could not refuse without facing grave consequences. Slidell was instructed by Buchanan on Polk's authority to describe those claims as "injuries and outrages" that could not be endured unless Mexico either paid up—which it could not do because it was bankrupt—or ceded all its territory within the Rio Grande to the United States. If Mexico failed to come to terms, Polk wrote Slidell, "we must take redress for the wrongs and injuries we have suffered into our own hands, and I will call on Congress to provide the proper remedies," which would mean war. Other nations had similar financial claims against Mexico. French forces had bombarded and occupied Veracruz in 1838 to compel payment of claims by French citizens, including a pastry chef who accused Mexican officers of wrecking his restaurant. Mexicans had viewed that so-called Pastry War as a brazen imperial assault on their country. Yet Polk, who cited the Monroe Doctrine when denying Britain or other European powers any right to colonize Oregon or California, was now asserting America's right to colonize Mexican territory by claiming it as indemnity for financial "outrages" that included failure to pay Parrott's claim, described by one American diplomat as inflated to "a disgusting degree."[28]

The peremptory tone of Slidell's instructions made it highly unlikely that Mexico would accept the terms proposed, and his mission was hampered when he was designated by Polk as "Envoy Extraordinary and Minister Plenipotentiary," which meant that Mexico by accepting him would be withdrawing its protest against American annexation of Texas and restoring diplomatic relations. Polk wrote Slidell that Mexico was "ready to receive a Minister from the United States," based on a report from the U.S. consul in Mexico City, John Black, who in fact stated that Mexico would accept a commissioner, a lower-level envoy with whom talks could be held without restoring relations.[29] Receiving a minister from the United States was a concession that President José Joaquín de Herrera could ill afford to make, for he was under pressure to respond forcefully to the loss of Texas and at risk being overthrown by General Mariano Paredes y Arrillaga, who opposed yielding to the United States. To make matters worse, Polk assigned the abrasive and unwelcome Parrott to join Slidell as secretary of the legation.

While this abortive effort to settle with Mexico was proceeding, the dispute with Britain over Oregon was intensifying. But Polk's response to that crisis—which combined due regard for British might with a refusal to be cowed by it—was more flexible. Without retreating publicly from his campaign pledge to acquire all of Oregon, he authorized Buchanan in July 1845 to propose a compromise to Pakenham that would divide American from British territory at the forty-ninth parallel and allow British ships access to ports at the southern tip of Vancouver Island, situated below that line. Aware that London was intent on retaining full possession of Vancouver Island and securing free navigation of the Columbia River, which Polk did not offer, Pakenham rejected the offer without referring it to his superiors. Offended by that response, Polk then proposed reiterating America's claim to all of Oregon. Buchanan warned against risking war over Oregon without first resolving the Texas dispute. Polk, as recorded in his diary, replied that he "saw no necessary connection between the two questions; that the settlement of the one was not dependent on the other; that we should do our duty towards both Mexico and Great Brittain and firmly maintain our rights, & leave the rest to God and the country."[30]

Polk had been encouraged to stand firm against Britain in one of the last letters he received from Andrew Jackson before Old Hickory died in June 1845. Do not be intimidated by the "rattling of the British drums," Jackson urged him. "War is a blessing compared with national degradation." And if Polk maintained "a bold and undaunted front," he added, conflict could be avoided. "England with all hear Boast dare not go to war."[31] To be sure, Britain had twice gone to war with the United States and might do so again if its vital interests were at stake. But its interests in Oregon were largely those of the Hudson's Bay Company, which would not be threatened by a settlement similar to the American proposal so long as Vancouver Island remained fully on the British side of the boundary and the company's ships had access to the Columbia River, which originated above the forty-ninth parallel. The British had not yet made such a counteroffer, however, and Polk was not yet ready to concede that much. He worried that if he or Congress showed any further inclination to compromise, "John Bull would immediately become arrogant and more grasping in his demands."[32] So he instead sought to pressure John Bull by terminating the joint occupation of Oregon—a step he proposed in his first annual message to Congress on December 2, 1845, which revealed that his administration was at odds with Mexico as well as Britain.

In that message, Polk tried to sweeten the bitter disclosure that Mexican-American relations were at a dangerous impasse by claiming that Texas was no longer in dispute and had been drawn peacefully into the Union pending congressional approval of its application for statehood later that month. "This accession to our territory has been a bloodless achievement," he declared. "The sword has had no part in the victory. We have not sought to extend our territorial possessions by conquest, or our republican institutions over a reluctant people." Anglo-Texans indeed welcomed annexation, as Polk claimed, but Hispanics living in Mexican towns within the Rio Grande boundary would be brought under American rule whether they liked it or not. That this might not be a bloodless achievement, after all, was signaled when Polk acknowledged that Mexico had assumed "an attitude of hostility toward the United States" and the U.S. Army had been "ordered to take position in the country between the Nueces and the [Rio Grande] Del Norte, and to repel any invasion of the Texan territory which might be attempted by the Mexican forces."[33] Mexicans had good reason to consider American troops invaders if they ventured beyond the Nueces. General Taylor knew that an advance to the Rio Grande might be so construed and remained with his forces in Corpus Christi, at the mouth of the Nueces. He would not advance farther south "without authority from the War Department."[34]

No less ominous than Polk's announced intention to send troops into territory that Mexico had not yet ceded to the United States was the emphasis he placed on the "unredressed injuries" suffered by American citizens with financial claims against Mexico. His lengthy discussion of those claims was accurate as far as it went, noting that a joint commission had examined them and awarded Americans some $2 million, which Mexico had agreed to pay in installments with interest but remained largely unpaid. By stressing that debt, however, and referring menacingly to Andrew Jackson's hyperbolic assertion in 1837 that Mexico's failure to redress such "outrages" on American citizens "would justify in the eyes of all nations immediate war," Polk was seeking justification for a conflict that Jackson had avoided. He informed Congress that the Mexican government had agreed to renew diplomatic relations and "accredit a minister from the United States," but that was not the case and would make Mexico's refusal to receive Slidell in that capacity appear unwarranted and insulting to Americans.[35]

Not long after Polk sent his message to Congress, Slidell's mission collapsed. By the time he reached Mexico City in December, word that Polk was bidding for Mexican territory extending beyond Rio Grande to California had leaked out. President Herrera declined to receive Slidell as a minister, but that did not prevent Herrera from being ousted by General Paredes. He too would refuse to receive Slidell, and the unwelcome envoy would leave Mexico in a huff. "Depend upon it," he would write in a dispatch to Washington that echoed Parrott's dismissive view of Mexicans, "we can never get along well with them, until we have given them a good drubbing."[36]

When Polk learned in January 1846 that Slidell had been rebuffed by Herrera, he had Secretary of War William L. Marcy order Taylor to advance from Corpus Christi toward the Rio Grande. Critics of Polk would view that as inviting conflict with Mexico, and it indeed set the stage for hostilities. But he did not yet know that Paredes would refuse to negotiate with Slidell and learned in February of another possible means of securing Mexican territory without waging war, suggested to him by Alexander Atocha, a Spanish-born American citizen who served as emissary to Polk from former Mexican president Santa Anna, in exile in Cuba. Atocha stated that Santa Anna might soon return to power in Mexico and would then cede all the territory Polk sought for $30 million, so long as it appeared he was forced to make that concession. Santa Anna's message to Polk, as conveyed by Atocha, was to "take strong measures, and such a Treaty can be made & I will sustain it."[37] Having already taken a strong measure by ordering Taylor to advance, Polk would send an envoy to Havana to meet with Santa Anna in July.

In early April 1846, Polk learned that Slidell's mission had failed and concluded that the time had come "to take the remedy for the injuries and wrongs we had suffered into our own hands."[38] Seeking a declaration of war because Mexico rejected Slidell and refused to honor American financial claims would have met with considerable opposition in Congress, but Polk was spared from committing that blunder by the ongoing dispute with Britain. After much debate, Congress terminated the joint occupation of Oregon but attached a resolution urging compromise and inviting Britain to respond to the proposal rejected by Pakenham with a counteroffer. Polk delayed action on Mexico while awaiting that response, which would avert conflict when accepted by giving the British full possession of Vancouver Island and allowing ships of the Hudson's Bay Company access to the Columbia while otherwise drawing the boundary at the forty-ninth parallel. In the meantime, Polk was urged to ease pressure on Mexico by some in Congress, including Senator Calhoun, whose support for annexing Texas did not extend to grabbing large portions of Mexico. Polk's willingness to compromise on Oregon led congressman and newspaper editor John Wentworth of Illinois to pose a pointed question in print: "Why should we not compromise our difficulties with Mexico as well as with Great Britain?"[39] Among the factors that led to peace in one case and war in the other were British strength as opposed to Mexican vulnerability, respect for rival Anglos in the ancestral British homeland of many white Americans as opposed to disdain for Hispanics, and the crucial fact that yielding part of Oregon was no great loss for Britain, whereas ceding territory from Texas to California would be an excruciating blow to Mexico, which would submit only if invaded and defeated.

Among those Americans who blamed the conflict that loomed on the exorbitant territorial demands of their nation and its president was Colonel Ethan Allen Hitchcock, who advanced below the Nueces toward the Rio Grande with Taylor's forces. "We have not one particle of right to be here," he concluded in his diary, and he feared that Taylor's four thousand troops were insufficient for an invasion that was sure to be opposed. "It looks as if the government sent a small force on purpose to bring on a war," he ventured, "so as to have a pretext for taking California and as much of the country as it chooses."[40] By April, Taylor had reached the Rio Grande and placed artillery within range of Matamoros, a large Mexican town on the south bank that was cut off from the Gulf of Mexico by an American naval blockade at the river's mouth. General Mariano Arista concluded that his country was under assault and sent troops across the Rio Grande to repulse Taylor. On April 25, two companies of U.S. dragoons (mounted infantry) were surprised and routed by a larger force of Mexican cavalrymen, who killed or wounded sixteen Americans and captured more than twice that number.

On Saturday, May 9, Polk received word from Taylor that hostilities had commenced. Two days later he asked Congress to approve a bill funding the war effort and authorizing him to summon fifty thousand volunteers. With American troops already embattled, skeptical congressmen found it hard to oppose the bill and its contentious preamble, which stated that war existed "by the act of the Republic of Mexico." One Whig who believed otherwise, Representative Garrett Davis of Kentucky, protested that Polk had begun the war by sending American forces across the Nueces into Mexican territory. But Davis then backed those troops by joining the overwhelming majority in the House and Senate who supported the bill and thus authorized war. Polk prevailed with his assertion that "Mexico has passed the boundary of the United States, has invaded our territory and shed American blood upon the American soil."[41] Yet suspicions would linger that war had been proclaimed on false pretenses—and that what Polk touted as a defense of the nation's rights was a blatant assertion of its might for gains that a republic increasingly at odds over slavery was ill-prepared to handle.

Continental Conquests

At a cabinet meeting on May 13, 1846, one day after the Senate joined the House in authorizing war on Mexico, Secretary of State Buchanan proposed informing foreign governments that the United States did not intend "to dismember Mexico . . . that in going to war we did not do so with a view to acquire either California or New Mexico or any other portion of the Mexican territory." Polk refused to make any such commitment. He told Buchanan that "though we had not gone to war for conquest, yet it was clear that in making peace we would if practicable obtain California and such other portion of the Mexican territory as would be sufficient to indemnify our claimants on Mexico, and to defray the expense of war which that power by her long continued wrongs and injuries had forced us to wage."[42] Polk remained willing to pay Mexico far more than it owed Americans for the losses they claimed if it yielded to his demands, indicating that he insisted on indemnity to cast blame on Mexico for the war he waged and make that nation cede territory.

Polk had long been planning to seize California if Mexico refused to yield and hostilities ensued. In June 1845, at Polk's initiative, Navy Secretary Bancroft had ordered Commodore John D. Sloat of the U.S. Pacific Squadron in the event of war to promptly "possess yourself of the port of San Francisco, and blockade or occupy such other ports as your force may permit."[43] Later that year, alarmed by unsubstantiated rumors that Britain had designs on California, Polk had directed Buchanan to make Thomas Larkin, U.S. consul at Monterey, a confidential agent, whose instructions included warning Californios against "European dominion" and assuring them that should they "desire to unite their destiny with ours, they would be received as brethren."[44]

Another American who would help loosen Mexico's hold on California was newly promoted Captain John Frémont, who had embarked from Missouri in June 1845 on his third expedition across the West. Although his official orders from Colonel Abert of the Corps of Topographical Engineers made no mention of California, Frémont later stated that he was authorized to enter that Mexican territory by his father-in-law, Senator Benton, "and other governing men in Washington."[45] Benton, who backed the war reluctantly rather than jeopardize his political career, met with Polk at the White House in October 1845 and discussed Frémont's expedition to California and Polk's fear of British interference there. Polk told Benton that "the U.S. would not willingly permit California to pass into the possession of any new colony planted by Great Brittain or any foreign monarchy." In thus asserting the Monroe Doctrine, Polk added, he had "the fine bay of San Francisco as much in view as Oregon." Benton predicted that Americans would settle along the Sacramento River "and ultimately hold the country." In fact, hundreds of Americans had already settled in the vicinity of Sutter's Fort near that river and were growing rebellious. Frémont would become involved in their uprising against Mexican authorities after being briefed by Lieutenant Archibald H. Gillespie of the Marine Corps, with whom Polk held a "confidential conversation" after meeting with Benton and before Gillespie left on a secret mission to California with instructions for Frémont.[46]

Aware when he departed Missouri that the dispute over Texas might lead to conflict, Frémont began defying Mexican authorities not long after he reached California in December 1845 and well before he heard from Gillespie. After stopping at Sutter's Fort, as he had during his previous expedition, he proceeded to Monterey for the avowed purpose of obtaining more supplies than were available at that fort. His ulterior motive was to confer with Larkin and learn where things stood with Mexico. Larkin as yet had no indication that war was imminent and worried that Frémont's arrival would antagonize José Castro, California's military chief, who was at odds with authorities in Mexico City after overthrowing their appointee, Governor Manuel Micheltorena. Castro had achieved that coup with Pío Pico, a confederate who was now his rival after assuming the governorship in Los Angeles, which briefly supplanted Monterey as California's capital. With few troops at hand, Castro did not want Frémont and his 60 well-armed men to camp near Monterey. Frémont lingered in the vicinity, however, awaiting word of hostilities that might arrive by ship. In March 1846 he openly defied Castro by assuming a fortified position atop Gavilán Peak (known later as Frémont Peak), not far from Monterey, and raising the American flag. "I am making myself as strong as possible," he wrote Larkin, "in the intention that if we are unjustly attacked we will fight to the extremity and refuse quarter."[47]

Frémont was risking battle without knowing whether his country was at war with Mexico. Larkin persuaded him to back down by warning that Americans in California would be in danger if he clashed with Mexican troops. "My sense of duty did not permit me to fight them," Frémont wrote his wife, Jessie, "but we retired slowly and growlingly," a flattering description that likened the retreating Americans to the formidable grizzlies that still roamed California. He headed north and crossed into Oregon in early May near Upper Klamath Lake, where Gillespie, who had arrived in Monterey by ship in April, caught up with him. Gillespie knew by then that Slidell's mission had failed and that conflict was likely. Whatever he conveyed in the way of confidential instructions from Washington led Frémont to conclude that he was relieved of his "duty as an explorer" and authorized to serve as an officer whose government "intended to take California."[48]

Frémont returned to the vicinity of Sutter's Fort as American settlers there were on the verge of rebelling. Unauthorized immigrants who did not obtain Mexican citizenship and thus could not legally acquire land there, they could be expelled at any time and credited rumors that Castro was inciting Indians to attack and drive them out. In early June they launched the Bear Flag Revolt, so called for the grizzly depicted on their banner, and induced Frémont to serve as their chief. The revolt was of little strategic significance compared with the seizure of Monterey in early July by Commodore Sloat. But it set a hostile precedent for what Larkin hoped would be a tranquil takeover. Former governor Mariano Vallejo—who had aided Americans in California, Larkin noted, and was "always speaking in their favour"—was seized by Bear Flag rebels at his home in Sonoma along with several relatives and associates and imprisoned at Sutter's Fort, where their jailers referred to them as "damned greasers," a slur that gained currency among Anglos during the war. Critics would fault Frémont for abetting an unruly uprising before he knew war had been declared, but he claimed to be acting on Gillespie's assurance that "to obtain possession of California was the chief object of the President."[49]

While the Bear Flag Revolt unfolded, Polk was taking additional steps to obtain California with the aid of Frémont's father-in-law, who furthered Polk's plans for a far-reaching military campaign from Missouri to New Mexico, from which some of the troops involved would then advance to help secure California. Long supportive of trade between Missouri and New Mexico, Benton viewed the campaign as way of protecting merchants who would follow the Santa Fe Trail that summer and using their commercial ties with New Mexicans to ease the military occupation of that territory. As he stated in a letter to Governor John C. Edwards of Missouri, New Mexicans would be encouraged to "remain

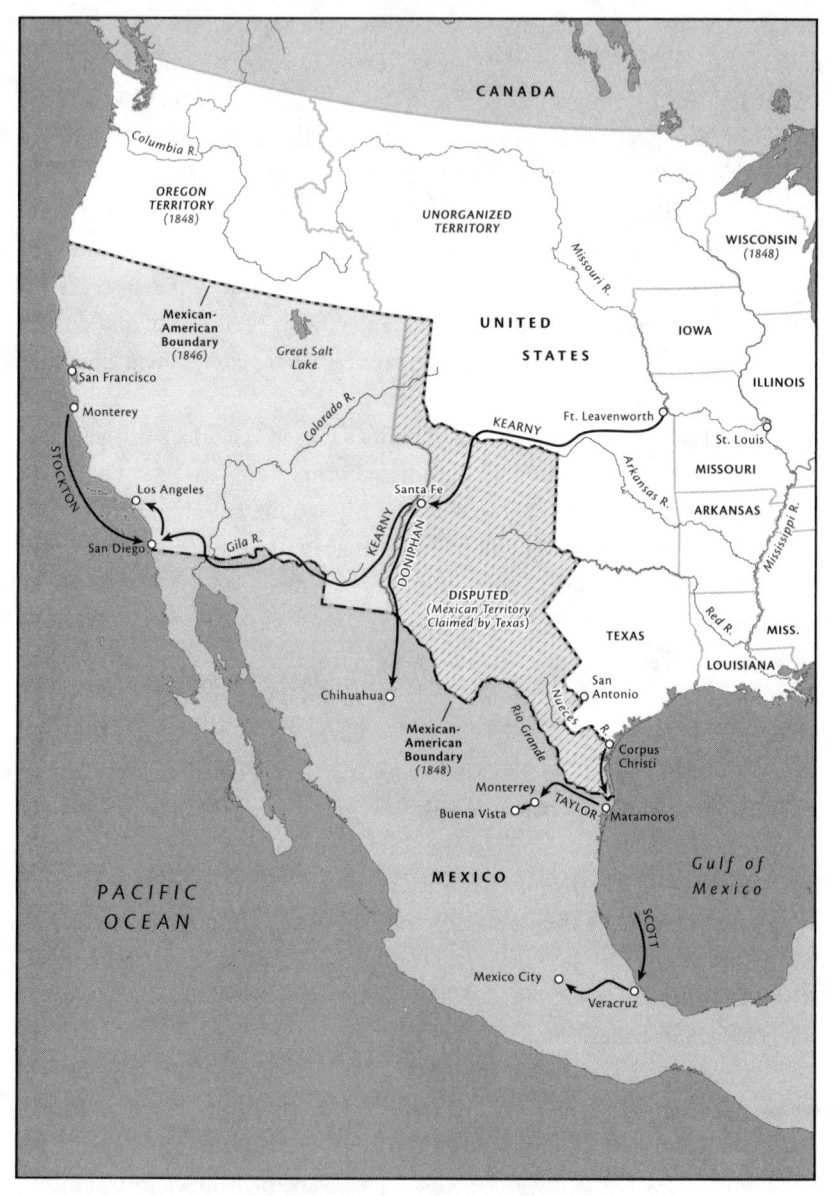

The Mexican-American War, 1846–1848

quiet and continue trading with us as usual, upon which condition they shall be protected in all their rights and be treated as friends. . . . This military movement will be to make sure of the main object, to wit: peace and trade, to be secured peaceably if possible, forcibly if necessary."[50]

That ambiguous campaign, in which the promise of peace was backed by the threat of force, reflected Benton's ambivalent position as an advocate of commercial expansion who was now advancing a war of conquest. While Polk used Mexico's delinquency in the payment of financial claims to justify armed expansion, Benton hoped to use trade between Americans and Mexicans to soften aggression and appease those subject to occupation. Even a commander possessing a rare combination of military skill and diplomatic finesse would have been hard-pressed to fulfill that prescription for benign conquest. The officer assigned to occupy New Mexico and continue on to California, General Stephen Watts Kearny, was further burdened by Polk's decision to establish temporary civil governments in those occupied territories before Mexico admitted defeat and ceded them to the United States. Although Polk considered conferring civilian rule and American citizenship on the people of New Mexico and California a generous alternative to military rule, it defined those who remained loyal to embattled Mexico and opposed American authority as traitors, subject to execution. Not until late in the war would Secretary of War Marcy rule that Mexican territory occupied by American troops was not yet part of the United States and its inhabitants were not yet American citizens.

Kearny's grandly titled Army of the West numbered only about 1,650 men, including 300 dragoons of the regular army and the newly recruited First Regiment of Missouri Mounted Volunteers under Colonel Alexander W. Doniphan. Some of those Missourians were slaveholders, and some of their officers were accompanied by enslaved manservants—one of whom rescued a major who awoke one morning to find a rattlesnake coiled beside his leg by promptly removing the reptile. Few Missourians, however, enlisted with the intention of extending slavery to New Mexico. Like volunteers in neighboring Illinois who invaded the Mexican heartland, they were motivated largely by military adventurism and boisterous patriotism. Kearny's forces set out from Fort Leavenworth on Missouri's western frontier in early July 1846 and followed the Santa Fe Trail to the Arkansas River, which had formed the Mexican-American boundary on the Great Plains for the past quarter century. Late that month, accompanied by the merchant caravan, they reached Bent's Fort, whose proprietors William and

Charles Bent abetted the campaign. When the troops and merchants left that trading post on the north bank of the Arkansas in early August and crossed the shallow river, they were entering territory claimed by Texas and the United States. But most still regarded it as Mexico. Young Susan Shelby Magoffin, who had wed trader Samuel Magoffin shortly before embarking on this arduous journey and suffered a miscarriage at Bent's Fort, described the crossing in her diary as a rite of passage, "separating me from my own dear native land. . . . Perhaps I have left it for not only the first, but the last time."[51]

The feeling among the traders and soldiers that they were in a foreign land grew stronger after they traversed Raton Pass and reached Las Vegas, the first substantial New Mexican settlement on the trail, where Kearny assembled the inhabitants and informed them through an interpreter that their country no longer belonged to them. "We consider it, and have done so for some time, a part of the territory of the United States," proclaimed the general, who went on to "absolve" his listeners "from all allegiance to the Mexican government." Kearny did not mention that Las Vegas, Santa Fe, and other New Mexican towns east of the Rio Grande were also considered part of Texas. In fact, his occupation raised a vexing question that would prove deeply divisive in years to come: whether American authorities would honor New Mexico's historical and cultural boundaries or place most of its settlements and inhabitants under the jurisdiction of Texans, whose past intrusions made New Mexicans wary of them.

As called for in his instructions from Polk, Kearny concluded the ceremony in Las Vegas by deputizing the town's alcalde, who served in effect as mayor, and two New Mexican militia captains as American officials and having them swear allegiance to the United States, a ceremony he adapted to appeal to Catholics by concluding the oath "in the name of the Father, Son, and Holy Ghost—Amen."[52] Captain Philip St. George Cooke, who served under Kearny, took a dim view of thrusting American citizenship on people he characterized scathingly as "mongrels who cannot read—who are almost heathens,—the great mass reared in real slavery, called peonism, but still imbued with enough patriotism to resent this outrage of being forced to swear an alien allegiance, by an officer who had just passed their frontier."[53] Cooke was wrong in describing the "great mass" of New Mexicans as peons and in equating peonage with "real slavery" as practiced in his native Virginia, but he rightly concluded that forcing American government and allegiance on them might breed resentment and defiance.

The American occupation of New Mexico went smoothly at first because Governor Manuel Armijo chose not to resist the invaders and withdrew southward with those few troops he considered battle-worthy. Kearny served briefly in Santa Fe as military governor and drew up a law code for New Mexicans. Based partly on the laws of Missouri and Texas, the code made no mention of slavery but stated that those serving as trial jurors should be "free male citizens of the territory."[54] Kearny prepared to depart for California with his dragoons in late September by designating Charles Bent as civil governor. Bent had a New Mexican wife and associates in Taos, but he also had bitter enemies there among New Mexicans and Pueblo Indians who feared losing out under American rule, which he came to personify. At odds with an influential priest, Padre Antonio José Martínez, and others in Taos, he had written recently that Mexicans were "not fit to be free, they should be ruled by others than themselves. . . . The Mexican caracter is made up of stupidity, Obstanacy, Ignorance duplicity and vanity."[55]

Bent's appointment did not bode well for the peaceful occupation envisioned by Polk and Benton. And as governor he would have to maintain order without the presence of Kearny and other officers. Colonel Doniphan and his regiment would head south in November on El Camino Real, the old royal road to Chihuahua, along which his troops would repulse two sharp challenges from Mexican troops wielding inferior weaponry. Doniphan's forces would be replaced in New Mexico by the Second Regiment of Missouri Mounted Volunteers under Colonel Sterling Price, a stern commander and future Confederate general who would repay blows struck against American occupiers several times over. Soon after Kearny departed for California, Cooke set out for San Diego along a different route with the Mormon Battalion—volunteers who hoped their service would help win official American support for a homeland in the West for Mormons who had recently fled Nauvoo, Illinois. (In 1847, Brigham Young would select a site for their new Zion along the Great Salt Lake.) Polk, for his part, hoped by enlisting Mormons to "attach them to our country, & prevent them from taking part against us."[56]

Kearny and his dragoons had not ventured far beyond Santa Fe in early October when they encountered a raucous party of mountain men serving as American scouts under Kit Carson, who had accompanied Frémont to California and was returning east with dispatches. He told Kearny that California had been secured by Commodore Robert F. Stockton, who had relieved Commodore Sloat at Monterey in July, enlisted Frémont's Bear Flag rebels as regular American troops, and prompted commandant Castro and Governor Pico to withdraw from California without doing battle. Anticipating no opposition, Kearny sent most of his men back to Santa Fe before proceeding west with one hundred dragoons, unaware that an uprising was under way in Los Angeles against the overbearing Lieutenant Gillespie, placed in charge there by Stockton. Among the insurgents was the departed governor's brother, Andrés Pico, who led a company of mounted lancers. They were guarding a pass in California's coastal range at San Pasqual when Kearny approached late that year. His overeager dragoons, some of them mounted on mules, rushed into battle early on December 6 against foes he later described as "the best horsemen in the world," who feigned a retreat before turning on the Americans and thrusting with their lances.[57] Kearny held his ground at San Pasqual after Pico's resilient company rode off, but eighteen of his dragoons were killed and nearly as many wounded. Army surgeon John Griffin, who treated the wounded, wrote that "we suffered most terribly in this action."[58]

Kearny then joined forces with Stockton, who had landed in San Diego with reinforcements and was preparing to reclaim Los Angeles, where the insurgents made their last stand in January 1847 before laying down their arms. Frémont, who was approaching Los Angeles from the north with several hundred men, met with leaders of the uprising at Cahuenga Pass and concluded a peace treaty stating that no Mexican citizen would have to pledge allegiance to the United States while it remained at war with Mexico. He was subsequently appointed governor by Stockton and sided with him in a bitter jurisdictional dispute with Kearny, who asserted his authority, ousted Frémont as governor, and charged him with insubordination, for which he was later court-martialed. In a proclamation to Californios, Kearny negated Fremont's assurance that they could remain loyal to their country in wartime by absolving them "from any further allegiance to the republic of Mexico" and pronouncing them "citizens of the United States." Referring to frequent power struggles in Hispanic California, Kearny stated that "civil wars have been the poisoned fountains which have sent forth trouble and pestilence over her beautiful land. Now those fountains are dried up; the star-spangled banner floats over California."[59] Yet Kearny engaged in his own power struggle with Stockton and Frémont, and the American conquest of California would not bring an end to trouble or civil strife.

Soon after armed resistance to American occupiers ended in California, Governor Charles Bent came under attack in Taos after traveling there from Santa Fe without a military escort. He had recently suppressed a planned uprising by New Mexicans in the capital, for which one suspect later won acquittal in a military court when the American officer defending him argued that he was innocent of treason, having never pledged allegiance to the United States. But Bent faced more determined opposition in Taos, and those who defied him would not be spared retribution. Upon arriving in his hometown, he refused demands that he release men from Taos Pueblo who had been jailed for theft and were subject to justice as administered by Sheriff Stephen L. Lee and others linked to Bent. On January 19, defiant Pueblos and New Mexicans took up arms and killed Bent, Lee, and three other men associated with the governor. The uprising spread to other settlements in northern New Mexico, where a number of Americans were slain. Colonel Price responded with a punishing campaign, during which he clashed twice with New Mexicans on the road to Taos before attacking insurgents holed up in the church at Taos Pueblo, where 150 of them died in a battle that cost Price over 50 casualties and left that ancient Pueblo community in mourning.

Thus ended tragically what had been touted as a peaceful takeover. "The number of troops engaged was comparatively small," Polk wrote when he learned of Price's battle at Taos, "but I consider this victory one of the most signal which has been gained during the War."[60] Harder campaigns were waged and bloodier battles fought as U.S. troops led by Zachary Taylor and Winfield Scott penetrated the Mexican core, an invasion whose ultimate purpose was to compel Mexico to yield formally by treaty what it had lost to Kearny and other American officers before Scott's forces entered Mexico City in September 1847. Such was the indemnity demanded by Polk. But a price would be exacted from Americans as well for the land, lives, and liberties they took while expanding their domain. The nation would pay dearly for the vast new territories it forcibly acquired when its elected representatives could no longer agree where to draw the line between freedom and slavery there.

CHAPTER 11

Wilmot's Proviso and the Free Soil Movement

E ven as Polk prosecuted the war, he hoped to bring it to a swift conclusion by inducing Mexican leaders to cede territory extending to the Pacific. Having been informed that Santa Anna planned to return to Mexico and was willing to come to terms with the United States, Polk allowed him to pass through the U.S. naval blockade of Veracruz in early August 1846 and reach that port on Mexico's Gulf Coast. Polk also requested an appropriation of $2 million from Congress for negotiating a boundary with Mexico, which he would compensate for yielding territory beyond the Rio Grande. He intended those funds as a down payment for concessions made either by Paredes, who resigned as president under pressure in late July, or by Santa Anna, whom Polk expected to regain power once he returned to Mexico. In that case, the $2 million would enable Santa Anna to pay his troops and suppress Mexican opposition to ceding territory. No Mexican leaders who yielded to the United States, Polk wrote, would "long maintain power unless they could receive, at the time of making the treaty, money enough to support the army."[1] Polk lost his bet on Santa Anna, who after landing at Veracruz went on to lead troops against American forces. Furthermore, the funds requested for boundary negotiations provoked a defiant response in Congress from a Democrat deemed loyal to the administration, Representative David Wilmot of Pennsylvania, who exasperated Polk by linking the war effort to slavery.

Since taking his seat in the House in 1845, Wilmot had backed Polk by approving the annexation of Texas and the war that resulted, endorsing the Oregon treaty with Britain—to which many other northern Democrats objected because it retreated from the party's pledge to acquire everything up to 54°40'—and backing a substantially lower tariff that diminished protection for industries in Pennsylvania and other northern states. There was little industry in Wilmot's district, but that stance exposed him to withering criticism in the state capital. "This recreant son who basely betrayed Pennsylvania's interests and voted with the other free traders should be banished from her territory," declared the *Harrisburg Telegraph*. "His infamous treachery should be revenged by disowning and turning him upon the South for support."[2] Wilmot's willingness to side with Polk and other southern Democrats on Texas and the reduced tariff may have earned him the right to speak when the House took up the $2 million appropriation bill on the evening of August 8, 1846, shortly before the first session of the Twenty-Ninth Congress adjourned. Hugh White of New York, a Whig who opposed slavery and its extension, opened the debate by calling Mr. Polk's War "unnecessary, uncalled for, and wholly unjustifiable." The House had already granted the president $30 million to wage war, noted White, who suspected that Polk wanted additional funds so he could bribe Mexican leaders to admit defeat and cede territory:

> Is the mode of warfare to be changed from fighting to purchasing? Who is to be bought? . . . Is this to be a corruption fund in the hands of the President, to use at his pleasure and discretion? . . . I have no confidence in this application for money; territory is what is sought after, and I cannot give my sanction to this appropriation, unless the bill now upon your table shall be so amended as to forever preclude the possibility of extending the limits of slavery.

White concluded by calling "on the other side of the House to propose such an amendment." He may have been aware that some Democrat who shared his views might do so. But the Democrat serving as chairman of the proceedings that night had no reason to suspect that Wilmot would embarrass Polk by raising the contentious issue of slavery and called on him to speak. The thirty-two-year-old Pennsylvanian began by affirming his support for the war, which he considered "necessary and proper," and stating that he had been willing to admit Texas as a slave state "because slavery had already been established there." But if Polk was seeking funds to acquire "free territory," where slavery was prohibited under Mexican law, Wilmot would not be complicit in "planting this institution upon it." He then introduced an amendment providing that "neither slavery nor involuntary servitude shall ever exist" in any territory obtained from Mexico, except for those duly convicted of crime.[3] The House adopted Wilmot's amendment as part of the appropriations bill along sectional rather than party lines, with nearly all northern Democrats and Whigs in favor. Stephen Douglas was one of the few northerners to vote against the bill with the proviso attached.

Known thereafter as the Wilmot Proviso, that historic amendment was in fact a collective effort by Wilmot and several other northern Democrats, including Representatives Preston King of New York, Jacob Brinkerhoff of Ohio, and James Thompson of Pennsylvania. Brinkerhoff later claimed that he drafted the proviso, but Wilmot said it was "the result of our united labors."[4] Its authorship mattered little because it was based on the Northwest Ordinance of 1787. A similar amendment based on that ordinance, which prohibited slavery in Oregon Territory, had been proposed a few days earlier by Thompson and approved by a wide margin in the House with the consent of more than a few southerners. Neither Thompson's proviso nor Wilmot's became law because the Senate adjourned without acting on the Oregon bill or the $2 million bill. But Wilmot's amendment had far-reaching implications because his fellow northern Democrats in the House broke with southerners in their party, whose leadership was consistently proslavery. If those free-state Democrats formed a durable antislavery alliance with northern Whigs, who had opposed annexing Texas, that coalition could dominate the House, where congressmen from the less populous South were outnumbered.

Some Democrats who backed the Wilmot Proviso were motivated less by an aversion to slavery, however, than by disdain for Polk's tariff bill, his willingness to compromise with Britain over Oregon while risking war with Mexico, and his perceived indifference to the party's disaffected Van Buren faction, to which Wilmot and his associates belonged. Still smarting over the rejection of their candidate at the Democratic convention in 1844, Van Burenites faulted Polk for not granting them enough cabinet or patronage positions and for exposing them to abuse from antislavery northerners as lackeys of an administration beholden to the South and its slaveholders. Van Buren's defiant supporters in New York, known as Barnburners for tactics rival Democrats there considered incendiary, distanced themselves from the administration by endorsing the Wilmot Proviso. That rift in the former Jackson–Van Buren alliance between southern and northern Democrats alarmed Polk, as did any suggestion that his war effort involved slavery.

Not about to concede to defiant northern Democrats, Polk raised the stakes by requesting $3 million for negotiations with Mexico during the second session of the Twenty-Ninth Congress, which convened in December 1846. Undeterred,

Preston King and Wilmot broadened the proviso to prohibit slavery in "any territory on the continent of America which shall hereafter be acquired by or annexed to the United States." That was blocked in the Senate, where southerners had more leverage than in the House. During the session, Wilmot met with Polk, who told him that he opposed linking the objectionable proviso to the appropriation bill because those funds would help bring peace with Mexico. As Wilmot recalled, Polk claimed that he did not want slavery "extended one foot beyond its present limits; that he was conscious it could not be done without endangering the peace and safety of the Union."[5] Whether he meant that or just said that to suggest there was no need for the proviso, Polk stood firm against any legislative language on slavery in territory acquired from Mexico, which suited those southerners who did not want any restriction on slavery there.

In March 1847, under pressure from the administration, the House fell into line with the Senate by narrowly voting to strip the proviso from the $3 million appropriation. Addressing the House in February before that vote was cast, Wilmot countered charges that he was promoting abolitionism: "I have stood up at home, and battled, time and again, against the Abolitionists of the North. I have assailed them publicly, on all occasions, when it was proper to do so. . . . Sir, I was in favor of the annexation of Texas. I supported it with my whole influence and strength. . . . The Democracy of the North, almost to a man, went for annexation. Yes, sir, here was an empire larger than France given up to slavery. Shall further concessions be made by the North? Shall we give up free territory, the inheritance of free labor? Must we yield this also? Never, sir, never, until we ourselves are fit to be slaves."

Americans engaged in actual or rhetorical conflicts often equated yielding to their foes with enslavement. Patrick Henry had implored colonists not to be slaves to the British, and that cry was taken up by Texans who rebelled against Mexican rule and later by secessionists who warned that President Lincoln and his fellow Republicans in Congress would reduce white southerners to slaves. Wilmot spoke to that same anxiety among northerners who resented southern dominance of leadership positions in Congress and the presidency (held by men from slave states during all but a few terms since Washington assumed that office). Unlike those southerners who believed that white liberty and equality depended on Black slavery, he argued that free white labor could be honored and protected only in free territory, where there were no slaves to degrade such labor. "I have no squeamish sensitiveness upon the subject of slavery," he declared, "no morbid sympathy for the slave. I plead the cause and the rights of white freemen.

I would preserve to free white labor a fair country, a rich inheritance, where the sons of toil, of my own race and own color, can live without the disgrace which association with negro slavery brings upon white labor. . . . Where the negro slave labors, the free white man cannot labor by his side without sharing in his degradation and disgrace."[6]

Such were the views of many who joined the emerging free-soil movement as the nation reckoned with the consequences of Mr. Polk's War. Like Wilmot, they deplored not just economic competition from Black slaves but their very presence. Indeed, preserving what Wilmot called "a fair country" for those of his own race and color could mean excluding not only slaves but also Black people who were free or seeking freedom, as indicated by statutes prohibiting or discouraging them from settling in various northern states. Some free-soilers opposed such strictures against African Americans, and many later joined the new Republican Party, as Wilmot did, and made common cause with those who sympathized with slaves and hoped to emancipate them. Wilmot called slavery "a great social and political evil" when addressing the House in February 1847 and stated later that year, as Lincoln would subsequently, that prohibiting its extension to American territories would ultimately cause it to expire in the South and thus ensure "the redemption of the Negro from his bondage in chains."[7] As indicated when Wilmot spoke of "degradation and disgrace," however, the free-soil movement originated as a defiant response to the Slave Power, which meant keeping free territories unpolluted by slave owners as well as those they enslaved, whose proximity was deemed powerful enough to demean white workers.

An Unsettling Victory

The Wilmot Proviso was never enacted, but it focused attention keenly on the divisive issue of slavery in lands acquired during the war. As Wilmot pointed out, northerners as well as southerners paid in blood for those acquisitions, and that made the issue more contentious than if they were obtained peacefully through purchase. By early 1847 American forces were delving deeper into Mexico and suffering significant casualties in battle and substantial losses to dysentery, yellow fever, and other diseases. In February, Zachary Taylor's troops advanced from Monterrey and repulsed Santa Anna's army in a close-fought battle at Buena Vista, impelling Santa Anna to pull back to his capital. In March, Winfield Scott's forces landed near Veracruz and bombarded the port, taking a steep toll among the populace there before advancing on Mexico City. Other Mexican civilians

Winfield Scott's forces landing at Veracruz, March 9, 1847. Courtesy Library of Congress Prints and Photographs Division (LC-USZ62-14216).

were attacked by vengeful American troops, including Texans who regarded this conflict as an extension of their border war with Mexico. Taylor complained of "outrages committed by the Texas volunteers" and had little sympathy for their state's claim to New Mexican territory thereafter.[8] Scott was alarmed by attacks on his forces by Mexican partisans and wary of prolonging the conflict to secure additional territory that would bring American occupiers nothing but trouble, a feeling shared by some on the home front who viewed Mexico as not worth the price paid to conquer it.

In Washington, Sarah Polk—who served as an astute political aide to her husband while also performing social functions expected of her as First Lady—paid a visit to a mother who lost her son in the war and proved inconsolable. "Tell me madam, if you can," she asked, "for what was this wicked war brought upon our country? Why was my noble son sent to be murdered in that barbarous country?"[9] James Polk received a reproving letter in January 1847 from a correspondent identifying herself as a "Quaker Woman" who wrote: "Have not thousands of thy fellow men within the last year been strewn on the field of battle, and the cries of the widdow and the captive gone up before that God whom thou professes to serve. . . . And, art thou not accessory to these evils?" A more scathing rebuke arrived for him in the mail that April—an inscribed leather medal proclaiming

Polk "the great American Caesar" for his "bloody conquests in Mexico," including the slaughter of "defenseless women and children at the siege of Vera Cruz."[10]

Some Americans hoped that all of Mexico would be conquered and annexed, but others abhorred that prospect, among them John Calhoun. On February 9, 1847, soon after Wilmot addressed the House on behalf of free labor in free territory, Calhoun warned the Senate against conquering a country the Union could not absorb without drastic consequences. "Mexico is to us the forbidden fruit; the penalty of eating it would be to subject our institutions to political death," he declared. (That was one of the few opinions he held in common with an ardent opponent of the war, Ralph Waldo Emerson, who wrote that "Mexico will poison us.") Calhoun did not want the nation to absorb millions of Mexicans "so dissimilar from us in every respect—so little qualified for free and popular government." A more pressing concern for him, however, was how to incorporate Mexican territory without sectional strife. "Shall it be for the benefit of one part of the Union to the exclusion of the other?" he asked. If northerners sought to deny the South and its slaveholders "all benefit in the acquired territory," then they would insist on their right to share in the fruits of conquest. "Be assured," he warned northerners, "if there be stern determination on one side to exclude us, there will be determination still sterner on ours, not to be excluded."[11]

Calhoun went to the heart of the matter that would plague the Union until it broke apart fourteen years later. But he failed to acknowledge that Americans had already eaten forbidden fruit by occupying Mexican territory from the Rio Grande to the Pacific—land he favored holding by adopting a defensive strategy until Mexico ceded that territory. His proposal to avoid further conquest would not avert the political struggle he anticipated. That conflict was already under way, as indicated by his insistence that slave owners have unrestricted access to occupied territories such as New Mexico and California from which free-soilers hoped to bar them. Benton, in his memoirs, cited a letter in which Calhoun credited the Wilmot Proviso with "forcing the issue," which Benton believed meant forcing southerners to consider separating from the Union unless they were granted the right to settle with slaves in any American territory, even if it lay north of the line formed by the Missouri Compromise. In Benton's view, Calhoun was carrying nullification, which he had asserted to justify South Carolina's rejection of the federal tariff, to calamitous extremes by proposing to nullify a compromise that kept the nation intact. Benton faulted Wilmot, on the other hand, for abetting the abolitionist cause that he professed to disdain. "Truly the abolitionists and the nullifiers were necessary to each other," wrote

Benton. They were like "the two halves of a pair of shears, neither of which could cut until joined together," which might then allow them to sever the Union.[12]

Both Wilmot and Calhoun had reason to worry when defeat loomed for Mexico and it risked losing additional territory to the United States where slavery might then be allowed or prohibited by Congress. Even before Polk learned that Mexico City had fallen to Scott's forces in September 1847, he told his cabinet that if Mexico remained obstinate he was "decidedly in favour of insisting on the acquisition of more territory."[13] He would not go as far as Treasury Secretary Robert Walker, who had agitated for "reannexation" of Texas and now favored taking all of Mexico. But in October Polk recalled Nicholas P. Trist, whom he had dispatched to negotiate with Mexico but concluded was too soft to drive a hard territorial bargain. Trist ignored the letter recalling him and signed a treaty at Guadalupe Hidalgo on February 2, 1848, that settled for Polk's original objectives. It established what would become the enduring Mexican-American boundary following the Gadsden Purchase Treaty, concluded in 1854, which added slightly to the vast area acquired from Mexico under the treaty ending the war. Polk was furious with Trist but submitted to the Senate the pact he negotiated, which secured a monumental cession for $15 million—less than Polk was originally prepared to offer and far less than the deal was worth to Americans as mineral wealth was uncovered in the ceded Mexican territory.

That the nation's continental ambitions were satisfied without a deeper and more divisive conquest of Mexico suited Secretary of State Buchanan, although he had argued in cabinet meetings for seeking more territory. He hoped to be nominated to succeed Polk at the Democratic convention in Baltimore in May 1848. Like Polk, he favored extending the Missouri Compromise line to the Pacific and thought that would be equitable within the nation's new boundaries, allowing Oregon to be organized as free territory, for example, while enabling slave owners to settle in New Mexico. But Buchanan's position alienated northern Democrats who backed the Wilmot Proviso as well as Calhounites who wanted no restriction on slavery anywhere in the Mexican Cession. Furthermore, California posed a problem because it would be bisected at 36°30' (a line reaching the Pacific near the town of Monterey). As it turned out, allowing slavery anywhere in California would be opposed by most of those who rushed there by land or by sea after gold was discovered at Sutter's Mill in January 1848 and subsequent strikes were publicized. Some slaveholders entered California during the gold rush, bringing with them more than one thousand enslaved people by some estimates. But they and their owners were unwelcome in goldfields, where nonslaveholding white fortune seekers abhorred such competition and often resented working near people of other races or nations. Thomas Jefferson Green, a venturesome Texan who with others from his state staked claims in California worked by more than a dozen of their slaves, was warned by an opposing prospector to leave the diggings "or by tomorrow morning you will not have one slave left, for the miners will run them out and you will never get them back."[14]

That California might pose an obstacle to extending the Missouri Compromise line to the Pacific was not foreseen when Buchanan proposed doing so. But the precise divide he favored proved less appealing to Democrats seeking middle ground between the positions staked by Wilmot and Calhoun than the vague compromise backed by Senator Lewis Cass of Michigan, who had served as secretary of war under President Jackson. Cass endorsed popular sovereignty, or allowing the inhabitants of American territories to decide whether to permit or prohibit slavery there. He did not indicate just how or when they would make that crucial decision. A senator close to Cass, Daniel S. Dickinson of New York, argued that territorial legislatures could decide the matter. But Calhoun and his cohorts insisted that not until a territory applied for statehood and drafted a constitution could it prohibit slavery, which would thus have more time to take hold there before its fate was determined. Calhoun did not want territories ceded by Mexico allowed to make that determination while they were still largely populated by Mexicans, whom he assumed were "all abolitionists" because their government had prohibited slavery.[15] "Popular sovereignty" was a new term for a concept at least as old as the American Revolution, when colonists asserted their right to self-government. When applied to slavery, it meant shifting a problem that bedeviled the nation's elected leaders in Washington to remote territories, where those who could not resolve the issue with ballots might resort to bullets. By settling nothing when enacted, however, it offered those on either side of the debate over slavery in the Mexican Cession something: hope of prevailing eventually in places where their cause might be lost if the Missouri Compromise line was extended.

In years to come, Stephen Douglas would surpass Cass as a proponent of popular sovereignty. But in 1848 the sixty-five-year-old Cass was more prominent and opportunistic than the thirty-five-year-old Douglas, who was new to the Senate. Both were avid expansionists, but Douglas favored taking all of Mexico before he and others in Washington learned of the Treaty of Guadalupe Hidalgo, whereas Cass altered his position and opposed doing so. Douglas considered that stance "unwise as an act of patriotism as well as policy" and voted against the treaty, while Cass helped provide the two-thirds majority in the Senate required to ratify it.[16] Cass proved more attuned than Douglas to their fellow Democrats, most of whom opposed a larger land grab in Mexico either to avoid absorbing its racially diverse and presumably antislavery populace or to avoid acquiring more territory where slavery might be introduced. Cass's endorsement of popular sovereignty helped him prevail at a Democratic convention that opposed both the Wilmot Proviso—which he had once favored but now pledged to veto if adopted by Congress—and the Alabama Platform, a guarantee for slavery in the Mexican Cession backed by William Lowndes Yancey, a future secessionist who if he could not make the party adamantly proslavery would break the party.

Whigs, for their part, had tried to avoid controversy by urging that no Mexican territory be annexed, a proposal advanced by two Georgians, Senator John M. Berrien and Representative Alexander H. Stephens, who hoped to reconcile northern and southern Whigs at odds over the Wilmot Proviso. Endorsed by prominent northern Whigs such as Senators Daniel Webster of Massachusetts and Thomas Corwin of Ohio, who said he feared disunion within his party "as much as dismemberment of the States," that "No Territory" option was nullified by the treaty Trist negotiated.[17] But Whigs continued to skirt the dispute over slavery in the Mexican Cession by nominating for president a war hero who took no stand on that issue, Zachary Taylor. Most southern Whigs assumed that Taylor, a slaveholder from Louisiana, would oppose an outright prohibition of slavery in territory acquired from Mexico of the sort applied to Oregon, which Congress organized as a free territory in August 1848. Some northern Whigs were reassured by the fact that Taylor was backed by Senator William Seward of New York, an antislavery stalwart, and had a running mate from that pivotal state, Millard Fillmore. That was not enough to soothe so-called Conscience Whigs like Charles Francis Adams, who upheld the principles of his recently deceased father, John Quincy Adams, by refusing to support a candidate who remained mute on the issue of slavery and might extend that deplorable institution. Adams joined the incipient Free Soil Party and became the running mate of its presidential nominee, Martin Van Buren, who ran under the slogan "Free Soil, Free Speech, Free Labor, and Free Men."[18]

Some of Van Buren's Barnburners who bolted the 1848 Democratic Convention and helped form the Free Soil Party were more interested in repaying Democrats for spurning him in 1844 than in halting the spread of slavery. But many were angered by Cass's rejection of the Wilmot Proviso, an amendment they hailed in print as shielding any Mexican territory acquired by the United

States "from the pollution of slavery."[19] That statement, drafted by Van Buren, contrasted with his tolerance for the South's peculiar institution as president. Long intent on suppressing sectional differences, he accentuated them when his new party absorbed the Liberty Party and adopted a platform urging no more slave states or territories and an end to slavery in the District of Columbia. The Free Soil campaign thus brought those like Wilmot who wanted western territories reserved for free white labor under the same tent with abolitionists Wilmot had recently deplored.

Assailing the Slave Power

Merging with the Free Soil Party brought an end to the Liberty Party, whose chief legacy was to make the Slave Power a vivid threat, against which ardent abolitionists and free-soilers with little concern for Black people could unite in opposition. One of the first public figures to apply that term to slave owners and their representatives was Thomas Morris of Ohio, the Liberty Party vice presidential candidate in 1844 and a former Jacksonian Democrat who denounced the Slave Power as intently as he did the so-called Money Power that Jackson assailed when he targeted the national bank. Morris had departed the U.S. Senate in 1839 with a defiant farewell speech in which he defended the right of abolitionists to speak freely without being attacked—and to submit petitions to Congress without having them tabled, as were those he presented to the Senate even though it had no formal gag rule. Unlike Wilmot, Morris openly sympathized with enslaved people and lamented their plight, but he anticipated the free-soil movement by portraying the Slave Power as a menace not just to those in bondage but to free labor and free speech. "I am not now contending for the rights of the negro—rights which his Creator gave him, and which his fellow-man has usurped or taken away," he declared. "No, sir; I am contending for the rights of the white person in the free States, and am endeavoring to prevent them from being trodden down and destroyed by that power which claims the black person as *property*."[20]

Foes of the gag rule, who considered it a violation of the First Amendment right to "petition the Government for a redress of grievances," were further antagonized in 1840 when Congressman William Cost Johnson, a Whig from Maryland, succeeded in requiring that antislavery petitions not even be received in the House. Johnson added insult to injury by advising women who signed and submitted such petitions to "attend to knitting their own hose and darning their stockings, rather than come there and unsex themselves, be laid on the table, and sent to a committee to be reported on."[21] The gag rule was repealed in 1844 by the House, in which representatives from free states formed an increasing majority. But proslavery southerners and northerners allied with them retained their grip on the Senate, the presidency, and the federal judiciary. The annexation of Texas and other Mexican territories to which Calhounites insisted that slaveholders be admitted suggested to many in the North that the Slave Power was on the rise.

Editor Joshua Leavitt, a leading member of the Liberty Party, understood that antipathy to the Slave Power could link abolitionists not just to Whigs and Democrats morally opposed to slavery but to those northerners who viewed southern expansionism as a threat to their own territorial ambitions and political interests, which were closely linked because territories could eventually become states and alter the balance of power in Washington. Members of that larger group also cared about free labor and free speech, but it was free soil that mattered most to them when they opposed the Slave Power. Wilmot spoke for them when he declared before the House in February 1847: "Free territory shall not be fettered, it shall not be trampled upon; it is ours, and we will hold on to it with a grasp that shall bid defiance to the slave power."[22] As Leavitt wrote in July 1848: "The *Slave Power* is now indissolubly incorporated in the political nomenclature of this country, & will be inscribed indelibly upon the historic page. We must make the most of that word." It was not necessary "that they who use it should ever know who taught it to them," he added, "but the incessant use of the term will do much to open the eyes & arouse the energies of the people."[23]

To expand their struggle against the Slave Power, Leavitt and other prominent Liberty Party abolitionists cast their lot with the Free Soil Party and backed Van Buren. One Liberty Party principle not upheld by the new party they joined was civil rights for free Blacks. Several Black abolitionists, including Frederick Douglass, Henry W. Bibb, and Samuel R. Ward, attended the Free Soil convention at Buffalo in August 1848, and Douglass and Bibb addressed the gathering. But their insistence that true emancipation meant acknowledging freedmen as full-fledged American citizens found little support among Van Buren's Barnburners, viewed by Ward as opportunists who espoused liberty but would "rob black men of their rights."[24] Douglass did not join the Free Soil Party but eventually endorsed its ticket, signaling that he was no longer strictly aligned with the radical abolitionist William Lloyd Garrison, who thought nothing worthwhile could be accomplished politically under a U.S. Constitution that shielded slavery and who would burn a copy of that document publicly. Some abolitionists who doubted that Van Buren was truly antislavery backed Gerrit Smith, presidential candidate of the Liberty League, which had recently separated from the Liberty Party. Smith garnered few votes but distinguished his campaign by advocating universal suffrage regardless of race or gender—a cause advanced by his cousin, abolitionist and feminist Elizabeth Cady Stanton, who figured prominently at the first American convention for women's rights, held at Seneca Falls, New York, one month before the Free Soil convention.

In the presidential election that fall, Van Buren received nearly three hundred thousand votes, almost five times the Liberty Party tally in 1844 and 10 percent of the popular vote nationwide. Enough Conscience Whigs abandoned Taylor for Van Buren and Adams in Ohio to tip that state to the Democrat Cass. But the defection of Democrats to the Free Soil campaign in New York, the Barnburner stronghold, helped Taylor win that state—one of three along with Massachusetts and Vermont where Van Buren finished second, ahead of Cass—and boosted the tight-lipped Whig nominee to victory.

News of Taylor's triumph added to the despondency of outgoing President Polk, who rather than basking in a military victory that extended the nation across the continent was distressed to find Congress more resistant to his leadership than when he entered the White House. As he remarked to his cabinet in December 1848, he feared that no action would be taken during "the present session of Congress for the Government of California & New Mexico" and worried that those territories "might be lost to the Union." He regarded Whigs as akin to the Federalists who had opposed Jefferson and the Louisiana Purchase. When Congress reconvened under the next president in 1849, Polk predicted, "the leading Federalists (alias Whigs) would be glad to avail themselves of the opportunity to give up the country [acquired from Mexico] for the purpose of relieving Gen'l Taylor of his embarrassments upon the Wilmot Proviso." Polk never admitted that the issue raised by Wilmot was worth quarreling over. "What connection slavery had with making peace with Mexico it is difficult to conceive," he wrote when he first learned of the proviso in August 1846." In January 1847, as debate over the proviso intensified, he denounced it even more emphatically. "Slavery has no possible connection with the Mexican War," he complained. "Its introduction in connection with the Mexican War is not only mischievous but wicked." Slavery would "probably never exist" in New Mexico or California, he added, "and therefore the question would never arise."[25] By endorsing extension of the Missouri Compromise line to the Pacific before he left office, however, he proposed allowing slavery in a large part of California and nearly all of New Mexico. And by upholding the claim of Texas to Santa Fe and other New Mexican settlements east of the Rio Grande prior to the war, Polk had tacitly acknowledged the right of Texans and other southerners to introduce Black bondage there even if the Missouri Compromise line was not extended.

In a message to the House of Representatives in July 1848, Polk obscured the fact that he had sided unequivocally with Texas in its boundary dispute with Mexico. With newfound impartiality, he stated that the state's claim to eastern New Mexico was never confirmed by "actual occupancy and possession." Until the war ended by treaty, Polk remarked, "New Mexico never became an undisputed portion of the United States, and it would therefore have been premature to deliver over to Texas that portion of it on the east side of the Rio Grande, to which she asserted a claim." He believed that claim to be "well founded," but he cited a letter sent at his direction to the governor of Texas in 1847 indicating that the boundary question "more properly belongs to the legislative than the executive branch of the Government."[26] Before the war began, however, he had ignored the joint resolution of Congress making the admission of Texas subject to the adjustment "of all questions of boundary with other Governments." Heedless of the legislative branch, he had pledged to defend the boundary claimed by Texas in its entirety despite Mexico's objections, thus encouraging Texans to approve annexation. Many of them considered that commitment binding on the government when the war ended—and some would threaten to fight for eastern New Mexico if denied possession by those in Congress opposed to extending slavery there under Texas jurisdiction.

Politically shrewd in other respects, Polk appeared oblivious to the implications of his expansionist agenda for a nation convulsed by slavery. He tried to distance himself from that topic publicly even as he continued to purchase slaves for his Mississippi plantation privately. That he feared disapproval should those purchases become known was indicated by his instructions to his agent to act discreetly and the fact that he avoided using his salary as president to obtain slaves. Polk's reluctance to admit that his private actions and public policies furthered slavery was not unusual among politically prominent planters, but his evasiveness, defensiveness, and duplicity marred his presidency and his legacy. The territory he acquired during his four years in the White House, including Oregon, Texas, and the Mexican Cession, surpassed what Jefferson gained through the Louisiana Purchase. But Polk would not be celebrated by Americans in posterity, in part because the crisis that shattered the Union in 1861 stemmed from a war he waged without acknowledging its true causes or perilous consequences.

"Death of Lt. Col. Henry Clay, Jr., at Buena Vista." Lithograph by Butler and Lewis.
Library of Congress Prints and Photographs Division (LC-USZ62-15642).

Polk's reputation suffered lasting damage when he drew the nation into war by
declaring that Mexicans had shed American blood on American soil. That claim
was questioned not only by later historians but also by his skeptical contempo-
raries, including Abraham Lincoln, whose main concern as a representative in
the Thirtieth Congress, which convened in December 1847, was to demonstrate
that the spot on which the war began was in fact Mexican soil, to which neither
Texas nor the United States then had rightful claim. Lincoln's "Spot Resolutions"
did not address slavery, and he was not yet staunchly antislavery like some of
his fellow northern Whigs. A great admirer of Henry Clay, he would long favor
efforts to colonize emancipated slaves abroad, which Clay advocated. But Lincoln
was also greatly influenced by a fervent speech against the war and the extension
of slavery that he heard Clay deliver at Lexington, Kentucky, in November 1847,
nine months after Clay's eldest son, Henry Jr., died while leading a Kentucky
regiment in battle at Buena Vista. Clay denounced Whigs as well as Democrats
in Congress for approving a war resolution that falsely blamed Mexico for the
"deadly and unprofitable" conflict that ensued. Congress should disavow as he
did, Clay told an audience that included many slave owners, any intention of
acquiring Mexican territory "for the purpose of introducing slavery into it."[27] To
that end, Lincoln backed the Wilmot Proviso after taking his seat in the House,

and he faulted Polk for enforcing the provocative boundary claim of slaveholding Texas. "I more than suspect already," he said of Polk before the House, "that he is deeply conscious of being in the wrong; that he feels the blood of this war, like the blood of Abel, is crying to Heaven against him."[28]

Polk would not admit to any such offense, but Lincoln was arguing figuratively that he had misled Congress and bore responsibility for the bloodshed by assailing a kindred republic (known formally as the United States of Mexico) much as Cain had assailed his brother Abel. In applying that biblical analogy, Lincoln may also have been alluding to a prophetic warning voiced by some who opposed Mr. Polk's War: that seizing Mexican territory would aggravate sectional tensions and cause civil strife, pitting brother against brother. The mark that God placed on Cain after he shed Abel's blood was misinterpreted by some in Lincoln's time as a curse, supposedly bequeathed to Cain's enslaved African descendants in the form of dark skin. Lincoln may not have had that myth in mind when he spoke, but Polk's sternest critics viewed his accursed war as staining Americans with blood spilled wrongfully to uphold slavery. An editor in Ohio who linked Polk to the "slave oligarchy of the South" wrote that northern Democrats who submitted slavishly to his war effort "should be marked with the curse of Cain."[29]

Polk firmly believed that he served the interests of the nation as a whole by extending its dominion to the Pacific. Yet the controversial war he waged and its caustic aftermath took a heavy toll on him. Already in poor health, he contracted cholera and died three months after stepping down in March 1849, having left his mark on a nation whose citizens no longer viewed expansion as an unalloyed blessing. As his career drew to a close, he had reason to fear that compromises of the sort he praised in his inaugural address as enabling "our fathers to form a common Constitution" might not be capable of closing the rift between North and South—a gap that widened and deepened as this nation dedicated to liberty and gravely compromised by slavery assumed continental proportions.

CHAPTER 12

Douglas's Southern Exposure
and Popular Sovereignty

The political ascent of Stephen A. Douglas followed the trajectory foreseen by Martin Van Buren when he envisioned the Democratic Party as an alliance between the plain Republicans of the North and the planters of the South. Born in 1813 on a farm in Vermont among staunch Republicans who scorned Federalists elsewhere in New England for opposing Mr. Madison's War against the British, Douglas came of age idolizing Andrew Jackson, headed west to practice law in Illinois, won election there to Congress as a Democrat at the age of thirty, and advanced to the Senate in 1847 as a supporter of Mr. Polk's War. By then, he had forged ties with the South not only politically by opposing the Wilmot Proviso but also personally by wedding Martha Martin of North Carolina, whose father had a plantation there and another in Mississippi, which he offered the couple as a wedding present.

Reluctant to be identified as a slave owner, Douglas declined that gift from Robert Martin but suggested it might be offered as a bequest. At his death in June 1848, Martin left the Mississippi plantation and the many enslaved people who labored there to Martha, to be bequeathed to her children at her death. Should she have no surviving offspring, Martin instructed that proceeds from the plantation be used to emancipate the slaves and send them to Liberia. "Nearly every head of a family among them have expressed to me a desire to belong to you and your children rather than go to Africa," he told Martha in his will. Yet he believed that they could not live peaceably among white people if emancipated and saw no alternative but to ship them to Africa if his daughter died childless. "To set them free where they are," he insisted, "would entail on them a greater curse."[1]

That bequest from his father-in-law entailed on Douglas advantages as well as liabilities. He was designated in Martin's will as manager of the plantation and earned 20 percent of its proceeds. Like Jefferson, Jackson, and Polk, he did not want to be viewed as mistreating slaves, and he received assurances to that effect from their overseer. They were in fine health, he wrote Douglas. The children were "increasing very fast & doing well," he claimed, and were "just as fat as you ever saw hogs."[2] Few plantations prospered, however, without overseers who whipped slaves if they lagged in their labors or tried to escape. The Douglases could say as Polk did that slavery was "entailed upon us by our ancestors," but they in turn entailed that curse on enslaved African Americans and their children.

Martha Douglas died in early 1853, shortly after giving birth to a daughter who did not long outlive her. Four years later, all 142 enslaved people under Douglas's management, valued at $113,300, were uprooted and set to the hard task of establishing a new plantation in Mississippi on land owned by his partner in that business, James A. McHatton. Douglas held his share of that plantation in trust for his two young sons by Martha, Robert and Stephen Jr., and left it in the hands of McHatton and overseers. Not until Douglas was informed by a merchant in Mississippi that slaves there were poorly fed and clothed and that some might "die if there is not a change in management" did he visit the plantation and revise his agreement with McHatton to specify that they be "properly cared for."[3] Robert and Stephen Douglas Jr. would later file suit seeking $250,000 in damages for more than a thousand five-hundred-pound bales of cotton and other goods confiscated by the Union Army during the Civil War from their property, which they described as one of Mississippi's "largest and most productive" plantations.[4] Those whose forced labor created that wealth were eligible for no such compensation.

That Douglas and his family were slaveholders did not go unnoticed. In 1850 he responded to a newspaper article describing him as an owner of slaves by stating that his wife had exclusive title to them and implying that he had little financial interest in her father's bequest. In 1855 he would rebut an accusation leveled by Senator Benjamin F. Wade of Ohio that Douglas's involvement in slavery influenced him politically. Wade quoted loosely from the Bible: "Where a man's treasure is, there will his heart be also." Douglas's reply was deceptive. "I am not the owner of a slave and never have been," he said, "nor have I ever received, and appropriated to my own use, one dollar earned by slave labor."[5] He described his father-in-law's bequest to his late wife and their two sons but made no mention of his share in the plantation's profits, which benefited him whether the income went for family expenses like his sons' education or for his own use. He could have denied that he had a "mercenary motive" for his policies more forthrightly by citing his legislative record. Before and after the bequest from his father-in-law, he backed measures favored by southerners such as the annexation of Texas while also serving northern interests by advancing bills to organize Oregon and Minnesota as free territories.

Douglas would go beyond that balancing act, however, by allowing slavery in territory where it had been forbidden under the Missouri Compromise and authorizing settlers and their elected legislators to decide whether to perpetuate or prohibit it—a policy he might not have advanced so boldly were he not conditioned to managing a plantation and complacent about holding Black people in bondage. By endorsing popular sovereignty, which gave southerners who controlled slave labor as he did access to American territories without ensuring that their peculiar institution would prevail there, he hoped to induce them to remain loyal Unionists and preserve the republic, an objective he said was "worth more to humanity than the whole black race."[6] As slavery's northern opponents and southern defenders grew increasingly fervent and intransigent, he would entrust that volatile issue to the inhabitants of newly organized territories—an expedient that he considered democratic and equitable but would further divide his party and nation.

The Grudging Compromise of 1850

Some northerners faulted Douglas for yielding to the South when he opposed the Wilmot Proviso and later endorsed popular sovereignty. Many southerners felt a similar sense of betrayal when newly elected President Zachary Taylor of Louisiana acted against the perceived interests of his section and fellow slaveholders. Not long after his inauguration in March 1849, Taylor declared in Pennsylvania that northerners "need have no apprehension of the further extension of slavery."[7] He saw no point in prolonging rancorous debate over admitting that institution to far western territories widely considered unsuitable for plantations of the sort worked by the more than one hundred enslaved people he owned. He hoped to end the stalemate in Congress over that issue by encouraging Californians and New Mexicans to hold conventions, adopt constitutions, and seek admission to the Union, entering as free states if they so wished. That inhabitants of a prospective state had the right to decide for or against slavery when they sought admission had been confirmed by Congress in Missouri's case, and the two would-be states favored by Taylor were both populous enough to join the Union. The gold rush had swelled California's non-Indian population from less than ten thousand before that upheaval began in 1848 to more than ninety thousand, of whom nearly one thousand were Black people, according to the 1850 census. New Mexico had been the most populous territory on Mexico's northern frontier and now had at least sixty thousand non-Native inhabitants, of whom only about two dozen were Black, according to the census.

Taylor sent emissaries to California and New Mexico to promote statehood. Californians needed little prompting and elected delegates to a constitutional convention that met at Monterey in late 1849. Although seventeen of the forty-eight delegates came from slave states, they bowed to the demand for free labor in the goldfields by resolving unanimously that neither slavery nor involuntary servitude, except for the punishment of crimes, "shall ever be tolerated in this State."[8] Taylor's urging had more impact on New Mexicans, who initially favored territorial status but would adopt a state constitution at Santa Fe in May 1850 that prohibited servitude for men aged twenty-one or older and women eighteen or older unless they were "bound by their own consent." That provision would allow New Mexicans to continue holding adults in peonage or debt servitude, including Indians who had been captured or purchased. But it was not meant to condone African American slavery, which the delegates called a "curse and a blight" inimical to New Mexico and "naturally impracticable" there.[9]

Lending urgency to that application for statehood was the fear that Santa Fe and other traditional Mexican settlements east of the Rio Grande might be seized by Texans, whose claim there had been endorsed by Polk prior to the Mexican-American War but was viewed skeptically by Taylor. He wanted New Mexico on either side of the Rio Grande to remain under the control of U.S. occupation forces until its status was determined by Congress and its boundary with Texas was delineated. In the meantime, he would not tolerate armed resistance to federal authority there by Texans, whose border dispute with New Mexico was among the hot issues that prompted calls for a convention of southern delegates to be held at Nashville in June 1850. Some who urged that convention were threatening secession if Texans seeking to enforce their Rio Grande boundary were opposed by U.S. troops, or if the nation's fifteen slave states were outnumbered by free states—as they would be if California was admitted—or if Congress prohibited slavery in territory ceded by Mexico by enacting the Wilmot Proviso.

Taylor reckoned that he could admit California and New Mexico as states without igniting conflict or secession if he stood firm against disunion, as Andrew Jackson did against the nullifiers in South Carolina. But this dispute was broader and deeper than that, and Jackson had been backed by Congress, which offered little comfort now to the politically inexperienced Taylor. He had alienated many southerners in his own party and had few allies among Democrats, who controlled the Senate and slightly outnumbered Whigs in the House, which also included several members of the Free Soil Party when Congress convened in December 1849 and embarked on its most tumultuous session since the Missouri crisis. Among those offering alternatives to Taylor's plan was Douglas. In the previous session, he had proposed admitting the entire Mexican Cession as a single state, which faltered for lack of support from northerners who wanted the Wilmot Proviso applied there and from southerners who feared that any such state would be dominated by Californians opposed to slavery. He now proposed territorial status for New Mexico as well as Deseret, the Mormon settlement along the Great Salt Lake that would be organized as Utah Territory. As yet, it had only about eleven thousand non-Native inhabitants, including about fifty free or enslaved African Americans. Douglas believed that New Mexico and Utah would eventually become free states but favored applying popular sovereignty there. Allowing slavery to be decided by the inhabitants would, he reckoned, lessen southern opposition to organizing those territories while leading to the likely outcome that northerners sought. Henry Clay, the preeminent Whig who was back in the Senate after losing his bid for the presidency to Polk in 1844, was thinking along similar lines and combined a proposal like Douglas's with other initiatives to offer a grand compromise, which he hoped would resolve "all questions in controversy between the free and the slave States, growing out of the subject of slavery."[10]

Clay's compromise included admitting California without congressional restriction as to slavery, thus making it a free state by its own choice, and organizing other territories acquired from Mexico on the same nonrestrictive basis, although he specified that slavery "does not exist by law and is not likely to be introduced" there. Clay also proposed excluding a large area east of the Rio Grande from the bounds of Texas while assuming its heavy public debt, passing a "more effectual" fugitive-slave law, and prohibiting the slave trade in the District of Columbia while barring the abolition of slavery there without its consent and that of neighboring Maryland and "just compensation" for the district's slave owners.[11] Many northerners would object to prolonging slavery in the nation's capital and placing no congressional restriction on slavery in territories within the Mexican Cession. But the swiftest and most fervent opposition to Clay's compromise came from the South. No sooner had he introduced his resolutions to the Senate in late January 1850 than several southern Democrats shot back. Jefferson Davis of Mississippi insisted that territory ceded by Mexico was no longer subject to that nation's prohibition of slavery and was now governed by the U.S. Constitution, which acknowledged slavery. He believed that institution was viable in the far Southwest and said he would never accept anything less "than the Missouri compromise line extended to the Pacific." Solomon W. Downs of Louisiana dismissed Clay's plan as "no compromise at all. What, sir, does it grant to the South?"[12] Andrew P. Butler of South Carolina echoed that complaint and suggested that Clay was offering southerners no more than what they were already entitled to while asking major concessions from them in return.

The case against making any further concessions to the North was summed up in early March by John Calhoun, who was dying of tuberculosis and entrusted delivery of his speech to Senator James M. Mason of Virginia. Unlike Davis, Calhoun saw nothing to be gained by extending the Missouri Compromise, which he denounced along with the earlier Northwest Ordinance as discriminatory acts "by which the South has been excluded from the common territory belonging to all of the States." In fact, such acts did not exclude southerners, many of whom had migrated to the Northwest Territory without slaves. Equating the interests and grievances of slave owners with the concerns of the nonslaveholding majority of southerners was a device employed by Calhoun and other proslavery ideologues to foster southern solidarity and defiance. He considered admitting California, where prospectors from the South were among those who wanted slavery pro-hibited, an affront to southerners as a whole that would destroy "equilibrium between the sections." Such equilibrium was not required by the Constitution, but Calhoun warned that unless it was preserved by Congress or guaranteed by constitutional amendment, southerners might soon have to choose between "submission or disunion."[13]

Some northerners expected a forceful rebuttal to Calhoun on their behalf by Daniel Webster, an eloquent Whig who had backed the Wilmot Proviso and earlier rebuked nullifiers in South Carolina for placing their liberty and rights above preservation of the Union, to which he responded famously: "Liberty *and* Union, now and forever, one and inseparable!"[14] When Webster addressed the Senate in 1850, however, he urged those opposed to slavery in the Mexican Cession to desist in a struggle that he considered settled by nature:

Now, as to California and New Mexico, I hold slavery to be excluded from those territories by a law even superior to that which admits and sanctions it in Texas—I mean the law of nature—of physical geography—the law of the formation of the earth. That law settles forever, with a strength beyond all terms of human enactment, that slavery cannot exist in California or New Mexico. . . . I would put in no Wilmot proviso, for the purpose of a taunt or reproach . . . to wound the pride of the gentlemen who belong to the southern States . . . every foot of territory in the States, or in the Territories, has now received a fixed and decided character.[15]

Similar arguments were advanced by others who saw no need to regulate slavery in the Mexican Cession because it was prohibited there by nature. As Clay told southerners opposed to his compromise: "If nature has pronounced the doom of slavery in these territories—if she has declared, by her immutable laws, that slavery cannot and shall not be introduced there—who can you reproach but nature and nature's God?"[16] But as Webster admitted, neither climate nor terrain had excluded involuntary servitude in California or New Mexico. The geography of the Far West indeed offered few opportunities for lucrative plantations like those in the South, but nature did not prevent southerners from settling there with slaves they employed as miners, field hands, or domestic servants. The chief obstacle to African American slavery in the Mexican Cession was that many of the region's Hispanic and incoming Anglo inhabitants opposed it—for reasons that included racial antagonism and fear of economic competition from slaveholders—and thus might forbid it under territorial or state law. Extending the Missouri Compromise line to the Pacific, as Jefferson Davis urged, would allow slave owners to settle in territories below 36°30' without being subjected to antislavery statutes. Congress's refusal to extend that line did not stop proslavery politicians from proposing to divide California and allow Black bondage to the south. Efforts to project slavery and southern dominion across the continent would persist.

By the time Douglas joined the debate on Clay's proposals in mid-March, the Senate's most influential figures had spoken, among them William Seward, who cheered antislavery northerners and appalled their southern opponents by invoking "a higher law than the Constitution"—a moral imperative that prompted some northerners to defy the fugitive-slave law and led Seward to oppose making concessions to slaveholders. California should be admitted as a free state, he concluded, "without conditions, without qualifications, and without compromise."[17] Although Douglas was twelve years younger than Seward and more than thirty years younger than Clay, Webster, and Calhoun, he was emerging as the Senate's "Little Giant," short of stature but formidable in debate and relentless in pursuit of his legislative goals and his party's interests. Far from deferring to the renowned Webster, with whom he shared a desire to compromise, Douglas chided that Whig for suggesting that northern Democrats who had supported annexing Texas as a slave state had no moral basis for restricting slavery in far western territories. Douglas insisted that they had embraced Texas strictly to enlarge and enhance the Union, but tolerating slavery in the Southwest had in fact been part of their congressional bargain with southern Democrats, who in return tolerated the extension of free territory in the Northwest.

Douglas also took issue with Calhoun by denying that congressional acts such as the Northwest Ordinance actually prohibited slavery and were thus an affront to the South. Settlers rather than Congress determined whether slavery would prevail, asserted Douglas, who claimed that "a law passed by the national legislature to operate locally upon a people not represented, will always remain practically a dead letter upon the statute book, if it be in opposition to the wishes and supposed interests of those who are to be affected by it, and at the same time charged with its execution."[18] This flawed argument for popular sovereignty ignored the fact that congressional prohibition of slavery in the Northwest Territory, although circumvented by some officials and inhabitants, discouraged slaveholders wary of that legal barrier from settling there and encouraged many people without slaves to do so, thus fostering free states above the Ohio River. Douglas stated that Illinois became a slaveholding territory "in utter defiance" of the Northwest Ordinance. But slavery had existed there before Illinois became American territory, and the ordinance helped prevent it from prevailing there despite the efforts of politically influential slave owners to the contrary. Less than 2 percent of Illinois's population was enslaved in 1820, making it freer at that time than New Jersey, where nearly 3 percent remained in bondage. Douglas's belief that disputes over slavery in territories could be resolved by withholding congressional judgment and conferring sovereignty on settlers would lead him dangerously astray in years to come.

Douglas played a less conspicuous role initially in efforts to resolve the congressional dispute over slavery than Senator Henry S. Foote of Mississippi, who favored preserving the equilibrium in the Senate by creating a second slave state within Texas, whose population now exceeded two hundred thousand. That proposal languished for lack of support, so Foote turned his attention to ensuring that Congress did not admit California without offering concessions to the South. To that end, Foote proposed forming a select committee that would draw up an omnibus bill combining various elements of Clay's compromise to be voted on as a whole. Several senators objected to that approach, including

Douglas—who helped craft parts of the omnibus and anticipated that pro- and antislavery forces would defeat them if combined—and Thomas Hart Benton, who opposed linking California's admission as a free state to resolutions involving slavery elsewhere.

Benton's support for admitting California with no strings attached and his opposition to Texas's Rio Grande boundary claim set him at odds with proslavery expansionists in Congress and the Missouri state legislature, which would deny him another term in the Senate the following January. In contrast to Calhoun—whose defiant "Southern Address" in 1849 had urged southerners to unite politically against northern intimidation and defend their "property, prosperity, equality, liberty, and safety"—Benton saw no need for Congress to protect the South and its peculiar institution other than by strengthening enforcement of the existing fugitive-slave law.[19] Calhoun's death on March 31, 1850, did not stop Benton from disparaging his Southern Address a few weeks later as reckless "agitation," which implied falsely that southern rights were being denied by Congress. Foote, who had earlier accused Benton of "treachery to the South," then rose to the defense of the "late illustrious Senator from South Carolina" and rebuked Benton, prompting him to leave his seat and advance menacingly toward Foote, who drew a pistol on the combative Missourian. "Let him fire!" Benton shouted as senators rushed to restrain him and disarm Foote. "I have no pistols! . . . Stand out of the way, and let the assassin fire!"[20] Senator Dickinson ended the confrontation without bloodshed by seizing Foote's pistol.

Defying Calhoun's detractor at gunpoint helped bolster Foote against southern charges that he was yielding to the North by pursuing compromise. Clay needed his support and agreed to form a select committee of thirteen, which proposed an omnibus bill in May that combined admitting California as a free state, organizing New Mexico and Utah as territories under popular sovereignty, and imposing a boundary settlement that left Texas more ground than Clay's original proposal but denied it historically New Mexican territory in exchange for debt relief. (Other bills barring the slave trade in the District of Columbia and proposing a stricter fugitive-slave law would be voted on separately.) Prospects for a settlement in Congress improved somewhat that summer. In June, southern delegates at Nashville passed resolutions far less incendiary than hoped for by the so-called ultras or fire-eaters who threatened secession. In July, legislators who opposed organizing territories within the Mexican Cession where slavery might prevail under popular sovereignty lost support at the highest level when Zachary Taylor fell ill following festivities on Independence Day and died soon

after. His successor, President Millard Fillmore of New York, signaled support
for compromise by appointing Webster secretary of state. Fillmore faced an
immediate crisis in New Mexico, however, one that menaced the Union and
could not be ignored. Though he did not support New Mexico's application for
statehood, he sent additional troops there to deter a possible invasion by Texans,
who were vowing to fight for their Rio Grande boundary claim. That raised the
specter of civil war if other southern states backed Texas against federal forces.
Georgia Whig Alexander Stephens, who was no fire-eater in 1850, warned in a
letter published on July 4 that "the cause of Texas, in such a conflict, will be the
cause of the entire South."[21]

The boundary dispute was thus the most urgent matter before Congress. It was
also the most muddled. Admitting California as a free state was a clear choice on
which ardent pro- and antislavery factions in Congress differed sharply. But both
groups shared an aversion to compromise and would unite against the omnibus
by exploiting the tangled Texas boundary question. That issue was debated at
length in the Senate, which acted on the compromise before the House did and
considered various amendments to the committee's boundary proposal that
were more or less favorable to Texas. Publicly, Texas senators Sam Houston and
Thomas Jefferson Rusk backed their state's full claim. Houston indicated that
if push came to shove, he might once again lead Texans in battle. But he cared
more about preserving the Union than about extending slavery, on which he
relied substantially after he wed Margaret Lea of Alabama in 1840 and employed
an overseer to manage their slaves at Raven Hill, a plantation in Texas that
served as the family's first home. Although Houston never renounced slavery
and opposed the Wilmot Proviso, he took issue with Calhoun's Southern Address
and annoyed that senator by joining Benton in casting decisive votes in favor of
organizing Oregon as a free territory. During the debate over Clay's proposals,
Houston endorsed compromise in principle by stating, as Lincoln would eight
years later, that a nation "divided against itself cannot stand."[22] Privately, both
he and Rusk were prepared to settle for a western boundary short of the upper
Rio Grande in exchange for debt relief, an accommodation with considerable
support among Texans wary of civil war.

Where to draw that line and how much to offer Texas for retracting its claim
remained thorny issues complicated by pressure from lobbyists for the state's
bondholders, who wanted more than some speculators had paid for those risky,
discounted bonds. On July 30 the Senate narrowly approved an amendment that
would grant Texas jurisdiction over New Mexican settlements east of the Rio

Grande until a commission determined the boundary line and compensation for Texas. That exasperated James A. Pearce of Maryland, a Whig who disdained what he considered a reckless land grab by Texans and worried that they would never surrender jurisdiction. On July 31, against Clay's urging, Pearce proposed eliminating the New Mexico–Texas plank from the omnibus, which he would then move to restore without the objectionable amendment. As Clay feared, anti-compromise senators, including men as far apart on slavery as Jefferson Davis and William Seward, helped Pearce excise that section but denied him the votes needed to restore it as he wished. They then proceeded to demolish Clay's compromise piece by piece. By day's end, the temporary alliance of pro- and antislavery senators—joined by Benton and a few others who believed that seeking a grand compromise on slavery would only exacerbate the issue—had rejected everything but territorial status for Utah. "The omnibus is overturned," Benton exulted, "and all the passengers spilled out but one."[23]

Clay was devastated and left Washington to recuperate. He had not commanded full support within the southern wing of his party or induced many northern Whigs with antislavery convictions to compromise. His departure left Douglas to pick up the pieces of the shattered omnibus and advance them separately, as Clay had done three decades earlier when securing the Missouri Compromise. Douglas was aided by a Democratic majority in the Senate whose northern members largely followed his lead. The sudden collapse of the omnibus, which left the boundary dispute unresolved and threats of secession unmuffled, increased fears that the Union was at risk of fracturing, causing some senators previously opposed to Clay's effort to back compromise measures or abstain when Douglas renewed the effort. Fillmore helped out by affirming his intention to defend all of New Mexico, including its settlements east of the Rio Grande, against any effort by "trespassers" from Texas to assert authority there before the boundary dispute was settled, which he urged on Congress.[24] Douglas then advanced a new motion crafted by Pearce, who had been blasted by Clay for wrecking the omnibus and made amends by offering a solution that satisfied many of his fellow Whigs as well as most northern Democrats. It gave Texas its enduring shape and $10 million in debt relief, half of which was set aside to satisfy bondholders.

Both Texas senators helped pass that boundary bill by a margin of ten votes, and Sam Houston went on to support all planks of the Compromise of 1850. He and Benton were the only slave-state Democrats in the Senate to vote with the majority in favor of statehood for California, which drew a heated protest from

Jefferson Davis and nine other southerners, all but one of them Democrats. Denying the South equilibrium in the Senate and equal access to American territory by admitting California as a free state was, they declared ominously, "fatal to the peace and *equality* of the States which we represent, and must lead, if persisted in, to the *dissolution* of that confederacy in which the slaveholding States have never sought more than *equality*, and in which they will not be content to *remain* with less."[25] By "confederacy," they meant a compact from which southern states were entitled to withdraw if denied political equality—not the perpetual Union that Jackson defended against the nullifiers.

The senators who lodged that protest spoke for southerners unappeased by a compromise that did not prohibit slavery in Utah and New Mexico Territories but left open the possibility that legislators there might outlaw it. Language that would have barred them from doing so was stricken from acts organizing those territories, which stated simply that when admitted as states they "shall be received into the Union, with or without slavery, as their constitution may prescribe."[26] Davis and like-minded southerners doubted that slavery would take hold in western territories unless it was exempted from prohibition before they achieved statehood. Allowing land-hungry settlers with little property or respect for property rights to bar slavery there was not popular sovereignty, they complained, but squatter sovereignty—an epithet applied as well by northern-ers who feared that proslavery intruders might decide the issue. Northerners also had misgivings about other parts of the compromise, notably the stricter fugitive-slave law. Solid northern opposition would have defeated that measure, which authorized federal marshals to require citizens in free states to serve on posses that pursued fugitives. But more than fifty northern representatives voted in favor, abstained, or missed the House vote in September (as Douglas did when the Senate approved that law in August). Congressman Thaddeus Stevens of Pennsylvania, a Whig who voted no, suggested sarcastically that those who had dodged the roll call should be informed that "the fugitive slave bill has been disposed of, and that they may now come back into the Hall."[27]

Despite such qualms, many in Washington and the country at large were relieved when Douglas pushed through the compromise, which enhanced his stature. By succeeding where Clay had faltered, he became a leading actor on the national stage, central to the dramatic political disputes that convulsed the republic for the next decade. He hoped to end sectional strife and win election as president. To rally his party and achieve its nomination, however, he would have to retain the loyalty of northern Democrats while placating powerful and

Stephen Douglas (1813–1861)
as U.S. senator from Illinois,
circa 1860. Courtesy Library
of Congress Prints and
Photographs Division
(LC-ppmsca-53278).

potentially rebellious southern Democrats dismayed by the Compromise of 1850,
a grudging settlement that also strained the Whig Party internally. The crucial
bill whose passage in the House on September 6 made New Mexico a territory
under popular sovereignty, defined its boundary with Texas, and cleared the way
for approval of the compromise as a whole was opposed by only a few southern
Whigs but by more than forty northern Whigs with antislavery convictions.

An Irrepressible Controversy

Millard Fillmore spoke for Americans who dreaded disunion when he urged
Congress in December 1850 to end the divisive debate over slavery and recognize
the compromise achieved that year as "final and irrevocable."[28] Douglas, for
his part, hoped "never to make another speech on the slavery question." But he
was soon denouncing Seward and other antislavery senators for encouraging
defiance of the 1850 fugitive-slave act in Boston, where protesters led by free
Black men broke into a courtroom in February 1851 and liberated Shadrach
Minkins, a fugitive whose owner in Virginia was seeking to reclaim him. "I hold

white men now within the range of my sight responsible for the violation of the law at Boston," Douglas declared before the Senate. "It was done under their advice, under their teaching, under their sanction, under the influence of their speeches."[29] Yet Douglas used his own influence to placate southern Democrats dissatisfied with the compromise he achieved. When he began campaigning in 1851 for the Democratic presidential nomination the following year, he broke with tradition by choosing his own running mate: Senator Robert M. T. Hunter of Virginia, a disciple of the late Calhoun whose selection indicated how far Douglas would go to secure the support of the party's proslavery hard-liners.

Amid a crowded field that included such notable candidates as James Buchanan of Pennsylvania, Lewis Cass of Michigan, and William Marcy of New York, Douglas briefly led the balloting at the Democratic convention in Baltimore in June 1852. But neither he nor his announced rivals could achieve the required two-thirds majority. After more than fifty ballots, the exhausted delegates turned to a dark horse, Franklin Pierce of New Hampshire. Pierce was a "doughface"—a northerner whose sympathy for the South and slavery was well known to associates like Jefferson Davis—but it was not so blatant as to spoil his chances in his own region. He was also vigorous enough at forty-seven to appeal to the Young America movement, whose unbridled expansionism lost some of its appeal during the Mexican-American War but rebounded following the Compromise of 1850. Ambitious Young Americans were intent on rejuvenating the Democratic Party, reinforcing its commitment to extending the nation's boundaries, and reframing its domestic agenda by supporting land grants for frontier settlers, financial incentives for the construction of railroads, and other federally backed internal improvements that many old-line Jacksonians resisted. As a reporter at the 1852 Democratic convention observed, Young Americans there were "opposed to old men, old fogies, old principles, and in favor of new men, young fogies, new measures, and new principles, including the great measure of the extension of the republic in every direction."[30]

Douglas, eight years younger than Pierce, had attached himself to the movement hoping it would help propel him to the presidency. He was endorsed by publisher George Nicholas Sanders, a Kentuckian who purchased the *Democratic Review* in 1851 with Douglas's encouragement and restored John O'Sullivan as its editor. Douglas echoed O'Sullivan when he stated that "a young nation, with all of her freshness, vigor, and youth, desires no limits fixed to her greatness, no boundaries to her future growth."[31] Not everyone was impressed when the Little Giant (sized up by one observer as "five feet nothing, or thereabouts") touted the nation's gigantic potential for growth and his own capacity to lead that great country. As Benton said tauntingly of Douglas's persistent presidential ambitions: "He thinks he can bestride this continent with one foot on the shore of the Atlantic, the other on the Pacific. But he can't do it. . . . His legs are too short. . . . That part of his body, sir, which men wish to kick, is too near the ground."[32] Douglas was not too short to lead the nation, but he was too young and brash in 1852 to suit his elders in the Democratic establishment. They resented being portrayed as old fogies but gave Young Americans an expansionist to their liking by nominating Pierce.

Although the nation was at peace in 1852 and relatively prosperous, thanks in part to an infusion of gold from California, that did not help Whigs retain the presidency. They flourished only in opposition and had neither a depressed economy to blame on the Democrats, as in 1840, nor the contentious aftermath of Mr. Polk's War to exploit, as in 1848. They tried to close the widening sectional gap within their party by dropping President Fillmore—whose efforts to enforce the stringent new fugitive-slave law offended many northern Whigs—and once again nominating a national hero like the late Zachary Taylor, General Winfield Scott. But southern Whigs were reluctant to embrace that politically inept sixty-six-year-old Virginian, fearing that he, like Taylor, might be influenced by the antislavery Seward. The last presidential candidate of his faltering party, Scott was defeated when Van Burenites who had bolted to the Free Soil Party in 1848 returned to the Democratic fold, helping Pierce win all but four states that November. Losses in congressional and state races further demoralized the Whigs and led Seward to ask plaintively: "Was there ever such a deluge since Noah's time?"[33]

In his inaugural address, Pierce warned against sectionalism but placed the burden of averting disunion largely on northerners by urging compliance with the fugitive-slave law and recognition of slaveholders' rights in southern states and American territories. "I believe that involuntary servitude, as it exists in different States of this Confederacy, is recognized by the Constitution," he declared. "I hold that the laws of 1850, commonly called the 'compromise measures,' are strictly constitutional and to be unhesitatingly carried into effect. I believe that the constituted authorities of this Republic are bound to regard the rights of the South in this respect as they would view any other legal and constitutional right." Pierce asked northerners to acknowledge southern rights "cheerfully," but he favored enlarging the nation in a way that would alienate them when his intentions became clear. His administration, he vowed, would "not be controlled by any timid forebodings of evil from expansion." Without mentioning Cuba, he added that "our attitude as a nation and our position on the globe render the acquisition of certain possessions not within our jurisdiction eminently important for our protection, if not in the future essential for the preservation of the rights of commerce and the peace of the world."[34]

Annexing slaveholding Cuba would surely arouse sectional tensions of the sort Pierce warned against. Yet support for doing so came not just from southerners who viewed the island as a prospective slave state but from northern Democrats like Douglas and O'Sullivan who envisioned Cuba as an alluring extension of the American empire, situated too close to the nation's shores to be allowed to remain under Spanish rule. In May 1848, Douglas and O'Sullivan had called on President Polk and urged him to purchase Cuba from Spain. A month later O'Sullivan tried to interest Polk in backing Venezuelan-born revolutionary Narciso López, who hoped to free Cuba from Spain. Polk refused to support armed intervention there "or even wink at such a movement," but he would gladly have purchased the island if Spain had been willing to part with it.[35] Neither Taylor nor Fillmore favored annexing Cuba, a move that would have alarmed northern Whigs averse to slavery and aggravated the crisis Congress faced in 1850. Both the Taylor and Fillmore administrations took legal action and naval precautions against a filibuster by López, who nonetheless succeeded in landing twice on Cuba with recruits he hailed as "sons of Washington," embodying the spirit of 1776.[36] Embarking from New Orleans in May 1850 with volunteers drawn largely from the South, he cut short his first invasion when Cubans failed to come to his aid and Spanish troops closed in. Returning to the island in August 1851, he was routed and executed along with Colonel William L. Crittenden of Kentucky and fifty of Crittenden's men.

Undeterred by that debacle, Pierce reversed the policy of his Whig predecessors by seeking possession of Cuba. He may have encouraged—and long did nothing to thwart—a would-be filibuster by a fellow Democrat, former Mississippi governor John A. Quitman, who planned to liberate Cuba from Spain while preserving slavery there. Some southerners aware of Quitman's well-funded, ill-concealed project opposed it on principle or because they feared competition from Cuba's sugar planters if that island became American territory. But reports that Spanish authorities were freeing some Cuban slaves and arming them to resist invasion brought Quitman support from fellow slaveholders intent on seizing the island before emancipation and armed Black resistance there inspired rebellion on southern plantations. The seizure in Havana harbor of the American merchant ship *Black Warrior* in early 1854 offered a pretext for Quitman's invasion, but he failed to act on it. Meanwhile, Pierce came to view purchasing Cuba as the safer option. Secretary of State Marcy, an ardent expansionist who had served as Polk's secretary of war, instructed the American minister to Spain, Pierre Soulé, to offer up to $130 million for Cuba. Marcy added provocatively that if the bid failed, Soulé might turn to "the next desirable object, which is to detach that island from the Spanish dominion."[37]

The hot-tempered Soulé, who as a Democratic senator from Louisiana had joined Jefferson Davis in protesting California's admission as a free state, was on poor terms with Spanish officials in Madrid when he received those instructions and made no headway in negotiations for Cuba. He then met in October 1854 at Ostend, Belgium, with two other American diplomats: James Buchanan, minister in London, and John Y. Mason, minister in Paris. The three men signed a document stating that if the American offer for Cuba was refused, "we shall be justified in wresting it from Spain." Their indiscreet Ostend Manifesto—which warned that unless Cuba was annexed by the United States it might be "African-ized and become a second St. Domingo, with all its attendant horrors to the white race"—was soon published.[38] The ensuing uproar in the North ended any prospect that Cuba would be obtained by Pierce, who had by then squelched Quitman's expedition by vowing to crack down on filibustering.

In May 1856, however, Pierce would endorse a filibuster in Nicaragua by William Walker after that notorious Tennessean intervened with his recruits in a civil war there and seized control as commander in chief while his Nicaraguan ally, Patricio Rivas, served as president. Nicaragua and Panama had been of interest to Americans since the onset of the gold rush, when California-bound prospectors began crossing those Central American countries to avoid lengthy voyages around Cape Horn. Douglas asserted in 1853 that the United States was entitled to control Panama and Nicaragua and command "every great route between our two great shores," and he later pressured Pierce to recognize the Walker-Rivas regime.[39] Soon after Pierce did so, Walker lost official American support by breaking with Rivas and assuming the presidency. He was then opposed militarily by other Central American nations and sought additional recruits from southern states by reinstituting slavery in Nicaragua. Ousted from that country in 1857, he was executed in Honduras in 1860, having tarnished what little idealistic luster Manifest Destiny retained.

Pierce's pursuit of Cuba, which if annexed would have provoked another convulsive struggle over slavery in Congress, demonstrated that he and other Democratic leaders did not in fact consider the Compromise of 1850 final, as they claimed. It failed to appease influential southern Democrats like future Confederate president Davis, now serving as secretary of war. And that led ambitious northern Democrats like Douglas to offer further concessions to the South—as he did fatefully in 1854 while the bid for Cuba was unraveling by proposing to organize two territories above the Missouri Compromise line, Kansas and Nebraska, that would be open to slavery under popular sovereignty. Although he argued that the Missouri Compromise had been nullified by the Compromise of 1850, the consensus in Congress was that the earlier compromise remained in effect within territory encompassed by the Louisiana Purchase unless repealed. Douglas had stated in 1849 that "no ruthless hand would ever be reckless enough to disturb" the Missouri Compromise, but he was now prepared to sweep it aside. Enabling settlers in American territories to allow or forbid slavery as they saw fit would, he predicted rashly, "destroy all sectional parties and sectional agitation."[40]

CHAPTER 13

Conceiving "Bleeding Kansas"

Stephen Douglas did not set out to enact legislation that would raise hell in Kansas and infuriate those who expected everything above the Missouri Compromise line to remain free soil. His original intention was to link the Midwest to the Far West by organizing Nebraska as a single large territory extending across the Great Plains from the western frontier of Missouri and Iowa, admitted as a free state in 1846. The eastern fringe of that expanse, all of which had been reserved for Indian tribes, was verdant prairie that could be cultivated. Organizing Nebraska would bring federal pressure to bear on tribes to relinquish that fertile country and other land suitable for settlement or the construction of railroads that would parallel paths like the Oregon Trail along the Platte River and the Santa Fe Trail along the Arkansas River.

Douglas had promoted and profited from the development of railroads east of the Mississippi, notably the Illinois Central, which received valuable land grants along a route linking his home state to the South. He would further benefit financially and politically if Chicago, where he resided when Congress was not in session and invested in real estate, became the eastern terminus of a transcontinental railroad, as he urged. But others were competing for that prize, including Congressman Benton, who had returned to Washington as a representative from Missouri and sought an iron road to the Pacific emanating from St. Louis. A bill passed by Congress in 1853 authorized surveys of several possible paths for railroads across the West. Secretary of War Jefferson Davis, who oversaw those surveys, favored the southernmost route, from Texas to southern California, which gained traction when his appointee James Gadsden of South

Carolina, who promised to advance the interests and "principles of the South," negotiated a treaty by which the United States purchased from Mexico land below the Gila River in New Mexico well suited for laying tracks to the Pacific.[1] Some northerners in Congress opposed that treaty and the route it facilitated, fearing that such a railroad would enable the South to exert influence across the continent and extend slavery, as Davis and Gadsden hoped it would. But Douglas backed the Gadsden Purchase and proposed avoiding sectional rivalry by approving central and northern routes in addition to the southern route. Uncertain that the central route he favored from Chicago across Nebraska would prevail, Douglas hedged his bets by investing in property along Lake Superior that would rise in value if Congress approved a transcontinental route near the Canadian border like that surveyed by Isaac Stevens, the future governor of Washington Territory, which was divided from Oregon Territory with Douglas's help in 1853.

Douglas was among those in Congress who had cozy dealings with railroad promoters, land speculators, and other moneymen seeking political favors. The banker William W. Corcoran advanced him $10,000 to purchase shares in the town site that became Superior, Wisconsin, envisioned as the future link between ships traversing the Great Lakes and what Douglas thought might become "the greatest railroad in the world."[2] Like Douglas's management of the plantation his late wife inherited in Mississippi, however, his investments in land and railroads reinforced rather than dictated his policy of soliciting southern support for organizing and developing western territories. So eager was he to transform that unorganized Indian country called Nebraska as Illinois had been transformed by white settlers, speculators, and investors in canals, railroads, and telegraph lines that he might well have made some concessions to southerners in Congress to achieve that goal even if he had no involvement in slavery and nothing to gain financially if tracks were laid across that territory. As remarked by Senator John Bell of Tennessee, who would later oppose Douglas in the 1860 presidential contest, he had "a passion, amounting to a sort of mania, for the organization of new Territories, and the founding of new States."[3]

Much like Jefferson, Douglas viewed the West as "the hope of this nation," a land of promise and regeneration where disputes over slavery and other contentious issues plaguing the Union could be transcended, or so he believed. As he reckoned in 1852, sectional strife between North and South "would ere this have dissolved this glorious Union had it not been for the Great West."[4] Douglas had transcended his own difficult upbringing in Vermont—where his father died soon after he was born and he rebelled against an uncle he deemed a "hard master" for exploiting his farm labor—by heading west by way of upstate New York to Illinois, where he arrived shortly before his twenty-first birthday and proudly proclaimed himself a "*Western* man."[5] Illinois seemingly confirmed his view that sectional tensions could be resolved in the West, for the state was settled by northerners and southerners alike and brought what slavery existed there gradually to an end while remaining a Democratic stronghold sympathetic to the South until the new Republican Party emerged in the mid-1850s. That new party opposed to Douglas's Democracy was fostered in large part by his mistaken belief that those migrating to territory above the Missouri Compromise line from free states and slave states could resolve the issue of slavery as he did, by viewing the fate of Black people held in bondage as insignificant compared with preserving a Union that upheld the rights of white Americans.

Douglas was not alone in seeking to organize Nebraska. Others in the House and Senate introduced bills to that effect, but such legislation was routinely referred to the Senate Committee on Territories, which he chaired. In February 1853 a bill establishing Nebraska Territory on which he collaborated with the chairman of the House Committee on Territories, fellow Illinoisan William A. Richardson, passed the House by a wide margin. That outcome reflected overwhelming support from the northern majority there for an act that did not mention slavery or apply popular sovereignty and would presumably make Nebraska a free territory under the Missouri Compromise. Douglas tried to push that bill through the Senate before the Twenty-Seventh Congress came to a close in March. Some senators complained that organizing Nebraska would deny Indians title to land guaranteed them by treaty. For Sam Houston that was a crucial objection, because the Cherokee tribe to which he felt indebted was assigned land at the southeastern corner of the proposed Nebraska Territory. But David Atchison of Missouri expressed the fundamental southern objection that the bill would preclude slaveholders from entering Nebraska unless the Missouri Compromise was repealed. Mindful that many Missourians without slaves were "ready and anxious" to emigrate there, Atchison reluctantly supported the legislation.[6] Senators from other slave states, however, combined with several northern Whigs to table a bill they opposed either because it implicitly prohibited slavery in Nebraska or failed to do so expressly.

Douglas concluded that he could not achieve his goal without attracting southern support, which meant circumventing the Missouri Compromise and allowing slaveholders access to Nebraska under popular sovereignty. He saw an opportunity to enact such legislation when the Twenty-Eighth Congress convened in December 1853 with a comfortable Democratic majority in the Senate and a hefty one in the House. Confident of prevailing, Democrats at odds with those in their ranks who had favored the Wilmot Proviso welcomed a bill that would test the loyalty of such free-soilers and marginalize those who failed to support popular sovereignty as applied in the Compromise of 1850. While revising the Nebraska legislation, Douglas conferred with influential southern senators, notably Atchison, who presided over the Senate following the death of Vice President William R. King of Alabama in April 1853 and favored those who shared his proslavery convictions with choice committee assignments. He and three senators he roomed with at house on F Street in the capital—Andrew Butler of South Carolina, James Mason of Virginia, and Douglas's would-be running mate in 1852, Robert M. T. Hunter of Virginia—had joined Jefferson Davis and others in protesting California's admission to the Union and warning that slave states would leave the Union if denied political equality with free states. Known collectively as the "F Street Mess," they exerted pressure on Douglas, who later denied Atchison's claim that he shaped the Nebraska bill. "It was written by myself, at my own house, with no man present," insisted Douglas.[7] But Atchison and his F Street messmates had significant input as the legislation evolved.

The revised bill that Douglas introduced in early January 1854 enlarged Nebraska Territory by extending it northward to the Canadian border and used the same language applied to Utah and New Mexico Territories in 1850, stating that the territory when applying for statehood "shall be received into the Union, with or without slavery," as its constitution may prescribe. An additional section, attached to Douglas's bill soon after it was first published, stated that all legal cases involving "title to slaves" and "questions of personal freedom" were to be decided in local courts, with the right of appeal to the U.S. Supreme Court. Douglas said that section was omitted from the bill as originally published by a clerical error, but he may have added it to assure southern senators that slaveholders would have legal standing in Nebraska from the territory's inception. Antislavery senators like Salmon P. Chase of Ohio recognized that the bill effectively nullified the longstanding prohibition of slavery in territories above the Missouri Compromise line. Douglas had "outSouthernized the South," complained Chase, but some southerners would not be satisfied with the legislation unless it explicitly repealed the Missouri Compromise.[8]

In mid-January, Senator Archibald Dixon of Kentucky, a Whig who took Henry Clay's seat following his death in 1852, proposed an amendment stating that the Missouri Compromise would no longer apply and that citizens "shall be at liberty to take and hold their slaves" in Nebraska and any other American territory. Some Democrats thought that sweeping amendment was a Whig scheme to divide their party over Nebraska. Dixon agreed to withdraw his amendment, however, if Douglas could find a way of rescinding the Missouri Compromise that would satisfy southerners without making the bill toxic to northerners. Atchison and his colleagues favored language crafted by Representative Philip Phillips of Alabama that alluded to the Missouri Compromise by stating that any congressional act infringing on the right of those in the territory to enact laws consistent with the U.S. Constitution (which recognized slavery) was "inoperative, void and of no force and effect."[9] Similar terms had been used by legislators in Kentucky to dismiss the Alien and Sedition Acts without explicitly nullifying them. But the precise language would have to be approved by President Pierce, who was wary of scrapping a compromise that had prevailed for more than three decades.

On Sunday, January 22, one day before the Senate took up the revised Nebraska bill, Douglas, Atchison, Hunter, and others involved in crafting the legislation met at the White House with Pierce, who normally refrained from such business on the Sabbath but was persuaded by his friend and advisor, Jefferson Davis, to make an exception. Like Douglas, Pierce felt compelled to allay the grievances of southern Democrats such as Davis and senators of the F Street Mess who had warned of secession if slave owners' rights were denied. Pierce reluctantly agreed to state that the Missouri Compromise was superseded by the Compromise of 1850 and "declared inoperative and void."[10] That was not the only bitter pill for antislavery legislators to swallow when Douglas unveiled his newly titled Kansas-Nebraska Act, which organized Kansas Territory west of Missouri and Nebraska Territory west of Iowa and Minnesota Territory. Douglas said he added Kansas to the bill to satisfy Missourians and Iowans, who preferred separate territories. But opponents of the act suspected that forming Kansas Territory adjacent to a slave state and accessible to its slaveholders was another concession by Douglas to the South.

Proslavery senators exacted a steep price from Douglas, and antislavery stalwarts in Congress would take their toll on him as well. One day after he proposed the Kansas-Nebraska Act, a blistering attack on the Nebraska bill he had introduced earlier that month, providing for popular sovereignty there, appeared in the *Daily National Era*, an abolitionist newspaper that was also published as a weekly edition. Several of those responsible for the article had ties to the defunct Free Soil Party, including Senator Chase and Representative Joshua R. Giddings of Ohio and Senator Charles Sumner of Massachusetts. "We arraign this bill," they declared, "as a gross violation of a sacred pledge; as a criminal betrayal of precious rights; as part and parcel of an atrocious plot to exclude from a vast unoccupied region, immigrants from the Old World and free laborers from our own States, and convert it into a dreary region of despotism, inhabited by masters and slaves." Without naming Douglas, they disparaged "demagogues" who maintained that the Union could be preserved "only by submitting to the demands of Slavery."[11] In a postscript aimed at the Kansas-Nebraska Act, they dismissed its claim that the Compromise of 1850 had rendered the Missouri Compromise inoperative.

Privately, Douglas complained to an acquaintance from Illinois that he was being vilified for engaging in political give-and-take, which involved doing "what you can do" when bargaining with others rather than "what you might prefer to do if free to choose."[12] But publicly he gave no hint that he had not freely agreed to declare the Missouri Compromise inoperative. Addressing the Senate on January 30, he insisted that his purpose in revising the bill was to uphold popular sovereignty as enshrined in the Compromise of 1850, which affirmed the "great principle of self-government—that the people should be allowed to decide the questions of their domestic institutions for themselves." He went on to blast Chase and Sumner for accusing him of engaging in "an atrocious plot against the cause of free government." His attack grew so heated that Chase interrupted him, but Douglas refused to yield the floor to a senator who had "violated all the rules of courtesy and propriety."[13]

Douglas's combative speech, laced with profanity that was audible in the gallery but omitted from the congressional record, foretold a bitter struggle for him and his party that would continue long after the Senate passed the Kansas-Nebraska Act by a substantial margin in the early hours of March 4. Sam Houston was one of the few southern Democrats in that chamber to oppose the bill, which he warned would violate tribal rights and prove "fatal to the future harmony and well-being" of the country as a whole.[14] As he predicted, the act would strain his party by subjecting northern members who backed it to fierce criticism from their constituents. The bill was approved in the House in May with grudging support from half of the chamber's northern Democrats. That vote that cost the party most of their seats, some of which went to candidates who ran as opponents of the Kansas-Nebraska Act rather than as Democrats or Whigs, whose party collapsed when its northern and southern branches split irrevocably over that legislation.

Douglas's convulsive act would shift the weight of the Democratic Party southward as it attracted southern Whigs with its increasingly proslavery agenda and contended with the new Republican Party, which emerged in opposition to the bill and absorbed northern Whigs who lost their party and northern Democrats who left their party. That outcome pleased eager Republican converts like Chase and Sumner but spelled trouble for a persistent northern Democrat like Douglas. Far from faulting southerners for seeking changes that made the bill repugnant to northerners, he claimed it was all his doing. "I passed the Kansas-Nebraska Act myself," he wrote. "I had the authority and power of a dictator throughout the whole controversy in both houses." He sought full credit and received full blame from free-soilers who shouted him down when he tried to defend his bill in Chicago and torched him symbolically elsewhere. As he stated sardonically, "I could travel from Boston to Chicago by the light of my own effigy."[15] Such was the impact of the Kansas-Nebraska Act on Douglas's historical reputation that those were among his most memorable words.

Vying for Kansas

Unlike New Mexico, Kansas and Nebraska had few non-Indian inhabitants when organized under popular sovereignty, meaning that slavery would be allowed or prohibited there largely by newcomers. The Kansas-Nebraska Act prescribed no waiting period before the territorial governor, appointed by the president, conducted a census, formed legislative districts, and held an election for the legislature in which all free white male citizens twenty-one or older could participate if they were "actual" residents of the territory. Those provisions suited Douglas's belief that popular sovereignty should apply to slavery and other vital issues as soon as a territorial legislature was elected rather than later, when the territory held a constitutional convention and applied for statehood. Promptly instituting what Douglas called the "great principle of self-government" would, the act stated, leave the "people perfectly free to form and regulate their domestic institutions in their own way, subject only to the Constitution of the United States."[16] On that same basis, he exempted laws passed by the legislature from congressional review, to which territories organized previously were subject. He imagined that citizens endowed with popular sovereignty would determine the fate of the South's peculiar institution wisely and peacefully. But the hasty election of legislators by voters new to the territory prompted a race between pro- and antislavery forces to dominate Kansas, which unlike Nebraska was susceptible to slavery under neighboring Missouri's influence. "We will engage in competition for the virgin soil of Kansas," declared William Seward on behalf

Slavery in the West, 1855

of those determined to allow only free labor there, "and God give the victory to the side which is stronger in numbers as it is in the right."[17]

Having helped ignite that dispute by pressuring Douglas to nullify the Missouri Compromise, David Atchison added fuel to the fire by urging Missourians to defeat northern "fanatics and demagogues" who threatened to "abolitionize Kansas." He was seeking reelection to the Senate and faced a challenge from Benton, who had opposed the Kansas-Nebraska Act in the House. Benton remained popular in St. Louis and elsewhere in eastern Missouri among German immigrants and others who resented the inordinate political clout of the state's slaveholding minority, concentrated in western Missouri where Atchison held sway. Planters who had settled there in fertile country bordering the Missouri

River feared that a free Kansas would box them in and tempt their slaves to flee across the border. Additional support for Atchison's campaign came from restless white men who were not slave owners but made common cause with them to obtain land in Kansas or scourge abolitionists, viewed as potential instigators of slave rebellions. In fact, abolitionists made up a small fraction of those who migrated to Kansas from free states beginning in 1854. But the well-publicized efforts of the New England Emigrant Aid Company, led by Eli Thayer of Massachusetts, fed fears of an abolitionist invasion, which Atchison vowed to repulse. If proslavery forces triumphed in Kansas, he wrote his F Street messmate Hunter, they could "carry slavery to the Pacific Ocean."[18] But if they were defeated, he warned, slavery would be imperiled not just in Missouri but in Arkansas and Texas.

The territorial governor appointed by President Pierce, Andrew H. Reeder of Pennsylvania, implemented popular sovereignty in Kansas without delay. After conducting a census that revealed a population of 8,600, of whom nearly 3,000 were eligible to vote, he held an election for the territorial legislature in March 1855, just ten months after the Kansas-Nebraska Act was signed. That gave an advantage to Missourians, who were among the first to arrive and made up about half the residents. Few of them were slave owners, who were reluctant to migrate to Kansas if it might end up a free territory. (The initial census there recorded just 192 enslaved inhabitants.) Some if not most of the Missourians in Kansas favored slavery, however, and they and other residents from southern states might have installed a proslavery legislature in a fair election. But Atchison took no chances. On election day, nearly 6,000 ballots were cast, thousands of them by proslavery men who crossed over from Missouri along with armed "Border Ruffians," who intimidated legitimate voters in antislavery districts. "We had at least 7,000 men in the territory on the day of the election," Atchison boasted to Hunter, "and one third of them will remain there."[19]

This was not popular sovereignty or squatter sovereignty, as skeptics referred irreverently to Douglas's hallowed principle, but sheer electoral fraud that embittered those who hoped to keep Kansas free of slavery, raising tensions in the territory. Reeder's requirement that voters swear under oath they were actual residents did little to stop intruders from Missouri from casting ballots. One proslavery newspaper in Atchison, Kansas—a town named for the senator and situated just across the Missouri River from the state he represented—assured readers beforehand that "every man in the Territory on the day of the election is a legal voter, if he have not fixed a day for his return to some other home."

Unidentified border
ruffians with swords, circa
1857. Courtesy Library
of Congress Prints and
Photographs Division
(LC-ppmsca-40662).

At some polling places, judges overseeing the election dispensed with the oath willingly or under pressure from Border Ruffians. "All voted that pleased," one observer stated, "no objections, no swearing in voters."[20] Reeder ordered new elections in several districts where the fraud was glaring, but that did not prevent the stacked legislature from enacting an aggressive proslavery agenda, including laws that made composing or circulating antislavery tracts punishable by two years' hard labor and prescribed the death penalty for those who encouraged slaves to rebel or helped them escape.

That legislative coup did not stop emigrants from free states from settling in Kansas or wealthy patrons from providing them with rifles and other weapons. Eli Thayer denied that the New England Emigrant Aid Company armed settlers, but he and Amos A. Lawrence—the company's main benefactor, heir to a fortune made in Massachusetts from cloth woven of cotton produced by slave labor—were among those who helped supply weapons. "That a revolution must take place in Kansas is certain," wrote Lawrence. "When farmers turn soldiers they must have *arms*."[21] Northerners soon made up the majority in Kansas, fewer of whom came from New England than from Illinois, Indiana, and other midwestern states. Most did not have strong moral objections to slavery, but they wanted Kansas to be free soil. Alarmed by a legislature they deemed hostile and illegitimate, they sent delegates to a convention at Topeka in October who drew up a free-state constitution. Some of those delegates were earnest antislavery men, notably Charles Robinson of Massachusetts, a prominent member of Thayer's company. Others abhorred slaves and slaveholders alike and wanted Kansas reserved for white settlers reliant on their own labor. Their spokesman was James H. Lane, a feisty former congressman from Indiana who backed a clause in the Topeka constitution barring all Black people from Kansas, free or enslaved. The convention also instituted an opposition government in the territory, which had no legal standing under Douglas's act but gained more support in Kansas than the improperly elected legislature. Disputes over land claims aggravated tensions between members of the opposing factions. By late 1855 they were sharply at odds in the vicinity of Lawrence, Kansas, home to Lane and other free-state firebrands who acted as envisioned by Amos Lawrence, for whom the town was named, and took up arms.

Like President Pierce, Douglas denounced the Topeka statehood movement and proposed legislation in March 1856 that would nullify its bid by postponing the admission of Kansas to the Union until it had a larger population and held a legitimate constitutional convention. The Topeka free-state constitution had no chance of winning approval in the Senate, where Democrats remained in control, but newly enlisted Republicans who favored it like Senators Sumner and Seward blamed the turmoil in what soon became known as "Bleeding Kansas" on Douglas and the southern Democrats who helped frame his act. On May 19, Sumner indicted them in his visceral "Crime Against Kansas" speech, focusing his wrath on Andrew Butler of South Carolina, held responsible along with his F Street messmate Atchison and others for "the rape of a virgin Territory, compelling it to the hateful embrace of Slavery." Those words evoked well-founded accusations that slave owners often forced themselves on women they held in bondage. Sumner alluded to that again in a scathing attack on Butler, whom he likened to Don Quixote lusting after Dulcinea:

> The Senator from South Carolina has read many books of chivalry, and believes himself a chivalrous knight, with sentiments of honor and courage. Of course he has chosen a mistress to whom he has made his vows, and who, though ugly to others, is always lovely to him; though polluted in the sight of the world, is chaste in his sight—I mean the harlot, Slavery. . . .

If the slave States cannot enjoy what, in mockery of the great fathers of the Republic, he misnames equality under the Constitution—in other words, the full power in the National Territories to compel fellow-men to unpaid toil, to separate husband and wife, and to sell little children at the auction block—then, sir, the chivalric Senator will conduct the State of South Carolina out of the Union!

This verbal assault was aimed not just at Butler but at his state, which had embraced nullification as conceived by its favorite son, Calhoun, and would before long be the first to embrace secession. Sumner could have focused his fury instead on Atchison or launched a fiercer attack than he did on Douglas, whom he belittled as Butler's Sancho Panza, "the squire of Slavery . . . ready to do all its humiliating offices."[22]

Douglas had received worse insults than that from his detractors, from whom he sought satisfaction not by thrashing or dueling with them but by striking back rhetorically, as he did when he rebutted Sumner's speech and said of him: "Is it his object to provoke some of us to kick him as we would a dog in the street, that he may get sympathy upon the just chastisement?"[23] Sumner risked such chastisement by fixing on Butler as a personification of South Carolina, the state with the largest share of enslaved people (who made up nearly 60 percent its population in 1850) and more than its share of proslavery hotspurs, quick to assail those who threatened their interests or insulted their honor. As Douglas said of Sumner when he lambasted Butler, who was ailing and not present, "That damn fool will get himself killed by some other damn fool."[24]

Douglas's prediction was nearly fulfilled a few days later when Butler's cousin, Congressman Preston Brooks of South Carolina, entered the chamber after the Senate adjourned and struck the seated Sumner repeatedly with a cane. By his own account, Brooks gave Sumner "about 30 first rate stripes." Sumner collapsed on the floor and lay "senseless as a corpse for several minutes," a congressman who intervened related, "his head bleeding copiously from the wounds."[25] Sumner said that when he regained consciousness, he saw Douglas standing beside Brooks, which suggested that he had failed to stop the attack and might have encouraged it. Douglas explained that he was in the Senate reception room when told of the assault and did not intervene because "my relations with Mr. Sumner were such that if I came into the Hall, my motives would be misconstrued, perhaps." Although witnesses confirmed that he did not enter the chamber until the attack was over, a pastor in Chicago condemned him in the pulpit and in print as *"Douglas, of giant Infamy,"* who stood by impassively while Sumner was bludgeoned.[26]

The assault on Sumner, who would not fully resume his Senate duties for several years, did as much to set North and South bitterly at odds as any act of violence committed in Kansas. Brooks was censured by the House and resigned his seat, but he was lionized in South Carolina, where constituents reelected him to Congress and presented him with a new cane inscribed "Hit him again." They and other southerners reckoned that Sumner deserved to be beaten like an insubordinate slave. "These vulgar abolitionists in the Senate must be lashed into submission," declared the *Richmond Enquirer.* "Sumner, in particular, ought to have nine-and-thirty every morning. He is a great strapping fellow, and could stand the cowhide beautifully."[27] Few white southerners acknowledged what Mary Boykin Chesnut stated privately in her diary. "Sumner said not one word of this hated institution which is not true," she wrote of slavery and the license it gave men to take women they enslaved as mistresses. "God forgive us, but ours is a *monstrous* system and wrong and iniquity."[28]

Northerners responded publicly to the attack with scathing denunciations of slavery and those who practiced it. That Sumner was caned for expressing his opinions, however vitriolic, revived earlier complaints aroused by the gag rule on antislavery petitions that southerners would not tolerate free speech on that subject. Must northerners "speak with bated breath in the presence of our Southern masters?" asked editor William Cullen Bryant of the *New York Evening Post.* "Are we to be chastised as they chastise their slaves?"[29] Some concluded that the North could not coexist with the South unless its peculiar and barbaric institution was abolished. "I do not see how a barbarous community and a civilized community can constitute one state," declared Ralph Waldo Emerson. "I think we must get rid of slavery, or we must get rid of freedom."[30]

In Kansas on the night of May 24, two days after Brooks caned Sumner, abolitionist John Brown set out with four of his sons and three other armed men to "fight fire with fire," as he put it, and scourge proslavery men living along Pottawatomie Creek.[31] He was incensed by a recent raid on the town of Lawrence by proslavery forces—who burned down the Free State Hotel, among other buildings, and wrecked the offices and equipment of two antislavery newspapers—and by court proceedings against him and his sons involving three men he targeted that night. They were among five victims whose mutilated bodies, slashed by swords, were found along the creek the next day. Although Brown and his accomplices escaped punishment, he was credited with the slayings in press accounts and went on to wage guerrilla warfare against proslavery men that summer. A new governor with military experience, John W. Geary of Pennsylvania, helped stanch the bleeding in Kansas that fall by using federal troops to prevent a concerted attack on Lawrence and deter reprisals by antislavery forces.

For all the controversy aroused by Douglas's ill-fated application of popular sovereignty to that hotly contested territory, his Kansas-Nebraska Act was endorsed by Democrats at their convention in Cincinnati in June 1856. And he once again competed for the nomination, picking up many of the delegates pledged to Pierce when he withdrew in the face of northern opposition and became the seventh president since Andrew Jackson to serve a single term or less. Douglas ultimately lost out to James Buchanan, whose diplomatic mission in London distanced him from the furor over slavery in the West and made him a safer choice for a party that did not want to lose the presidency over Kansas as it had recently lost control of the House.

Despite that congressional setback, Democrats had the advantage of competing in 1856 not with the once-formidable Whig Party, ripped apart by sectional tensions, but with two parties of recent vintage—one of which would collapse even more quickly than it arose. Known officially as the American Party, it appealed to nativist Anglo-Protestants alarmed by the influx of immigrants of other origins and faiths, notably Irish Catholics, many of whom began casting ballots as Democrats in cities like Boston and New York soon after they arrived from Ireland. Some northern Whigs who abhorred such immigrants turned temporarily to the American Party when their own party crumbled. Some southern Whigs and Democrats also embraced that new party, particularly in Maryland, where nativists clashed frequently with immigrants in Baltimore. One mayoral candidate there who challenged an American Party incumbent and his intimidating supporters conceded defeat at noon on Election Day to prevent "loss of life."[32] Secret rituals enhanced the mystique of the party, whose adherents were dubbed Know-Nothings for remaining mum about those rites. But the solidarity of their secret society could not withstand sectional disputes exacerbated by conflict in Kansas. When Know-Nothings from northern states lost a platform fight to denounce the Kansas-Nebraska Act at the party's 1856 convention, most of them departed to hold their own convention. Delegates from New York remained behind and joined southerners in nominating former president Millard Fillmore, who received one-fifth of the popular vote that November but won only Maryland. Many southern Whigs who had joined the short-lived American Party subsequently became Democrats.

Far more enduring was the Republican Party, which competed effectively for the presidency in 1856 just two years after forming. The party's unifying principle was opposition to slavery in existing American territories as well as any new ones that might be acquired if Democrats had their way, notably Cuba, targeted by Buchanan when he signed the provocative Ostend Manifesto. Lincoln, a newly enlisted Republican, warned that if the nation continued in the direction Douglas charted for Kansas, slavery would become the "very figure-head of the ship of State," allowed wherever American colonizers planted their flag.[33] Republicans absorbed northern Know-Nothings when their nominee, Speaker of the House Nathaniel P. Banks of Massachusetts, withdrew from the race in favor of Republican candidate John Frémont, who had helped detach California from Mexico before serving as one of the state's first U.S. senators. His nomination dismayed his Democratic father-in-law, Benton, whose bid to return to the Senate had failed when he and Atchison deadlocked in 1855. (The Missouri legislature eventually settled on a third candidate, James S. Green.) Benton feared that Frémont's party, as conspicuously northern as it was antislavery, would spawn a defiantly southern proslavery party of the sort envisioned by the late Calhoun, whom he reviled. Benton's breach with his son-in-law also distanced him from his daughter Jessie, who wrote her father often while aiding her husband's campaign but was met with silence. "He always drops me that way when he is offended with Mr. Frémont," she noted.[34] Hoping that Democrats could preserve national unity, Benton backed Buchanan, but that old Jacksonian from Pennsylvania owed his victory that fall largely to the slave states, carrying all of them but Maryland.

Douglas was relieved when Illinois became one of five free states that backed Buchanan, along with Pennsylvania, New Jersey, Indiana, and California. By overturning the Missouri Compromise and fostering Bleeding Kansas, however, Douglas had so swelled the ranks of Republicans that they would need to capture only a few of the northern states they lost in 1856 to win the presidency in 1860. Echoing Douglas's overconfident prediction when he framed the Kansas-Nebraska Act, Buchanan resolved to end agitation over slavery as president and "destroy sectional parties."[35] Yet his own party was increasingly southern and proslavery.

Buchanan began favoring the slaveholding South before he was inaugurated in March 1857. He knew that the Supreme Court under Chief Justice Taney would soon rule in the case of Dred Scott, a slave in Missouri who had been taken by his owner to the free state of Illinois and the free territory of Wisconsin. For that

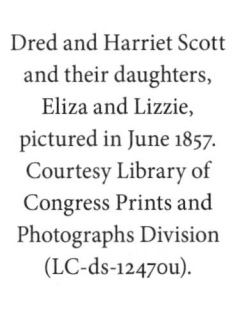

Dred and Harriet Scott
and their daughters,
Eliza and Lizzie,
pictured in June 1857.
Courtesy Library of
Congress Prints and
Photographs Division
(LC-ds-12470u).

reason Scott claimed freedom, which if granted by the court would also promise freedom for his wife, Harriet, an enslaved woman he had wed in Wisconsin, and their two daughters. Buchanan anticipated a broad proslavery decision that he hoped would settle the dispute in Kansas and went so far as to urge his fellow Pennsylvanian, Justice Robert C. Grier, to join the Supreme Court's southern majority in that verdict. At his inauguration, Buchanan said that the question of when the people of a territory could allow or prohibit slavery would soon be decided by the Supreme Court and added that he would "cheerfully submit" to the court's decision. In fact, the ruling would go beyond the question of when slavery could be resolved to whether it could be prohibited in Kansas or any other American territory. Despite expressing hope that the "long agitation" over slavery would soon end, Buchanan implicitly sided with southerners who blamed abolitionists for encouraging slaves to rebel when he warned that "should the agitation continue it may eventually endanger the personal safety of a large portion of our countrymen where the institution exists."[36]

Taney could have denied Scott's appeal by upholding the decision against him by the Missouri Supreme Court and citing as precedent a U.S. Supreme Court ruling in 1851 that states had jurisdiction in such cases. Instead, he ruled that Scott did not have standing in the case because no Black person, free or enslaved, was entitled to American citizenship and qualified to sue in federal courts. Taney argued that the rights and privileges enshrined in the Constitution and the Declaration of Independence were not intended for Black people because "they were at that time considered as a subordinate and inferior class of beings, who had been subjugated by the dominant race, and, whether emancipated or not . . . had no rights or privileges but such as those who held the power and the Government might choose to grant them." The founders would have deserved "universal rebuke and reprobation," he added, if they had included among those created equal and entitled to liberty members of "the negro race, which, by common consent, had been excluded from civilized Governments and the family of nations, and doomed to slavery . . . and were never thought of or spoken of except as property."[37] Benjamin R. Curtis of Massachusetts—one of two Supreme Court justices along with John McLean of Ohio who offered dissenting rather than concurring opinions—noted that free Blacks had legal rights when the republic was founded, including the right to vote in some states, and concluded that "color was not a necessary qualification of citizenship."[38]

Taney's dismal conclusion that Black people must remain legally "subjugated by the dominant race" because they were viewed at the nation's inception as property or a lower class of beings appalled those like Abraham Lincoln who believed that the Declaration of Independence promised liberty for all and that the framers of the Constitution avoided mentioning slavery by name because they knew it was antithetical to the freedom they cherished. Taney rendered his ruling all the more objectionable to free-soilers by declaring that owners retained property rights in slaves like Scott when taking them to territories where slavery had been prohibited under the Missouri Compromise, which he deemed unconstitutional. His conclusion that the Constitution "distinctly and expressly affirmed" the right to hold people as property implied that territorial legislatures could not prohibit slavery and sent shock waves across the North because the same argument might be used to challenge state prohibitions of slavery.[39]

Defying Buchanan and Debating Lincoln

Douglas was not among those northerners outraged by Taney's ruling. "No one can vindicate the character, motive and conduct of the signers of the Declaration of Independence," he stated, "except upon the hypothesis that they referred to the white race alone, and not to the African, when they declared men to have been created free and equal."[40] Like other Democrats, he faulted Republicans for denouncing Taney's opinion and slighting the Supreme Court. Lincoln, who often took issue with Douglas and planned to challenge him when he sought reelection in 1858, responded that Republicans would do what they could to have the court overrule this decision. That meant electing Republican presidents whose appointments would end southern dominance of the court and its allegiance to the Slave Power.

Before taking on Lincoln, Douglas broke with Buchanan over Kansas, where Robert Walker began serving as governor of the territory in May 1857. Like Buchanan, Walker was a Pennsylvania Democrat sympathetic to the South, having represented Mississippi in the Senate before joining Buchanan in Polk's cabinet. Although he had zealously promoted annexing Texas as a slave state, Walker was wary of the proslavery minority in Kansas, whose legislators had clashed with his predecessor Geary before he resigned. Walker accepted the governorship only after Buchanan agreed that any constitution drawn up there should be ratified by the territory's "actual *bona fide* residents" before Kansas applied for statehood.[41] In a vote held in June that was boycotted by free-staters who feared a repetition of the fraudulent legislative election in 1855, proslavery delegates won control of a constitutional convention that met at Lecompton a few months later. The constitution they framed defined those enslaved in Kansas, whose numbers had not much increased since the first census, as the permanent, legal property of their owners and contained other provisions objectionable to free-staters, who were asked to vote not on the constitution as a whole but strictly on the question of whether more slaves could be brought to Kansas once it became a state. Walker had by then persuaded free-staters to take part in a new election, which gave them control of the legislature after he invalidated blatantly fraudulent returns favoring proslavery candidates in two districts. He wanted the entire constitution adopted at Lecompton to be submitted for a vote but no longer had Buchanan's support. Walker resigned in December 1857, citing his "unfortunate difference of opinion" with the president.[42]

Douglas opposed the limited referendum offered by the Lecompton convention as contrary to popular sovereignty. That vote, held in late December, was shunned by free-staters and confirmed a constitution allowing more slaves to be introduced to Kansas. Despite a subsequent election sponsored by the free-state legislature in which far more Kansans opposed the proslavery constitution than had earlier endorsed it, Buchanan sought admission for Kansas as a slave state. He was paying his dues to southerners who were largely responsible for his election. For Douglas, however, the calculation was quite different. His legislative concessions to southern Democrats had not been reciprocated by ultras like Atchison, whose provocations in Kansas brought popular sovereignty into disrepute. Although Douglas had dutifully joined Buchanan in supporting the *Dred Scott* decision, that ruling further alienated northerners alarmed by the Kansas-Nebraska Act. The rapid gains made in Illinois by Republicans placed his reelection there in doubt, and his prospects would worsen if Kansas became a slave state. When he defied Buchanan and repudiated the Lecompton constitution, he was not only upholding popular sovereignty or what he called "that great principle" of his party, "which allowed all white men to form and regulate their domestic institutions to suit themselves"; he was also fighting for his political life. As one supporter in Illinois wrote him, "I don't see how you could have taken any other course, and sustained yourself at home."[43]

Douglas's opposition to the Lecompton bid did not prevent the Senate from approving it, but the northern-dominated House balked, resulting in a congressional compromise that offered a revised referendum to voters in Kansas, whose free-state majority would reject statehood under the Lecompton constitution decisively in August 1858. Douglas did not have to wait until that vote occurred to receive credit in Illinois and elsewhere in the North for opposing the Lecomptonites. Some Republicans thought he might join their party, but Douglas hoped to lure Democrats who had defected to them back to the Democracy, win reelection to the Senate, and secure in 1860 the party's presidential nomination denied him previously. Among his assets in that pursuit was his second wife, Adele Cutts Douglas, whom he wed in late 1856. Unlike his late wife, Martha Martin Douglas, who had preferred to remain at her father's North Carolina estate when Congress was in session, she was thoroughly at home in Washington, where her father, James Madison Cutts, a descendant of prominent families on both sides of the Mason-Dixon Line, served in the Treasury Department. Although half Douglas's age and concerned that her Catholicism might be a political liability for him—to which he responded that one's faith was a matter "no one else has a right to interfere with"—she was poised and politically astute and had the potential to be as accomplished a First Lady as her great-aunt, Dolley Madison.[44] Before she and Douglas could enter the White House, however, he had several hurdles to clear. Standing in his way in 1858 was the Republican senatorial candidate in Illinois, Lincoln, a far less seasoned politician. But Douglas had crossed paths with Lincoln frequently since they first met in Illinois in the 1830s and knew him to be a keen and agile opponent.

When Lincoln proposed in July 1858 that the two candidates debate at various towns in Illinois, Douglas readily accepted. Although he risked giving the lesser-known Lincoln a boost, Douglas relished political combat and trusted that his long experience sparring with opponents in Congress would serve him well. He set the tone in their first debate, held at Ottawa on August 21, by assailing the "house divided" speech Lincoln delivered when accepting the Republican nomination. Why, Douglas asked, could the Union not remain "divided into free and slave States?" The nation's founders had "left each State perfectly free to do as it pleased on the subject of slavery," he added. "Why can it not exist on the same principles on which our fathers made it?" Lincoln replied that the founders intended to restrict slavery to the states where it then existed and place it on the course of ultimate extinction—a questionable assertion, considering that as many slave states as free states had entered the Union under Presidents Washington, Adams, Jefferson, and Madison without objections from those founders. He spoke with more authority when he said that slavery had always been "an apple of discord, and an element of division in the house." Douglas warned that seeking to make the nation's house all free, as Lincoln proposed by confining slavery to the South, would "bring about a dissolution of the Union." Lincoln would later argue to the contrary that restricting slavery geographically, as the Missouri Compromise did, eased sectional strife, whereas allowing it to enter Kansas convulsed the Union. "Why, when we had peace under the Missouri Compromise," he asked Douglas, "could you not have let it alone?"[45] Yet that compromise was meant to preserve the nation part slave and part free, which Lincoln deemed unsustainable. Intent on blaming Douglas and the Kansas-Nebraska Act for the crisis facing the nation, Lincoln ignored how slavery and its extension had long been driving a wedge through the Union.

Having spent much of the first debate on the defensive, Lincoln pressed Douglas when they next met, at Freeport, to reconcile his commitment to popular sovereignty with his support for Taney's decision that slaves remained the rightful property of their owners when taken to American territories. When asked if that ruling left settlers any lawful way of prohibiting slavery in territories before they achieved statehood, Douglas said that the inhabitants could effectively exclude slaveholders by denying them a slave code and law enforcement. Slavery could not exist "a day or an hour anywhere," he stated, "unless it is supported by local police regulations." This so-called Freeport Doctrine received far more notice during the debates than when Douglas made the same argument previously, and it would dim his presidential prospects by alienating southern Democrats who insisted that a territory's inhabitants had no sovereign right to inhibit or prohibit slavery until they applied for statehood. Yet Lincoln recognized that the Freeport Doctrine might help Douglas among free-soilers in Illinois and later countered it by arguing that Taney's decision left settlers who wanted to exclude slavery from a territory no recourse. There was "vigor enough in slavery," he claimed, "to plant itself in a new country" without laws and law enforcement, which were required rather to keep slavery out.[46]

Lincoln also countered Douglas's appeal to Illinoisans who might give him credit for opposing the proslavery Lecompton constitution in Kansas by asking at Freeport if he was in favor of acquiring additional American territory, regardless of how that would "affect the nation on the slavery question." Douglas was known to favor annexing slaveholding Cuba and the nation's right to expand southward into Mexico and Central America, where any U.S. territories established would be open to slavery under the *Dred Scott* decision. He defended his stance by stating that to "increase, and multiply, and expand, is the law of this nation's existence." Whenever Americans required more territory on which to settle, Douglas added, whether "in the North, in the South, or on the Islands of the ocean, I am for it." And he would leave the people there "free to do as they please on the subject of slavery and every other question." Lincoln did not rebut that statement at Freeport, but at their fifth meeting, in Galesburg, he warned that if Douglas's expansionist agenda prevailed, "the next thing will be a grab for the territory of poor Mexico, an invasion of the rich lands of South America," and other imperial acquisitions offering "additional slave fields."[47]

Lincoln suggested at the close of the Freeport debate that Douglas had defied Buchanan and opposed the Lecomptonites in an effort to seduce Republicans and make their party "the tail of his new kite." But if Douglas ever harbored such an ambition, he had forsaken it by the time he faced Lincoln and blasted what he and other Democrats dubbed the "Black Republican Party." Douglas used that racially charged label repeatedly, causing some Republicans in the crowd at Freeport to shout in protest, "White, white," and one listener to ask sarcastically, "Couldn't you modify and call it brown?"

"Not a bit," replied Douglas, who said that since Republicans were committed to abolitionism he must call them "black and not brown." He made much of the fact that Lincoln was supported by the renowned Black abolitionist Frederick Douglass, who had parted ways with William Lloyd Garrison and now believed that slavery could be restricted and ultimately eliminated under the Constitution. (Whether by coincidence or calculation, Stephen Douglas had dropped the final s in his original surname "Douglass" not long after Frederick Douglass's autobiography was published.) Douglas also claimed at Freeport that another Black orator in Illinois he left unnamed was touting "his friend Lincoln as the champion of black men."

"What have you to say against it?" one of Lincoln's supporters shouted. To which Douglas replied that "those of you who believe that the negro is your equal and ought to be on an equality with you socially, politically, and legally, have a right to entertain those opinions, and of course will vote for Mr. Lincoln."[48]

Douglas's race-baiting continued in the third debate, held at Jonesboro in that far southern part of Illinois Douglas called "lower Egypt." He recalled confronting Lincoln and other leaders of the "Black Republican Party" at a debate in Springfield, among them the antislavery stalwart Salmon Chase, now governor of Ohio. "Why didn't you shoot him?" someone in the crowd yelled. Likening his words to bullets, Douglas replied that because he was "single-handed against the white, black and mixed drove, I had to use a shot-gun and fire into the crowd instead of taking them off singly with a rifle." On a more sober note, he declared that states' rights protected not just slaveholders in the South but free-soilers in the North, enabling Illinoisans to prohibit slavery but decide that "the negro shall not be a citizen within our limits; that he shall not vote, hold office, or exercise any political rights."[49]

Lincoln was no abolitionist. He repeatedly stated that Republicans would not, and could not under the Constitution, interfere with slavery in states where it was lawful. Even if slavery was prohibited elsewhere on American soil and confined to those states, as Republicans intended, he said it might linger in the South for a century before it expired. Lincoln was no champion of free Black people and their civil rights either. Mindful that Douglas had insinuated he might deny his

"Abolition platform" when addressing listeners with southern sympathies at Jonesboro, he held back there and waited until the next debate, at Charleston in central Illinois, before stating unequivocally that he was not in favor of "making voters or jurors of negroes," as some in his party were, "nor of qualifying them to hold office, nor to intermarry with white people." The white and Black races were not meant to live together "on terms of social and political equality," he added, and opposing slavery did not mean endorsing racial amalgamation. Because he did not want "a negro woman for a slave," he said, it did not follow he wanted her "for a wife." Yet Lincoln clung to his assertion—reiterated when he and Douglas met at Alton in October for their seventh and final debate—that though all people were not "equal in color, size, intellect," or other attributes, they were equally entitled to those inalienable rights enshrined in the Declaration of Independence, which set a lofty goal for humanity that was "constantly spreading and deepening its influence and augmenting the happiness and value of life to all people, of all colors, every where."[50]

Douglas succeeded during the debates in focusing attention on race—where he felt much better positioned than Lincoln to sway white voters—and in diverting attention from the issue of preserving American territories as free soil, a cause that Republicans championed and northerners who had little sympathy for enslaved or free Black people could embrace. But Lincoln's party had moved beyond the narrow racial appeals of free-soil pioneers like David Wilmot, who sought to ensure that laborers of his own race could inhabit American territories without being disgraced by "association with negro slavery." Some Republicans clung to that dogma, and Lincoln invoked it occasionally, as when he told white New Englanders in March 1860 that he favored keeping territories free so that those who moved west would "not be degraded, not have your family corrupted by forced rivalry with negro slaves."[51] Yet Lincoln's hope that forbidding slavery in the West would ultimately eradicate it in the South and free Black people held in bondage there was shared by many Republicans, including Wilmot, who would help draft the party's 1860 platform. Whether influenced by sentimental antislavery literature like Harriet Beecher Stowe's *Uncle Tom's Cabin* or by fervent abolitionists like Frederick Douglass and Gerrit Smith whose speeches drew curious listeners of various persuasions—including Adele Douglas, who attended a lecture by Smith in Chicago without her husband—Illinoisans proved more receptive to Lincoln's view that all people were entitled to life, liberty, and the pursuit of happiness than Stephen Douglas calculated when appealing to their baser instincts. The November balloting for state legislators, who would then determine which candidate was elected senator, was extremely close. Republicans cast about as many votes as Democrats did, but Democrats won more legislative seats and returned Douglas to the Senate. The tight race indicated that Republicans were within striking distance of taking Illinois in 1860—and made Lincoln a national figure who would contend for the Republican presidential nomination and the chance to deny Douglas the ultimate prize he sought.

CHAPTER 14

Deconstructing the Democracy

Stephen Douglas viewed popular sovereignty as the essence of democracy and the principle on which the party known as the Democracy must stand or fall. By upholding that principle, he believed he was honoring the values of the nation's founders and his party's founder, Andrew Jackson. Northerners such as Lewis Cass and Franklin Pierce who followed Jackson as Democratic standard-bearers had embraced popular sovereignty no less than Douglas did. Even Jackson's vice president and immediate successor, Martin Van Buren, who defected to the Free Soil Party in 1848, returned to the Democratic fold four years later and backed the Compromise of 1850, which left slavery in New Mexico and Utah to be determined by their inhabitants. By 1859, however, Douglas's insistence that the *Dred Scott* decision did not nullify popular sovereignty and require settlers in American territories to uphold slavery there had transformed him from a trusted ally of many southern Democrats to their despised rival, whose bid for the party's presidential nomination in 1860 would split the Democracy and leave the democratic nation it had dominated politically since Jackson's presidency on the brink of fracturing.

Senator James Mason of Virginia, one of those who had pressured Douglas to repeal the Missouri Compromise, spoke for many southern Democrats who felt betrayed by his Freeport Doctrine that settlers could refuse slaveholders legal protection in western territories. As Mason declared in February 1859, "You promised us bread, and you have given us a stone; you promised us a fish, and you have given us a serpent; we thought you had given us a substantial right, and you have given us the most evanescent shadow and delusion."[1] Some northern

Democrats also turned against Douglas after he broke with Buchanan over admitting Kansas as a slave state. Buchanan loyalists in Illinois had retaliated by entering another Democrat in the senatorial race there, but he received few votes and did not affect the outcome.

Characteristically, Douglas responded to such political attacks by fighting back. He resolved to capture the nomination in 1860 that the sixty-eight-year-old Buchanan was not seeking but hoped to deny him, as did numerous southern Democrats in Congress and in state offices. He waged that fight not only in defiance of his political adversaries—who removed him as chairman of the Senate Committee on Territories—but also in defense of his convictions, including his belief that Buchanan had yielded too much to proslavery extremists and given northern Democrats little chance of stemming the rising Republican tide. If the party's next presidential nominee was a doughface like Buchanan or an ardent defender of southern rights like Jefferson Davis, Republicans might sweep the North and win the election, giving fire-eaters in the South cause to foment secession.

Douglas was intent on preventing that outcome, but his determination to do so by seeking the Democratic nomination was not based on a realistic assessment of his prospects. His position was comparable to that of Republican William Seward, an apparent front-runner who was too close to the abolitionist fringe of his party and too outspoken—as evidenced by his notable speech in October 1858 proclaiming an "irrepressible conflict" between the slaveholding South and free-labor North—to appeal to moderates in Illinois, Pennsylvania, and other states bordering the South that were crucial to Republican chances in the general election. Douglas, for his part, was now too close to the free-soil fringe of his party—or those who believed American territories should be free of Black slaves and their owners if white settlers so wished—to attract enough southern Democratic delegates to clinch the nomination, which required a two-thirds majority. Front-runners who fell short of that high standard in the early balloting often lost out to compromise candidates. Douglas was in no mood to yield, however, without fighting for a nomination he felt he deserved and a platform that upheld his doctrines. If in the process he stirred a rebellion by southern Democrats, he and those who had backed his Kansas-Nebraska Act before turning against him would have the unenviable distinction of contributing to the emergence of the opposing Republicans in 1854 and the breakup of their own party in 1860.

Recruiting southern support became even harder for Douglas following John Brown's raid on the federal arsenal at Harpers Ferry, Virginia, in October 1859.

Accompanied by twenty-one men, including several free Black recruits, Brown intended to seize weapons there and distribute them to slaves he hoped would rebel in response to his raid. No such uprising occurred, however, and U.S. Marines led by Lieutenant Colonel Robert E. Lee overwhelmed the raiders and captured Brown, who was executed on December 2 after declaring in his last testament that he was "now quite certain that the crimes of this guilty land will never be purged away but with blood."[2] Brown's attempt to incite a slave rebellion was all the more alarming to white southerners because he was funded by northern abolitionists and hailed as a martyr at his death by northern sympathizers. In the wake of his raid, the ongoing dispute in Congress over slavery in the territories took on broader significance as southern Democrats challenged northerners in their party to denounce abolitionism and protect slavery in existing states as well as American territories. Unlike fire-eaters intent on secession, such as Robert Barnwell Rhett of South Carolina and Edmund Ruffin of Virginia, prominent southern Democrats in Congress like Davis were not yet prepared to abandon the Union. But they were under pressure to mount a stronger defense of slavery than Douglas would allow if he became their party's leader.

In February 1860, Davis introduced a resolution in the Senate that called on the federal government to protect "the constitutional right of any citizen of the United States to take his slave property into the common Territories . . . if experience should at any time prove that the judiciary does not possess power to insure adequate protection." Although Davis insisted that he was seeking "no slave code" for the territories, his proposal that Congress intervene "when personal and property rights in the Territories are not protected" meant upholding and enforcing slavery there by federal law if necessary.[3] Such intervention—long opposed by southerners who feared congressional prohibition of slavery in American territories but favored now by those emboldened by Taney's *Dred Scott* decision—would obliterate popular sovereignty as Douglas conceived it. His opponents knew he could not lead the party if delegates endorsed a prospective federal slave code at the forthcoming Democratic convention at Charleston, South Carolina.

Charleston was a hotbed of southern defiance and separatism in 1860. As an aide to Douglas noted, it was "the last place on Gods Earth where a national convention should have been held."[4] Just over half the delegates who convened there in April supported Douglas, not nearly enough to ensure his nomination and barely enough to withstand a determined effort by their opponents to insert in the party platform a plank favoring a federal guarantee for slavery in the territories. Leading that drive was fire-eater William Yancey, who was prepared to break with northern Democrats if they won the platform fight. On April 27, he addressed a hall packed with delegates and proslavery Charlestonians and portrayed the issue before the convention as a contest between two societies, one that reduced poor white laborers to drudges or wage slaves and another that upheld white liberty and racial supremacy. As he declared to northern delegates in support of the proslavery plank:

> If you desire the good of your country—if you desire the welfare of this union . . . then I would say to you: "Hands off and let us work our own row in these Territories." If you beat us at the end you will be entitled to the palm of victory. If we beat you, we will give you good servants for life and enable you to live comfortably, and we will take your poor white man and elevate him from the office of boot-black, and from other menial offices . . . we will elevate him to a place amongst the master race and put the negro race to do this dirty work which God designed they should do.[5]

Yancey's diatribe, which echoed the assertion of proslavery ideologue George Fitzhugh that there were no "white slaves in the South, because we have black ones," was sure to rile northern delegates who scorned the claim that only in slave states practicing so-called master race democracy were all white men truly free and equal.[6] Yancey's further claim that Democrats had lost ground to Republicans in the North because they apologized for slavery rather than defending it manfully brought a blistering response from Senator George E. Pugh of Ohio. Pugh rightly attributed those Republican gains to costly concessions that northern Democrats made to southerners in their party, including repealing the Missouri Compromise and thus enabling proslavery forces to infiltrate Kansas and skew elections there. As Pugh declared, "We adhered to your cause, gentlemen of the South, in supporting the Kansas-Nebraska bill; we have adhered ever since—until from such heights of power, and influence, and almost absolute domination, at home, we have fallen to what we are now." Northern Democrats would not have another proslavery initiative foisted on them that would further weaken them at home and bolster their Republican foes. Do you think us so craven, Pugh asked, as to submit to such demands and "place our hands on our mouths and our mouths in the dust? Oh, gentlemen of the South—once and for all!—you entirely mistake us. We are not of that sort; we cannot do what you seem to desire—and we will not!"[7]

There was more at stake here for Yancey and Pugh and the factions they represented than whether Congress would grant legal protection in the form of a federal slave code to those planters inclined to migrate to western territories—or to foreign lands the United States might annex such as Cuba or Mexico, where Buchanan had recently proposed intervening to suppress "anarchy and violence," to which Americans were contributing along the border.[8] Yancey linked the dispute at the convention to the wider grievances of white southerners who felt demeaned and threatened by verbal assaults on their way of life by northerners. Pugh, for his part, voiced the indignation of northern Democrats who loathed being portrayed as lackeys of slaveholders who were now demanding federal protection for their notorious institution. That some southern Democrats driven by what Pugh called the "urgency of fanaticism" were threatening secession if denied such protection further aggravated Douglas's supporters by tainting their party with disunion. Federal support for slavery had become a matter of honor whose acceptance or rejection would be intolerable to one side or the other. Yancey's Alabamans and other southern delegates vowed to bolt if that proslavery plank was rejected, and some northern delegates threatened to do likewise if it was approved. Echoing Seward, journalist Murat Halstead of Cincinnati wrote that there was an "irrepressible conflict" within the Democracy at Charleston.[9]

Douglas's supporters won the vote, prompting nearly fifty southern delegates to walk out. Most of those who bolted came from the seven states of the Lower South that would initiate the Confederacy in February 1861: Texas, Louisiana, Mississippi, Alabama, Florida, Georgia, and South Carolina. Douglas's cause was then stymied when delegates who remained in the hall upheld a ruling—favored by many from New York and the Upper South who were seeking a compromise candidate—that required approval of the nominee by two-thirds of the convention's 303 delegates before the walkout. After 57 ballots, Douglas remained stuck at barely half that number, and the convention adjourned. It reconvened in Baltimore in June after pro-Douglas delegations were organized in several states whose delegates had bolted the Charleston convention. Many of those absconders then appeared at Baltimore and demanded to be seated in place of the newly recruited delegates. Douglas recognized that his party was on the verge of breaking apart and reluctantly offered to withdraw his candidacy. But his supporters in Baltimore were not about to concede defeat and voted to exclude from the convention enough of those seeking reentry who opposed him to ensure Douglas's nomination. That in turn caused most of the remaining southern delegates to withdraw in protest. Soon after the convention backed Douglas, defiant southern Democrats split the party by nominating their own presidential candidate: Buchanan's vice president, John C. Breckinridge of Kentucky.

Slavery's Long Reach

Among those who joined southerners in bolting the Baltimore convention were delegates from California and Oregon, which despite their status as free states proved receptive to proslavery politicians of southern origin like Joseph Lane, Breckinridge's running mate. Born in North Carolina, Lane settled in Indiana and commanded troops during the Mexican-American War before becoming governor of Oregon Territory in 1849. When Oregon achieved statehood a decade later, he entered the U.S. Senate and allied with southern Democrats. Voters in Oregon rejected a proposal Lane favored to legalize slavery in their state, but they approved a clause in their constitution excluding free Black people. Oregon thus became the only free state to join the Union with that restriction, although several northern states enacted exclusionary laws after being admitted. When accepting the nomination for vice president, Lane called for enforcing the *Dred Scott* decision by stating that the "Judicial authority, as provided by the Constitution," must be upheld "in regard to the rights of property in the Territories as in all other matters."[10]

California attracted many southerners, who made up about one-third of its population when it achieved statehood in 1850. Its first elected governor, Peter H. Burnett, was a former slave owner born in Tennessee who practiced law in Missouri before emigrating to Oregon, where he joined its provisional government and enacted a statute in 1844 requiring emancipated slaves to leave the state or be whipped. Burnett moved to California during the gold rush and helped develop the boomtown of Sacramento. During his brief term as governor, which ended in 1851, he failed to win legislative approval for a law excluding Black people from California. In 1852, however, California assemblyman Henry A. Crabb—a native of Tennessee who would be executed in Mexico five years later for filibustering with armed American recruits in Sonora—won passage of a draconian fugitive-slave act that denied freedom to those who had fled bondage in California before it entered the Union and allowed them to be seized and reenslaved in the South. Furthermore, the law as amended allowed those in violation of the state's poorly enforced prohibition of slavery to remain for up to three years before returning to southern states with the people they held in bondage. How in supposedly free California, asked the antislavery weekly *National Era*, were those still enslaved "to know their rights, and who is there to assert them?"[11]

The powerful, proslavery wing of the Democratic Party in California that backed Crabb's fugitive-slave act and other repressive measures was known as the Chivalry and led by U.S. Senator William M. Gwin, a former congressman from Mississippi who continued to own slaves in that state after moving to California in 1849 and who later backed Breckinridge for president. Gwin used his influence with the southern-leaning Pierce and Buchanan administrations to establish a customhouse and U.S. mint in San Francisco and pack them with federal employees loyal to the Chivalry. He and his allies in the state legislature reached beyond their southern base by catering to white Californians in general with laws that imposed prohibitive taxes on miners from Mexico, China, and other foreign countries and subjected Indians to forced labor. The Chivalry also gained support among some prominent Californios, including Andrés Pico, a former foe of American occupation forces. Pico was appointed a tax collector by Gwin and introduced a bill in 1859 to divide the state and make southern California a separate American territory. Pico and other landholders there touted the plan as a way of obtaining relief from burdensome state taxes on their property, but critics suspected it would also serve the purposes of politicians like Gwin and Henry Foote of Mississippi, who described it as laying the foundation for "a slave State in Southern California."[12] The bill was passed by the state legislature and approved by voters in the south but then died in Congress.

That and other Chivalry initiatives were opposed by the northern wing of California's Democratic party led by U.S. senator David C. Broderick, a combative veteran of ward politics in New York who backed Douglas when he broke with Buchanan over the proslavery Lecompton constitution in Kansas. In September 1859, Broderick faced off against a formidable Chivalry foe: California's former chief justice David S. Terry, born in Kentucky, raised in Texas, and intent on advancing the southern expansionist agenda that Broderick reviled. Terry killed him in a duel emblematic of the mounting antagonism between northern and southern Democrats nationwide.

In the presidential election of 1860, roughly 60 percent of those who cast ballots in California and Oregon would vote for one of the two Democratic candidates, Douglas or Breckinridge. Had Democrats coalesced behind a single candidate, they could have won both states, which went to Lincoln narrowly. Instead, the party split over an issue that was extraneous to free states—granting slaveholders in American territories federal protection—and offered little benefit to slave states, where few planters found those territories alluring. The more southern Democrats focused on extending slavery, the more they antagonized northern Democrats and left their fractious party vulnerable to the cohesive Republicans. A federal slave code would likely have done little to help slavery as practiced in the South prevail in western territories, as indicated in Utah and New Mexico, where such codes were enacted.

In February 1852 the Utah territorial legislature passed "An Act in Relation to Service," which affirmed the right of masters to the labor and services of those "justly bound to them." An amended version of a bill entitled "An Act in Relation to African Slavery," the revised code followed the example of Brigham Young when he addressed that subject by making no mention of "slaves" or "slavery" and emphasizing the obligations of masters, who had to send their "servants of the African race" to school for at least eighteen months before they turned twenty-one and would forfeit any such enslaved people they had sex with, punished unreasonably, or treated cruelly.[13] Slave owners in Utah did not always honor that code, but few of them settled in Utah before or after the act was passed. According to the federal census, which was inexact when counting the population of far western territories and distinguishing free Black people from those enslaved, the number of slaves in Utah barely increased from twenty-six in 1850 to twenty-nine in 1860. There may have been twice as many African Americans in bondage there as those records indicate, but enactment of the slave or "service" code did little to increase their numbers.

The marginal existence of slavery in Utah was largely ignored amid the national furor over polygamy there. When delegates to the first Republican presidential convention in 1856 railed in their platform against those "twin relics of barbarism—Polygamy and Slavery," their concern was plural marriage in Utah rather than Black bondage there.[14] President Buchanan, elected that fall, sent troops to Utah in 1857, not to end slavery or polygamy but to force Brigham Young to resign as territorial governor after he clashed with federal officials. As sectional rivalry for control of American territories increased in the late 1850s, Republicans grew more concerned about New Mexico, where the territorial legislature in early 1859 passed a much harsher slave code than instituted in Utah. Entitled "An Act to Provide for the Protection of Property in Slaves in this Territory," it applied to enslaved Black people rather than Indians or mestizos, who if held in bondage legally in New Mexico were deemed peons or indentured servants and covered under a separate act governing "contracts between masters and servants."[15] Among other provisions, the New Mexico slave code prohibited emancipating enslaved Black people, imposed severe penalties for aiding or encouraging them to escape, and called for slaves who were insolent or committed other offenses to be whipped or branded. Editor Horace Greeley denounced the code as "most inhuman and piratical" and warned that it was "widening the base of the Slave Power."[16]

The instigator of that controversial act was Miguel Antonio Otero, New Mexico's nonvoting delegate to Congress, who had recently wed the daughter of a South Carolina slave owner and was aligned with southern Democrats in the House. Enacting a slave code in New Mexico would "tend to elevate our own class of free laborers," wrote Otero, who also thought it would be politically advantageous for the territory.[17] At his suggestion, officials appointed by Buchanan pressed the legislature to adopt the act, which was drafted by territorial secretary Alexander M. Jackson of Mississippi and based in part on that state's slave code. The legislators, many of whom were Hispanic New Mexicans, may have concluded as Otero did that the act, which was rammed through without a roll call, would put their territory in the good graces of an administration that supported the Lecompton constitution and the *Dred Scott* decision. The punitive code did not reflect enthusiasm among the populace as a whole for African American slavery, which New Mexican delegates had opposed when they sought admission to the Union unsuccessfully in 1850. According to the 1860 census, there were fewer than one hundred Black people in the territory, free or enslaved.

In mid-1860, Republican representative John A. Bingham of Ohio secured passage in the House of a bill to nullify New Mexico's slave code, but it died in the Senate. As secession gained momentum at year's end, some Republicans would consider offering New Mexico statehood without restriction on slavery to appease southern Democrats, who might assume that a territory with a slave code would seek admission as a slave state. The *Chicago Tribune*'s editor feared that outcome and urged Republicans not to surrender New Mexico to the "powers of darkness."[18] But the slave code imposed there did not alter conditions inhospitable to southern planters and their peculiar institution in a land where water was scarce and irrigated fields were precious resources for New Mexicans. Legislators in Santa Fe who sought favor with the proslavery Buchanan administration might change their tune under Lincoln. In any case, statehood for New Mexico as a sop to the South would be abandoned in Congress as efforts to avert secession collapsed in early 1861. Late that year, New Mexico's territorial legislature would signal its loyalty to the Union by repealing the slave code. Nothing short of an invasion by Confederates could impose their proslavery regime there—and that would be repulsed during the war that resulted when southerners fractured the Democracy in pursuit of a federal slave code and went on to fracture the Union.

Southern hopes for a slaveholding empire extending to the Pacific were not mere pipe dreams. The lowermost portion of New Mexico, situated in and around the Gadsden Purchase and encompassing the towns of Mesilla and Tucson, attracted a significant number of southerners, many of them prospectors from Texas. By the mid-1850s, they made up roughly half the ten thousand or so non-Native inhabitants there and were seeking to form a territory of their own called Arizona. Few of them held Black slaves, which may have helped them attract support from Hispanics in the area, but their sympathies lay so firmly with the South that Arizona would later secede from a Union that did not recognize its existence. The legislature in Santa Fe opposed their efforts to separate from New Mexico Territory, and their appeals to Congress for separate territorial status encountered the same barriers that stalled the application from southern California, including Republican resistance and Democratic reluctance to provoke another bitter sectional dispute like that over Kansas. Had the Democracy held together in 1860 and won the presidency and control of Congress, however, both territories might perhaps have been organized, providing a southern-dominated corridor across the lower United States. As Jefferson Davis hoped, a transcontinental railroad could then have been built along that corridor by slave labor, thus accomplishing what one promoter, Thomas Jefferson Green, envisioned as a "great slavery road" from the Atlantic to the Pacific.[19]

The differing expansionist agendas of northern and southern Democrats might have prevented such an outcome even if their party had remained united and triumphed in 1860. But by insisting on congressional protection for slavery in American territories, southern expansionists broke the Democracy in two and helped Lincoln, Greeley, and other influential Republicans focus their party intently on thwarting slavery and southern intrigue in the West. Without challenging the *Dred Scott* decision, Republicans could by prevailing at the polls in 1860 oust proslavery territorial officials in New Mexico, deny patronage to Gwin and his Chivalry machine, and prevent Arizona and southern California from becoming territories. They were aided in pursuing such objectives by southern Democrats, who had long opposed congressional efforts to regulate slavery in American territories but now proposed asserting federal authority there so blatantly in support of slave owners that they alienated northern Democrats and made any real or potential gains by southern expansionists live ammunition for Republican attacks.

Campaigning against Secession

The nomination of Breckinridge by southern Democrats in June 1860 was both a curse and a blessing for Douglas. It left him no chance of winning states in the Lower South that went solidly for Pierce and Buchanan in the past two presidential elections. His hopes rested on winning over those in the Upper South and in northern states bordering it who feared for the Union if either the fire-eaters backing Breckinridge or their Republican opponents emerged victorious. Douglas faced stiff competition for those votes, however. Rivaling him in the Upper South was John Bell of Tennessee, former senator and Speaker of the House and nominee of the newly formed Constitutional Union Party, which appealed to many in the region hoping to avoid secession and civil war. Vying with Douglas in Illinois and other states bordering the South was his old foe Lincoln, whose managers skillfully promoted him as the moderate alternative to Seward at the Republican convention in Chicago in early May. Nominated on the third ballot after Seward faltered, Lincoln led a party united in opposition to the fractured Democracy and eager to exploit its breakup. That he was likely to win most northern states and sure to be elected if he won them all worked against Douglas, who if he carried even a few free states might deny Lincoln an electoral-vote majority and leave the decision to the House of Representatives, where Breckinridge might prevail by securing the vote of every slave state as well as California and Oregon. The political rebellion of southern Democrats thus hurt Douglas in the North as well as the South. Yet it also freed him from the burden of straddling the sectional divide within his party. No longer in the same camp with ultra-proslavery men inclined to secede if Lincoln won, he emerged as an eloquent Unionist—a role that seemed natural to him because he was not introspective or mindful of how he had helped foster disunion by making concessions that failed to appease those ultras while arousing adamant northern opposition to their demands.

Campaigning energetically, Douglas divided his time between the North and Upper South until early October, when Republicans swept congressional and local elections in two states that Buchanan won in 1856, Pennsylvania and Indiana. If Lincoln prevailed there and in the other free states that Frémont carried in 1856, he would be the next president. Douglas had little doubt that would be the outcome and spent the last few weeks of the campaign speaking on behalf of the Union and against secession to large crowds in Missouri, Tennessee, Alabama, and Georgia, home to his running mate and former governor of that state, Herschel V. Johnson. Douglas's last-ditch campaign against disunion was his finest effort as a public figure, but he changed few minds. Many Democrats in the Lower South considered him little better than Lincoln and bristled when he affirmed his earlier declaration at Norfolk, Virginia, that a Republican victory would not justify secession and that the president, "whoever he may be, should treat all attempts to break up the Union, by resistance to its laws, as Old Hickory treated the Nullifiers in 1832."[20] Such Jacksonian Unionism no longer appealed to southerners alarmed by a Republican candidate who believed that preserving the nation half slave and half free as it expanded was not just unsustainable but unconscionable.

Lincoln's victory on November 6—with only 40 percent of the popular vote but 60 percent of the electoral vote, coming entirely from free states—triggered the reaction Douglas feared. South Carolina seceded on December 20, and the six other states of the original Confederacy followed suit over the next six weeks. Douglas viewed the Confederate rebellion as a plot that began when fire-eaters like Yancey split the Democratic Party, increasing the likelihood of a Republican victory, which then served as their pretext for dividing the nation. Secession from the party, he declared after southern Democrats nominated Breckinridge, meant "secession from the federal Union." Speaking in Alabama as the campaign drew to a close, he warned that there was "a conspiracy on foot to break up this Union."[21] Some southern Democrats who backed Breckinridge were indeed fomenting what Yancey, after bolting the Charleston convention, touted as a "new revolution," prompting the crowd he addressed there to give "three cheers for the Independent Southern Republic."[22] Such fire-eaters welcomed a Republican victory if that would give birth to secession. But other southern Democrats hoped to deny Lincoln an electoral majority and defeat him in the House. In the South as a whole, far more voters wanted to avoid a Republican triumph than hoped to enable one. When that victory occurred, many found it so intolerable that support for secession spread far beyond those militants who were seeking a second American revolution in the South.

The sudden emergence of the Confederacy following Lincoln's election was remarkable considering that Democrats still controlled the Senate and Democratic-appointed justices still dominated the Supreme Court. The resignation of secessionist Democrats from the Senate and Lincoln's appointments to the high court in years to come would enhance his authority and effectively nullify the *Dred Scott* decision upholding slavery in American territories. But there were few things Lincoln could do under the Constitution to interfere with slavery in southern states. He could appoint Republican postmasters in the South, which secessionists and those who would soon join them like Senator Thomas L. Clingman of North Carolina warned would flood slave states with incendiary "abolitionist pamphlets."[23] As commander in chief, Lincoln could also place officers loyal to his administration in command of federal forts in the South, which fire-eaters envisioned as hostile government strongholds and havens for fugitive slaves if the forts were not soon seized by Confederates. Secessionists won support for their cause less by stressing what Lincoln and his antislavery party could do constitutionally, however, than by stoking white fears of a calamitous Black rebellion incited by so-called Black Republicans.

Southern dread of being hemmed in by hostile forces had deep roots in American history and the American psyche. In colonial times, the great fear was of tribal hostilities aroused by foreign powers, as during the French and Indian War. That anxiety persisted through the Revolutionary War and the War of 1812, both of which set Americans against the British and their Indian allies and also prompted enslaved people to seek freedom behind British lines, where some enlisted to fight opposing Americans. Subsequent warnings that the British might throttle the slaveholding South by winding about it "like the terrible anaconda," as Michael Hoke of North Carolina imagined, later served as a rationale for annexing Texas and preserving it as an outlet for surplus slaves who might otherwise rebel. By 1860 the Black Republicans had replaced the British as the bêtes noires of white southerners, threatening to trap them amid millions of slaves, who might then lash out. That threat was conveyed most vividly by a metaphor employed by various northern opponents of slavery, including Thaddeus Stevens of Pennsylvania, who reportedly vowed that he and his fellow Republicans would "encircle the slave States of this Union with free States as a cordon of fire, and that slavery, like a scorpion, would sting itself to death."[24] The implication for anxious white southerners—particularly those living where they were in the minority—was that they might perish along with slavery when caught in that ring of fire and targeted by rebellious slaves.

States intent on secession sent commissioners to urge southerners elsewhere to abandon the Union rather than risk disaster under Republican rule. Stephen F. Hale, Alabama's commissioner to Kentucky, assured that state's governor that whites would be "degraded to a position of equality with free negroes." Other secessionists warned that Republican domination and forced emancipation would lower white southerners who had been spared menial labor to "hewers of wood and drawers of water" like the subjugated Gibeonites reduced to slavery in the

Bible (Joshua 9:23). Hale and like-minded secession commissioners predicted an even more alarming outcome if the South succumbed to Lincoln's party: an apocalyptic race war. Although Hale claimed that enslaving Black people improved their "moral, physical, and intellectual condition," he warned that they would savagely attack whites when exposed by Republicans to abolitionism. A "dark pall of barbarism" would descend on the South, he stated, and the "horrors and crimes" of the revolution in Haiti would be reenacted, consigning white men to death and their "wives and daughters to pollution and violation to satisfy the lust of half-civilized Africans." Another secession commissioner, Andrew Pickens Calhoun, son of the late senator, urged those in other states to join South Carolinians in resisting "degradation and annihilation" at the hands of Black Republicans and Black people they incited. White southerners who embraced the Confederate cause would, he vowed, fight and "die freemen rather than live slaves."[25]

Those promoting secession had reason to fan the fears of whites living in slave states, but warnings of racial amalgamation or annihilation if slaves were emancipated or encouraged to seek freedom had long been issued by leaders loyal to the Union. Jefferson's dismal assumption that allowing emancipated Blacks to inhabit the same country as whites would "produce convulsions which will probably never end but in the extermination of the one or the other race" led him to accept the existence and extension of slavery until a practical scheme of colonizing most freed slaves abroad could be instituted, which meant prolonging Black bondage indefinitely.[26] Jackson asserted that proposing even gradual emancipation over the course of several decades, as Congressman Tallmadge did when Missouri sought admission to the Union, would incite slaves to "masacre."[27] Such fears led many Jacksonians to rule out any remedy for the problem that ultimately shattered the Union other than preserving roughly half slave and half free a republic whose geography and demography—notably the widening gap between the surging northern population and the smaller southern population—doomed that precarious balancing act as the nation developed. Douglas believed that slavery had little chance of prevailing in western territories but denounced efforts to prohibit it there as part of a radical Black Republican agenda that supposedly included promoting racial amalgamation, which would taint "not only the purity of the blood, but the purity of the government," he claimed, and cause national "degeneration, demoralization, and degradation."[28] By branding Lincoln during their well-publicized debates as an agent of abolition and amalgamation, Douglas arguably did more to reinforce southern resistance to Republican rule than he later did to discourage secession.

That southern politicians continued until the eve of secession to seek guarantees for slavery in western territories largely ill-suited for plantation slavery
indicated how much they feared being hemmed in and trapped like scorpions in
a ring of fire. Whether a Republican administration not confronted with armed
Confederate resistance would have pursued abolition, as fire-eaters warned,
remains a matter of conjecture because secession led quickly to civil war and
a nightmare of another sort for southerners who dreaded constriction: the
Union's wartime Anaconda Plan, which called for blockading southern ports,
seizing control of the Mississippi, and throttling the Confederacy. But even
catastrophic defeat for the South did not produce the murderous apocalypse they
feared. Rather than wreaking wholesale vengeance on white civilians when the
Confederacy began crumbling, enslaved people would instead deprive owners
of their labor and seek refuge behind Union lines, where some would enlist as
soldiers and "die freemen rather than live slaves" in battle against Confederates
who allowed them no quarter.

A Crisis beyond Compromise

During the "secession winter" that followed Lincoln's election, Douglas was
encouraged when states in the Upper South refrained from joining the Confederacy. He was among thirteen senators who served on a committee led by
Senator John J. Crittenden of Kentucky, a founder of the Constitutional Union
Party, who hoped to keep those states loyal and coax others that seceded back
into the Union by fashioning a grand compromise in the tradition of the late
Henry Clay. Like Douglas, Crittenden held slaves and believed that tolerating
slavery and enforcing Black subservience were essential to preserving a nation
organized by and for white men, a bias evident in their proposals. Douglas put
forward constitutional amendments designed to appeal to southerners as well as
northerners who disdained free African Americans. One would have prohibited
"persons of the African race" from voting or holding office in any American
jurisdiction, which contradicted his long-held view that such matters were
for those in territories or states to determine. Another would have authorized
the United States to acquire districts "in Africa and South America, for the
colonization, at the expense of the Federal Treasury, of such free negroes and
mulattoes as the several States may wish to have removed from their limits"
or whom Congress might remove from the District of Columbia and other
places under its jurisdiction.[29] All five Republicans on the committee opposed
those amendments, and they were not presented to the Senate by Crittenden.

They were included, however, in a compromise that the House rejected in late February 1861.

The most significant constitutional amendment proposed by Crittenden would have nullified the *Dred Scott* decision by forbidding slavery in American territories above 36°30', the former Missouri Compromise line, while upholding slavery in territories below that line. Republicans who felt that some concessions were in order did not insist on prohibiting slavery in new western territories that attracted few slaveholders such as Colorado and Nevada, which like California were initially settled largely by prospectors and merchants who supplied them. Soon after Kansas was admitted to the Union as a free state in late January 1861 by a Congress from which prominent southern secessionists had resigned, Colorado, Nevada, and Dakota Territories were organized without reference to slavery, which if prohibited there would have been at odds with the *Dred Scott* decision. Crittenden's proposed amendment went beyond that neutral stance, however, by stating that in all territories south of 36°30' "slavery of the African race is hereby recognized as existing, and shall not be interfered with by Congress; but shall be protected as property by all the departments of the territorial government during its continuance."[30] Douglas endorsed the amendment even though it nullified popular sovereignty there.

Lincoln, born in Kentucky and wed to a Kentuckian, Mary Todd Lincoln, understood Crittenden's desire to avert a conflict that threatened to tear that border state apart. He was willing to compromise on some divisive issues, such as upholding a modified fugitive-slave law. But he could not accept Crittenden's amendment recognizing slavery and slaveholders' presumed property rights in existing American territories or those that might be "hereafter acquired" below 36°30', which would allow for annexing Mexico, Cuba, or other foreign lands as slaveholding territories. Lincoln would not allow for the extension of slavery. "On that point hold firm, as with a chain of steel," he insisted. Mindful of the encouragement that Pierce and Buchanan had given to southern expansionism in the Far West and Latin America, Lincoln told Seward he opposed any deal that "would put us again on the high-road to a slave empire."[31]

Other amendments Crittenden proposed were also opposed by Republicans, including one that barred Congress from abolishing slavery in the District of Columbia as long as it existed in Virginia and Maryland. That none of Crittenden's amendments could ever be nullified by future amendments increased resistance to his compromise as a whole, which was rejected by the House on March 1 and narrowly defeated by the Senate in the early hours of March 4, 1861, Lincoln's

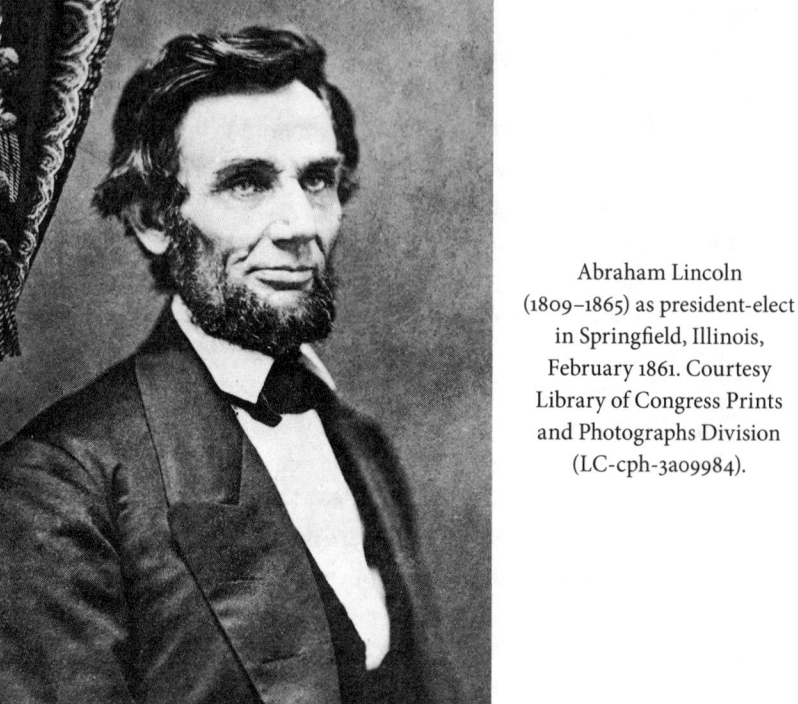

Abraham Lincoln
(1809–1865) as president-elect
in Springfield, Illinois,
February 1861. Courtesy
Library of Congress Prints
and Photographs Division
(LC-cph-3a09984).

inaugural day. The only constitutional amendment approved by Congress before it adjourned ruled out congressional interference with slavery in states where it existed, a measure Lincoln accepted because he disclaimed any such intention or authority. As president, however, he was free to alter his stance because the amendment was not adopted by the states.

Douglas was pleased when Lincoln struck a conciliatory note in his inaugural address and told southerners: "We must not be enemies. Though passion may have strained, it must not break our bonds of affection." But Lincoln also vowed to "hold, occupy, and possess the property, and places belonging to the government," which included Fort Sumter in Charleston Harbor, where the first shots of the Civil War would soon be fired.[32] Douglas and other compromisers would have surrendered the fort rather than the risk that outcome, but Lincoln rejected that option. His Democratic predecessor, James Buchanan, notorious for his concessions to southerners, had nonetheless sent two hundred troops to reinforce Sumter in a merchant ship that was repulsed in January before it reached the fort. Lincoln felt he could do no less than reprovision soldiers stranded there, who would have to surrender if they did not receive rations. That put the onus on South Carolinians if they attacked. On orders from Confederate president Jefferson Davis, they bombarded Fort Sumter on April 12 before it could be resupplied and accepted its surrender a day later.

On April 14, Lincoln met with Douglas in the White House and told him he would summon troops the following day to defend the Union, a call to arms that would prompt four more states—Virginia, North Carolina, Tennessee, and Arkansas—to join the Confederacy. Lincoln said he was asking for 75,000 state militiamen. "I would make it 200,000," remarked Douglas, who urged "prompt action" to preserve the Union.[33] Although still vigorous enough to deliver a rousing speech on his return to Chicago in which he insisted that there "can be no neutrals in this war, *only patriots—or traitors*," Douglas had less than two months to live.[34] He had long suffered from an ulcerated throat, aggravated perhaps by his overindulgence in whiskey and cigars, and from bouts of rheumatic fever, which led to his death on June 3. His career ended in defiance of secessionists, and his legacy to his embattled republic included substantial support from two new states he had organized as territories, Kansas and Minnesota, which provided tens of thousands of Union troops by war's end. But Douglas's concessions to slavery, intended to placate southerners, had instead emboldened future secessionists like David Atchison, who would battle Unionists in Missouri during the Civil War. And though Douglas conceded in a speech at Springfield, Illinois, on April 25 that he may have erred by "leaning too far to the southern section of the Union against my own," he would have readily embraced a compromise that allowed slavery in American territories, particularly if the agreement upheld popular sovereignty there. Supporting Lincoln's war effort did not mean supporting the president's party, whose policies Douglas deplored. As he stated at Springfield, he stood "in equal, irreconcilable, and undying opposition both to the Republicans and Secessionists."[35]

Douglas remained true to the Democratic Party forged by Jackson and dedicated to life, liberty, and the pursuit of happiness for white Americans, whether they labored on free soil or relied freely on slave labor. (Those formerly in that party's antislavery minority were now mostly Republicans.) Although the Democracy was strained by Mr. Polk's War and fractured when the party's southern wing demanded too great a concession from Douglas and his supporters, it endured in the wartime North, where its representatives would largely oppose efforts by Republicans to use leverage they gained when southern Democrats left Congress to end slavery, which Douglas warned against. "No adjustment will restore & preserve peace," he wrote shortly after South Carolina seceded, "*which does not banish the slavery question from Congress power* and place it beyond the reach of Federal Legislation."[36] Had he lived to witness the congressional prohibition of slavery in American territories in June 1862 and Lincoln's subsequent emancipation proclamation, Douglas would likely have deplored those momentous advances. His premature death at the age of forty-eight thus spared him from being remembered as a wartime opponent of a president hailed as the Union's savior and Great Emancipator.

Douglas was a more tragic figure than Lincoln, who acquired that aura because of his travails as commander in chief and his assassination at war's end. Before Lincoln died, however, he had the satisfaction of defeating the Confederacy and securing passage of the Thirteenth Amendment, abolishing slavery. And he was mercifully free of a trait long associated with those who brought tragedy on themselves and others: hubris. Douglas possessed hubris in abundance. His assurance that he knew how to heal the nation did not waver even when his prescription made the patient worse. As he said of his adherence to self-rule and popular sovereignty, which caused turmoil in Kansas and heightened tensions between North and South: "I knew I was right—I knew my principles were sound—I knew that the people would see in the end that I had done right, and I knew that the God of Heaven would smile upon me if I was faithful in the performance of my duty."[37] Such hubris could lead one astray even when right, and Douglas was right when he advocated nurturing self-government in American territories and allowing their inhabitants a say in matters that affected them but did not affect "the general welfare of the Republic," which he acknowledged was Congress's responsibility.[38] Yet he was tragically wrong when he enabled the intensifying dispute over slavery, an issue crucial to the nation's welfare, to be thrashed out by opposing factions in territory where slavery was previously forbidden.

Douglas was insensitive to the evils of slavery and the hazards of abetting it, perhaps because he profited from it at a remove. His emotional detachment from the core problem of his era and his career was greater than that of Jefferson, Jackson, or Polk, products of the South who were deeply involved in its peculiar institution. Yet they all maintained as much distance as they could from the harsh realities and unsettling consequences of slavery while relying on it personally and advancing it materially. Despite their devotion to the Union and their determination to enhance it, their efforts furthered slavery and compounded that fault in the nation's foundation, which could not support the weight of the continental expansion they collectively engineered and fractured disastrously in 1861.

The dilemma for those master builders of the house divided, and for earnest compromisers like Henry Clay, was that efforts to maintain the nation part slave and part free compromised the Union structurally and made it more fragile as it expanded. The Missouri Compromise, by partitioning the West, sustained the conflicted slaveholding empire of liberty that Jefferson enlarged in 1803, but that pact could not withstand further American expansion and aroused bitter recriminations when Polk annexed Texas and seized New Mexico and California. Southern expansionists such as Jefferson Davis believed that projecting the Missouri Compromise line to the Pacific honored that agreement in principle, and they would accept nothing less. Northern restrictionists believed that the Compromise of 1820 placed firm limits on slavery and were irate when the Compromise of 1850 exceeded those limits and the Kansas-Nebraska Act erased them.

By early 1861 there was little chance that a nation severed by secessionists could be patched back together by any compromise, let alone one that would negate Lincoln's commitment to contain slavery and rededicate the nation to liberty, which he believed Jefferson enshrined in the Declaration of Independence as a promise for "all men and all times."[39] As Lincoln faced a second American revolutionary struggle that would prove far deadlier and more agonizing than the first, he drew inspiration from Jefferson the revolutionary idealist—who declared that enslaved Africans were robbed of their rightful liberty and proposed prohibiting slavery in the West he prized—rather than from Jefferson the opportunistic nation builder who purchased Louisiana and enlarged the domain in which Americans were free to deny people freedom. Lincoln took the stand that Jefferson had abandoned and refused to allow an institution destructive of liberty to advance, which set him unalterably at odds with defiant southerners. As Lincoln wrote Alexander Stephens not long before he became Confederate vice president and declared that enslavement by the "superior race" was the "natural and normal condition" of the Black race: "You think slavery is *right* and ought to be extended; while we think it is *wrong* and ought to be restricted. That I suppose is the rub."[40]

The fearsome Civil War that resulted would be regarded by some who experienced or later studied it as a needless tragedy that could have been avoided if compromisers "groping for some middle ground between the right and the wrong," in Lincoln's words, had prevailed and preserved the Union part slave and part free.[41] But that tragic conflict was a necessary ordeal if Americans were ever to fulfill their pledge thereafter and form one nation indivisible, with liberty and justice for all.

Notes

Acknowledgments

I would like to thank Executive Editor J. Kent Calder for welcoming my proposal and making this my third book published by the University of Oklahoma Press; Christopher Childers and a second authoritative reader for their constructive critiques of my manuscript and suggestions for improving it; copy editor David Chesanow for his close attention to matters of substance as well as style; cartographer Erin Greb for her exemplary maps—and above all my wife and mainstay, D'Vera, for keeping me going through the depths of the pandemic, when much of this book was written. While research libraries were closed, I relied extensively on the wealth of historical documents, pamphlets, articles, and books in the public domain made available online by scholars, editors, librarians, and other contributors. I'm grateful to all those involved in such projects and to the many historians whose works cited here guided me on this journey.

Preface

1. Jefferson in Richardson, *Compilation of the Messages and Papers of the Presidents*, 1:379; Meinig, *Shaping of America*, 2:13–14; Wood, *Empire of Liberty*, 357. Jefferson referred to the United States alternately as an "empire of liberty" or an "empire for liberty." See Jefferson to George Rogers Clark, December 25, 1780 ("Empire of liberty"), National Archives, Founders Online, https://founders.archives.gov /documents/Jefferson/01-04-02-0295; Jefferson to Madison, April 27, 1809 ("empire for liberty"), National Archives, Founders Online, https://founders.archives.gov /documents/Madison/03-01-02-0163.
2. Quincy in *Annals of Congress*, 11th Cong., 3rd Sess., 524–27 (1811); Meinig, *Shaping of America*, 2:17.
3. Lincoln, *Collected Works*, 7:17–19.

Introduction

1. Douglas in Johannsen, *Lincoln-Douglas Debates*, 42; Greenberg, *A Wicked War*, 248–51.
2. Lincoln in Johannsen, *Lincoln-Douglas Debates*, 14.
3. Lincoln in Johannsen, *Lincoln-Douglas Debates*, 14, 18; Varon, *Disunion!*, 315–17; Richards, *Slave Power*, 11–16; McPherson, *Battle Cry of Freedom*, 170–82. Johannsen

follows Lincoln's acceptance speech as reported verbatim in a newspaper article that Lincoln kept in his debate scrapbook. See also Lincoln, *Collected Works*, 2:462–69, which collates that text with another transcript of the speech and differs somewhat in wording, altering "chief architects" to "chief bosses."

4. Douglas in Johannsen, *Lincoln-Douglas Debates*, 91; Johannsen, *Stephen A. Douglas*, 668–69; Quitt, *Stephen A. Douglas*, 4–5.

5. Calhoun in *Congressional Globe*, 31st Cong., 1st Sess., 453–54 (1850); Varon, *Disunion!*, 11–12, 216.

6. Jefferson to Wilson Cary Nicholas, September 5, 1799, National Archives, Founders Online, https://founders.archives.gov/documents/Jefferson/01-31-020151; Koch and Ammon, "Virginia and Kentucky Resolutions," 165–68; Wood, *Empire of Liberty*, 270–71; Onuf, *Jefferson's Empire*, 144–45.

7. Taney, *Dred Scott*, para. 26.

8. Clark, *Dear Brother*, 172–73.

9. Jackson in Belohlavek, *Andrew Jackson*, 18; Brands, *Andrew Jackson*, 71–73.

10. Greeley in McPherson, *Battle Cry of Freedom*, 49.

11. Atchison in Etcheson, *Bleeding Kansas*, 55; "Remonstrance of the People of Louisiana," *Annals of Congress*, 8th Cong., 1st Sess., app., 1597–1606 (1804); Hammond, *Slavery, Freedom, and Expansion*, 48.

12. Lincoln to William Seward, February 1, 1861, *Collected Works*, 4:183; Waite, *West of Slavery*, 1–6.

13. Seward in Levine, *Half Slave and Half Free*, 15; Varon, *Disunion!*, 12, 317–20.

Chapter 1. Jefferson's Abandoned Stand against Slavery

1. Jefferson to John Holmes, April 22, 1820, National Archives, Founders Online, https://founders.archives.gov/documents/Jefferson/03-15-02-0518; Ellis, *American Sphinx*, 316–18; Onuf, *Jefferson's Empire*, 109–17.

2. Report of the Committee, March 1, 1784, National Archives, Founders Online, https://founders.archives.gov/documents/Jefferson/01-06-02-0420-0004; Ordinance of 1784 (without Jefferson's proposed slavery prohibition), National Archives, Founders Online, https://founders.archives.gov/documents/Jefferson/01-06-02-0420-0006; Peterson, *Thomas Jefferson and the New Nation*, 281–84.

3. Jefferson to James Madison, April 25, 1784, National Archives, Founders Online, https://founders.archives.gov/documents/Madison/01-08-02-0009; Smith, *Republic of Letters*, 1: 309.

4. Jefferson to Jean Nicolas Démeunier, June 22, 1786, National Archives, Founders Online, https://founders.archives.gov/documents/Jefferson/01-10-02-0001-0005; Ellis, *American Sphinx*, 80.

5. Pickering in Wills, *"Negro President,"* 22; North Carolina cession of western territory, *United States Statutes at Large*, 1:106–8.

6. Northwest Ordinance, *United States Statutes at Large*, 1:50–53; Finkelman, "Slavery and the Northwest Ordinance," 348–49; Childers, *Failure of Popular Sovereignty*, 13–16; Fehrenbacher, *Slaveholding Republic*, 253–56.

7. Madison, *Journal of the Debates*, 1:278, 361–62; Feldman, *Three Lives of James Madison*, 142, 148; Wilentz, *No Property in Man*, 58.

8. Morris in Madison, *Journal of the Debates*, 1:340; Constitution of the United States, *United States Statutes at Large*, 1:10–22 (all subsequent quotes from the Constitution that appear in the text are from this source); Wilentz, *No Property in Man*, 65; Richards, *Slave Power*, 28–34, 46–51.

9. Peter Jefferson in Stanton, *"Those Who Labor for My Happiness,"* 56, 58, 107–13; Malone, *Jefferson the Virginian*, 31–32, 114; Wiencek, *Master of the Mountain*, 32–33.

10. Jefferson, *Notes on the State of Virginia*, 162.

11. Polk in *Register of Debates*, House, 19th Cong., 1st Sess., 1649; Sellers, *James K. Polk: Jacksonian*, 107–8.

12. Brewer, "Entailing Aristocracy in Colonial Virginia," 313–15; Malone, *Jefferson the Virginian*, 251–57.

13. Petition of the House of Burgesses in Du Bois, *Suppression of the African Slave-Trade*, 13–14, Du Bois concludes that "whatever opposition to the slave-trade there was" in Virginia and other southern "planting colonies was based principally on the political fear of insurrection" (15).

14. Wayles and Randolph in Randall, *Thomas Jefferson*, 177; Gordon-Reed, *Hemingses of Monticello*, 68–69; Wiencek, *Master of the Mountain*, 70–71.

15. Jefferson's "original Rough draught" of the Declaration of Independence, National Archives, Founders Online, https://founders.archives.gov/documents/Jefferson/01 -01-02-0176-0004; Declaration of Independence, *United States Statutes at Large*, 1:1–3; Ellis, *American Sphinx*, 56; Peterson, *Thomas Jefferson and the New Nation*, 91–92; Gordon-Reed, *Hemingses of Monticello*, 134–35.

16. Jefferson, "Notes of Proceedings in the Continental Congress, 7 June–1 August 1776," National Archives, Founders Online, https://founders.archives.gov/documents /Jefferson/01–01–02–0160.

17. Jefferson, *Notes on the State of Virginia*, 137–43; Baptist, *The Half Has Never Been Told*, xxv, 48; "An Act to Prohibit the Importation of Slaves" *United States Statutes at Large*, 2:426–30.

18. Chesnut, *Mary Chesnut's Civil War*, 29.

19. Jefferson's proposed law in Finkelman, *Slavery and the Founders*, 207; Wiencek, *Master of the Mountain*, 56–57; Stanton, *"Those Who Labor for My Happiness,"* 195–96; Gordon-Reed, *Hemingses of Monticello*, 536–39, 645–62.

20. Gibson and Jung, "Historical Census Statistics on Population Totals by Race, 1790 to 1990," Table 32, Kentucky. All subsequent references to the total population or the enslaved or free Black population of American states or territories are from this source.

21. Madison to Jefferson, August 12, 1786, National Archives, Founders Online, https:// founders.archives.gov/documents/Jefferson/01–10–02–0154; Smith, *Republic of Letters*, 1:396, 431; Linklater, *Artist in Treason*, 79.

22. Wilkinson in Shepherd, "Wilkinson and the Beginnings of the Spanish Conspiracy," 496–502; Narrett, "James Wilkinson," 106–10; Linklater, *Artist in Treason*, 81–87.

23. Kentucky's 1792 constitution, in Wood, *Empire of Liberty*, 531; Linklater, *Artist in Treason*, 93; Hudson, "Slavery in Early Louisville and Jefferson County, Kentucky," 258, 272–73.

24. Senate Resolution on William Blount, July 4, 1797, in editor's note, National Archives, Founders Online, https://founders.archives.gov/documents/Jefferson/01–29–02–0371.

25. Ellicott in Hammond, *Slavery, Freedom, and Expansion*, 13–22; Childers, *Failure of Popular Sovereignty*, 20–22.

26. Kentucky Resolutions, including Jefferson's draft and resolutions adopted by the Kentucky General Assembly, November 10, 1798, National Archives, Founders Online, https://founders.archives.gov/ancestor/TSJN-01-30-02-0370; Virginia Resolutions, December 21, 1798, National Archives, Founders Online, https://founders.archives .gov/documents/Madison/01-17-02-0128; Wood, *Empire of Liberty*, 267–71; Peterson, *Thomas Jefferson and the New Nation*, 613–17.

27. Jefferson to Madison, August 23, 1799, National Archives, Founders Online, https:// founders.archives.gov/documents/Jefferson/01–31–02–0145; Jefferson to Wilson Cary Nicholas, September 5, 1799, National Archives, Founders Online, https://founders .archives.gov/documents/Jefferson/01–31–02–0151; Koch and Ammon, "Virginia and Kentucky Resolutions," 165–68; Feldman, *Three Lives of James Madison*, 417–20.

28. Jefferson in Richardson, *Compilation*, 1:378; Stanton, *"Those Who Labor for My Happiness,"* 71–89; Gordon-Reed, *Hemingses of Monticello*, 508–10.

29. Jefferson to Jeremiah A. Goodman, March 5, 1813, National Archives, Founders Online, https://founders.archives.gov/documents/Jefferson/03–05–02–0558; Jefferson to Joel Yancey, January 17, 1819, National Archives, Founders Online, https://founders .archives.gov/documents/Jefferson/03–13–02–0522; Wiencek, *Master of the Mountain*, 92–102; Howe, *What Hath God Wrought*, 59.

30. Jefferson to Thomas Mann Randolph, June 5, 1805, National Archives, Founders Online, https://founders.archives.gov/documents/Jefferson/99–01–02–1850; Jefferson to James Dinsmore, December 1, 1802, National Archives, Founders Online, https:// founders.archives.gov/documents/Jefferson/01–39–02–0081; Wiencek, *Master of the Mountain*, 120–23; Gordon-Reed, *Hemingses of Monticello*, 577–83; Stanton, *"Those Who Labor for My Happiness,"* 13–15, 178.

31. Jefferson to Holmes, April 22, 1820; Freehling, "Louisiana Purchase and the Coming of the Civil War," 69–72.

32. Pinckney in Wood, *Empire of Liberty*, 533–34.

Chapter 2. A Contested Purchase

1. *National Intelligencer and Washington Advertiser*, July 4, 1803 (notice of Louisiana Purchase Treaty), July 8, 1803 ("proud day" for the president); Malone, *Jefferson the President: First Term*, 284, 296–98; Weber, *Spanish Frontier*, 290–93.

2. Jefferson's proposed constitutional amendment, circa July 9, 1803, in National Archives, Founders Online, https://founders.archives.gov/documents/Jefferson /01-40-02-0523-0003; Malone, *Jefferson the President: First Term*, 311–15; Wallace, *Jefferson and the Indians*, 251–55.

3. Louisiana Purchase Treaty, *United States Statutes at Large*, 8:200–202; Malone, *Jefferson the President: First Term*, 316.

4. Jefferson to Madison, August 24, 1803, National Archives, Founders Online, https://founders.archives.gov/documents/Madison/02-05-02-0362; Malone, *Jefferson the President: First Term*, 316.

5. Wills, *"Negro President,"* 1–13; *Senate Executive Journal*, 8th Cong., 1st Sess., 450 (Senate vote confirming treaty on October 20, 1803).

6. Callender, "The President, Again"; Ellis, *American Sphinx*, 258–62; Gordon-Reed, *Hemingses of Monticello*, 554–58.

7. Lyon in Wood, *Empire of Liberty*, 229, 262.

8. Lyon and Griswold in *Annals of Congress*, 8th Cong., 1st Sess., 386 (1803: Griswold's original resolution), 390 (Lyon's objection), 419 (vote on amended resolution).

9. Griswold in *Annals of Congress*, 8th Cong., 1st Sess., 462 (1803).

10. Rodney in *Annals of Congress*, 8th Cong., 1st Sess., 472–73 (1803).

11. Jefferson to Madison, October 1, 1792, National Archives, Founders Online, https://founders.archives.gov/documents/Madison/01-14-02-0339; Wood, *Empire of Liberty*, 294; Chernow, *Alexander Hamilton*, 352.

12. Mitchill in *Annals of Congress*, 8th Cong., 1st Sess., 478 (1803).

13. La Salle in Sprague, *So Vast So Beautiful a Land*, 3–4.

14. Jefferson to Harrison, February 27, 1803, National Archives, Founders Online, https://founders.archives.gov/documents/Jefferson/01-39-02-0500; Wallace, *Jefferson and the Indians*, 248–51; Wilentz, *Rise of American Democracy*, 149–50.

15. White and Pickering in *Annals of Congress*, 8th Cong., 1st Sess., 33, 45–47 (1803).

16. Tracy in *Annals of Congress*, 8th Cong., 1st Sess., 45, 56–58 (1803).

17. Breckinridge in *Annals of Congress*, 8th Cong., 1st Sess., 60, 65 (1803).

18. Wilkinson in Linklater, *Artist in Treason*, 202–9; Narrett, "James Wilkinson," 120–21; Weber, *Spanish Frontier*, 292–94.

19. Jefferson to Breckinridge, November 24, 1803, in National Archives, Founders Online, https://founders.archives.gov/documents/Jefferson/01-42-02-0030; Malone, *Jefferson the President: First Term*, 351–52.

20. Cocke, Anderson, and Pickering in Plumer, *Memorandum*, 111; *Annals of Congress*, 8th Cong., 1st Sess., 233–34 (1804); Brown, *Constitutional History of the Louisiana Purchase*, 105–7.

21. Hillhouse in Plumer, *Memorandum*, 125; *Annals of Congress*, 8th Cong., 1st Sess., 240–42 (1804); Malone, *Jefferson the President: First Term*, 354 (Jefferson proposed that slaves not be imported to Louisiana "except from such of the U.S. as prohibit importation"); Wilentz, *No Property in Man*, 173–81; Fehrenbacher, *Slaveholding Republic*, 259–61; Brown, *Constitutional History of the Louisiana Purchase*, 101–20.

22. Jackson and Dayton in Plumer, *Memorandum*, 119.

23. Adams in Traub, *John Quincy Adams*, 127–28.

24. Hillhouse in Plumer, *Memorandum*, 124.

25. Hillhouse amendment, *Annals of Congress*, 8th Cong., 1st Sess., 243–44 (1804); Plumer, *Memorandum*, 127.

NOTES TO CHAPTER 2

26. Maryland statute in Rothman, *Slave Country*, 20.
27. Jackson in Plumer, *Memorandum*, 125, 127–28.
28. Jefferson in Hammond, *Slavery, Freedom, and Expansion*, 47; Claiborne in Kastor, *Nation's Crucible*, 91; Wood, *Empire of Liberty*, 372–74.
29. Breckinridge in Plumer, *Memorandum*, 129; Wilentz, *Rise of American Democracy*, 338–40.
30. Turner in Howe, *What Hath God Wrought*, 324–25.
31. A Virginian and a slave trader in Rothman, *Slave Country*, 51, 53.
32. Breckinridge amendment in *Annals of Congress*, 8th Cong., 1st Sess., 243 (1804).
33. Bradley in Plumer, *Memorandum*, 113. Wilentz, *Rise of American Democracy*, 136–37. Wilentz remarks that "even while Jefferson was president, antislavery Jeffersonians offered an alternative to Jefferson's own gloominess, discretion, and paralysis; and to the obdurate pro-slavery views of other southern Republicans. And Jefferson never tried to disown these antislavery men."
34. Claiborne in Hammond, *Slavery, Freedom, and Expansion*, 48.
35. Anonymous to Jefferson, September 11, 1804, National Archives, Founders Online, https://founders.archives.gov/documents/Jefferson/01-44-02-0342; "Remonstrance of the People of Louisiana," *Annals of Congress*, 8th Cong., 2nd Sess., app., 1597–1606 (1804). Madison to Jefferson, August 13, 1804, editor's notes 6–9, National Archives, Founders Online, https://founders.archives.gov/documents/Jefferson/01-44-02-0213.
36. Notices in the *Louisiana Gazette* in Rothman, *Slave Country*, 86–87; Hammond, *Slavery, Freedom, and Expansion*, 50–54. The 1805 governance act for Orleans Territory made no mention of slavery but stated that the inhabitants were entitled to "all the rights, privileges, and advantages" of the people of Mississippi Territory, where the domestic slave trade was permitted but the international slave trade was prohibited (*United States Statutes at Large*, 2:322–23). The 1805 governance act for the District of Louisiana did not mention slavery or the rights of the people of Mississippi Territory, thus placing no restriction on the slave trade in that district before the international trade was outlawed throughout American territory in 1808 (*United States Statutes at Large*, 2:331–32). For links to those and other acts relating to the Louisiana Purchase, see Library of Congress, https://memory.loc.gov/ammem/amlaw/lwlaw3.html.
37. Pickering in Wills, "*Negro President*," 133.
38. Plumer, *Memorandum*, 517–18; Isenberg, *Fallen Founder*, 252–53.
39. Hamilton, *Papers of Alexander Hamilton*, 26: 189; Chernow, *Alexander Hamilton*, 671–79.
40. Cheetham in Chernow, *Alexander Hamilton*, 673; Isenberg, *Fallen Founder*, 254–55; Kennedy, *Burr, Hamilton, and Jefferson*, 94–95.
41. Burr in Isenberg, *Fallen Founder*, 255.
42. Published letter of Dr. Charles Cooper in Chernow, *Alexander Hamilton*, 681.
43. Burr and Hamilton in Chernow, *Alexander Hamilton*, 685–86.
44. Plumer, *Memorandum*, 213; Wood, *Empire of Liberty*, 421–24; Wilentz, *Rise of American Democracy*, 126–28.

45. Jackson to George Washington Campbell, January 15, 1807, *Papers of Andrew Jackson*, 2:149; Remini, *Andrew Jackson and the Course of American Empire*, 150–51; Burstein, *Passions of Andrew Jackson*, 68–85.

46. Daveiss to Jefferson, July 14, 1806, National Archives, Founders Online, https://founders.archives.gov/documents/Jefferson/99-01-02-4028; Malone, *Jefferson the President: Second Term*, 223–25; Isenberg, *Fallen Founder*, 301, 306. Although the July 14 letter from Daveiss to Jefferson implicates "Burr's relations" rather than Burr himself, Daveiss had previously accused Burr of plotting with Wilkinson to form a "new Government" in the West. See Daveiss to Jefferson, February 10, 1806, National Archives, Founders Online, https://founders.archives.gov/documents/Jefferson/99-01-02-3210.

47. Wilkinson and Adair in Linklater, *Artist in Treason*, 215, 220; Narrett, "James Wilkinson," 123–27.

48. Merry and Adams in Isenberg, *Fallen Founder*, 290, 365; Linklater, *Artist in Treason*, 218; Dumas Malone, *Jefferson the President: Second Term*, 247–65; Wood, *Empire of Liberty*, 384–85; Wilentz, *Rise of American Democracy*, 128–30. The evidence as to Burr's intentions is contradictory, and historians have drawn various conclusions. As Wood notes, "Since Burr said so many different things to so many different people, his ultimate aim has never been entirely clear." Isenberg concludes that Burr's abortive expedition in 1806 was not intended to separate the American West from the Union. Malone and Wilentz conclude that Jefferson had reason to believe Burr posed a serious threat to the republic.

49. Wilkinson and Dearborn in Pike, *Journals of Zebulon Montgomery Pike*, 2:101; Malone, *Jefferson the President: Second Term*, 228–30; Isenberg, *Fallen Founder*, 296–97.

50. Wilkinson to Jefferson, October 21, October 26, November 12, and November 28, 1806, in National Archives, Founders Online, https://founders.archives.gov/documents/Jefferson/99-01-02-4459, 99-01-02-4476, 99-01-02-4537, 99-01-02-4604; Linklater, *Artist in Treason*, 249–50; Isenberg, *Fallen Founder*, 312–15.

51. Wilkinson in Linklater, *An Artist in Treason*, 252; Malone, *Jefferson the President: Second Term*, 246–47.

52. Jefferson to U.S. Congress, January 22, 1807, National Archives, Founders Online, https://founders.archives.gov/documents/Jefferson/99-01-02-4925; Malone, *Jefferson the President: Second Term*, 263–65; Isenberg, *Fallen Founder*, 309–10, 319–23; Wood, *Empire of Liberty*, 384–85; 439–40.

53. Jefferson to Charles Clay, January 11, 1807, National Archives, Founders Online, https://founders.archives.gov/documents/Jefferson/99-01-02-4842.

54. Marshall in Tarrant, "To 'Insure Domestic Tranquility,'" 110–12. Isenberg, *Fallen Founder*, 335–36.

55. Jefferson to Wilkinson, June 21, 1807, National Archives, Founders Online, https://founders.archives.gov/documents/Jefferson/99-01-02-5788; Randolph in Isenberg, *Fallen Founder*, 349–51; Linklater, *Artist in Treason*, 270.

56. Burr in Isenberg, *Fallen Founder*, 342.

57. Wickham in Linklater, *An Artist in Treason*, 266, 271; jury's verdict in Isenberg, *Fallen Founder*, 362; Malone, *Jefferson the President: Second Term*, 363.

58. Jefferson to William Thomson, September 26, 1807, National Archives, Founders Online, https://founders.archives.gov/documents/Jefferson/99-01-02-6452; Jefferson to William Branch Giles, April 20, 1807, National Archives, Founders Online, https://founders.archives.gov/documents/Jefferson/99-01-02-5478 ; Malone, *Jefferson the President: Second Term*, 339–46; Onuf, *Jefferson's Empire*, 132–35.

59. Sedition Act of 1798, http://www.let.rug.nl/usa/documents/1786-1800/the-sedition-act-of-1798.php; Tarrant, "To 'Insure Domestic Tranquility,'" 111.

Chapter 3. Lewis and Clark, William Henry Harrison, and the Northwestern Frontier

1. Clark in Lewis and Clark, *Journals*, 478.

2. Toast to American states in Ambrose, *Undaunted Courage*, 413.

3. Clark in Lewis and Clark, *Journals*, 49; Betts, *In Search of York*, 16–19; Ambrose, *Undaunted Courage*, 180.

4. Clark in Betts, *In Search of York*, 25, 27, 29.

5. Kennerly and Russell, *Persimmon Hill*, 19.

6. Clark, *Dear Brother*, 139.

7. Clark, *Dear Brother*, 160, 172–73, 183, 201.

8. O'Fallon in Betts, *In Search of York*, 113.

9. Irving, *Journals*, 3:112.

10. Jefferson to Lewis, June 20, 1803, National Archives, Founders Online, https://founders.archives.gov/documents/Jefferson/01-40-02-0136-0005; Wallace, *Jefferson and the Indians*, 244.

11. Clark in Wallace, *Jefferson and the Indians*, 271–72.

12. Clark in Aron, *American Confluence*, 148.

13. Lewis in Aron, *American Confluence*, 139.

14. Opponents of Indiana Territory indenture law in Owens, *Mr. Jefferson's Hammer*, 112; Hammond, *Slavery, Freedom, and Expansion*, 96–120; Fehrenbacher, *Slaveholding Republic*, 256–59.

15. Harrison to Jefferson, August 29, 1805, National Archives, Founders Online, https://founders.archives.gov/documents/Jefferson/99-01-02-2320; Owens, *Mr. Jefferson's Hammer*, 106; Van Atta, *Securing the West*, 66–67, 78–79.

16. Harrison in Barce, "Governor Harrison and the Treaty of Fort Wayne," 364.

17. Tecumseh in Harrison, *Messages and Letters*, 1:465–69; Wood, *Empire of Liberty*, 675–76; Wilentz, *Rise of American Democracy*, 148–53.

18. Harrison to Eustis, August 7, 1811, in Harrison, *Messages and Letters*, 1:549.

19. Harrison to Eustis, August 7, 1811, in Harrison, *Messages and Letters*, 1:548; Owens, *Mr. Jefferson's Hammer*, 211–20.

20. Madison in Owens, *Mr. Jefferson's Hammer*, 222.

21. Jackson to Harrison, November 28, 1811, *Papers of Andrew Jackson*, 2:270; Owens, *Mr. Jefferson's Hammer*, 221, 223–31; Wilentz, *Rise of American Democracy*, 153–60.

22. Perry in Wood, *Empire of Liberty*, 686; Wilentz, *Rise of American Democracy*, 153–60.

23. Southern Illinoisan in Etcheson, *The Emerging Midwest*, 118; Snively, "Slavery in Illinois," 52–59.

Chapter 4. Jackson's Southern Strategy

1. Jackson in Remini, *Andrew Jackson and the Course of American Empire*, 190; Burstein, *Passions of Andrew Jackson*, 97–100; Wood, *Empire of Liberty*, 686–87; Braund, "Creek War of 1813–14"; Waselkov, "Fort Mims Battle and Massacre."

2. Sevier in H. W. Brands, *Andrew Jackson*, 106; Burstein, *Passions of Andrew Jackson*, 41–49.

3. Jackson in Reid and Eaton, *Life of Andrew Jackson*, 190–91; Remini, *Andrew Jackson and the Course of American Empire*, 229.

4. North Carolinian in Rothman, *Slave Country*, 183; Howe, *What Hath God Wrought*, 125–27; Meinig, *Shaping of America*, 2:232–33.

5. Hammond in *Congressional Globe*, 35th Cong., 1st Sess., 961 (1858); Baptist, *Half Has Never Been Told*, 114 (cotton production table), 317–19.

6. Jackson in Burstein, *Passions of Andrew Jackson*, 59.

7. Jackson in Belohlavek, *Andrew Jackson*, 18; Brands, *Andrew Jackson*, 71–73, 148–52, 365–66.

8. Jackson to Graves W. Steele, November 7, 1829, *Papers of Andrew Jackson*, 7:539–40.

9. Jackson in Hay, "'And Ten Dollars Extra,'" 468–78; Belohlavek, *Andrew Jackson*, 18–19; Hopkins, "Enslaved Household of Andrew Jackson."

10. Report of the Hartford Convention in Wood, *Empire of Liberty*, 694; Wilentz, *Rise of American Democracy*, 162–68, 175–76; Feldman, *Three Lives of James Madison*, 552–55.

11. Adams in Traub, *John Quincy Adams*, 194.

12. Terms of the Treaty of Ghent in Howe, *What Hath God Wrought*, 75.

13. Jackson to Gaines, April 8, 1816, *Correspondence of Andrew Jackson*, 2:238–39; Jackson to Mauricio de Zuñiga, April 23, 1816, *Papers of Andrew Jackson*, 4:22–23; Remini, *Andrew Jackson and the Course of American Empire*, 344–47; Fehrenbacher, *Slaveholding Republic*, 98–101; Howe, *What Hath God Wrought*, 76–77; Meinig, *Shaping of America*, 2:24–32.

14. Jackson to Monroe, January 6, 1818, *Papers of Andrew Jackson*, 4:166–67.

15. Monroe to Jackson, December 28, 1817, in Remini, *Andrew Jackson and the Course of American Empire*, 348–49; Howe, *What Hath God Wrought*, 98–100.

16. Andrew Jackson to Rachel Jackson. June 2, 1818, *Papers of Andrew Jackson*, 4: 212; Jackson in Remini, *Andrew Jackson and the Course of American Empire*, 363–64; Brands, *Andrew Jackson*, 340; Belohlavek, *Andrew Jackson*, 36.

17. Clay in *Annals of Congress*, 15th Cong., 2nd Sess., 631–55 (1819); Heidler and Heidler, *Henry Clay*, 142.

18. Adams in Edel, *Nation Builder*, 152–53.

19. Monroe in Howe, *What Hath God Wrought*, 104.

20. Adams, *Memoirs*, 4: 239.

21. Adams in Edel, *Nation Builder*, 155; Remini, *Andrew Jackson and the Course of American Empire*, 389–90.

22. Jackson to Calhoun, December 21, 1820, *Papers of Andrew Jackson*, 4:409–10; Howe, *What Hath God Wrought*, 684.

Chapter 5. Missouri Compromised

1. Benton in Mueller, *Senator Benton and the People*, 72; Bay, *Reminiscences of the Bench and Bar*, 10–11. Bay was not a witness to the dispute he describes between Lucas and Benton, with whom the author did not become acquainted until many years later. But Lucas offered a similar account of the incident, stating that he challenged Benton's right to vote, "asking if he had paid his taxes on property that included his slaves" (Mueller, 66–67).

2. Tallmadge amendment in *Annals of Congress*, 15th Cong., 2nd Sess., 1170 (1819); Mueller, *Senator Benton*, 79–81, 86; Forbes, *Missouri Compromise*, 35–37.

3. Clay quoted by Taylor in *Annals of Congress*, 15th Cong., 2nd Sess., 1177 (1819); Heidler and Heidler, *Henry Clay*, 143–44.

4. Act authorizing admission of Ohio, *United States Statutes at Large*, 2:173–74.

5. Taylor in *Annals of Congress*, 15th Cong., 2nd Sess., 1172–74 (1819); Forbes, *Missouri Compromise*, 35–37; Howe, *What Hath God Wrought*, 147–50.

6. Tallmadge rebutting Colston on "servile war" in *Annals of Congress*, 15th Cong., 2nd Sess., 1203–5 (1819).

7. Barbour, Scott, and Tallmadge in *Annals of Congress*, 15th Cong., 2nd Sess., 1188, 1202, 1204 (1819); Forbes, *Missouri Compromise*, 39–45; Richards, *Slave Power*, 52–54, 72–78.

8. Edwards in Snively, "Slavery in Illinois," 55; *Annals of Congress*, 15th Cong., 2nd Sess., 273, 1214 (1819: Senate and House votes on Tallmadge Amendment); Freehling, *Road to Disunion*, 1:144–52.

9. Clay, Blunt, and *St. Louis Enquirer* in Van Atta, *Wolf by the Ears*, 1–2, 76–77, 86–87; Heidler and Heidler, *Henry Clay*, 147; Wilentz, *Rise of American Democracy*, 228–31.

10. Clay in Heidler and Heidler, *Henry Clay*, 95.

11. Taylor's amendments to bill organizing Arkansas Territory in *Annals of Congress*, 15th Cong., 2nd Sess., 1235–39; 1272–74, 1280–82 (1819); *Annals of Congress*, 16th Cong., 1st Sess., 468–69 (1820: Senate vote on compromise); Forbes, *Missouri Compromise*, 45–46, 92–98; Richards, *Slave Power*, 75–76, 80.

12. Taylor in Forbes, *Missouri Compromise*, 99; *Annals of Congress*, 16th Cong., 1st Sess., 1586–88 (1820: House votes on compromise measures); Heidler and Heidler, *Henry Clay*, 147–48; Freehling, *Road to Disunion*, 1:152–54.

13. Missouri state constitution in Aron, *American Confluence*, 182.

14. Pinckney in *Annals of Congress*, 16th Cong., 1st Sess., 1134–35 (1821); Forbes, *Missouri Compromise*, 112–15.

15. Clay's compromise resolution in *United States Statutes at Large*, 3:645.

16. Benton in Mueller, *Senator Benton*, 186–87.

17. Ritchie in Childers, *Failure of Popular Sovereignty*, 76.

18. Jackson to Andrew Jackson Donelson, April 16, 1820, *Papers of Andrew Jackson*, 4:366–67.

Chapter 6. Stephen Austin's Invasive Texas Colony

1. Moses Austin to Stephen Austin, May 22, 1821, in Barker, *Austin Papers*, 1:393; Cantrell, *Stephen F. Austin*, 84–88.

2. Stephen Austin in Weber, *Mexican Frontier*, 13; Cantrell, *Stephen F. Austin*, 93–94.

3. Austin to Iturbide, May 25, 1822, in Barker, *Austin Papers*, 1:518–19; Cantrell, *Stephen F. Austin*, 113–14, 124.

4. Austin to Edward Lovelace, November 22, 1822, in Barker, *Austin Papers*, 1:554–55; Cantrell, *Stephen F. Austin*, 123–24.

5. Austin and Mexican colonization bill in Bugbee, "Slavery in Early Texas," 394–95; Cantrell, *Stephen F. Austin*, 123–27, map 163 (showing the extent of Austin's original colony).

6. Austin to William H. Wharton, April 24, 1829, in Barker, *Austin Papers*, 2: 209–11; Weber, *Mexican Frontier*, 162–66; Cantrell, *Stephen F. Austin*, 182–87.

7. Austin to Gonzáles, April 4, 1825, in Barker, *Austin Papers*, 1:1065–67; Torget, *Seeds of Empire*, 85–87.

8. Austin in Cantrell, *Stephen F. Austin*, 155–56, 177–79.

9. Austin to Saucedo, September 11, 1826, in Barker, *Austin Papers*, 1: 1452; Cantrell, *Stephen F. Austin*, 145–46 (Austin's slave code), 190–92, 204 (purchase of "forty-year-old domestic servant"), 315–16, 328 ("bodyservant Simon"); Torget, "Stephen F. Austin's Views on Slavery," 107–28.

10. *New Orleans Halcyon and Literary Repository*, May 25, 1828, in Torget, *Seeds of Empire*, 135; Cantrell, *Stephen F. Austin*, 203–4.

11. Terán in Weber, *Mexican Frontier*, 167; Terán in Cantrell, *Stephen F. Austin*, 209–21.

12. Austin in Cantrell, *Stephen F. Austin*, 223–24; Torget, *Seeds of Empire*, 152; Weber, *Mexican Frontier*, 170–72.

13. Austin in Cantrell, *Stephen F. Austin*, 115; Weber, *Myth and the History of the Hispanic Southwest*, 153–68.

14. Austin to Thomas F. Leaming, June 14, 1830, in Barker, *Austin Papers*, 2: 413–15.

15. Austin to S. Rhoads Fisher, June 17, 1830, in Barker, *Austin Papers*, 2: 423–27.

16. Austin to Holley, December 29, 1831, in Barker, *Austin Papers*, 2:726–30; Cantrell, *Stephen F. Austin*, 242–45.

17. Austin to Wiley Martin, May 30, 1833, in Barker, *Austin Papers*, 2:977–81.

18. Téran in Cantrell, *Stephen F. Austin*, 255–57; Weber, *Mexican Frontier*, 172–73, 246–47; Davis, *Lone Star Rising*, 74–90.

19. Austin to Thomas F. Leaming, June 14, 1830, in Barker, *Austin Papers*, 2: 415.

20. Austin in Cantrell, *Stephen F. Austin*, 271; Austin to Ayuntamiento of [San Antonio de] Bexar, October 2, 1833 (letter in Spanish), in Barker, *Austin Papers*, 2:1007; Weber, *Mexican Frontier*, 242–44, 251–54.

21. General Cos and the Liberty Committee of Public Safety in Campbell, *An Empire for Slavery*, 40–41; Howe, *What Hath God Wrought*, 661–62 (Texas slave uprising in October 1835).

22. Austin to Holley, August 21, 1835, *Austin Papers*, 3: 101–3; Cantrell, *Stephen F. Austin*, 308–11.

23. Austin to Columbia Committee, September 19, 1835, in Barker, *Austin Papers*, 3:129; Cantrell, *Stephen F. Austin*, 312–13.
24. Austin to Senator Lewis F. Linn, May 4, 1836, in Barker, *Austin Papers*, 3:344–45; Cantrell, *Stephen F. Austin*, 344.

Chapter 7. Houston, Jackson, and the Southwestern Frontier

1. Sam Houston to Andrew Jackson, November 20, 1836, *Writings of Sam Houston*, 1:487; Library of Congress, https://www.loc.gov/item/maj015322 (photocopy of Houston's letter); Haley, *Sam Houston*, 171–74.
2. Houston to Jackson, November 20, 1836, *Writings of Sam Houston*, 1:487–88.
3. Houston to Jackson, December 18, 1817, in Haley, *Sam Houston*, 21–22. A photocopy of this letter is provided by Texas Library and Archives Commission, https://www .tsl.texas.gov/exhibits/presidents/houston1/sam_houston_dec18_1817_6.html.
4. Jackson and Clay in Remini, *Andrew Jackson and the Course of American Freedom*, 87, 104; Brands, *Andrew Jackson*, 389–90, Burstein, *Passions of Andrew Jackson*, 163–64.
5. Jackson as "King Andrew the First" in Remini, *Andrew Jackson and the Course of American Freedom*, 385; Library of Congress, https://www.loc.gov/pictures/item /2008661753/ (portrayed as "King Andrew the First"); Bowman, *At the Precipice*, 121–23.
6. Houston in Haley, *Sam Houston*, 41, 43–44; James, *The Raven*, 64–67; Campbell, *Sam Houston and the American Southwest*, 17–18.
7. Adams and Jackson in Wilentz, *Rise of American Democracy*, 281, 308. See also Wilentz, 183–202, on the expansion of white male suffrage and restriction of Black suffrage.
8. Houston to John Allen, April 9, 1829, *Writings of Sam Houston*, 1;130; Haley, *Sam Houston*, 53–61; Crook, "Sam Houston and Eliza Allen," 14; Campbell, *Sam Houston*, 23–26.
9. Berrien in James, *The Raven*, 156; Campbell, *Sam Houston*, 32–34.
10. Marshall in Howe, *What Hath God Wrought*, 355; Cornell Law School, Legal Information Institute, *"The Cherokee Nation v. The State of Georgia,"* https://www.law.cornell .edu/supremecourt/text/30/1.
11. Removal Act, *Senate Resolutions*, 21st Cong., 1st Sess., S. 102, Sec. 1; Wallace, *Long, Bitter Trail*, 124–25; Meinig, *Shaping of America*, 2:85–89.
12. Jackson in Richardson, *Compilation*, 2:458–59; Wallace, *Long, Bitter Trail*, 121–24.
13. Removal Act, *Senate Resolutions*, 21st Cong., 1st Sess., S. 102, Sec. 3; Wallace, *Long, Bitter Trail*, 125–26.
14. Frelinghuysen in *Register of Debates*, 21st Cong., 1st Sess., 312, 318–19 (1830); Wilentz, *Rise of American Democracy*, 322–27.
15. Lumpkin in *Register of Debates*, 21st Congress, 1st Sess., 1020–22 (1830). For the authorship of the pamphlet referred to by Lumpkin, see Cheever, "Removal of the Indians," 16.
16. Beecher in Hershberger, "Mobilizing Women, Anticipating Abolition," 28; Howe, *What Hath God Wrought*, 349–52.

17. Lumpkin in *Register of Debates*, 21st Cong., 1st Sess., 1021 (1830).

18. Garrison in Howe, *What Hath God Wrought*, 426; Hershberger, "Mobilizing Women, Anticipating Abolition," 35–37; Wilentz, *Rise of American Democracy*, 335–38; Forbes, "African-American Resistance to Colonization," 210–23.

19. Frelinghuysen in *Register of Debates*, 21st Cong., 1st Sess., 316 (1830); Ronda, "'We Have a Country': Race, Geography, and the Invention of Indian Territory," 739–41; Meinig, *Shaping of America*, 2:78–80.

20. Evans in *Register of Debates*, 21st Cong., 1st Sess., 1049 (1830).

21. Everett in *Register of Debates*, 21st Cong., 1st Sess., 1064, 1069 (1830); Howe, *What Hath God Wrought*, 343–44; *Register of Debates*, 21st Cong, 1st Sess., 383 (1830: Senate vote on Indian Removal Act); Richards, *Slave Power*, 89–90, 125–27.

22. Jackson and Calhoun in Howe, *What Hath God Wrought*, 372–73. Jackson altered "Our Union" to "Our federal Union" for publication; see his toast and Calhoun's toast as reported in *Niles' Weekly Register*, April 24, 1830, 38:153–54, in which the editor predicts that Jackson would "resist a *nullification* of the public law—else we much mistake his character."

23. Turnbull, *The Crisis*, 26.

24. Calhoun in Bartlett, *John C. Calhoun*, 144, 181; Howe, *What Hath God Wrought*, 395–404.

25. South Carolina nullification ordinance in Benton, *Thirty Years' View*, 1:297.

26. Jackson's proclamation against nullification on December 10, 1832, in *United States Statutes at Large*, 11 (proclamations since 1791):771–81; Wilentz, *Rise of American Democracy*, 379–89.

27. Jackson to John Coffee, April 9, 1833, and Jackson to Andrew Jackson Crawford, May 1, 1833, *Papers of Andrew Jackson*, 11:235, 284–85; Remini, *Andrew Jackson and the Course of American Democracy*, 42–43; Earle, *Jacksonian Antislavery*, 41–44, 110–11; Richards, *Slave Power*, 159–60; Wilentz, *Rise of American Democracy*, 410–25.

28. Derivation of "Mascogos" in Porter, "The Seminole in Mexico," 1n2.

29. Houston to Jackson, May 11, 1829, *Papers of Andrew Jackson*, 7:212–14.

30. Jackson to Houston, June 21, 1829, *Papers of Andrew Jackson*, 7:294–95; Haley, *Sam Houston*, 66–71.

31. Stanbery in *Register of Debates*, 22nd Cong., 1st Sess., 2321–22 (1832); James, *The Raven*, 163–72; Campbell, *Sam Houston*, 35–38. Eaton's resignation was followed by that of all members of the cabinet at Jackson's request to end a bitter dispute over Eaton's wife Marguerite (Peggy), whom Jackson defended but several members of the cabinet and their wives considered disreputable and refused to associate with.

32. Houston to Jackson, February 13, 1833, *Papers of Andrew Jackson*, 11:110–11; Haley, *Sam Houston*, 95–96; Campbell, *Sam Houston*, 40–41, 52–53.

33. Houston to James Prentiss, April 24, 1834, *Writings of Sam Houston*, 290–91; Haley, *Sam Houston*, 101; Campbell, *Sam Houston*, 55–56.

34. Haley, *Sam Houston*, 149–50; replica of battle flag at Library of Congress, https://www.loc.gov/item/2014633202.

35. Cass to Gaines in Brands, *Andrew Jackson*, 522; Jones and Jones, "Occupation of Nacogdoches," 20.

36. Excerpt from "the *National Intelligencer* of May 10" in *Niles' Weekly Register*, May 14, 1836, 50:185–86; Jones and Jones, "Occupation of Nacogdoches," 31.

37. Kendall and Jackson in Remini, *Andrew Jackson and the Course of American Democracy*, 361–62.

38. Van Buren to Thomas Ritchie, January 13, 1827, Papers of Martin Van Buren: http://vanburenpapers.org/document-mvb00528; Earle, *Jacksonian Antislavery*, 49–50; Bowman, *At the Precipice*, 119–21; Wilentz, *Rise of American Democracy*, 295–96.

39. Constitution of the Republic of Texas, General Provisions, Sec. 9, Tarlton Law Library, https://tarlton.law.utexas.edu/c.php?g=815580&p=5820525.

40. Adams in Brands, *Andrew Jackson*, 524; Traub, *John Quincy Adams*, 438.

41. Lamar in Waite, *West of Slavery*, 16.

Chapter 8. Benton, Frémont, and the Westward Course of American Empire

1. Benton, *Thirty Years' View*, 1:734; Mueller, *Senator Benton*, 48–53, 112–13, 132–34, 169–70, 192–94; Wilentz, *Rise of American Democracy*, 363.

2. Calhoun in *Congressional Globe*, 25th Cong., 2nd Sess., app., 29, 61, 70 (1838); Benton, *Thirty Years' View*, 2:134–39; Childers, *Failure of Popular Sovereignty*, 90–96.

3. Senate resolution in *Congressional Globe*, 25th Cong., 2nd Sess., app., 74 (1838).

4. Benton, *Thirty Years' View*, 1:628–29.

5. Democratic Party's *Address to the People of the United States* (1835) in Howe, *What Hath God Wrought*, 511; Richards, *Slave Power*, 109–12, 132–33. Analyzing voting records on crucial legislation related to slavery between the mid-1830s and mid-1850s, Richards concludes that if a northerner was "elected as a Whig, the chances that he would vote with the South in the next sectional crisis were at best one in twenty. If he was elected as a Democrat, the odds were one in two" (*Slave Power*, 112).

6. Davis, *History of the City of Memphis*, 72–73; Mueller, *Senator Benton*, 82–83, 273–74nn63–64. According to James D. Davis's account, published in 1873, Benton parted with a "beautiful French quadroon girl" named Mary before he got married and provided "liberally for her, giving her property and money," which he entrusted on her behalf to Major Marcus Brutus Winchester of Memphis. She may have been the same woman Winchester wed in 1823, Amarante (Mary) Loiselle of New Orleans.

7. Storrs in White, *News of the Plains and Rockies*, 2:84; Hyslop, *Bound for Santa Fe*, 47.

8. Benton, *Thirty Years' View*, 1:42; Mueller, *Senator Benton*, 183–86; Sibley, *Road to Santa Fe*, 5–6; Hyslop, *Bound for Santa Fe*, 47–51.

9. Smith in Weber, *Californios versus Jedediah Smith*, 50; Hyslop, *Contest for California*, 209–24.

10. Benton, *Thirty Years' View*, 1:671.

11. Becknell in White, *News of the Plains and Rockies*, 2:67; Weber, *Mexican Frontier*, 179–82, 195.

12. Smith, *Southwest Expedition*, 129–30; Hyslop, *Contest for California*, 216–21, 299.

13. Simpson, *Narrative of a Voyage*, 73–74; Hyslop, *Contest for California*, 288–89.

14. Benton in Mueller, *Senator Benton*, 230; Freehling, *Road to Disunion*, 1:541–44; Inskeep, *Imperfect Union*, 30–31. Inskeep notes that according to 1840 census records Benton owned six slaves at his home in St. Louis.

15. Jessie Benton Frémont, *A Year of American Travel*, 44; Denton, *Passion and Principle*, 19–21, 54–55, 79.

16. John C. Frémont, *Memoirs*, 65; Chaffin, *Pathfinder*, 19–39, 85–86.

17. Frémont, *Memoirs*, 70–71; Chaffin, *Pathfinder*, 95–99.

18. Walt Whitman, "Passage to India," *Leaves of Grass*, 317.

19. Miller in Goetzmann and Williams, *Atlas of North American Exploration*, 159.

20. *Niles' National Register* in Chaffin, *Pathfinder*, 146–47.

21. Marcus Whitman in Lavender, *Westward Vision*, 381.

22. Abert in Goetzmann, *Exploration and Empire*, 244.

23. Tyler in Richardson, *Compilation*, 4:258 ; Benton, *Thirty Years' View*, 2:565, 579.

24. Abert in Frémont, *Expeditions*, 1:344–45; Hyslop, *Contest for California*, 321–31.

25. Jessie Benton Frémont in Chaffin, *Pathfinder*, 150; Frémont, *Memoirs*, 167–68.

26. Benton, *Thirty Years' View*, 2:579–80; Chaffin, *Pathfinder*, 197–99.

27. Benton, *Thirty Years' View*, 2:580.

28. Frémont, *Memoirs*, 298.

29. Benton, *Thirty Years' View*, 2:580–81; Chaffin, *Pathfinder*, 209–25.

30. Carson, *Autobiography*, 79; Frémont, *Memoirs*, 317.

31. Preuss, *Exploring with Frémont*, 83.

32. Sutter in Hurtado, *John Sutter*, 58; Hyslop, *Contest for California*, 265–83.

33. Robinson in Weber, *Mexican Frontier*, 179, 343n1.

34. Larkin in Hurtado, *John Sutter*, 129.

Chapter 9. Tyler, Calhoun, and the "Reannexation" of Texas

1. Tyler to William Selden, February 12, 1820, National Union Catalog of Manuscript Collections, https://www.loc.gov/coll/nucmc/2011CivilWar/01_JohnTylerLetter.html.

2. Tyler in Crapol, *John Tyler*, 38–39, 59–62; Bowman, *At the Precipice*, 125–27, 130–31.

3. Tyler in Greenberg, *A Wicked War*, 11–12; Crapol, *John Tyler*, 202.

4. Tyler in Richardson, *Compilation*, 4:260; Benton, *Thirty Years' View*, 2:566.

5. Benton, *Thirty Years' View*, 2:602.

6. Lamar's proclamation to New Mexicans in Kendall, *Narrative of the Texan Santa Fé Expedition*, 1:270; Hyslop, *Bound for Santa Fe*, 275–91.

7. Miller in Haynes, "Anglophobia and the Annexation of Texas," 120–21; Campbell, *Sam Houston*, 129–31.

8. Adams in Crapol, *John Tyler*, 73; Hietala, *Manifest Design*, 15–20; Howe, *What Hath God Wrought*, 671–82.

9. Lord Aberdeen in Graebner, *Manifest Destiny*, xxx; Haynes, "Anglophobia," 119; Fehrenbacher, *Slaveholding Republic*, 119–26; Freehling, *Road to Disunion*, 1:388–401.

10. Houston in Haley, *Sam Houston*, 289.

11. Houston to Jackson, February 16, 1844, *Correspondence of Andrew Jackson*, 6:260–64; Campbell, *Sam Houston*, 133; Freehling, *Road to Disunion*, 1:416. On January 10, 1844, Senator Walker of Mississippi had urged Jackson to pressure Houston to accept annexation by the United States. "I think the annexation of Texas depends *on you*," Walker wrote Jackson. "Much as you have done for your country, this would be the crowning act" (*Correspondence of Andrew Jackson*, 6:255–56).

12. Jackson to Kendall, April 12, 1844, Library of Congress (letter as published), https://www.loc.gov/item/majo17633/; Haley, *Sam Houston*, 279–80; Hietala, *Manifest Design*, 24–26.

13. Hoke in Freehling, *Road to Disunion*, 1:424.

14. Ingersoll in Silbey, *Storm over Texas*, 37; Varon, *Disunion!*, 173–74.

15. Smith in Graebner, *Manifest Destiny*, 57.

16. Texas annexation treaty of 1844, Article II, Yale Law School, Avalon Project, https://avalon.law.yale.edu/19th_century/texano5.asp.

17. Upshur in Silbey, *Storm over Texas*, 43.

18. Calhoun in Wilentz, *Democracy in America*, 567; Bartlett, *John C. Calhoun*, 311.

19. Van Buren to William Henry Hammett, April 20, 1844, Papers of Martin Van Buren, http://vanburenpapers.org/document-mvbo3868; Richards, *Slave Power*, 143–45.

20. The 1844 Democratic Party platform in Sellers, *James K. Polk, Continentalist*, 99; Meinig, *Shaping of America*, 2:103–16.

21. Robert Walker, *Letter, of Mr. Walker, of Mississippi, Relative to the Annexation of Texas*, 6; Freehling, *Road to Disunion*, 1:418–23; Hietala, *Manifest Design*, 26–34.

22. Walker, *Letter*, 12–13.

23. Walker, *Letter*, 15; Howe, *What Hath God Wrought*, 682–85.

24. Walker, *Letter*, 19.

25. Polk advisor Cave Johnson and *New York Courier and Enquirer* in Sellers, *James K. Polk, Continentalist*, 109, 142.

26. Clay in Sellers, *James K. Polk, Continentalist*, 146; Heidler and Heidler, *Henry Clay*, 390; Howe, *What Hath God Wrought*, 435–36, 686–87; Silbey, *Storm over Texas*, 72–77; Freehling, *Road to Disunion*, 1:435–39.

27. Pike in Brown, *Life of Albert Pike*, 62, 282.

28. Birney in Rogers, *Apostles of Equality*, 139, 177.

29. Tyler in Silbey, *Storm over Texas*, 81.

30. Joint Resolution, *Congressional Globe*, 28th Cong., 2nd Sess., 362–63 (1845); Freehling, *Road to Disunion*, 1:440-43; Benton, *Thirty Years' View*, 2:632.

31. *Boston Daily Atlas*, December 23, 1845, in May, *Slavery, Race, and Conquest*, 32–36.

32. Adams in Traub, *John Quincy Adams*, 498, 501; Heidler and Heidler, *Henry Clay*, 196.

33. Barnard in Silbey, *Storm over Texas*, xviii.

34. Ellis in *Congressional Globe*, 28th Cong., 2nd Sess., app., 138–39 (1845); Graebner, *Manifest Destiny*, 70–74; Holt, *Fate of Their Country*, 12–14; Silbey, *Storm over Texas*, 82–88; Richards, *Slave Power*, 146–48.

35. Benton, *Thirty Years' View*, 2:634–35; Freehling, *Road to Disunion*, 1:446–447. Benton's initial proposal in December 1844 would have limited the state of Texas "to an extent

not exceeding that of the largest State in the Union" and would have prohibited slavery in other territory claimed by Texas "so as to divide, as equally as may be, the whole of the annexed country between slaveholding and non-slaveholding" areas (*Congressional Globe*, 28th Cong., 2nd Sess., 19). Benton eliminated that free-territory provision and any mention of slavery from his subsequent bill.

36. Benton, *Thirty Years' View*, 2:638; Mueller, *Senator Benton*, 209–12; Sellers, *James K. Polk, Continentalist*, 206–7, 215–20; Hietala, *Manifest Design*, 219–20.

Chapter 10. Mr. Polk's War and Manifest Destiny

1. Gag rule in Sellers, *James K. Polk: Jacksonian*, 314–15; Dusinberre, *Slavemaster President*, 121–24; Greenberg, *Lady First*, 21–27. Passed by the House in 1836 along with resolutions stating that "interfering with slavery in the states was unconstitutional and in the District inexpedient," the gag rule was reenacted when the Twenty-Fifth Congress convened in 1837. Democratic leaders met at "a presession caucus in Speaker Polk's apartment," where a new set of "gag resolutions was drafted carefully so as to deny to Congress the right to interfere with slavery anywhere, while avoiding the delicate constitutional question as to the District of Columbia" (Sellers, 337–38).

2. Elias Polk in Kinslow, "Enslaved and Entrenched"; Greenberg, *Lady First*, 239–41; Dusinberre, *Slavemaster President*, 77–78.

3. Long Harry to Polk, November 28, 1844, *Correspondence of James K. Polk*, 8:370; Dusinberre, *Slavemaster President*, 110–114.

4. Pillow and Polk in Dusinberre, *Slavemaster President*, 12, 14–15.

5. Caldwell and overseer in Dusinberre, *Slavemaster President*, 31–32, 37–39.

6. Polk to Campbell, January 31, 1846, November 14, 1846, and January 23, 1847, *Correspondence of James K. Polk*, 11:62–63, 394–95, 12:57; Campbell to Polk, January 9, 1847, *Correspondence of James K. Polk*, 12:37–42. In that January 9 letter to Polk itemizing his payments to slaves for cotton they cultivated, Campbell seldom used decimal points to distinguish dollars from cents. For instance, he listed the total payment for 1846 as "$13730," meaning $137.30 paid to the twenty enslaved people listed as recipients. See Dusinberre, *Slavemaster President*, 107–10.

7. Campbell to Polk, October 9, 1846, *Correspondence of James K. Polk*, 11:345–46; Dusinberre, *Slavemaster President*, 18–21.

8. Caroline and Jane Polk in Greenberg, *Lady First*, 53, 166–67; Dusinberre, *Slavemaster President*, 14, 94–95, 103–4. Dusinberre concludes that owning slaves helped "shape Polk's political vision" and instilled in him and other prominent planters a "defensive mentality, which boiled with resentment when outsiders suggested that the federal government had any right to interfere with the private business of a slavemaster" (168).

9. Polk's inaugural address in Richardson, *Compilation*, 4: 373–82; Leonard, *James K. Polk*, 1–5; Silbey, *Storm over Texas*, 91–96; Greenberg, *Wicked War*, xv, 108 ("Mr. Polk's War").

10. Bancroft in Sellers, *James K. Polk, Continentalist*, 213, Waite, *West of Slavery*, 19–22; Hietala, *Manifest Design*, 59–63, 83–93; Howe, *What Hath God Wrought*, 706–7.

11. Adams in *Congressional Globe*, 29th Cong., 1st Sess., 340–42 (1846); Graebner, *Manifest Destiny*, 103–9; Traub, *John Quincy Adams*, 511–13.

12. Austin in Cantrell, *Stephen F. Austin*, 202.

13. O'Sullivan, "Great Nation of Futurity," 426–30; Graebner, *Manifest Destiny*, 15–21; Eyal, *Young America Movement*, 93–95.

14. O'Sullivan, "Annexation," 5–10. The authorship of this unsigned editorial is discussed in Hudson, *Mistress of Manifest Destiny*, 60–62; and Sampson, *John L. O'Sullivan*, 244–45.

15. O'Sullivan, "White Slavery," 260–70; Hietala, *Manifest Design*, 95–100; Meinig, *Shaping of America*, 2:209–11.

16. O'Sullivan, "The Democratic Review and Mr. Calhoun," 107–8; Hietala, *Manifest Design*, 218–19.

17. O'Sullivan in Pratt, "John L. O'Sullivan and Manifest Destiny," 223–24.

18. Goodyear in *Congressional Globe*, 29th Cong., 1st Sess., app., 109–11 (1846); Graebner, *Manifest Destiny*, 110–12.

19. Emerson, "Young American," 484–93; Graebner, *Manifest Destiny*, 5–10; Eyal, *Young America Movement*, 3–5; Hietala, *Manifest Design*, 254. As published in April 1844, "The Young American" expanded on the text of a lecture Emerson delivered in Boston in February 1844.

20. Almonte in Sellers, *James K. Polk, Continentalist*, 221.

21. Donelson in Sellers, *James K. Polk, Continentalist*, 223; Leonard, *James K. Polk*, 77–80.

22. Polk to Houston, June 6, 1845, *Correspondence of James K. Polk*, 9:430–31.

23. Polk to Donelson, June 15, 1845, *Correspondence of James K. Polk*, 9:449–50; Sellers, *James K. Polk, Continentalist*, 227–30; Leonard, *James K. Polk*, 80–81.

24. Parrott in Sellers, *James K. Polk, Continentalist*, 262–63.

25. Polk, *Diary*, 1:199.

26. Parrott in Sellers, *James K. Polk, Continentalist*, 263.

27. Polk, *Diary*, 1:33–35.

28. Polk, Buchanan, and an American diplomat in Sellers, *James K. Polk, Continentalist*, 230, 337–38n50; Polk to Slidell, November 10, 1845, *Correspondence of James K. Polk*, 10:362–63.

29. Polk to Slidell, November 6 and 7, 1845, *Correspondence of James K. Polk*, 10:351, 355–56; Polk, *Diary*, 1:93; Leonard, *James K. Polk*, 150–51.

30. Polk, *Diary*, 1:4–5.

31. Jackson to Polk, May 2, 1845, *Correspondence of James K. Polk*, 9:332–41; Sellers, *James K. Polk, Continentalist*, 236.

32. Polk in Sellers, *James K. Polk, Continentalist*, 359.

33. Polk in Richardson, *Compilation*, 4:385–89, Sellers, *James K. Polk, Continentalist*, 339–43.

34. Taylor in Sellers, *James K. Polk, Continentalist*, 331.

35. Polk in Richardson, *Compilation*, 4:389–91; Leonard, *James K. Polk*, 147–49.

36. Slidell in Sellers, *James K. Polk, Continentalist*, 404; Leonard, *James K. Polk*, 150–53.
37. Polk, *Diary*, 1:222–25, 227–29.
38. Polk, *Diary*, 1:319; Sellers, *James K. Polk, Continentalist*, 404–5; Leonard, *James K. Polk*, 158–59.
39. Wentworth in Sellers, *James K. Polk, Continentalist*, 407; Hietala, *Manifest Design*, 152–57, 164.
40. Hitchcock, *Fifty Years in Camp and Field*, 213.
41. Polk in Richardson, *Compilation*, 4: 442; Polk in Sellers, *James K. Polk, Continentalist*, 409, 416–19; Leonard, *James K. Polk*, 159–61; Holt, *Fate of Their Country*, 16–18; Wilentz, *Rise of American Democracy*, 582–85.
42. Polk, *Diary*, 1:397; Sellers, *James K. Polk, Continentalist*, 409, 416–19; Leonard, *James K. Polk*, 167.
43. Bancroft in Sellers, *James K. Polk, Continentalist*, 227; Leonard, *James K. Polk*, 137–39.
44. Buchanan to Larkin in Sellers, *James K. Polk, Continentalist*, 334; Hyslop, *Contest for California*, 340.
45. Frémont, *Memoirs*, 423.
46. Polk, *Diary*, 1:71–72, 83–84; Sellers, *James K. Polk, Continentalist*, 335–36.
47. Frémont, *Memoirs*, 463; Leonard, *James K. Polk*, 139–43; Hyslop, *Contest for California*, 340–44.
48. Frémont, *Memoirs*, 460–61, 488.
49. Frémont, *Memoirs*, 489; Hyslop, *Contest for California*, 360–64 (Larkin on Mariano Vallejo, and Salvador Vallejo on the slur directed at him and others jailed by Bear Flag rebels). Polk wrote Benton on September 1, 1846, to inform him that Monterey had been occupied by the Pacific Squadron in July and Sonoma had been seized by Frémont's Bear Flag forces. Polk thought Benton "would be gratified to learn this intelligence, and particularly to learn Col. Fremont's whereabouts" (Polk, *Correspondence*, 11:299).
50. Benton in Smith and Judah, *Chronicles of the Gringos*, 112; Mueller, *Senator Benton*, 213–16; Hyslop, *Bound for Santa Fe*, 308, 400.
51. Magoffin, *Down the Santa Fe Trail*, 72; Hyslop, *Bound for Santa Fe*, 309–24.
52. Kearny in Emory, *Notes of a Military Reconnaissance*, 27–28; Hyslop, *Bound for Santa Fe*, 335–37.
53. Cooke, *Conquest of New Mexico and California*, 34–35.
54. Kearny Code, "Jurors," Sec. 9, Yale Law School, Avalon Project, https://avalon.law.yale.edu/19th_century/kearney.asp#jurors.
55. Bent, "Charles Bent Papers," 254; Hyslop, *Bound for Santa Fe*, 300–301.
56. Polk, *Diary*, 1:444.
57. Kearny in Bryant, *What I Saw in California*, 397; Harlow, *California Conquered*, 174–92; Hyslop, *Contest for California*, 391–94. Edwin Bryant, a journalist and editor from Louisville, Kentucky, who arrived overland in California in August 1846, included official records in his account of the American takeover there.
58. Griffin, *A Doctor Comes to California*, 46–47.

59. Treaty of Cahuenga and Kearny's proclamation in Bryant, *What I Saw in California*, 392, 431–32; Harlow, *California Conquered*, 193–243; Hyslop, *Contest for California*, 396–99.

60. Polk, *Diary*, 2:481–82; Hyslop, *Bound for Santa Fe*, 384–403.

Chapter 11. Wilmot's Proviso and the Free Soil Movement

1. Polk, *Diary*, 2:76–77; Sellers, *James K. Polk, Continentalist*, 430–32, 479–90.

2. *Harrisburg Telegraph* editorial in Duff, "David Wilmot," 285; Earle, *Jacksonian Antislavery*, 1–3, 129–31.

3. White and Wilmot in *Congressional Globe*, 29th Cong., 1st Sess., 1213–14, 1217–18 (1846); Morrison, *Slavery and the American West*, 39–41; Wilentz, *Rise of American Democracy*, 596–601; Howe, *What Hath God Wrought*, 766–68; May, *Slavery, Race, and Conquest*, 55–56.

4. Wilmot in Earle, *Jacksonian Antislavery*, 2; Sellers, *James K. Polk, Continentalist*, 479–84.

5. Wilmot on his conversation with Polk in *Congressional Globe*, 30th Cong., 2nd Sess., app., 139 (1849); revised Wilmot Proviso in *Congressional Globe*, 29th Cong., 2nd Sess., app., 318 (1847); Earle, *Jacksonian Antislavery*, 134–35; Richards, *Slave Power*, 152–53. The revised proviso offered by Wilmot on February 8, 1847, included a fugitive-slave clause for annexed territories where slavery would be prohibited under the amendment.

6. Wilmot in *Congressional Globe*, 29th Cong., 2nd Sess., app., 315–17 (1847).

7. Wilmot in *Congressional Globe*, 29th Cong., 2nd Sess., app., 318 (1847), and in Earle, *Jacksonian Antislavery*, 124; Hietala, *Manifest Design*, 122–27; Wilentz, *Rise of American Democracy*, 598–600.

8. Taylor in Greenberg, *A Wicked War*, 134; Stegmaier, *Texas, New Mexico*, 44.

9. Bereft mother to Sarah Polk in Greenberg, *Lady First*, 152.

10. Inscription on the medal sent to Polk and the letter accompanying that medal in *Correspondence of James K. Polk*, 12:xliv (introduction by editor Tom Chaffin), and 12:183–84; letter from "Quaker Woman," 12:7–8.

11. Calhoun in *Congressional Globe*, 29th Cong. 2nd Sess., app., 322–27 (1847); Emerson in McPherson, *Battle Cry of Freedom*, 51; Bartlett, *John C. Calhoun*, 340–41.

12. Benton, *Thirty Years' View*, 2:695.

13. Polk, *Diary*, 3:161; Leonard, *James K. Polk*, 176–80; Greenberg, *A Wicked War*, 238–40, 256–61.

14. Prospector Edwin Sherman to Thomas Jefferson Green in Waite, *West of Slavery*, 38.

15. Calhoun in Childers, *Failure of Popular Sovereignty*, 132.

16. Douglas to Samuel Treat, February 19, 1848, *Letters of Stephen A. Douglas*, 156–57; Hietala, *Manifest Design*, 161–64; *Senate Executive Journal*, 7:340 (vote ratifying Treaty of Guadalupe, March 10, 1848); May, *Slavery, Race, and Conquest*, 3, 41–44, 55–56. May characterizes Douglas as "Washington's most aggressive apostle of Manifest Destiny," whose expansionism embraced all of Mexico as well as Cuba and Central America: "At times he seemed to crave the whole hemisphere."

17. Corwin in Morrison, *Slavery and the American West*, 80; Holt, *Fate of Their Country*, 37–43.

18. Free Soil Party slogan in McPherson, *Battle Cry of Freedom*, 62; Earle, *Jacksonian Antislavery*, 74–77; Holt, *Fate of Their Country*, 44–49.

19. Barnburners' published address in Silbey, *Storm over Texas*, 126.

20. Morris in *Congressional Globe*, 25th Cong., 3rd Sess., app., 169 (1839); Earle, *Jacksonian Antislavery*, 37–48; Brooks, *Liberty Power*, 25–27.

21. Johnson in *Congressional Globe*, 26th Cong., 1st Sess., 150 (1840); Brooks, *Liberty Power*, 37; Varon, *Disunion!*, 145–46, 186–88; Richards, *Slave Power*, 145–46.

22. Wilmot in *Congressional Globe*, 29th Cong., 2nd Sess., app., 317 (1847).

23. Leavitt in Brooks, *Liberty Power*, 130.

24. Ward in Earle, *Jacksonian Antislavery*, 168–69; Wilentz, *Rise of American Democracy*, 617–32; Howe, *What Hath God Wrought*, 831–40. On Gerrit Smith, Elizabeth Cady Stanton, and universal suffrage, see Wellman, *Road to Seneca Falls*, 173–76.

25. Polk, *Diary*, 2:75, 308; 4:231. Polk reiterated his support for extending the Missouri Compromise line to the Pacific in his last annual message to Congress (Richardson, *Compilation*, 4:641–42).

26. Polk in Richardson, *Compilation*, 4:594–98; Stegmaier, *Texas, New Mexico*, 31.

27. Clay in Greenberg, *A Wicked War*, 229–34.

28. Lincoln in *Congressional Globe*, 30th Cong., 1st Sess., app., 95 (1848); Greenberg, *A Wicked War*, 248–50.

29. Editor of the *Cleveland Plain Dealer* in Silbey, *Storm over Texas*, 113–14. On Polk's last months in office and his death in June 1849, see Haynes, *James K. Polk*, 201–13.

Chapter 12. Douglas's Southern Exposure and Popular Sovereignty

1. Martin in Johannsen, *Stephen A. Douglas*, 211; Johannsen, *The Frontier, the Union, and Stephen A. Douglas*, 189–90.

2. Overseer to Douglas in Johannsen, *Stephen A. Douglas*, 337.

3. Merchant's report and Douglas's revised partnership agreement in Quitt, *Stephen A. Douglas*, 190–91; May, *Slavery, Race, and Conquest*, 53–54.

4. Robert and Stephen A. Douglas Jr., *Claim of Rob't and Stephen A. Douglas*, 7; Quitt, *Stephen A. Douglas*, 186–87.

5. Wade and Douglas in *Congressional Globe*, 33rd Cong., 2nd Sess., app., 222, 330 (1855); Quitt, *Stephen A. Douglas*, 188–89; Johannsen, *Frontier*, 189–91.

6. Douglas in Johannsen, *Stephen A. Douglas*, 419.

7. Taylor in Holt, *Fate of Their Country*, 59; Potter, *Impending Crisis*, 87.

8. California state constitution in Harlow, *California Conquered*, 338–42.

9. Address "to the people of New Mexico" by delegates at its constitutional convention in Stegmaier, *Texas, New Mexico*, 119.

10. Clay in *Congressional Globe*, 31st Cong., 1st Sess., 244 (1850).

11. Clay in *Congressional Globe*, 31st Cong., 1st Sess., 246–47 (1850).

12. Davis and Downs in *Congressional Globe*, 31st Cong., 1st Sess., 249–51 (1850).

13. Calhoun in *Congressional Globe*, 31st Cong., 1st Sess., 451–55 (1850).

14. Webster in Howe, *What Hath God Wrought*, 368–71.

15. Webster in *Congressional Globe*, 31st Cong., 1st Sess., 476–81 (1850).

16. Clay in *Congressional Globe*, 31st Cong., 1st Sess., app., 126 (1850); Waite, *West of Slavery*, 30–32.

17. Seward in *Congressional Globe*, 31st Cong., 1st Sess., app., 265–69 (1850).

18. Douglas in *Congressional Globe*, 31st Cong., 1st Sess., app., 369–70 (1850); Quitt, *Stephen A. Douglas*, 114–16; Finkelman, *Slavery and the Founders*, 46–48.

19. Calhoun in Holt, *Political Crisis of the 1850s*, 69.

20. Benton and Foote in *Congressional Globe*, 31st Cong., 1st Sess., 762 (1850); Mueller, *Senator Benton*, 229–34; Hamilton, *Prologue to Conflict*, 52, 62.

21. Stephens in Stegmaier, *Texas, New Mexico*, 160, 167–71.

22. Houston in Haley, *Sam Houston*, 304–5; Campbell, *Sam Houston*, 145–53; Stegmaier, *Texas, New Mexico*, 90, 136, 154–56.

23. Benton in Hamilton, *Prologue to Conflict*, 110, 191–200 (House and Senate votes on compromise measures); Stegmaier, *Texas, New Mexico*, 167–200.

24. Fillmore in Stegmaier, *Texas, New Mexico*, 209–10.

25. Protest of Davis and other southern senators in Benton, *Thirty Years' View*, 2:769–70.

26. *U.S. Statutes at Large*, 31st Cong, 1st Sess., 9:453; Childers, *Failure of Popular Sovereignty*, 198, 306n65; Potter, *Impending Crisis*, 115–116.

27. Stevens in Hamilton, *Prologue to Conflict*, 162: Landis, *Northern Men With Southern Loyalties*, 31–36

28. Fillmore in Richardson, *Compilation*, 5:93; Potter, *Impending Crisis*, 121.

29. Douglas in Johannsen, *Stephen A. Douglas*, 303, 340.

30. *New York Herald*, June 3, 1852, in Eyal, *Young America Movement*, 208, 210–17; Landis, *Northern Men with Southern Loyalties*, 66–76.

31. Douglas in Johannsen, *Stephen A. Douglas*, 326; May, *Slavery, Race, and Conquest*, 97. Douglas spoke those words in 1853 while assailing the Clayton-Bulwer Treaty by which the United States and Great Britain pledged not to occupy or colonize any part of Central America. His statement was consistent with expansionist views and statements that made him the "darling of the Young Americans" when he sought the Democratic nomination in 1852 (May, 69).

32. Benton in Johannsen, *Frontier*, 87; Benton in Johannsen, *Stephen A. Douglas*, 446–47; Quitt, *Stephen A. Douglas*, 80.

33. Seward in Wilentz, *Rise of American Democracy*, 665.

34. Pierce in Richardson, *Compilation*, 5:199, 202.

35. Polk, *Diary*, 3:446, 476–78; May, *Slavery, Race, and Conquest*, 62–67; Wilentz, *Rise of American Democracy*, 668–70; Meinig, *Shaping of America*, 2:154–58.

36. López in Chaffin, "'Sons of Washington,'" 89.

37. Marcy in Potter, *Impending Crisis*, 188; Freehling, *Road to Disunion*, 2:103–16.

38. Ostend Manifesto in May, *Slavery, Race, and Conquest*, 115–16; Fehrenbacher, *Slaveholding Republic*, 129–30; Potter, *Impending Crisis*, 190.

39. Douglas in May, *Slavery, Race, and Conquest*, 88–89, 116–30.

40. Douglas in Johannsen, *Stephen A. Douglas*, 255, 431; Quitt, *Stephen A. Douglas*, 113.

Chapter 13. Conceiving "Bleeding Kansas"

1. Gadsden in Waite, *West of Slavery*, 51.

2. Douglas in Johannsen, *Stephen A. Douglas*, 436; Goetzmann and Williams, *Atlas of North American Exploration*, 166–67; Morrison, *Slavery and the American West*, 142–43; Eyal, *Young America Movement*, 47–49, 70–71.

3. Bell in *Congressional Globe*, 33rd Cong., 1st Sess., app., 409 (1854); Johannsen, *Frontier*, 106.

4. Douglas in Johannsen, *Frontier*, 84.

5. Douglas in Quitt, *Stephen A. Douglas*, 17, 38–39, 43; Johannsen, *Frontier*, 105.

6. Atchison and Houston in *Congressional Globe*, 32nd Cong., 2nd Sess., 1111–16 (1853); Malavasic, *F Street Mess*, 74–76.

7. Douglas in Johannsen, *Stephen A. Douglas*, 407; Malavasic, *F Street Mess*, 87–89; Holt, *Fate of Their Country*, 99–101.

8. Chase in Johannsen, *Stephen A. Douglas*, 409; Nebraska bill in Malavasic, *F Street Mess*, 88–90.

9. Dixon amendment and proposed Phillips amendment in Johannsen, *Stephen A. Douglas*, 411, 413; Malavasic, *F Street Mess*, 91–95.

10. Pierce in Malavasic, *F Street Mess*, 98.

11. "Appeal of the Independent Democrats in Congress to the People of the United States: Shall Slavery Be Permitted in Nebraska?," *Daily National Era*, January 24, 1854, https://chroniclingamerica.loc.gov/lccn/sn86053546/1854-01-24/ed-1/seq-2/; Johannsen, *Stephen A. Douglas*, 418–19; Holt, *Fate of Their Country*, 106–12; Earle, *Jacksonian Antislavery*, 192–95.

12. Douglas in Malavasic, *F Street Mess*, 112–13.

13. Douglas in *Congressional Globe*, 33rd Congress, 1st Sess., 275–76 (1854); Johannsen, *Stephen A. Douglas*, 419–21.

14. Houston in *Congressional Globe*, 33rd Cong., 1st Sess., app., 340–42 (1854); Haley, *Sam Houston*, 321–26; Campbell, *Sam Houston*, 158–60.

15. Douglas in Johannsen, *Stephen A. Douglas*, 434, 451; Landis, *Northern Men with Southern Loyalties*, 126–29.

16. Kansas-Nebraska Act in *United States Statutes at Large*, 10:279, 289; Johannsen, *Frontier*, 112–13. The act allowed the territorial governor to veto bills passed by the legislature but did not give Congress the veto power granted it under earlier territorial organic acts.

17. Seward in Johannsen, *Stephen A. Douglas*, 472; Morrison, *Slavery in the West*, 144–52.

18. Atchison in Malavasic, *F Street Mess*, 146; Atchison in Reynolds, *John Brown, Abolitionist*, 140–41.

19. Atchison in Johannsen, *Stephen A. Douglas*, 474; Etcheson, *Bleeding Kansas*, 29–30, 59.

20. Poll observer and the *Atchison Squatter Sovereign* in Etcheson, *Bleeding Kansas*, 57, 63.

21. Lawrence in Etcheson, *Bleeding Kansas*, 76–77.

22. Sumner in *Congressional Globe*, 34th Cong., 1st Sess., app., 530–31 (1856).

23. Douglas in *Congressional Globe*, 34th Cong., 1st Sess., 545 (1856); Etcheson, *Bleeding Kansas*, 99.

24. Douglas in Johannsen, *Stephen A. Douglas*, 503.

25. Brooks and Representative Edwin B. Morgan in Donald, *Charles Sumner and the Coming of the Civil War*, 247–48.

26. Douglas in Johannsen, *Stephen A. Douglas*, 504; Douglas to J. E. Roy, July 4, 1856 (rebutting a sermon preached by Roy and published in the *Chicago Times*), *Letters of Stephen A. Douglas*, 363–65.

27. *Richmond Enquirer* in Donald, *Charles Sumner*, 256–57.

28. Chesnut in *Mary Chesnut's Civil War*, 29; Klein, *Days of Defiance*, 67–73.

29. Bryant in McPherson, *Battle Cry of Freedom*, 150; Wilentz, *Rise of American Democracy*, 691–93.

30. Emerson in Donald, *Charles Sumner*, 260.

31. Brown in Reynolds, *John Brown, Abolitionist*, 171–78; Etcheson, *Bleeding Kansas*, 107–11, 131–38.

32. Mayoral candidate Colonel Schutt in Ford, "Gangs of Baltimore"; Wilentz, *Rise of American Democracy*, 681–84, 693–95.

33. Lincoln in May, *Slavery, Race, and Conquest*, 109–10.

34. Jessie Benton Frémont in Chaffin, *Pathfinder*, 441; Mueller, *Senator Benton*, 253–54; Inskeep, *Imperfect Union*, 300–301.

35. Buchanan in Johannsen, *Stephen A. Douglas*, 538.

36. Buchanan in Richardson, *Compilation*, 5:431–32; Varon, *Disunion!*, 295–300.

37. Taney, *Dred Scott*, para. 26, 48–50.

38. Curtis in Varon, *Disunion!*, 297.

39. Taney in Wilentz, *No Property in Man*, 245; Fehrenbacher, *Slaveholding Republic*, 280–83.

40. Douglas in Johannsen, *Stephen A. Douglas*, 570.

41. Walker in Johannsen, *Stephen A. Douglas*, 564.

42. Walker, "Letter . . . Resigning the Office of Governor of Kansas," 15; Etcheson, *Bleeding Kansas*, 144–60; Richards, *Slave Power*, 201–5; Potter, *Impending Crisis*, 297–317.

43. Illinoisan to Douglas in Johannsen, *Stephen A. Douglas*, 601; Douglas in *Congressional Globe*, 35th Cong., 1st Sess., 15 (1857); Morrison, *Slavery and the American West*, 197–98.

44. Douglas to Adele Cutts in Quitt, *Stephen A. Douglas*, 59.

45. Douglas and Lincoln in Johannsen, *Lincoln-Douglas Debates*, 44, 53–54, 73, 135–36.

46. Douglas and Lincoln in Johannsen, *Lincoln-Douglas Debates*, 88, 147.

47. Douglas and Lincoln in Johannsen, *Lincoln-Douglas Debates*, 79, 91–92, 234–35; May, *Slavery, Race, and Conquest*, 146–50.

48. Douglas and Lincoln in Johannsen, *Lincoln-Douglas Debates*, 92–93, 97, 100, 114; Quitt, *Stephen A. Douglas*, 56.

49. Douglas in Johannsen, *Lincoln-Douglas Debates*, 118, 120, 128.

50. Lincoln in Johannsen, *Lincoln-Douglas Debates*, 41, 162–63, 304.

51. Lincoln in Bowman, *At the Precipice*, 92; Adele Cutts Douglas in *Letters of Stephen A. Douglas*, 384–85 (on lecture by Gerrit Smith); James L. Huston, foreword to Johannsen, *Lincoln-Douglas Debates*, xvii–xxviii.

Chapter 14. Deconstructing the Democracy

1. Mason in *Congressional Globe*, 35th Cong., 2nd Sess., 1249 (1859); Johannsen, *Stephen A. Douglas*, 695.
2. Brown in Reynolds, *John Brown, Abolitionist*, 395 (punctuation in Brown's note regularized).
3. Davis in *Congressional Globe*, 36th Cong., 1st Sess., 658, 1941 (1860); Morrison, *Slavery and the American West*, 212–18.
4. Democratic delegate to Douglas in Johannsen, *Stephen A. Douglas*, 748.
5. Yancey, "Speech of the Hon. William L. Yancey, " 7, 13; McPherson, *Battle Cry of Freedom*, 213–16.
6. Fitzhugh in Varon, *Disunion!*, 288.
7. Pugh, "Speech of George E. Pugh," 6, 16.
8. Buchanan in May, *Slavery, Race, and Conquest*, 170–73; Wilentz, *Rise of American Democracy*, 755–58.
9. Halstead in McPherson, *Battle Cry of Freedom*, 214–16.
10. Lane in Johannsen, *Frontier*, 65–66; Nokes, "Black Exclusion Laws in Oregon."
11. *National Era* in Waite, *West of Slavery*, 93, 98–100; Albin, "The Perkins Case," 215–27. Waite argues that proslavery "partisans transformed the southwest quarter of the nation—California, Arizona, New Mexico, and even parts of Utah—into an appendage of the slave states," to which they were linked by their "coercive labor regimes." But he adds that plantation slavery "never took root in the region, as some hoped, and others feared" (2).
12. Foote in Fehrenbacher, *Slaveholding Republic*, 294; Waite, *West of Slavery*, 107–21, 155–58; Pitt, *Decline of the Californios*, 203–5; Bowman, *At the Precipice*, 168–69; Stanley, "Senator William Gwin," 243–55.
13. Act in Relation to Service in Ricks, "Peculiar Place for the Peculiar Institution," 158–62; Waite, *West of Slavery*, 125–34.
14. Republican Party platform of 1856 in May, *Slavery, Race, and Conquest*, 127.
15. Act governing indentured servants in New Mexico in Reséndez, "North American Peonage," 604.
16. Greeley in Waite, *West of Slavery*, 123, 140.
17. Otero in Stegmaier, "A Law That Would Make Caligula Blush?," 59; Waite, *West of Slavery*, 134–41.
18. *Chicago Tribune* in May, *Slavery, Race, and Conquest*, 221; Waite, *West of Slavery*, 163–64. Lincoln indicated to Seward that he did not "care much about New Mexico, if further extension were hedged against" (Lincoln, *Collected Works*, 4:183). But offering New Mexico statehood without restriction as a concession to the South would have cost Republicans little if New Mexicans remained opposed to African American slavery, as in 1850, and prohibited it in their state constitution.

19. Green in Waite, *West of Slavery*, 41, 54–55, 69, 151–55.

20. Douglas in Johannsen, *Stephen A. Douglas*, 789; Potter, *Impending Crisis*, 441; Quitt, *Stephen A. Douglas*, 162–66; McPherson, *Battle Cry of Freedom*, 251–57.

21. Douglas in Johannsen, *Stephen A. Douglas*, 772, 800; Bowman, *At the Precipice*, 140–43.

22. Yancey in Johannsen, *Frontier*, 164; Potter, *Impending Crisis*, 414.

23. Clingman in Fehrenbacher, *Slaveholding Republic*, 305; Howe, *What Hath God Wrought*, 429–30.

24. Quote attributed to Stevens by Representative Sherrard Clemens of Virginia in Oakes, *Scorpion's Sting*, 24.

25. Andrew Calhoun and Hoke in Dew, *Apostles of Disunion*, 41–42, 119–21.

26. Jefferson, *Notes on the State of Virginia*, 138.

27. Andrew Jackson to Andrew Jackson Donelson, April 16, 1820, *Papers of Andrew Jackson*, 4:367.

28. Douglas in Johannsen, *Lincoln-Douglas Debates*, 34.

29. Douglas amendments in *Senate Joint Resolutions*, 36th Cong., 2nd Sess., S.R. 52, Article 14 (1860); House vote on compromise proposals in *Congressional Globe*, 36th Cong., 2nd Sess., 1260–61 (1861); Johannsen, *Stephen A. Douglas*, 816–18; Quitt, *Stephen A. Douglas*, 171–72.

30. Crittenden amendments in *Senate Joint Resolutions*, 36th Cong., 2nd Sess., S.R. 50 (1860).

31. Lincoln to Seward, February 1, 1861, in Lincoln, *Collected Works*, 4:183; Lincoln to Elihu B. Washburne, December 13, 1860, in Lincoln, *Collected Works*, 4:151; May, *Slavery, Race, and Conquest*, 206–20; Waite, *West of Slavery*, 6, 159–60.

32. Lincoln's first inaugural address, March 4, 1861, in Lincoln, *Collected Works*, 4:266–71.

33. Douglas in Johannsen, *Stephen A. Douglas*, 859–60 (meeting with Lincoln on April 14).

34. Douglas in Johannsen, *Stephen A. Douglas*, 868 (speech in Chicago on May 1); 484–85, 871–72 (illness and death on June 3); Quitt, *Stephen A. Douglas*, 183–84.

35. Douglas in Johannsen, *Stephen A. Douglas*, 866; Johannsen, *Frontier*, 187.

36. Douglas to Charles H. Lanphier, December 25, 1860, *Letters of Stephen A. Douglas*, 504; Bowman, *At the Precipice*, 140.

37. Douglas in Johannsen, *Lincoln-Douglas Debates*, 105.

38. Douglas in Johannsen, *Frontier*, 128.

39. Lincoln to Henry L. Pierce and others, April 6, 1859, in Lincoln, *Collected Works*, 3:376; Wilentz, *Rise of Democracy*, 790–93.

40. Lincoln to Alexander H. Stephens, December 22, 1860, in Lincoln, *Collected Works*, 4:160; Stephens in Levine, *Half Slave and Half Free*, 228; McPherson, *Battle Cry of Freedom*, 244–45.

41. Lincoln during his Cooper Institute address, February 27, 1860, in Lincoln, *Collected Works*, 3:550. For a discussion of historians' evolving views on the necessity of the Civil War, see Horwitz, "150 Years of Misunderstanding the Civil War." On the Civil War as a needless tragedy, see for example Hamilton, *Prologue to Conflict*, 189, where

he states: "If the Civil War was a needless tragedy (as I think it was), the biggest share of blame must be borne not by moderate men of good will but by firebrands of the North and South who never thought themselves culpable for four years of brutal bloodletting." Hamilton offered that assessment amid the centennial of the Civil War in 1963. The alternative view that the conflict was tragic but necessary to restore the continental Union and rededicate it to freedom was encouraged by those engaged then in the civil rights movement, who demanded fulfillment of the long-deferred promise of liberty and justice for African Americans embodied in the Thirteenth, Fourteenth, and Fifteenth Amendments, made possible when Unionists defeated the Confederacy in 1865.

Bibliography

Archival Sources Online

Austin, Stephen F. The Digital Austin Papers. http://digitalaustinpapers.org.

Jackson, Andrew. *The Papers of Andrew Jackson*. 11 vols. online (through 1833). Knoxville: University of Tennessee Press, 1980–2019. https://thepapersofandrewjackson.utk.edu.

Jefferson, Thomas. The Papers of Thomas Jefferson, Digital Edition. https://rotunda .upress.virginia.edu/founders/TSJN.html.

Library of Congress, *A Century of Lawmaking for a New Nation: U.S. Congressional Documents and Debates, 1774–1875*. Includes House and Senate bills and resolutions, joint resolutions, *United States Statutes at Large, Senate Executive Journal, Annals of Congress, Register of Debates*, and *Congressional Globe*. http://memory.loc.gov /ammem/amlaw/lawhome.html.

National Archives, Founders Online. Correspondence and other writings of George Washington, Benjamin Franklin, John Adams (and family), Thomas Jefferson, Alexander Hamilton, John Jay, and James Madison. Correspondence can be accessed at this site by author, recipient, and date, or by the URL provided for each letter cited in the notes. https://founders.archives.gov.

Polk, James K. *Correspondence of James K. Polk*. 14 vols. online. Knoxville: University of Tennessee Press, 1958–2020. https://trace.tennessee.edu/utk_polk.

Van Buren, Martin. The Papers of Martin Van Buren. https://vanburenpapers.org /documents.

Published Primary Sources

Adams, John Quincy. *Memoirs of John Quincy Adams, Comprising Portions of His Diary from 1793 to 1848*. 12 vols. Edited by Charles Francis Adams. Philadelphia: J. B. Lippincott, 1874–77.

Barker, Eugene C., ed. *The Austin Papers*. 3 vols. Washington, DC: Government Printing Office, 1924–28 (vols. 1–2); Austin: University of Texas Press, 1926 (vol. 3).

Bent, Charles. "The Charles Bent Papers." Edited by Frank D. Reeve. *New Mexico Historical Review* 30, no. 2 (July 1955).

Benton, Thomas Hart. *Thirty Years' View*. 2 vols. New York: D. Appleton, 1854.

Bryant, Edwin. *What I Saw in California*. 1848. Reprint. Lincoln: University of Nebraska Press, 1985.

Calhoun, John C. *The Works of John C. Calhoun.* 4 vols. New York: D. Appleton, 1854.

Callender, James Thomson. "The President, Again." *The Recorder; or, Lady's and Gentleman's Miscellany.* September 1, 1802. Reprinted in Encyclopedia Virginia. https:// encyclopediavirginia.org/entries/the-president-again-by-james-thomson-callender -september-1-1802/.

Carson, Kit. *Kit Carson's Autobiography.* Edited by Milo Milton Quaife. 1935. Reprint. Lincoln: University of Nebraska Press, 1966.

Cheever, George B. "The Removal of the Indians: An Article from the *American Monthly Magazine.*" Boston: Peirce and Williams, 1830.

Chesnut, Mary Boykin. *Mary Chesnut's Civil War.* Edited by C. Vann Woodward. New Haven, CT: Yale University Press, 1981.

Clark, William. *Dear Brother: Letters of William Clark to Jonathan Clark.* Edited by James J. Holmberg, with a foreword by James P. Ronda. New Haven, CT: Yale University Press, 2002.

Cooke, Philip St. George. *The Conquest of New Mexico and California: An Historical and Personal Narrative.* New York: Putnam, 1878.

Douglas, Robert, and Stephen A. Douglas Jr. "Claim of Rob't M. and Stephen A. Douglas." Washington, DC: Powell and Ginck, 1872.

Douglas, Stephen A. *The Letters of Stephen A. Douglas.* Edited by Robert W. Johannsen. Urbana: University of Illinois Press, 1961.

Emerson, Ralph Waldo. "The Young American." *Dial* 4, no. 4 (April 1844).

Emory, W. H. *Notes of a Military Reconnaissance, from Fort Leavenworth, in Missouri, to San Diego, in California.* Washington: Wendell and Van Benthuysen, 1848.

Frémont, Jessie Benton. *A Year of American Travel.* New York: Harper & Brothers, 1878.

Frémont, John C. *The Expeditions of John Charles Frémont.* 2 vols. Edited by Donald Jackson and Mary Lee Spence. Urbana: University of Illinois Press, 1970.

———. *Memoirs of My Life.* Chicago: Belford, Clarke, 1887.

Graebner, Norman A., ed. *Manifest Destiny.* Indianapolis: Bobbs-Merrill, 1968.

Griffin, John S. *A Doctor Comes to California: The Diary of John S. Griffin, Assistant Surgeon with Kearny's Dragoons, 1846–1847.* Edited by George Walcott Ames Jr. San Francisco: California Historical Society, 1943.

Hamilton, Alexander. *The Papers of Alexander Hamilton.* Edited by Harold C. Syrett. 27 vols. New York: Columbia University Press, 1961–1987.

Harrison, William Henry. *Messages and Letters of William Henry Harrison.* 2 vols. Edited by Logan Esary. Indianapolis: Indiana Historical Commission, 1922.

Hitchcock, Ethan Allen. *Fifty Years in Camp and Field.* Edited by W. A. Croffut. New York; G. P. Putnam's Sons, 1909.

Houston, Sam. *The Writings of Sam Houston, 1813–1863.* 8 vols. Edited by Amelia W. Williams and Eugene C. Barker. Austin: University of Texas Press, 1938–43.

Irving, Washington. *The Journals of Washington Irving.* 3 vols. Edited by William P. Trent and George S. Hellman. Boston: Bibliophile Society, 1919.

Jackson, Andrew. *Correspondence of Andrew Jackson.* 7 vols. Edited by John Spencer Bassett. Washington, DC: Carnegie Institution of Washington, 1926–35.

Jefferson, Thomas. *Notes on the State of Virginia.* Edited by William Peden. New York: W. W. Norton, 1972

Johannsen, Robert W., ed. *Lincoln-Douglas Debates of 1858.* Foreword by James L. Huston. New York: Oxford University Press, 2008.

Kendall, George Wilkins. *Narrative of the Texan Santa Fé Expedition.* 2 vols. New York: Harper and Brothers, 1844.

Lewis, Meriwether, and William Clark. *The Journals of Lewis and Clark.* Edited by Bernard DeVoto. Boston: Houghton Mifflin, 1953.

Lincoln, Abraham. *Collected Works of Abraham Lincoln.* 8 vols. Edited by Roy P. Basler. New Brunswick, NJ: Rutgers University Press, 1953. https://abrahamlincolnassociation.org/collected-works/.

Madison, James. *The Journal of the Debates in the Convention Which Framed the Constitution of the United States, May–September, 1787.* 2 vols. Edited by Gaillard Hunt. New York: G. P. Putnam's Sons, 1908.

Magoffin, Susan Shelby. *Down the Santa Fe Trail and into Mexico: The Diary of Susan Shelby Magoffin, 1846–1847.* Edited by Stella M. Drumm. 1926. Reprint, with a foreword by Howard R. Lamar. New Haven, CT: Yale University Press, 1962.

O'Sullivan, John, ed. "Annexation." *United States Magazine, and Democratic Review* 17, no. 1 (July–August 1845).

———. "The Democratic Review and Mr. Calhoun." *United States Magazine, and Democratic Review* 16, no. 2 (February 1845).

———. "The Great Nation of Futurity." *United States Magazine, and Democratic Review* 6, no. 5 (November 1839).

———. "White Slavery." *United States Magazine, and Democratic Review* 11, no. 3 (September 1842).

Pike, Zebulon Montgomery. *The Journals of Zebulon Montgomery Pike, with Letters and Related Documents.* 2 vols. Edited by Donald Jackson. Norman: University of Oklahoma Press, 1966.

Plumer, William. *William Plumer's Memorandum of Proceedings in the United States Senate, 1803–1807.* Edited by Everett Somerville Brown. New York: Macmillan, 1923.

Polk, James K. *The Diary of James K. Polk during His Presidency, 1845 to 1849.* 4 vols. Edited by Milo Milton Quaife. Chicago: A. C. McClurg, 1910.

Preuss, Charles. *Exploring with Frémont: The Private Diaries of Charles Preuss, Cartographer for John C. Frémont on his First, Second, and Fourth Expeditions to the Far West.* Translated and edited by Erwin G. Gudde and Elisabeth K. Gudde. Norman: University of Oklahoma Press, 1958.

Pugh, George E. "Speech of George E. Pugh, of Ohio, in the Democratic National Convention at Charleston, Friday, April 27, 1860." Available at HathiTrust Digital Library. https://babel.hathitrust.org/cgi/pt?id=uiuo.ark:/13960/t3mw9r04m&view=1up&seq=1&skin=2021.

Richardson, James D., ed. *A Compilation of the Messages and Papers of the Presidents, 1789–1897.* 10 vols. Published by Authority of Congress, 1899.

Sibley, George Champlin. *The Road to Santa Fe: The Journal and Diaries of George Champlin Sibley*. Edited by Kate L. Gregg. Albuquerque: University of New Mexico Press, 1952.

Simpson, Sir George. *Narrative of a Voyage to California Ports in 1841–1842*. 1847. Reprint. Fairfield, WA: Ye Galleon Press, 1988.

Smith, George Winston, and Charles Judah, eds. *Chronicles of the Gringos: The U.S. Army in the Mexican War, 1846–1848*. Albuquerque: University of New Mexico Press, 1968.

Smith, James Morton, ed. *The Republic of Letters: The Correspondence between Thomas Jefferson and James Madison, 1776–1826*. 2 vols. New York: W. W. Norton, 1995.

Smith, Jedediah. *The Southwest Expedition of Jedediah S. Smith: His Personal Account of the Journey to California, 1826–1827*. Edited by George R. Brooks. 1977. Reprint. Lincoln: University of Nebraska Press, 1989.

Taney, Roger B. "*Dred Scott, Plaintiff in Error, v. John F. A. Sandford.*" Cornell Law School, Legal Information Institute. https://www.law.cornell.edu/supremecourt/text/60/393.

Turnbull, Robert J. *The Crisis: or, Essays on the Usurpations of the Federal Government*. Charleston, SC: A. E. Miller, 1827.

Walker, Robert J. "Letter of Hon. Robert J. Walker, Resigning the Office of Governor of Kansas." Kansas Historical Society. https://www.kansasmemory.org/item/3863.

———. *Letter, of Mr. Walker, of Mississippi, Relative to the Annexation of Texas*. Philadelphia: Mifflin and Parry, 1844. https://www.tsl.texas.gov/exhibits/annexation/part4/walker_letter_1844_titlepage.html.

White, David A., ed. *News of the Plains and Rockies, 1803–1865*. 9 vols. Spokane, WA: Arthur H. Clark, 1996–2001.

Whitman, Walt. *Leaves of Grass*. Boston: James R. Osgood, 1881–82.

Yancey, William L. "Speech of the Hon. William L. Yancey, of Alabama, Delivered in the National Democratic Convention, Charleston, April 28th, 1860." https://babel.hathitrust.org/cgi/pt?id=hvd.32044011713724&view.

Secondary Sources

Albin, Ray R. "The Perkins Case: The Ordeal of Three Slaves in Gold Rush California." *California History* 67, no. 4 (December 1988).

Ambrose, Stephen E. *Undaunted Courage: Meriwether Lewis, Thomas Jefferson, and the Opening of the American West*. New York: Touchstone, 1996.

Aron, Stephen. *American Confluence: The Missouri Frontier from Borderland to Border State*. Bloomington: Indiana University Press, 2006.

Baptist, Edward E. *The Half Has Never Been Told: Slavery and the Making of American Capitalism*. New York: Basic Books, 2014.

Barce, Elmore. "Governor Harrison and the Treaty of Fort Wayne, 1809." *Indiana Magazine of History* 11, no. 4 (December 1915). https://scholarworks.iu.edu/journals/index.php/imh/article/view/5951.

Bartlett, Irving H. *John C. Calhoun: A Biography*. New York: W. W. Norton, 1993.

Bay, William Van Ness. *Reminiscences of the Bench and Bar of Missouri*. St. Louis: F. H. Thomas, 1878.

Belohlavek, John M. *Andrew Jackson: Principle and Prejudice*. New York: Routledge, 2016.

Betts, Robert B. *In Search of York: The Slave Who Went to the Pacific with Lewis and Clark*. Boulder: Colorado Associated University Press, 1985.

Bowman, Shearer Davis. *At the Precipice: Americans North and South during the Secession Crisis*. Chapel Hill: University of North Carolina Press, 2010.

Brands, H. W. *Andrew Jackson: His Life and Times*. New York: Anchor Books, 2006.

Braund, Kathryn. "Creek War of 1813–14." Encyclopedia of Alabama. http://encyclopediaofalabama.org/article/h-1820.

Brewer, Holly. "Entailing Aristocracy in Colonial Virginia: 'Ancient Feudal Restraints' and Revolutionary Reform." *William and Mary Quarterly* 54, no. 2 (April 1997).

Brooks, Corey M. *Liberty Power: Antislavery Third Parties and the Transformation of American Politics*. Chicago: University of Chicago Press, 2016.

Brown, Everett Somerville. *The Constitutional History of the Louisiana Purchase, 1803–1812*. Berkeley: University of California Press, 1920.

Brown, Walter Lee. *A Life of Albert Pike*. Fayetteville: University of Arkansas Press, 1997.

Bugbee, Lester G. "Slavery in Early Texas." 2 parts. *Political Science Quarterly* 13, nos. 3 (September 1898) and 4 (December 1898).

Burstein, Andrew. *The Passions of Andrew Jackson*. New York: Alfred A. Knopf, 2003.

Campbell, Randolph B. *An Empire for Slavery: The Peculiar Institution in Texas, 1821–1865*. Baton Rouge: Louisiana State University Press, 1989.

———. *Sam Houston and the American Southwest*. 3rd ed. New York: Pearson Longman, 2007.

Cantrell, Gregg. *Stephen F. Austin, Empresario of Texas*. Austin: Texas State Historical Association, 2016.

Chaffin, Tom. *Pathfinder: John Charles Frémont and the Course of American Empire*. New York: Hill and Wang, 2002.

———. "'Sons of Washington': Narciso López, Filibustering, and U.S. Nationalism, 1848–1851." *Journal of the Early Republic* 15, no. 1 (Spring 1995).

Chernow, Ron. *Alexander Hamilton*. New York: Penguin Books, 2004.

Childers, Christopher. *The Failure of Popular Sovereignty: Slavery, Manifest Destiny, and the Radicalization of Southern Politics*. Lawrence: University Press of Kansas, 2012.

Crapol, Edward P. *John Tyler, the Accidental President*. Chapel Hill: University of North Carolina Press, 2006.

Crook, Elizabeth. "Sam Houston and Eliza Allen: The Marriage and the Mystery." *Southwestern Historical Quarterly* 94, no. 1 (July 1990).

Davis, James D. *The History of the City of Memphis*. Memphis, TN: Hite, Crumpton & Kelly, Printers, 1873.

Davis, William C. *Lone Star Rising: The Revolutionary Birth of the Texas Republic*. College Station: Texas A&M University Press, 2006

Denton, Sally. *Passion and Principle: John and Jessie Frémont, the Couple Whose Power, Politics, and Love Shaped Nineteenth-Century America*. New York: Bloomsbury, 2007.

Dew, Charles B. *Apostles of Disunion: Southern Secession Commissioners and the Causes of the Civil War*. 2001. Revised ed. Charlottesville: University of Virginia Press, 2016.

Donald, David Herbert. *Charles Sumner and the Coming of the Civil War*. 1960. Reprint. Naperville, IL: Sourcebooks, 2009.

Du Bois, W. E. B. *The Suppression of the African Slave-Trade to the United States of America*. New York: Longmans, Green, 1904.

Duff, James H. "David Wilmot, the Statesman and Political Leader." *Pennsylvania History: A Journal of Mid-Atlantic Studies* 13, no. 4 (October 1946).

Dusinberre, William. *Slavemaster President: The Double Career of James Polk*. New York: Oxford University Press, 2003.

Earle, Jonathan H. *Jacksonian Antislavery and the Politics of Free Soil, 1824–1854*. Chapel Hill: University of North Carolina Press, 2004.

Edel, Charles N. *Nation Builder: John Quincy Adams and the Grand Strategy of the Republic*. Cambridge, MA: Harvard University Press, 2014.

Ellis, Joseph J. *American Creation: Triumphs and Tragedies at the Founding of the Republic*. New York: Vintage Books, 2007.

———. *American Sphinx: The Character of Thomas Jefferson*. New York: Vintage Books, 1998.

Etcheson, Nicole. *Bleeding Kansas: Contested Liberty in the Civil War Era*. Lawrence: University Press of Kansas, 2004.

———. *The Emerging Midwest: Upland Southerners and the Political Culture of the Old Northwest, 1787–1861*. Bloomington: Indiana University Press, 1996.

Eyal, Yonatan. *The Young America Movement and the Transformation of the Democratic Party, 1828–1861*. New York: Cambridge University Press, 2007.

Fehrenbacher, Don E. *The Slaveholding Republic: An Account of the United States Government's Relations to Slavery*. Completed and edited by Ward M. McAfee. New York: Oxford University Press, 2001,

Feldman, Noah. *The Three Lives of James Madison: Genius, Partisan, President*. New York: Random House, 2017.

Finkelman, Paul. *Slavery and the Founders: Race and Liberty in the Age of Jefferson*. 3rd ed. Armonk, NY: M. E. Sharpe, 2014.

———. "Slavery and the Northwest Ordinance: A Study in Ambiguity." *Journal of the Early Republic* 6, no. 4 (Winter 1986).

Foner, Eric. *Free Soil, Free Labor, Free Men: The Ideology of the Republican Party before the Civil War*. 1970. Revised ed. New York: Oxford University Press, 1995.

Forbes, Ella. "African-American Resistance to Colonization." *Journal of Black Studies* 21, no. 2 (December 1990).

Forbes, Robert Pierce. *The Missouri Compromise and Its Aftermath: Slavery and the Meaning of America*. Chapel Hill: University of North Carolina Press, 2007.

Ford, Martin. "Gangs of Baltimore." *Humanities* 29, no. 3 (May–June 2008). https://www.neh.gov/humanities/2008/mayjune/feature/gangs-baltimore.

Freehling, William W. "The Louisiana Purchase and the Coming of the Civil War." In *The Louisiana Purchase and American Expansion, 1803–1898*. Edited by Sanford Levinson and Bartholomew H. Sparrow. Lanham, MD: Rowman & Littlefield, 2005.

———. *The Road to Disunion*. Vol. 1: *Secessionists at Bay, 1776–1854*. New York: Oxford University Press, 1990.

———. *The Road to Disunion*. Vol. 2: *Secessionists Triumphant, 1854–1861*. New York: Oxford University Press, 2007.

Gibson, Campbell, and Kay Jung. "Historical Census Statistics on Population Totals by Race, 1790 to 1990, and by Hispanic Origin, 1970 to 1990, for the United States, Regions, Divisions, and States." U.S. Census Bureau, Population Division, Working Paper No. 56, September 2002. https://www.census.gov/content/dam/Census/library/working-papers/2002/demo/POP-twps0056.pdf.

Goetzmann, William H. *Exploration and Empire: The Explorer and the Scientist in the Winning of the American West*. New York: W. W. Norton, 1966.

Goetzmann, William H., and Glyndwr Williams. *The Atlas of North American Exploration: From the Norse Voyages to the Race to the Pole*. New York: Prentice Hall, 1992.

Gordon-Reed, Annette. *The Hemingses of Monticello: An American Family*. New York: W. W. Norton, 2008.

Greenberg, Amy S. *Lady First: The World of First Lady Sarah Polk*. New York: Vintage Books, 2019.

———. *A Wicked War: Polk, Clay, Lincoln, and the 1846 U.S. Invasion of Mexico*. New York: Vintage Books, 2012.

Haley, James L. *Sam Houston*. Norman: University of Oklahoma Press, 2002.

Hamilton, Holman. *Prologue to Conflict: The Crisis and Compromise of 1850*. New York: W. W. Norton, 1966.

Hammond, John Craig. *Slavery, Freedom, and Expansion in the Early American West*. Charlottesville: University of Virginia Press, 2007.

Harlow, Neal. *California Conquered: War and Peace on the Pacific, 1846–1850*. Berkeley: University of California Press, 1982.

Hay, Robert P. "'And Ten Dollars Extra, for Every Hundred Lashes Any Person Will Give Him, to the Amount of Three Hundred': A Note on Andrew Jackson's Runaway Slave Ad of 1804 and on the Historian's Use of Evidence." *Tennessee Historical Quarterly* 36, no. 4 (Winter 1977).

Haynes, Sam W. "Anglophobia and the Annexation of Texas: The Quest for National Security." In *Manifest Destiny and Empire: American Antebellum Expansion*. Edited by Sam W. Haynes and Christopher Morris. College Station: Texas A&M University Press, 1997.

———. *James K. Polk and the Expansionist Impulse*. 3rd ed. New York: Pearson Longman, 2006.

Heidler, David S., and Jeanne T. Heidler. *Henry Clay: The Essential American*. New York: Random House, 2010.

Hershberger, Mary. "Mobilizing Women, Anticipating Abolition: The Struggle against Indian Removal in the 1830s." *Journal of American History* 86, no. 1 (June 1999).

Hietala, Thomas R. *Manifest Design: American Exceptionalism and Empire*. 1985. Revised ed. Ithaca, NY: Cornell University Press, 2003.

Holt, Michael F. *The Fate of Their Country: Politicians, Slavery Extension, and the Coming of the Civil War*. New York: Hill and Wang, 2004.

———. *The Political Crisis of the 1850s*. New York: W. W. Norton, 1983.

Hopkins, Callie. "The Enslaved Household of Andrew Jackson." White House Historical Association. https://www.whitehousehistory.org/slavery-in-the-andrew-jackson -white-house.

Horwitz, Tony. "150 Years of Misunderstanding the Civil War." *Atlantic* (June 19, 2013). https://www.theatlantic.com/national/archive/2013/06/150-years-of-misunderstanding -the-civil-war/277022.

Howe, Daniel Walker. *What Hath God Wrought: The Transformation of America, 1815–1848*. New York: Oxford University Press, 2007.

Hudson, J. Blaine. "Slavery in Early Louisville and Jefferson County, Kentucky, 1780–1812." *Filson Club Historical Quarterly*, 73:3 (July 1999). https://filsonhistorical.org/wp -content/uploads/publicationpdfs/73-3-3_Slavery-in-Early-Louisville-and-Jefferson -County-Kentucky-1780-1812_Hudson-Blaine-J..pdf.

Hudson, Linda S. *Mistress of Manifest Destiny: A Biography of Jane McManus Storm Cazneau*. Austin: Texas State Historical Association, 2001.

Hurtado, Albert L. *John Sutter: A Life on the North American Frontier*. Norman: University of Oklahoma Press, 2006.

Hyslop, Stephen G. *Bound for Santa Fe: The Road to New Mexico and the American Conquest, 1806–1848*. Norman: University of Oklahoma Press, 2002.

———. *Contest for California: From Spanish Colonization to the American Conquest*. Norman: Arthur H. Clark and University of Oklahoma Press, 2012.

Inskeep, Steve. *Imperfect Union: How Jessie and John Frémont Mapped the West, Invented Celebrity, and Helped Cause the Civil War*. New York: Penguin Press, 2020.

Isenberg, Nancy. *Fallen Founder: The Life of Aaron Burr*. New York: Viking Penguin, 2007.

Jackson, Donald. *Thomas Jefferson and the Rocky Mountains: Exploring the West from Monticello*. 1981. Reprint, with a foreword by James P. Ronda. Norman: University of Oklahoma Press, 2002.

James, Marquis. *The Raven: A Biography of Sam Houston*. 1912. Reprint. Austin: University of Texas Press, 2019.

Johannsen, Robert W. *The Frontier, the Union, and Stephen A. Douglas*. Urbana: University of Illinois Press, 1989.

———. *Stephen A. Douglas*. 1973. Reprint. Urbana: University of Illinois Press, 1997.

Jones, Robert L., and Pauline Jones. "Occupation of Nacogdoches." *East Texas Historical Journal* 50, no. 2 (October 2012). https://scholarworks.sfasu.edu/cgi/viewcontent.cgi ?article=2669&context=ethj.

Karp, Matthew. *This Vast Southern Frontier: Slaveholders at the Helm of American Foreign Policy*. Cambridge, MA: Harvard University Press, 2016.

Kastor, Peter J. *The Nation's Crucible: The Louisiana Purchase and the Creation of America*. New Haven, CT: Yale University Press, 2004.

Kennedy, Roger G. *Burr, Hamilton, and Jefferson: A Study in Character*. New York: Oxford University Press, 2000.

Kennerly, William Clark, and Elizabeth Russell. *Persimmon Hill: A Narrative of Old St. Louis and the Far West*. Norman: University of Oklahoma Press, 1948.

Kinslow, Zacharie W. "Enslaved and Entrenched: The Complex Life of Elias Polk." White House Historical Association. https://www.whitehousehistory.org/enslaved-and -entrenched.

Klein, Maury. *Days of Defiance: Sumter, Secession, and the Coming of the Civil War*. New York: Vintage Books, 1999.

Koch, Adrienne, and Harry Ammon. "The Virginia and Kentucky Resolutions: An Episode in Jefferson's and Madison's Defense of Civil Liberties." *William and Mary Quarterly* 5, no. 2 (April 1948).

Landis, Michael Todd. *Northern Men With Southern Loyalties: The Democratic Party and the Sectional Crisis*. Ithaca: Cornell University Press, 2014.

Lavender, David. *Westward Vision: The Story of the Oregon Trail*. 1963. Reprint. Lincoln: University of Nebraska Press, 1985.

Leonard, Thomas M. *James K. Polk: A Clear and Unquestionable Destiny*. Wilmington, DE: Scholarly Resources, 2001

Levine, Bruce. *Half Slave and Half Free: The Roots of Civil War*. 1992. Revised ed. New York: Hill and Wang, 2005.

Linklater, Andro. *An Artist in Treason: The Extraordinary Double Life of General James Wilkinson*. New York: Walker, 2009.

Malavasic, Alice Elizabeth. *The F Street Mess: How Southerners Rewrote the Kansas- Nebraska Act*. Chapel Hill: University of North Carolina Press, 2017.

Malone, Dumas. *Jefferson the President: First Term, 1801–1805*. Boston: Little, Brown, 1970

———. *Jefferson the President: Second Term, 1805–1809*. Boston: Little, Brown, 1974.

———. *Jefferson the Virginian*. Boston: Little, Brown, 1948.

May, Robert E. *Slavery, Race, and Conquest in the Tropics: Lincoln, Douglas, and the Future of Latin America*. New York: Cambridge University Press, 2013.

McPherson, James M. *Battle Cry of Freedom: The Civil War Era*. New York: Oxford University Press, 1988.

Meinig, D. W. *The Shaping of America: A Geographical Perspective on 500 Years of History*. 4 vols. New Haven, CT: Yale University Press, 1988–2006.

Mieczkowski, Yanek. *The Routledge Historical Atlas of American Elections*. Edited by Mark C. Carnes. New York: Routledge, 2001.

Morrison, Michael A. *Slavery and the American West: The Eclipse of Manifest Destiny and the Coming of the Civil War*. Chapel Hill: University of North Carolina Press, 1997.

Mueller, Ken S. *Senator Benton and the People: Master Race Democracy on the Early American Frontiers*. DeKalb: Northern Illinois University Press, 2014.

Narrett, David E. "James Wilkinson, the Spanish Borderlands, and Mexican Indepen- dence." *William and Mary Quarterly* 69, no. 1 (January 2012).

Nokes, Greg. "Black Exclusion Laws in Oregon." Oregon Encyclopedia. https://www .oregonencyclopedia.org/articles/exclusion_laws/#.Y5LwdLgrySo.

Oakes, James. *The Scorpion's Sting: Antislavery and the Coming of the Civil War*. New York: W. W. Norton, 2014.

Oates, Stephen B. *With Malice toward None: A Life of Abraham Lincoln*. 1977. Reprint. New York: Harper Perennial, 1994.

Onuf, Peter S. *Jefferson's Empire: The Language of American Nationhood*. Charlottesville: University Press of Virginia, 2000.

Owens, Robert M. *Mr. Jefferson's Hammer: William Henry Harrison and the Origins of American Indian Policy*. Norman: University of Oklahoma Press, 2007.

Peterson, Merrill D. *Thomas Jefferson and the New Nation: A Biography*. New York: Oxford University Press, 1970.

Pitt, Leonard. *The Decline of the Californios: A Social History of the Spanish-Speaking Californians, 1846–1890*. 1966. Revised ed., with a foreword by Ramón A. Gutiérrez. Berkeley: University of California Press, 1998.

Porter, Kenneth W. "The Seminole in Mexico, 1850–1861." *Hispanic American Historical Review* 31, no. 1 (February 1951).

Potter, David M. *The Impending Crisis, 1848–1861*. Completed and edited by Don E. Fehrenbacher. New York: Harper & Row, 1976.

Pratt, Julius W. "John L. O'Sullivan and Manifest Destiny." *New York History* 14, no. 3 (July 1933).

Quitt, Martin H. *Stephen A. Douglas and Antebellum Democracy*. New York: Cambridge University Press, 2012.

Randall, Willard Sterne. *Thomas Jefferson: A Life*. New York: Henry Holt, 1993.

Reid, John, and John Henry Eaton, *The Life of Andrew Jackson, Major General in the Service of the United States*. Philadelphia: M. Carey and Son, 1817.

Remini, Robert V. *Andrew Jackson and the Course of American Empire, 1767–1821*. New York: Harper & Row, 1977.

———. *Andrew Jackson and the Course of American Freedom, 1822–1832*. New York, Harper & Row, 1981.

———. *Andrew Jackson and the Course of American Democracy, 1833–1845*. New York: Harper & Row, 1984

Reséndez, Andrés. "North American Peonage." *Journal of the Civil War Era* 7, no. 4 (December 2017).

Reynolds, David S. *John Brown, Abolitionist: The Man Who Killed Slavery, Sparked the Civil War, and Seeded Civil Rights*. New York: Alfred A. Knopf, 2005.

Richards, Leonard L. *The Slave Power: The Free North and Southern Domination, 1780–1860*. Baton Rouge: Louisiana State University Press, 2000.

Ricks, Nathaniel R. "A Peculiar Place for the Peculiar Institution: Slavery and Sovereignty in Early Territorial Utah." MA thesis, Brigham Young University, 2007. https://scholarsarchive.byu.edu/cgi/viewcontent.cgi?article=2006&context=etd.

Rogers, D. Laurence. *Apostles of Equality: The Birneys, the Republicans, and the Civil War*. East Lansing: Michigan State University Press, 2011.

Ronda, James P. "'We Have a Country': Race, Geography, and the Invention of Indian Territory." *Journal of the Early Republic* 19, no. 4 (Winter 1999).

Rothman, Adam. *Slave Country: American Expansion and the Origins of the Deep South*. Cambridge, MA: Harvard University Press, 2005.

Sampson, Robert D. *John L. O'Sullivan and His Times*. Kent, OH: Kent State University Press, 2003.

Sellers, Charles. *James K. Polk, Jacksonian, 1795–1843*. 1957. Reprint, Norwalk, CT: Easton Press, 1987.

———. *James K. Polk, Continentalist, 1843–1846*. Princeton, NJ: Princeton University Press, 1966.

Shepherd, William R. "Wilkinson and the Beginnings of the Spanish Conspiracy." *American Historical Review* 9, no. 3 (April 1904). https://www.jstor.org/stable/pdf /1833472.pdf.

Silbey, Joel H. *Storm over Texas: The Annexation Controversy and the Road to the Civil War*. New York: Oxford University Press, 2005.

Smith, Stacey L. *Freedom's Frontier: California and the Struggle over Unfree Labor, Emancipation, and Reconstruction*. Chapel Hill: University of North Carolina Press, 2013.

Snively, Ethan A. "Slavery in Illinois." *Transactions of the Illinois State Historical Society for the Year, 1901*. Springfield, IL: Phillips Bros., State Printers, 1901.

Sprague, Marshall. *So Vast So Beautiful a Land: Louisiana and the Purchase*. 1974. Reprint. Athens: Swallow Press/Ohio University Press, 1991.

Stanley, Gerald. "Senator William Gwin: Moderate or Racist?" *California Historical Quarterly* 50, no. 3 (September 1971).

Stanton, Lucia. *"Those Who Labor for My Happiness": Slavery at Thomas Jefferson's Monticello*. Charlottesville: University of Virginia Press, 2012.

Stegmaier, Mark J. "A Law That Would Make Caligula Blush?: New Mexico Territory's Unique Slave Code, 1859–1861." In *African American History in New Mexico: Portraits from Five Hundred Years*. Edited by Bruce A. Glasrud. Albuquerque: University of New Mexico Press, 2013.

———. *Texas, New Mexico, and the Compromise of 1850: Boundary Dispute and Sectional Crisis*. Lubbock: Texas Tech University Press, 2012.

Tarrant, Catherine M. "To 'Insure Domestic Tranquility': Congress and the Law of Seditious Conspiracy, 1859–1861." *American Journal of Legal History* 15, no. 2 (April 1971).

Torget, Andrew J. *Seeds of Empire: Cotton, Slavery, and the Transformation of the Texas Borderlands, 1800–1850*. Chapel Hill: University of North Carolina Press, 2015.

———. "Stephen F. Austin's Views on Slavery." In *This Corner of Canaan: Essays on Texas in Honor of Randolph B. Campbell*. Edited by Richard B. McCaslin, Donald E. Chipman, and Andrew J. Torget. Denton: University of North Texas Press, 2013.

Traub, James. *John Quincy Adams: Militant Spirit*. New York: Basic Books, 2016.

Van Atta, John R. *Securing the West: Politics, Public Lands, and the Fate of the Old Republic, 1785–1850*. Baltimore: John Hopkins University Press, 2014

———. *Wolf by the Ears: The Missouri Crisis, 1819–1821*. Baltimore: Johns Hopkins University Press, 2015.

Varon, Elizabeth R. *Disunion!: The Coming of the American Civil War, 1789–1859*. Chapel Hill: University of North Carolina Press, 2008.

Waite, Kevin. *West of Slavery: The Southern Dream of a Transcontinental Empire*. Chapel Hill: University of North Carolina Press, 2021.

Wallace, Anthony F. C. *Jefferson and the Indians: The Tragic Fate of the First Americans.* Cambridge, MA: Belknap Press of Harvard University Press, 1999.

———. *The Long, Bitter Trail: Andrew Jackson and the Indians.* New York: Hill and Wang, 1993.

Waselkov, Gregory A. "Fort Mims Battle and Massacre." Encyclopedia of Alabama. http://encyclopediaofalabama.org/article/h-1121.

Weber, David J. *The Californios versus Jedediah Smith, 1826–1827: A New Cache of Documents.* Spokane, WA: Arthur H. Clark, 1990.

———. *The Mexican Frontier, 1821–1846: The American Southwest under Mexico.* Albuquerque: University of New Mexico Press, 1982.

———. *Myth and the History of the Hispanic Southwest: Essays by David J. Weber.* Albuquerque: University of New Mexico Press, 1988.

———. *The Spanish Frontier in North America.* New Haven, CT: Yale University Press, 1992.

Wellman, Judith. *The Road to Seneca Falls: Elizabeth Cady Stanton and the First Woman's Rights Convention.* Urbana: University of Illinois Press, 2004.

Wiencek, Henry. *Master of the Mountain: Thomas Jefferson and His Slaves.* New York: Farrar, Strauss and Giroux, 2012.

Wilentz, Sean. *No Property in Man: Slavery and Antislavery at the Nation's Founding.* Cambridge, MA: Harvard University Press, 2018.

———. *The Rise of American Democracy: Jefferson to Lincoln.* New York: W. W. Norton, 2005

Wills, Garry. *"Negro President": Jefferson and the Slave Power.* New York: Houghton Mifflin, 2003.

Wood, Gordon S. *Empire of Liberty: A History of the Early Republic, 1789–1815.* New York: Oxford University Press, 2009.

Index